THE MORALITY OF FREEDOM

The Morality of Freedom

JOSEPH RAZ

CLARENDON PRESS · OXFORD
1986

Oxford University Press, Walton Street, Oxford OX2 6DP
Oxford New York Toronto
Delhi Bombay Calcutta Madras Karachi
Petaling Jaya Singapore Hong Kong Tokyo
Nairobi Dar es Salaam Cape Town
Melbourne Auckland
and associated companies in
Beirut Berlin Ibadan Nicosia

Oxford is a trade mark of Oxford University Press

Published in the United States
by Oxford University Press, New York

British Library Cataloguing in Publication Data
Raz, Joseph
The morality of freedom
1. Equality   2. Liberty
I. Title
323.4'01   IIM146
ISBN 0-19-824772-9

Library of Congress Cataloging in Publication Data
Raz, Joseph.
The morality of freedom.
1. Liberty.   2. Authority.   I. Title.
JC571.R39 1986   323.44   86-5296
ISBN 0-19-824772-9

Set at the University Press, Oxford
Printed in Great Britain by
Billing & Sons Ltd,
Worcester

Acknowledgements

The idea of writing a book on political theory was suggested to me in March 1980 by Henry Hardy of Oxford University Press. Later, when the book's shape changed, and it began to assume its present form, I was fortunate to have the quiet encouragement of Adam Hodgkin, who took over responsibility for the book on behalf of the Press. During the intervening years I incurred many other debts of gratitude. Several friends commented on drafts of papers which I wrote during the work on the book. They include J. Waldron, R. M. Dworkin, H. Oberdiek, H. Steiner, P. M. S. Hacker, W. Sumner, K. Campbell, M. Moore, C. L. Ten, M. Dan-Cohen, D. Sugarman, D. Regan, M. Farrell, J. Bell, R. Shiner. Others read drafts of chapters of the book and their comments were invaluable in the final revision. They include H. L. A. Hart, P. A. Bulloch, L. Green, A. Weale, P. Jones, G. A. Cohen, M. Gur-Arie, R. Gavison, J. Griffin, S. Scheffler, D. Heyd, S. Perry, and D. Wiggins.

I greatly benefited from the opportunity to use the drafts of the book in my teaching in Oxford and, during a sabbatical term in 1984, at Berkeley. I am grateful to the Dean and Faculty of the Law School at Berkeley, who provided me with the most agreeable environment in which to pursue my work during the Winter Term of 1984, and to the Master and Fellows of Balliol College, Oxford, who, by reducing my teaching load during 1984/5, enabled me to complete the final draft of the book.

Part One contains material previously published in 'Authority and Consent', *Virginia Law Review*, 1981, and in 'Authority and Justification', *Philosophy and Public Affairs*, 1985. Chapter 7 is a revised and expanded version of an article of the same name published in *Mind*, in 1984. Chapter 8 is a more substantially revised version of the article of the same name first published in J. Waldron (ed.), *Theories of Rights*, Oxford 1984. Chapters 5 and 6 contain material originally published as 'Liberalism, Autonomy, and the Politics of Neutral Concern', *Midwest Studies in Philosophy*, 7 (1982). Chapter 9 is based on 'Principles of Equality', *Mind*, 1978, which is here considerably revised and extended. Chapter 13 contains material used in my paper to the Aristotelian Society in February 1986, and published in its proceedings of that year. Chapters 14 and 15 contain material published in R. Gavison (ed.), *Issues in Contemporary Legal Philosophy: The Influence of H. L. A. Hart* (Oxford, forthcoming), ch. 8.1, 'Autonomy, Toleration, and the Harm Principle'. I am grateful for permission to use these articles.

Contents

III. Individualistic Freedom: Liberty and Rights

IV. Society and Value

V. Freedom and Politics

1

The Problem of Political Freedom

1. A Journey of Exploration

This is a book about political freedom. It is both an introduction and a contribution to the political theory of liberalism. Liberalism can be understood in historical terms.
It is a political tradition which has developed and become
one of the dominant political forces in what is known as the
Western world over the last three hundred years or so. It is
identified by a series of political causes espoused by liberals
over the centuries, by a variety of claims about the working
of society and the economy, and by a cluster of ideas concerning the fundamental principles of political morality. It
is probably true to say that no political cause, no one vision
of society nor any political principle has commanded the
respect of all liberals in any given generation, let alone
through the centuries.[1] But the liberal tradition displays a
considerable degree of unity and continuity which have enabled it to become one of the dominant and most formative
strands of Western culture.

This essay, however, will not pursue the historical trail.
It is addressed primarily to people who grew up in the embrace of the liberal tradition or who at least have felt its
attraction, to those who wish to define their own position
relative to that tradition. They hope to identify a coherent
body of ideas which places them somewhere inside the liberal
tradition, even though it may turn out to include elements
borrowed from other political traditions. It is, in other
words, an essay on the political morality of liberalism.
Though the ideas to be canvassed will presuppose certain
views concerning the nature and working of society, these
will largely remain the background. Though the conclusions
I will reach have implications for various political problems

[1] The range of liberal ideas is displayed in *Western Liberalism*, ed. E. K. Bramsted
and K. J. Melhuish, London, 1978.

such as the control of immigration, censorship and taxation, the implications will not be spelt out. Instead, the essay will concentrate on the moral principles of political action, on the political morality of liberalism, in an attempt to extract from them a coherent moral position.

In inviting the reader to join me on this voyage of exploration I have made it clear that our purpose is not that of those who set out to draw maps of the oceans and who have to record all their currents, islands and shores. Ours is a different mission. It is that of explorers looking for the best navigable channels to reach a destination, ours being a view of the ideal of individual freedom and its role in politics.

In recent years many philosophers have embarked on similar explorations. It is part of our endeavour to examine their efforts. We shall do so selectively and critically and only to the extent that we may be helped by their experiences. There is no doubt that their work enhances our prospects. From their misfortunes we will learn which routes lead to disaster, while their successes have charted paths to be followed and further explored.

Many of the recent contributions to liberal political theory consist in the development of theories of justice. Our aim is a theory of political freedom. The reason for this difference of goal and perspective is simple. A complete political morality must include a doctrine of justice. But any plausible view of justice rests on principles and doctrines which are neither uniquely liberal nor derivable from specifically liberal principles. The specific contribution of the liberal tradition to political morality has always been its insistence on the respect due to individual liberty. To the extent that liberal theories of justice present a distinctive conception of justice, this is due to the way their principles of political freedom feed into and shape their conception of justice. Indeed the argument of this book will demonstrate how far-reaching are the implications of political liberty, how they affect our conceptions of justice, equality, prosperity and other political ideals.

It is not our aim to examine all the aspects of political theory. It is ambition enough to argue for certain principles of political freedom and against others. Theories of justice and of other political ideals will be examined, but only in-asmuch as they embody a doctrine of political freedom. This book does not present a liberal political morality. It does, however, offer a liberal foundation for a political morality.

2. The Importance of Politics

Political theory can conveniently be divided into two parts: a political morality and a theory of institutions. Political morality consists in the principles which should guide political action. It provides the principles on the basis of which the theory of institutions constructs arguments for having political institutions of this character rather than that. Political morality also sets a goal as well as limits to the actions of those political institutions. But the principles of political morality themselves grow out of the concrete experience of a particular society with its own institutions. Their validity is limited by their background. In this way institutions shape the principles which are designed for the guidance and re-moulding of these institutions. Much of the day to day political activity of a country is concerned with the shaping of political institutions and procedures. Not uncommonly the best way to implement new policies is to create new public institutions or rearrange or reform old ones. And we are all aware of many cases where the best policies failed through the failure of the institutions which were charged with their implementation. In this book, however, we will not have the space to examine the way the principles we will canvass should be translated into political institutions.

I have referred several times to political morality as the morality which governs political action. It would be tedious to engage in lengthy argument on what action is political. For our purposes let us regard the term as referring to the action of political institutions, or any other action evaluation of which should assign significant weight to its likely effects on the constitution, composition, or action of political institutions. By 'political institutions' I will be referring primarily to the state and its organs, but also, somewhat more broadly, to all public authorities. So not all political organizations are political institutions. Political parties, in most democracies, are not. They are political organizations for it is their purpose to engage in political action.

Why concentrate on political morality? Why should there be moral principles which are special to political morality? In a way the second question is the subject of the book. It will be answered only at its conclusion. For in inquiring about the political conception of individual liberty we will be asking whether political respect for individual freedom is a simple case of applying general moral principles to political action, or whether it involves a more radical modification of or departure from general morality to suit the political context. Influential voices among political theorists argue for the existence of a relatively independent body of moral principles, addressed primarily to the government and constituting a (semi-)autonomous political morality. The critical evaluation of such views is one of the main tasks of this book. Their rejection means that the positive conclusions argued for in the book concerning the morality of political freedom are based on considerations of individual morality to a greater degree than is common in many contemporary works of political philosophy. It is a book on ethics, which concentrates on certain moral issues because of their political implications.

A word of explanation is, however, required to justify the concentration on political institutions. Those who object to this way of focusing the issues quite rightly point out that many private corporations and trade unions have as much, if not more, power than many public authorities. I wish neither to deny this nor to deny that their power subjects those private organizations to certain moral requirements concerning its exercise. In this respect they are like public authorities. Where they differ is in lacking authority, or at least lacking general authority. The authority the government of a state claims for itself is general in that it claims authority to regulate all aspects of life, including the terms of incorporation and the rules governing the activities of other corporations. We are not always willing to acknowledge that public authorities are entitled to the authority they claim. But we always judge them by their claims. We look to see whether their actions are such as to justify their own claims to general authority. This is the crucial difference between Parliament and a powerful private organization like the Miners' Union or Imperial Chemical Industries. The power of these organizations means that their actions affect the fate of many. They must therefore give adequate weight to the interest of those individuals in deciding on their actions. But essentially their responsibility is confined to the outcome of their own actions or that of their employees. Parliament, on the other hand, has the further responsibility of supervising the activities of all persons and organizations within its jurisdiction and seeing to it that they all conform to certain appropriate standards of behaviour. Other public authorities are assigned certain limited and partial responsibilities in discharging this general supervisory role. Our ordinary political judgments reflect these facts. We think that public authorities are to a certain extent responsible for the actions of others. A breakdown of law and order in a town is in part an indication of the failure of the police and other public authorities. Unemployment is a political problem, as is a worsening balance of trade, and the like.

There is a second consideration which combines with the first to make political authorities deserving of special consideration. They do not have a legitimate interest of their own. The only interest a government is entitled to pursue is that of its subjects. Talk of the interest of a government refers to its ability to pursue the interest of its subjects in the way it ought to. It does not have an interest independent of, one which is not a reflection of, the interests of its subjects. In this it differs from corporations and voluntary associations which may have independent interests which they may pursue within moral bounds. In its relations to those not subject to its authority, a government is in the same position as you or I or any corporation: that is, its actions must respect moral bounds which impose on us all certain responsibilities to others. But its duties to its subjects are much more extensive. It is misleading to say that a government may, like anyone else, pursue its own interest within the bounds imposed by moral respect for the rights and interests of its subjects and of others. For the government's own interest is only what serves its ability to promote and protect the interests of its subjects.

These are judgments based on controversial conceptions of the role of political institutions. We will examine theories which controvert them. I am here anticipating the later endorsement of these conceptions to illustrate the reason for focusing on political institutions. Because they are obligated to regulate the activities of those over whom they claim authority, by studying them we indirectly study the norms which they should impose on other corporations. This is the reason why our attention will be focused on political institutions. This way of posing the question does not imply that corporations and unions are not subject to stringent moral requirements in the conduct of their business.

3. The Revisionist Challenge

Much ink has been spilt in argument about political freedom. This is often felt to call for an apology for adding to the library. But the persistence of the issue is surely evidence of its elusiveness and difficulty. Indeed the difficulty is so great that several liberal political theorists doubt whether liberty, or political freedom, is valuable at all. They do not claim that all those people who cherished liberty, those who fought for it, and those who felt fortunate to have enjoyed it, had nothing valuable in mind when they wrote or thought of the value of liberty. Rather, these revisionist theorists claim that those who wrote and talked of the value of liberty really cherished not liberty but something else. Justice, equality, some list of rights such as the rights to freedom of worship, of expression and of association, are among the candidates for what liberals really value and to which they misleadingly refer as the value of liberty.[1]

Given my introductory remarks about the variety of political causes espoused in the name of freedom in the history

---

[1] The most explicit attack on the idea that liberty is of value was mounted by R. M. Dworkin. See in particular the essay 'What Rights Do We Have?' in *Taking Rights Seriously*, London, 1977. In denying the value of liberty as such Dworkin is following J. Rawls, whose *A Theory of Justice*, Oxford, 1971, understands 'Liberty' to refer to a list of basic liberties, which are not mere exemplifications of one distinctive value.

of the liberal tradition, such revisionist suggestions are not to be dismissed out of hand. It is possible and not at all implausible that a common political slogan such as 'Freedom' does not in fact refer to one distinct value. It may have a perfectly legitimate rhetorical use as a shorthand reference to a complex of values, or to certain values as they manifest, or ought to manifest, themselves in certain concrete situations. Indeed in Chapter 9 I will myself suggest that some such account is needed to make sense of the continued and pervasive popularity of 'Equality' as a political battle-cry. That is, I shall argue that when understood as a distinct value it has little appeal.

Furthermore, liberalism was long divided between those who regarded liberty as intrinsically valuable, and those who claimed that it is of instrumental value only. The latter include the utilitarians and the free-market economists. Their most powerful spokesman in recent times was F. A. Hayek, who drew on the impossibility of marshalling all the information required for the successful governing of a society in any way other than through the invisible hand of the market and the free interaction of people generally.[1] The instrumental approach lends itself more readily to the revisionist argument, for it naturally makes the value of liberty depend on other values. It is thus ready in principle to allow for exceptions and to admit that on occasion liberty is not merely overridden by other concerns but is devoid of all value.

The arguments for the instrumental value of liberty are crucially important. Without them no political morality is complete. In many areas they provide the weightiest arguments in support of liberty. Yet the focus of attention in this book is elsewhere. It denies the revisionist approach and affirms the intrinsic value of liberty. But first we should realize the strength of the revisionist challenge.

We can best do that by examining the difficulties that two simple attempts to provide a quick answer to the question of political freedom encounter. Cannot the value due to

---

[1] See, e.g., F. A. Hayek's *The Constitution of Liberty*, Chicago, 1960, and *Law, Legislation, and Liberty*, London, 1973. For an excellent discussion of Hayek's political thought see J. Gray, *Hayek*, Oxford, 1984.

liberty be expressed by one simple principle: the presumption of liberty,[1] that is the principle that there is a presumption against any political action which denies or restricts anyone's freedom in any way? Those who hold that no restriction of liberty is ever justified will endorse the presumption of liberty. They will add that the presumption is irrebuttable. Others who endorse the presumption may have their own views on its strength, that is on the circumstances in which it is justified for a political act to restrict freedom. But could not all those who cherish political freedom agree to the presumption of liberty as a minimal common denominator?

4. The Presumption of Liberty

The presumption of liberty is, indeed, sometimes presented as an uncontroversial common ground for all liberty lovers. But this is a case in which the desire for compromise and agreement leads astray. Talk of a presumption of liberty is misleading and confusing. Furthermore, it disguises rather than illuminates the problems the liberal position involves.

We talk of presumptions in three different senses. Two of them do not apply to the question of the foundations of political liberty. The third leads to an implausible doctrine. 'A presumption of . . .' is sometimes used to indicate that the burden of adducing evidence and marshalling arguments is on those who challenge the presumed view. It is often said that the presumption of liberty means that the burden of proof is on those who favour the restriction of liberty. The legal doctrine that the burden of proof lies on one party or the other is recognized to be complex. One element of it is the burden of adducing evidence.

At first one may wonder why this should matter. Should not all the parties to a trial have an equal commitment to the truth and an equal obligation to help the court to establish

---

[1] On the presumption of liberty see J. Feinberg, *Social Philosophy*, Englewood Cliffs NJ, 1979, pp. 18–20; S. I. Benn and R. S. Peters, *The Principles of Political Thought*, New York, 1959, p. 259. On most points my discussion follows closely D. N. Husak, 'The Presumption of Freedom' *Nous*, (1983). I have also been greatly influenced by E. Ullman-Margalit, 'On Presumptions', *Journal of Philosophy*, 80 (1983), 143. Presumptions in each of the three senses here distinguished can be either rebuttable or irrebuttable. But the distinction does not affect the argument in the text.

it? They may not be committed to the truth, but should they not be? A little reflection provides the answer. The burden of adducing evidence applies where one of the parties to a dispute or a disagreement is exempt from the duty to help establish the truth or at least where he is excused if he fails to comply with it. Courts are public official bodies. Why should a person be required to justify his conduct to the authorities and in public? Such a requirement, if not confined to exceptional circumstances, invades his privacy, offends his dignity, is expensive and disrupts his normal life. Hence the burden of adducing evidence is initially on the prosecution. It shifts to the accused only if the prosecution has established a strong case against him. If it fails to do so the judge should rule that there is no case to answer and direct the jury to acquit. There is a strong case for invoking such a presumption whenever one is concerned with the working of institutions which decide, or act on, potentially controversial propositions and whose actions are likely significantly to affect the life of particular persons.

Perhaps this is the reason why some political theorists have sought to rely on a presumption of liberty. They may have thought of it as a principle for the guidance of political institutions. There are objections to its blanket use in this role and some of them will emerge in our consideration of other senses of 'presumption'. Here it is enough to point out that we are not considering principles for the guidance of institutions, but principles to guide our own thoughts and actions. We are searching for an explanation of the nature and value of political freedom which will help us make up our minds about the merits of existing policies, laws and institutions as well as on proposals for changing them. We are, in other words, looking for the principles which may justify the imposition of rules concerning the burden of adducing evidence on certain institutions and exempting others from their application. (Courts are subject to such rules but parliaments are, normally, exempt. Why the difference?) When one asks for the ultimate principles of political freedom presumptions establishing a burden of adducing evidence are out of place.

There is a second sense of 'presumption'. Consider the

presumption of death. It says, roughly, that if the next of kin has no news of a person for so many years he is presumed dead. This means that one can then (usually after obtaining a judgment of a court) act as if he is dead. 'Presumption' in its second sense acts to sever the normal connection between belief and action. In the above example it is a licence to act as if a certain fact is the case in the absence of adequate evidence to support a belief that the fact is the case. Absence of news of a person during seven years, say, is some evidence of his death. But it is weak and insufficient evidence. There could normally be many other equally plausible explanations of the absence of news. Nevertheless, it is allowed to create a presumption of death because it is adequate evidence of the existence of a practical need to act as if he is dead (or to allow the persons affected to do so). At other times the presumption may act in the opposite direction. It may prohibit acting on a certain belief even though it is adequately supported. The presumption of innocence is of this kind. Notwithstanding that one may have evidence enough to believe that a person is guilty one is bound, if one is bound by it, to treat him as if he is innocent.

There is no sense in advocating a presumption of liberty in this sense of presumption. We are not concerned with an urgent practical problem which has to be settled one way or another even if the evidence is insufficient. Nor are we concerned with the distortions and mistakes that institutions are liable to if allowed to act on their own judgment, rather than defer to some specialist institutions (a person is deemed innocent unless convicted by due process of law), or if they are allowed to act on a judgment which is based on the balance of evidence rather than on a stiffer standard (proven beyond reasonable doubt). Ours is a theoretical inquiry. Rather than assume a licence or an obligation to act by special standards of argument, which either do not justify belief or require one to suspend action on one's belief even when it is justified, we should carry on our exploration in order to improve our understanding and to reach well founded conclusions.[1]

---

[1] I do not wish to deny that there are presumptions in this second sense which govern all rational inquiry and argument. My point is merely on the suggestion that there are presumptions special to arguments about liberty.

The first two senses are the main senses of 'presumption', as used in moral, political and legal contexts. Presumptions come into their own in the presence of practical and institutional concerns which require deviation from the (otherwise) normal course of rational inquiry and action. That is why talk of presumptions in abstract philosophical contexts is misleading. In common discourse the term is often used in a third sense (of which the second is perhaps a special institutional development). It commonly means the existence of an unrefuted reason for believing something which is just enough to justify the belief, though its weight is such that suspension of belief is also rational in the circumstances. When we say 'presumably he has reached his home by now' we indicate that what we know about his intentions, the weather, traffic conditions, etc. gives us reason to believe that he has reached home, and that reason is not refuted by anything we are aware of, but though this evidence is sufficient to justify the belief, it is not sufficient to reject as irrational the refusal to accept it which is typically expressed by saying: 'Let's wait a little longer to be sure that he is really there'.

Is this the meaning of the presumption of liberty? Does it simply mean that there is a reason which justifies, though it does not compel, a belief that denial or restriction of liberty is wrong? This claim is very weak, indeed it is so weak that it is no longer distinctively liberal, as many illiberal people will endorse it. But the fundamental objection to accepting this presumption as the fundamental principle of political freedom, or as a principle of liberty at all, is that understood in this way the presumption is grossly misleading. It is undiscriminating. It does not assign any greater weight to our concern for religious freedom or for freedom of expression or for the freedom to have a family than to the freedom to kill people we dislike, be cruel to animals, or spend a fortnight on the summit of Ben Nevis. The problem is not that the presumption of liberty compels us to assign the same importance to all these freedoms. It is that the presumption does not tell us anything about which freedoms are important, which are not, and why. It is a watered down principle to the extent that it loses sight of anything which is or ever was of concern to those who care about liberty. It bypasses rather than addresses the main liberal preoccupations.

5. The Simple Principle

Despite these criticisms of the doctrine of the presumption of liberty a nagging doubt remains. Has not something been overlooked? Can it be denied that any measure restricting liberty must be justified by strong arguments? And is not that what the presumption of liberty means? We have to tread carefully. The presumption of liberty should not be confused with the conservative presumption which says, roughly speaking, that one requires a reason for any change but not for its absence. This weak presumption (which belongs to the last of the three types analysed above) is based on the belief that there is generally a cost to any change. Therefore, the presumption allows one to believe that change is undesirable unless it is established either that in the case under consideration the change involves no cost, or that its benefits at least match its drawbacks. The conservative presumption entails that a proposal which restricts liberty shall not be accepted unless supported by good reasons. But it entails the same regarding a proposal to repeal a law which restricts freedom. So the principle is not a principle of liberty. By focusing attention exclusively on freedom-restricting changes one may create the false impression that the two presumptions are the same. But while the conservative presumption should have a modest place in our deliberations, there is no useful role for a presumption of liberty.

The preceding arguments are directed at the suggestion that the fundamental principle of political freedom, the principle which states the respect due to political freedom, is a presumption of liberty. Can these arguments be avoided and by-passed by endorsing a different fundamental principle, one making no mention of presumptions? Cannot one simply state that freedom is intrinsically valuable? I will call this the simple principle. If it is valid then it follows that there is a reason against every restriction of freedom. Hence every political act restricting anyone's freedom requires a justification which overcomes that reason against such acts. Is not that the intuition which the adherents of the presumption of liberty unsuccessfully sought to articulate?

One charge against the presumption of liberty was that, when understood as a fundamental political principle, in the only interpretation in which it is not false it is so diluted as to lose all distinctive liberal flavour. But a second, separate charge was that it fails to recognize, and therefore it serves to disguise, the problems a theory of political freedom has to contend with. This charge holds with the same force against the simple principle. I mentioned one of the problems which both the presumption of liberty and the simple principle distort. We feel intuitively that some liberties are more important than others. The restriction of the more important liberties is a greater restriction of liberty than that of the less important ones. This point is at the heart of the revisionist challenge. If the value of freedom depends on other values which having various freedoms serves, then freedom itself is not valuable. If liberty is intrinsically valuable then a theory of liberty will turn out not to be a theory of unrelated heterogeneous liberties. It will reveal the common thread which explains why the important liberties are important and why the others are not.

A second major problem (or cluster of problems) which helps to reinforce the revisionist challenge is encountered the moment we ask ourselves what counts as a restriction of freedom. Forcing someone to act in a certain way seems to qualify as a denial of freedom. But if the law requires me to wear a seat-belt when driving my car does it force me to do so? If not, does it restrict my freedom in some other way? Does need force a person to accept employment for a very low wage? If so does it mean that anyone has restricted his freedom? Is it his current employer, or his previous one who dismissed him and created his need, or the government which made the laws under which such events occur? If low wages restrict freedom, how about a person who has to sell his car quickly because he must go abroad within a week? He is forced to sell below market price. But does this indicate a restriction on his freedom? And who can be said to have restricted his freedom? Is it the person who created the circumstances which make him leave in a hurry? Does it matter if these result from the fact that he is sought by the police on suspicion of murder or that the government refused to renew his residence permit or that he has to be with his ailing father? If low wages restrict freedom is the same true of a sudden increase in the market price of an essential commodity such as bread? If not, where lies the difference? If one locks up a person one restricts his freedom. Does one do so by stealing his car? Or by frightening him so that he does not wish to leave the room? Does it matter if one frightens him by threatening him or by misleading him about the dangers awaiting him outside? Does one restrict his freedom even if one does sincerely believe in those dangers oneself?

In many ways these questions and similar ones are not difficult or complicated. They do need some careful sorting out to avoid confusion and incoherence. To a considerable extent articulating a theory of political freedom consists in sorting out the different answers to such questions. Neither proclaiming a presumption of liberty nor insisting on the simple principle advances this enterprise. Many theorists have argued that what is required is a clear definition of freedom. Once we have one the revisionist challenge will be met, the simple principle will become transparent and will qualify as the guiding principle of liberal thought.

6. *The Inadequacy Of Linguistic Analysis*

A voluminous literature on the concept of freedom has sprouted in the years since the publication in 1959 of Berlin's influential 'Two Concepts of Liberty'.[1] But neither a definition nor a conceptual analysis of 'freedom' can solve our problems. Consider the following four cases:

[1] Berlin's 'Two Concepts of Liberty' is reprinted in his *Four Essays on Liberty*, Oxford, 1969. For other very helpful discussions see G. C. McCallum, Jr., 'Negative and Positive Freedom', *Philosophical Review*, 76 (1967), 312; J. Feinberg, *Social Philosophy*, ch. 1, and S. I. Benn and W. L. Weinstein, 'Free to Act and Being a Free Man', *Mind*, 80 (1971) 194. On the difficulties of comparing the extent of different liberties see O. O'Neill, 'The Most Extensive Liberty', *Proceedings of the Aristotelian Society*, 80 (1979/80), 45. The most ingenious, but ultimately unsuccessful, attempt to solve these difficulties that I know of is in P. Jones and R. Sugden, 'Evaluating Choices', *International Review of Law and Economics*, 2 (1982), 47.

1. Hunger forces a person to take a job he does not like. He had no choice and his choice was not a free one. His action of taking the job was free and he did it out of his free will but he was not really free to do anything else.

2. A gunman forces a person to hand over his money by threatening his life. He has no choice and his choice is not a free one. Nor would we say that he acted out of his free will or freely when he handed over the money. Nor was he free to do anything else.

3. A person sells his car below market price in order to leave the country and go and stay with his ailing father. He was forced to do so. He had no other choice and he was not free to do anything else. But his choice was a free one, and he acted freely and out of his own free will.

4. A person stays indoors because he was misled into believing that there are poisonous fumes outside. The person who deceived him did so intentionally in order to make him stay indoors. The deceived person was not forced to stay indoors and he had a choice. But he did not act out of his free will and it was not his free choice.

The point of these examples is not to suggest that linguistic distinctions are arbitrary or inconsistent. They are not. The point is that they do not follow any consistent political or moral outlook. I trust that whatever your intuitions about the moral and political implications of these cases the linguistic distinctions do not reflect them. If by chance this is not revealed by these four examples then further different examples will make the point. My own gut reaction is that linguistic considerations will not suffice either to establish that the first two cases are morally alike (as most moral philosophers claim) or that they are not (as free marketeers contend). Moreover, case (3) seems to me irrelevant to political freedom whereas case (4) is highly relevant. Despite this much of the terminology of being denied freedom is appropriate in describing (3) but inapplicable to (4). What we need is not a definition nor mere conceptual clarity. Useful as these always are they will not solve our problems. What we require are moral principles and arguments to support them.

It has to be said that much that has been written in articles and books purporting to define and elucidate or analyse the concept of freedom will be helpful to anyone interested in the issues to be explored here. Philosophers and political theorists are sometimes better than their word. Much that is presented as conceptual analysis is really much more and includes advocacy of principles of political freedom. Moral and political philosophy has for long embraced the literary device (not always clearly recognized as such) of presenting substantive arguments in the guise of conceptual explorations. One may even say that the whole purpose of this book is to defend a concept of political freedom. It is only important to remember that that concept is a product of a theory or a doctrine consisting of moral principles for the guidance and evaluation of political actions and institutions. One can derive a concept from a theory but not the other way round.

7. Liberalism and Individualism

I have raised all these questions not in order to resolve them here, but to indicate the range and complexity of the issues which a doctrine of political freedom has to resolve. They form the subject of this book. All I hope to have established so far is that the analysis of the meaning of 'liberty' or of 'freedom' cannot answer the questions of which liberties are valuable, what counts as a restriction or interference with a person's freedom and how to judge what to do when considerations of freedom conflict with other considerations (which may or may not involve the interest of freedom in some other respect).

The failure of the linguistic approach leads, ultimately, to the demise of the simple principle. It shows again that there is no value-neutral definition of liberty; none, that is, which is of any interest for moral and political thought. It reaffirms the point made earlier that any assessment of degrees of liberty depends on the importance of various actions for the protection or promotion of values other than freedom. If so then the value of freedom depends on the other values which the freedom to perform some actions serves. It would seem plausible that the freedom to perform some actions is valueless. For it is plausible to assume that there are some actions such that neither their performance nor the ability to choose not to perform them has any value, unless the freedom so to choose is by itself independently valuable. The above remarks suggest that in that case it is without value, because freedom is valuable only if it serves other values. It is equally plausible to assume that some other measures can protect or promote various values in the very same way that certain freedoms can. None of this denies that the freedom to perform many acts is of great value. But it refutes the simple principle, which presupposes that freedom is an independent value. It seems to do more. It seems to refute the view that freedom itself is intrinsically valuable.

Freedom to perform certain actions in certain circumstances is valuable only if it serves other values. Does it follow that there is no distinct value in freedom as such? That is the challenge to traditional liberal belief in the value of liberty. It is a challenge posed, as we saw, not only by those who reject liberal values, but by several revisionist liberal theorists. The argument of this book strives to rehabilitate the traditionalist affirmation of the value of freedom. But it accepts the revisionist arguments against both the presumption of liberty and the simple principle, as well as their critique of linguistic analysis. In some ways my proposed defence of the traditional belief in the value of freedom is based on a radical departure from some historically central liberal doctrines. I shall anticipate the position to be advocated below by explaining the direction the argument of the book is to follow.

Historically, liberalism and individualism grew together. Similar social and economic forces have often combined to advance their cause in various countries. Yet they are distinct doctrines. Liberalism is a doctrine about political morality which revolves round the importance of personal liberty. Individualism is a moral doctrine. It is related to liberalism as liberalism is related to democracy, understood as a theory of political institutions. Liberalism can provide a foundation for democracy, though one can reach democratic conclusions from other foundations, each lending a somewhat different shape to the democratic theory it yields. Similarly an

individualist may endorse liberalism, as his political morality, but liberal conclusions can also be based on non-
individualistic premises. Also, just as a liberal may support
non-democratic institutions as the most suitable for some
societies, so an individualist may become not a liberal but a
libertarian, or an anarchist.

If there is one common thread to the argument of this
book it is its critique of individualism and its endeavour to
argue for a liberal morality on non-individualistic grounds.
Individualism, or moral individualism as understood in this
book,[1] is the doctrine that only states of individual human
beings, or aspects of their lives, can be intrinsically good or
valuable (to be precise, this is what characterizes humanistic
individualism). The critique of this plausible-sounding doctrine will take us away from direct political issues and on to
an examination of some fundamental moral issues. These
will be introduced in Chapter 8 (Rights-Based Moralities).
Elements of a non-individualist moral position will be described in Part Four (Society and Value).

Individualism tends to lead to a vision of liberalism as a
theory of limited government. It presents a view of political
liberty as a doctrine of what governments may not do, how
they may not treat their subjects, which areas of individual
conduct they should keep their hands off, and similar principles. Here too the connection is a loose one and one can
support a limited government interpretation of political liberty on non-individualist grounds as well.

The doctrine of limited government regards governments
as a threat to liberty. Its protection is in keeping governments confined within proper moral bounds. While not
denying that governments can and often do, pose a threat to
individual liberty, there is another conception which regards
them also as a possible source of liberty. They can create
conditions which enable their subjects to enjoy greater
liberty than they otherwise would. This second conception regards liberty as sometimes threatened by individuals
and corporations, not only by governments. It goes further
and claims that though governments sometimes abuse their

---

[1] On the various senses of 'individualism' see S. Lukes, *Individualism*, Oxford,
1973.

powers and trespass on individual liberty, in situations which are not all that rare they should act to promote freedom, and not only sit back and avoid interfering with it. They should keep off certain areas of life, or avoid interfering with them in certain ways, while acting in other areas and in other ways to promote freedom.

The interpretation of liberalism as the doctrine of limited government will come under scrutiny in Parts Two and Three of the book. These will examine two ways of limiting governmental authority. The first limits governments by denying their authority either to act in order to promote any conception of the good life, or to act in ways which help one conception of the good life more than others. The second is through a doctrine of fundamental rights which are not to be trespassed upon by governments, and which therefore set limits to their authority.

Doctrines of limited government are doctrines of political authority. They explain that political authority can go that far and no further. Their consideration will be prefaced by a first part which is a general doctrine of political authority. The first and last parts of the book (combined with the discussion of moral issues in Chapters 8 and 9) offer an interpretation of liberalism, based on a non-individualistic conception of morality, and a doctrine of political authority which rests on a perfectionist political defence and promotion of liberty and autonomy. The concluding chapter returns to the revisionist challenge: is freedom a distinct value? While giving an affirmative answer to that question I will not retract the points made in support of the revisionist challenge in this chapter. Freedom will be seen to be a distinct value, but one which is intimately intertwined with others, and cannot exist by itself.

I

THE BOUNDS OF AUTHORITY

The conclusions of the first chapter were negative. It rejected certain common approaches to the problem of liberty, and raised serious doubts concerning its intrinsic value. But the chapter also points in a positive direction. The doctrine of liberty consists in principles of political morality which require governments to protect and promote individual freedom. Not surprisingly the doctrine of liberty is part and parcel of the general doctrine of political authority. It contributes to the definition of its scope and duties. The question of political liberty does not arise unless the existence of political authorities is justifiable. Liberals believe that, at the very least given the prevailing circumstances of human life, human well-being can best be achieved in communities subject to political authorities. They also believe that those authorities are bound by principles requiring the promotion and protection of freedom. The two beliefs are connected in that violation of the principles of freedom may undermine the legitimacy of the authority. The doctrine of freedom is part of a view of the foundations of legitimacy of political authorities.

The following three chapters explore these foundations. Chapter Two vindicates the general view that having authority over another person implies a duty of obedience on his part. This view dictates the direction of the inquiry of Chapter Three which seeks to establish, at a fairly abstract level, the conditions which any authority must meet to enjoy legitimacy. Chapter Four considers the argument that any political authority, even one not meeting the conditions argued for in Chapter Three, is legitimate if it is based on the consent of the governed. It rejects this claim on the ground that consent is binding only if it meets certain conditions, and that in the case of consent to be governed by authority those are roughly the conditions establishing the legitimacy of an authority independently of consent. This chapter also applies the conclusions previously reached to present in outline a view as to whether existing political authorities are legitimate authorities enjoying a (moral) right to rule.

2

Authority and Reason

The doctrine of freedom is part of the doctrine of authority. It consists of principles binding political authorities to protect and promote the freedom of their subjects. These are some of the principles constituting the doctrine of authority, i.e. those which determine the conditions under which a person has legitimate authority and by which authorities should guide their actions.

The inquiry leads us to examine the foundations of political authority. It is common to regard authority over persons as centrally involving a right to rule, where that is understood as correlated with an obligation to obey on the part of those subject to the authority.[1] If that view is correct it provides the pivotal clue to the direction of the inquiry. It has to focus on the conditions under which one person can bind another. Since several writers have recently challenged the common view it is necessary to re-examine it. This is the purpose of the present chapter.

1. Authority and Justified Power

R. Sartorius is one of those who challenge the common view that legitimate authority held by A over B implies a duty on B to obey A.[2] He does, however, regard political authority as 'a morally justified form of authorship constituted by certain moral capacities, justification-rights, and claim-rights'.[3] A parent's authority is likewise regarded by him as

[1] See, e.g., J. Lucas, *The Principles of Politics*, Oxford, 1966, Tuck 'Why is Authority such a Problem?' in P. Laslett, W. G. Runciman and Q. Skinner (eds.), *Philosophy, Politics and Society*, 4th series, Oxford, 1972; G. E. M.Anscombe, 'On the Sources of the Authority of the State', *Ratio*, 20 (1978), 1; J. M. Finnis, *Natural Law and Natural Rights*, Oxford, 1980, ch. 9

[2] R. Sartorius, 'Political Authority and Political Obligation', *Virginia Law Review* 67 (1981), 3.

[3] Ibid., p. 5.

including the capacity (presumably moral) 'to issue binding directives to his or her children'.

The explanation of normative capacities gives rise to difficulties. The only explanation which has succeeded in withstanding objections and in gaining widespread acceptance explains them as, essentially, abilities to impose or revoke duties or to change their conditions of application.[1] The obligation to obey a person which is commonly regarded as entailed by the assertion that he has legitimate authority is nothing but the imputation to him of a power to bind. For the obligation to obey is an obligation to obey if and when the authority commands, and this is the same as a power or capacity in the authority to issue valid or binding directives. In the absence of an alternative explanation of capacities one must conclude that Sartorius's analysis of authority over persons in general does not accomplish its purpose.

Perhaps, however, political authority differs in that respect from other kinds of authority? Perhaps it can be understood independently of normative powers or capacities? An analysis along such lines is offered by Robert Ladenson. He regards political authority as a right to rule, 'that is to say, strong reasons can be advanced for holding that possession of the governmental power and acceptance by those one presumes to govern of its exercise jointly constitute a justification for coercive acts which would otherwise be immoral'.[2] Power over a person here is not normative power. It means 'the ability to make that person do what one wishes'.[3]

It is clear that not every power amounts to an authority. My neighbour can stop me from growing tall trees in my garden by threatening to burn rubbish by my border. He, therefore, has some power over me but no authority. Nor does his power turn into an authority just by the fact that I acquiesce and do not pick a fight with him. An authority, according to Ladenson, has a justification-right to possess and exercise its power. A justification-right is contrasted with a claim-right in not implying any obligations. My

[1] See H. L. A. Hart, *Essays on Bentham*, Oxford 1982, ch. 10.

[2] R. Ladenson, 'In Defense of a Hobbesian Conception of the State', *Philosophy and Public Affairs*, 9 (1980), 139.

[3] Ibid., p. 137.

neighbour's justification-right to threaten me does not mean that I have a duty to obey him. It merely means that he does no wrong in threatening me and this is compatible with my having a right to resist him.[1]

Let us therefore assume that such threats are in general wrong because they interfere with a person's use of his own property. Let us further assume that my neighbour has nevertheless the right to threaten me either because my behaviour will greatly harm his interests or for whatever other reason seems to you an acceptable justification provided it is compatible with our final assumption, i.e. that I have the right to resist him (both his and my rights being justification-rights). It seems clear that my neighbour does not have authority over me just because he can affect my behaviour and will be justified in doing so. If this is authority we all have authority over our neighbours. Nor is it clear whether Ladenson would deny that. He adds two further elements to his explanation of political authority. First, it is authority to use coercion. Second, it is justified by the fact that its possessor successfully exercises governmental power with the acquiescence of his subjects. It is tempting to say that these two conditions do not belong to an explanation of authority over persons generally. They simply establish which authorities are political authorities. But perhaps it is wrong to divide the explanation of political authority into two separate parts, an explanation of authority and of what makes it political. Let us therefore examine the two conditions that Ladenson requires.

It seems plain that the justified use of coercive power is one thing and authority is another. I do not exercise authority over people afflicted with dangerous diseases if I knock them out and lock them up to protect the public, even though I am, in the assumed circumstances, justified in doing so. I have no more authority over them than I have over mad dogs. The exercise of coercive or any other form of power is no exercise of authority unless it includes an appeal for

---

[1] If I understand his meaning Ladenson regards 'having a justification right to do A' as meaning being justified in doing A. This is to confuse 'having a right to do A' with 'doing A is all right'. But my argument does not depend on rejecting Ladenson's conception of rights.

compliance by the person(s) subject to the authority. That is why the typical exercise of authority is through giving instructions of one kind or another. But appeal to compliance makes sense precisely because it is an invocation of the duty to obey.

Some, particularly those with Hobbesian sympathies, may think that there is an alternative and better explanation of the fact that authority is usually exercised by issuing directives. These, they will say, are threats or coercive threats. There can indeed be no doubt that threats are another type of what may be loosely called 'appeals for compliance'. Nor do I doubt that all political authorities must and do resort to extensive use of and reliance on coercive and other threats. Yet it is clear that all legal authorities do much more. They claim to impose duties and to confer rights. Courts of Law find offenders and violators guilty or liable for wrongdoing.

None of these and similar claims has much to do with threatening people. To threaten is not to impose a duty, nor is it to claim that one does. None of this shows that legal authorities have a right to rule, which implies an obligation to obey. But it reminds us of the familiar fact that they claim such a right, i.e. they are *de facto* authorities because they claim a right to rule as well as because they succeed in establishing and maintaining their rule. They have legitimate authority only if and to the extent that their claim is justified and they are owed a duty of obedience. Ladenson's mistake is to think that since there can be political authority which is not owed a duty of obedience there can also be one which does not claim that it is owed such a duty.

It should be clear by now that Ladenson's last condition, that the authority has a justification-right to use coercion because it regularly exercises governmental power with the acquiescence of its subjects, cannot retrieve the situation. Acquiescence seems relevant to the explanation of *de facto* authority rather than to that of legitimate authority. To have effective political control requires, in the circumstances of our world, a high degree of acquiescence. Ladenson's conception of authority amounts to a claim that all *de facto* authorities are legitimate. It is a familiar Hobbesian view, which will be challenged in the next chapter. But can it really be claimed to be faithful to the main features of the notion of political authority prevalent in our culture?

To test it, try to imagine a situation in which the political authorities of a country do not claim that the inhabitants are bound to obey them, but in which the population does acquiesce in their rule. We are to imagine courts imprisoning people without finding them guilty of any offence; damages are ordered, but no one has a duty to pay them. The legislature never claims to impose duties of care or of contribution to common services. It merely pronounces that people who behave in certain ways will be made to suffer. And it is not merely ordinary people who are not subjected to duties by the legislature: courts, policemen, civil servants, and other public officials are not subjected by it to any duties in the exercise of their official functions either.

Two things stand out when contemplating a political system of this kind. First, it is unlikely that any such society ever existed. Societies we know about are invariably subject to institutions claiming a right to bind their subjects, and when they survive this is in part because at least some of their subjects accept their claim. Secondly, if such a society were to exist we would not regard it as being governed by authority. It is too unlike the political institutions we normally regard as authorities.

The two points are related. The second is a conceptual point. But we have the concept of authority that we do because in our world societies have governed by institutions claiming and being acknowledged to have the right to bind their subjects. Ladenson's analysis is not merely not an analysis of the concept of authority which is part of our cultural tradition. It is an analysis of a concept that does not have much use in our world.

To conclude: Ladenson offers an explanation of legitimate authority in terms of *de facto* authority. It is justified *de facto* authority. De facto authority is then understood as some form of power over people. The analysis fails because the notion of a *de facto* authority cannot be understood except by reference to that of legitimate authority. Having *de facto* authority is not just having an ability to influence people. It is coupled with a claim that those people are bound to obey.[1]

2. The Recognitional Conception

In the previous section I underlined the fact that the claims an authority makes for itself are part of what makes it an authority. One way of examining these claims, which I will follow in this and the next section, is to concentrate on the attitude of people who accept the legitimacy of the authority. One can then most clearly discern what authority is by seeing what one acknowledges when acknowledging that a person has legitimate authority.

The first point to emerge from the discussion so far is that the influence authorities intend to exert is direct and normative. Characteristically, it affects people's practical reasoning by means of authoritative utterances. A person is an authority or has authority only if some of his utterances are authoritative. Saying that the influence of an authoritative utterance is meant to be direct and normative means that a person who accepts the authority of another accepts the soundness of the arguments of the following form:

Y has authority;
Y decreed that X is to do A;
Therefore, X ought to do A.

Many conceptions of authority are different interpretations of this inference form. Before we are ready to accept the common view, which regards authorities as claiming the

---

[1] Sartorius has another string to his bow. On p. 8 of his article he makes a claim not about authority in general nor about political authority, but about legal governments. He follows H. L. A. Hart in identifying such a government as a body acting according to complex social practices whose acceptance does not involve moral approval by those who accept them. I have argued against Hart on this point before. See *The Authority of Law*, pp. 28, 155, and elsewhere. Hart replies to this criticism in his *Essays on Bentham*, pp. 153–61, and 264–8. For my rejoinder see 'Hart on Moral Rights and Legal Obligations' *Oxford Journal of Legal Studies*, 4 (1984), 123.

The arguments of this section do not affect those who hold that 'has a duty' and all other normative terms just mean 'has been threatened', etc. They do not refute those willing to endorse the semantic view that normative terms generally are to be explained in terms of threats and coercion. Such a reductionist semantic view, though wrong, does not concern us here for it does not challenge the relation between a right to rule and an obligation to obey.

right to impose duties, we should consider some of the alternatives. One conception, which I shall call the recognitional
conception, holds that to accept an utterance as authoritative
is to regard it as a reason to believe that one has a reason
to act as told. On this account authoritative utterances are
reasons, but they are reasons for belief, not for action. Therefore, regarding someone as an authority does not entail a
belief that one has a reason to obey him, since reasons for
obedience are reasons for action. The account applies to
theoretical authorities as well as to practical ones. But we
will examine its success in explaining practical authority
only.

This explanation regards practical authorities as theoretical authorities of a special kind. Practical authority is
authority affecting what is to be done. According to the
recognitional conception, the utterances of legitimate authorities do not affect the balance of reasons. They are not
themselves reasons for action, nor do they create any such
reasons. They merely provide information about the balance
of reasons as they exist separately and independently of such
utterances. Suppose that the question is whether to make a
particular contract in writing or be satisfied with an oral
agreement. There are reasons for and against each course.
The right decision is that which is supported by the better
reasons. Let us assume that Parliament, whose authority we
acknowledge, has decreed that it is an offence to make such
contracts, except in writing. The recognitional conception
denies that this law is a reason for making such contracts in
writing. It is said to be a reason for believing that there are
(other) reasons for making a written contract. Authoritative
utterances, you may say, are held not to affect the balance of
reasons on the main issue (what to do) but on the subsidiary
issue of the evidence concerning the main issue (they are
reasons to believe in reasons for action).

This is not to make light of the importance of authority as
interpreted by this conception. After all, people act not on
the reasons there are but on those they believe there are (in so
far as they act on reason at all). Therefore, the recognitional
conception has an explanation to offer as to how it is that
authoritative utterances, though not themselves reasons for

action, can affect one's reasoning about practical problems. Practical authority is reinterpreted as theoretical authority concerning belief in deontic propositions. The authoritative utterances of practical authorities are reasons to believe that one ought to do that which the utterance says one is to do.

Such an account of practical authority is fundamentally flawed. It leads to the *no difference thesis*, i.e. the view that authority does not change people's reasons for action. There is nothing which those subject to authority ought to do as a result of the exercise of authority which they did not have to do independently of that exercise, they merely have new reasons for believing that certain acts were prohibited or obligatory all along. I shall return to the no difference thesis in the next chapter where a relatively detailed examination of its shortcomings will help explain the conception of authority which I will defend. For the moment it is enough to point to one central function of authority which the recognition conception cannot explain.

It fails, for example, to explain the role of authority in the solution of co-ordination problems. Those are problems where the interests of members of the group coincide in that, among a set of options, the members prefer that which will be followed by the bulk of the members of the group above all else. One does not mind whether one drives on the left or the right provided everyone else does the same. There are many such problems of great importance to the orderly conduct of any society. A wise man can tell me which options belong to that set, but he cannot tell me which of the options to choose before it is known what others will do. Sometimes that can be known on the basis of existing facts. Many people are likely to believe that many will choose a particular option and therefore they will choose it themselves; hence one has reason to follow them and choose it as well. Sometimes, however, there is no option in the designated set that will be the obvious choice. In such cases, what one needs is something that will make a particular option the one to follow.

This is something practical authorities often do (or attempt to do). They designate one of the options as the one to be chosen and, if their action is regarded as a reason to adopt that course of action, then a successful resolution of the problem is found. Since solving co-ordination problems is one of the important tasks of political and many other practical authorities, and as their relative success in it can only be explained by regarding authoritative utterances as reasons for action, one must reject the recognitional account of practical authority.[1]

3. The Inspirational Conception

The conception that I will call inspirational is perhaps marginal, but presents interesting features. It can best be introduced by reflecting on the well-known apparent dilemma in explaining the moral authority of God. Either the moral law is valid because it emanates from God's will or its validity is independent of God. If the latter is the case, then God is not the ultimate moral authority. His own goodness and the justice of His commands has to be tested by the independent criterion of their conformity to the moral law. Morality is independent of belief in God, since agnostics and atheists can accept the independently valid moral law. God is irrelevant to morality.

On the other hand, how can the fact that the moral law is God's will endow it with validity? Why should one obey God's will? Admittedly He is omnipotent and can punish those who disobey Him. It may therefore be prudent to obey Him, but this can hardly endow His command with moral character. To reply that His will is to be obeyed because it is good is to presuppose an independent moral standard by which God's will is measured. To do this is to return to the first horn of the dilemma. Therefore, on either possibility God is irrelevant to morality. His will and command provide people neither with a standard that one has any reason to call moral nor with a motive for action that can be regarded as a moral motive.

There are various traditional ways of struggling with the dilemma. I shall not examine them, for my interest is not theological. One answer, which I think is the best and most promising one, is of present interest for the light it sheds on authority generally. According to it, all who know God love

---

[1] See further the arguments against the no difference thesis in the next chapter.

Him. It is possible to doubt or even to deny God's existence. Those who do so obviously do not love Him. Given human nature, however, it is impossible for those who believe in His existence not to love Him. Loving Him includes wanting to do His will. This is a purely non-self-interested motivation and therefore a moral one. According to this view, God's will sets moral standards; it does not merely reflect independently valid standards. They are valid because they express His will. There is, however, no difficulty concerning the motivation to obey. The love that He inevitably inspires in all who believe in Him is that motivation. (This does not mean that those who love Him will always obey Him, for they may be overcome by other motives.) The unselfish, non-self-interested character of the motivation assures both it and the command toward which it is directed of a moral character.

This is inspirational authority, for the reason we ought to obey it is that we want to and the wish to do so is not preconceived, is not derived from our other interests and needs. It is inspired by the recognition of the nature of the person or body in authority. If this is the character of God's authority, is it the model on which all human authority should be understood?

Similar attitudes are found in human relations. As we all know from our experience, affection for another often leads people to conceive desires and wishes, because the person toward whom they have the affection would be pleased if they had such wishes and tastes or acted on them. The appearance of such desires is one necessary mark for affection to count as love. The desires I have in mind are to be strictly distinguished from desires to do certain things in order to please the other person. Obviously lovers want to please their loved ones and sometimes act for that reason. This is common in all friendly relations between people. I am referring to a much rarer phenomenon existing paradigmatically in loving relations, and not very frequently even there, in which one comes to desire something for its own sake because one knows that this will please the loved one.

One may, for example, come to enjoy Byrd's music because one's lover does and would be pleased if this taste were shared. The point is that one comes to enjoy Byrd's music in itself. One does not merely like to listen to it because one's desire to listen to it pleases the loved one. On the other hand, the pleasure in Byrd's music was induced neither suggestively by one's trust in one's friend's musical taste nor subconsciously. The 'because he would have wanted me to' is not merely a non-reason-giving explanation. It is a reason, but a reason for liking Byrd's music in itself, a reason for wanting to listen to it because one enjoys it. For it is only this that the loved person wishes.

He may be pleased that I want to listen to Byrd to please him, but he does not want me to listen to Byrd for that reason. He simply wants me to listen to Byrd, and since doing so to please him is doing it, it pleases him. On the other hand, he has another wish, namely that I should like Byrd. It is a wish that I should like listening to Byrd in itself, for the pleasure it gives. Here he wishes me to do it for a particular reason. Doing it for another reason would not be doing as he wishes. The fact that I love him and that he wishes it is for me a second-order reason—a reason to act for that reason.

That second-order reason is not a desire to please him but a desire to have the desires and tastes that it would please him for me to have, because I love him. It does not matter whether doing so would please him. It may not please him, for he may never know of it. Indeed, often people are motivated in the way I have described after the death of a person they love. It is rare to find such wishes and desires even in love. This rarity does not, however, diminish the importance of the phenomenon to our understanding of love. It seems to me to represent the spiritual aspect of the image of the lovers merging to become one. Aspiring to such fusion includes the desire to have one will, not only through gradual adaptation, but also by the more immediate transformation of the will through love.

What are the implications of this to our understanding of authority? Do the led love their leaders? A charismatic leader inspires enthusiasm and devotion, which can take many practical and psychological forms that are often combined. Among these, the one sometimes called blind devotion is characteristic. It is the feeling that one will follow one's leader to the end of the world. This attitude often involves unbounded trust, namely confidence that the leader knows best and that he has the right goals at heart. But it does characteristically involve more—the feeling that he is so unique and outstanding that one wants to do as he commands, because then one would be at one with him. Since charismatic leaders often influence masses of people, there is often the additional feeling of being united with one's community by embracing the leader's will. In such cases I feel no hesitation in saying that the attitude of the people to their leader is one of love or devotion reinforced by love of the community that he represents. (None of this is meant to suggest that there is no more to love than the desire to unite one's will with that of the loved one. I am only suggesting that when this desire is present so are, in the normal case, the other elements of love.)

I said that this attitude is often regarded as blind devotion. My explanation of it makes it appear no blinder than any other love. It is not inherently irrational, as one is often inclined to think. If it is generally undesirable, this could only be because one's attitude to one's leaders and community should not be one of love, because love is appropriate in personal relations but not in politics, or because all-embracing love is out of place in politics. Be that as it may, since not all authority is political, there may be proper room for inspirational authority in other contexts. Could it be, for example, that parental authority is sometimes quite properly of this kind? Here we face a major difficulty in the inspirational conception of authority.

First, even if some authorities are of this mould, it is clear that many are not, and it is arguable that many should not be. Most political authorities are not recognized through love and are not inspirational in character; perhaps none should be. Second, even when love and authority are combined, as in the case of some parental relations, the two are distinct and should not be confused. After all, parents' love of their children can be every bit as great as and of a similar character to children's love for their parents. Yet parents do not as a rule admit that their children have authority over them. More generally, many loving relations involving the occasional transformation of the will that was described above do not involve any recognition of authority. It follows that even where, as in some cases of charismatic authority, the inspirational conception does illuminate an important aspect of the authority relation, it fails to explain why it is an authority relationship at all. It merely explains some features that may sometimes accompany its instantiation.

4. Content-Independent Reasons

If the harvest our inquiry has so far yielded is meagre, it is nonetheless of great importance. A person has (practical) authority, we have concluded, only if his authoritative utterances are themselves reasons for action. This is not enough to identify authoritative utterances, for many utterances which are not authoritative meet this condition. One important idea was suggested by H. L. A. Hart.[1] Authoritative utterances can be called 'content-independent' reasons.

A reason is content-independent if there is no direct connection between the reason and the action for which it is a reason. The reason is in the apparently 'extraneous' fact that someone in authority has said so, and within certain limits his saying so would be reason for any number of actions, including (in typical cases) for contradictory ones. A certain authority may command me to leave the room or to stay in it. Either way, its command will be a reason. This marks authoritative reasons as content-independent. By this feature they can be distinguished from many reasons, including various other kinds of utterances that are reasons.

There are, however, other content-independent reasons, and to be complete a characterization of authoritative utterances must distinguish them. One group, including promises and vows, is clearly different in that its members are reasons for the agent alone. It is interesting to compare threats and offers with authoritative utterances. Threats are meant to be taken as reasons and credible threats are reasons,

---

[1] In *Essays on Bentham*, ch. 10. I am indebted to Dr. L. Green whose paper on content-independent reasons helped clarify my thoughts on the subject.

and they are content-independent. They are reasons to believe that a certain unwelcome eventuality will come about,
if something that the threatened person is alleged to have at
least a chance of controlling will occur (the triggering event).
It is the conditional occurrence of that unwelcome event,
and not the threat, that is the reason for avoiding the condition that will bring it about. Threats differ from ordinary
communications of information about undesirable future events conditional on the addressee's action, for it is alleged
that the occurrence of the undesirable future event is under
the control of the person making the threat (or at least that
he has a chance of controlling it), that he has decided to
prevent it only if the threatened person will prevent the
triggering event, and that this decision was taken in order to
try to get the threatened person to prevent the triggering
event by threatening him. In the absence of the last condition
the utterance is not a threat but a warning.

Threats (and, for similar reasons, offers) are content-
independent reasons for belief. Hence one does not need
practical authority to make them. Nor does one need to have
theoretical authority. It is only metaphorically that a person
is an authority regarding his own intentions.

Requests are another kind of content-independent reason.
It would be wrong to regard requests as mere communication of information that the speaker, or someone else
in whose interests the request is made, needs or wants something and that the speaker wants the addressee to help in
getting it. Although every request at least implies such information, it is possible to communicate the information
without requesting. This is admittedly rare, since under-
standably a conventional way of requesting is by telling a
person that one would like him to do something. It is possible, however, to tell a person that, while I would like him
to do something for me, I am not asking and am not going
to ask him to do it. This may be said, for example, to a
close friend with whom relations are temporarily somewhat
strained. The point of the distinction thus drawn is that,
while one would be pleased if one's need moves the friend
into action, one would be displeased if it takes a request to
do so. This presupposes that the request is intended to be

regarded as a reason over and above the need and the desire to be helped by a friend. This account explains why one might request even when one knows that the other person knows of one's need and of one's desire for help and that he and others know that one knows.

None of this is meant to deny that requesting involves stating or implying that there is a reason for the addressee to act as requested. But the specific quality of requests is that they are acts intended to communicate to their addressee the speaker's intention that the addressee shall regard the act of communication as a reason for a certain action. The speaker's intention is not to make the addressee act as requested, but merely to create a reason for such action. The speaker realizes that there may be overwhelming reasons against acceding to the request, and he does not wish the addressee to do as requested in such a case. The speaker leaves it to the addressee to judge what is right. He intends to influence him only by tipping the balance somewhat in favour of the requested act.

Orders and commands are among the expressions typical of practical authority. Only those who claim authority can command. As we saw, in requesting and in commanding the speaker intends the addressee to recognize the utterance as a reason for action. The difference is that a valid command (i.e. one issued by a person in authority) is a peremptory reason. We express this thought by saying that valid commands or other valid authoritative requirements impose obligations. The next chapter explores the special nature of these obligations.

3

The Justification of Authority

This chapter develops and defends the conception of the nature of practical authority outlined in the previous chapter, i.e. authority as involving essentially the power to require action. The explanation proceeds through normative theses of three kinds. One concerns the type of argument required to justify a claim that a certain authority is legitimate. The second states the general character of the considerations which should guide the actions of authorities. The last concerns the way the existence of a binding authoritative directive affects the reasoning of the subjects of the authority. The explanation and defence of the three theses is preceded by an introductory section defending the general approach to the analysis of authority adopted here, and introducing some of the themes which are explored in greater detail later in the essay.

1. 'Surrendering One's Judgement'

How is authority to be related to the nebulous notion of a valid requirement for the obedience of one's subjects? As Richard Flathman disapprovingly remarked, 'There has been a remarkable coalescence of opinion around the proposition that authority and authority relations involve some species of "surrender of judgment" on the part of those who accept submit or subscribe to the authority of persons or a set of rules and offices. From anarchist opponents of authority such as William Godwin and Robert Paul Wolff through moderate supporters such as John Rawls and Joseph Raz and on to enthusiasts such as Hobbes, Hannah Arendt and Michael Oakeshott, a considerable chorus of students have echoed the refrain that the directives . . . of authority are to be obeyed by B irrespective of B's judgments of their merits'.[1]

---

[1] Richard E. Flathman, *The Practice of Political Authority*, Chicago 1980, p. 90.

But what is 'a surrender of judgment'? H. L. A. Hart, who has recently added his voice in support of this kind of analysis, provides the following explanation: 'The commander characteristically intends his hearer to take the commander's will instead of his own as a guide to action and so to take it in place of any deliberation or reasoning of his own: the expression of the commander's will . . . is intended to preclude or cut off any independent deliberation by the hearer of the merits pro and con of doing the act.'[1] Understood literally, this explanation is, however, implausible. Surely what counts, from the point of view of the person in authority, is not what the subject thinks but how he acts. I do all that the law requires of me if my actions comply with it. There is nothing wrong with my considering the merits of the law or of action in accord with it. Reflection on the merits of actions required by authority is not automatically prohibited by any authoritative directive, though possibly it could be prohibited by a special directive to that effect.

Richard Friedman offers an explanation aimed at the same target which avoids this objection:

The idea being conveyed by such notions as the surrender of private judgment . . . is that in obeying, say, a command simply because it comes from someone accorded the right to rule, the subject does not make his obedience *conditional* on his own personal examination and evaluation of the thing he is being asked to do. Rather, he accepts as a sufficient reason for following a prescription the fact that it is prescribed by someone acknowledged by him as entitled to rule. The man who accepts authority is thus said to surrender his private or individual judgment because he does not insist that reasons be given that he can grasp and that satisfy him, as a condition of his obedience.[2]

Is this conception of authority correct? One point to remember (it is consistent with Friedman's account) is that a person may have limited authority (e.g., in matters concerning football only, or in military affairs but not in the

[1] H. L. A. Hart, *Essays on Bentham*, p. 253. I used to hold a similar view. See my 'Reasons, Requirements, and Practical Conflicts', in S. Korner (ed.), *Practical Reasoning*, Oxford 1974.

[2] R. B. Friedman, 'On the Concept of Authority in Political Philosophy', R. E. Flathman (ed.), *Concepts in Social and Political Philosophy*, Macmillan, NY, 1973, p. 129.

conduct of the economy). It should be noted that Friedman's explanation shows how misleading the metaphor of 'surrendering one's judgment' can be. Unlike Hart's, Friedman's explanation shifts the emphasis from the subjects' deliberations to their action. The subjects accept that someone has authority over them only if their willingness to do his bidding is not conditional on their agreement on the merits of performing the actions required by the authority.

This condition is open to two interpretations. The minimalist interpretation maintains that they are willing to obey if they have no judgment of their own on the merits of performing the required action. They will not then defer decision until they form their own judgment. The maximalist interpretation claims that the subjects accept that they should obey even if their personal belief is that the balance of reasons on the merits is against performing the required act.

The minimalist interpretation is too weak since it assumes that people are never bound by authority regarding issues on which they have firm views. The maximalist interpretation is more promising, and the views to be argued for in the rest of this chapter explore and develop it. Either way no surrender of judgment in the sense of refraining from forming a judgment is involved. For there is no objection to people forming their own judgment on any issue they like. Nor does one surrender one's judgment if that means acting against one's judgment. For an authority is legitimate only if there are sufficient reasons to accept it, i.e. sufficient reasons to follow its directives regardless of the balance of reasons on the merits of such action.

There are more ways than one in which a metaphor can mislead. It can sometimes mislead people who perceive clearly the fallacies the metaphor invites and therefore reject it altogether, turning a blind eye to the true insight it encapsulates. This has happened to the many theorists who thought they had a simple explanation for the confusion of thought which led to the surrender of judgment metaphor. According to them, to accept the legitimacy of an authority is simply to accept that whatever other reasons there may be for a certain action, its being required by the authority is an additional reason for its performance. Inasmuch as that additional reason may tip the balance one can perhaps over-dramatize the situation by saying that an authoritative requirement is a reason to act against the balance of reasons on the merits of the case. This means no more than that the authoritative requirement is an additional factor. Much the same can be said of any reason for action. The fact that it will rain tomorrow, for example, may mean that I should not go to London, even though the balance of reasons on the merits of my going (i.e. all the reasons pro and con but the rain) suggest that I should go.

This description of the relevance of authority to practical reasoning is profoundly misguided. It is wrong not in what it says but in what it leaves out and implicitly denies. To be sure, if a person accepts the legitimacy of an authority then its instructions are accepted by him as reasons for conforming action. But until we understand how and why they are such reasons and how they differ from ordinary reasons we will not begin to understand the nature of authority. Perhaps the point can be best brought out by considering first authority as it functions in one, not untypical, context.

Consider the case of two people who refer a dispute to an arbitrator. He has authority to settle the dispute, for they agreed to abide by his decision. Two features stand out. First, the arbitrator's decision is for the disputants a reason for action. They ought to do as he says because he says so. But this reason is related to the other reasons which apply to the case. It is not (like the rain in the example of my going to London) just another reason to be added to the others, a reason to stand alongside the others when one reckons which way is better supported by reason. The arbitrator's decision is meant to be based on the other reasons, to sum them up and to reflect their outcome. For ease of reference I shall call both reasons of this character and the reasons they are meant to reflect dependent reasons. The context will prevent this ambiguity from leading to confusion. Notice that a dependent reason is not one which does in fact reflect the balance of reasons on which it depends: it is one which is meant to do so.

This leads directly to the second distinguishing feature of

the example. The arbitrator's decision is also meant to replace the reasons on which it depends. In agreeing to obey
his decision they agreed to follow his judgment of the balance
of reasons rather than their own. Henceforth, his decision
will settle for them what to do. Lawyers say that the original
reasons merge into the decision of the arbitrator or the judgment of a court, which, if binding, becomes *res judicata*.
This means that the original cause of action can no longer
be relied upon for any purpose. I shall call a reason which
displaces others a pre-emptive reason.[1]

It is not that the arbitrator's word is an absolute reason
which has to be obeyed come what may. It can be challenged
and justifiably refused in certain circumstances. If, for example, the arbitrator was bribed, or was drunk while considering the case, or if new evidence of great importance
unexpectedly turns up, each party may ignore the decision.
The point is that reasons that could have been relied upon
to justify action before his decision cannot be relied upon
once the decision is given. Note that there is no reason for
anyone to restrain their thoughts or their reflections on the
reasons which apply to the case, nor are they necessarily
debarred from criticising the arbitrator for having ignored
certain reasons or for having been mistaken about their significance. It is merely action for some of these reasons which
is excluded.

The two features, dependence and pre-emptiveness, are
intimately connected. Because the arbitrator is meant to decide on the basis of certain reasons, the disputants are excluded from later relying on them. They handed over to him
the task of evaluating those reasons. If they do not then deny
them as possible bases for their own action they defeat the
very point and purpose of the arbitration. The only proper
way to acknowledge the arbitrator's authority is to take it to
be a reason for action which replaces the reasons on the basis
of which he was meant to decide.

2. The Dependence Thesis

The crucial question is whether the arbitrator's is a typical
authority, or whether the two features picked out above are

---

[1] In ch. 1 of *The Authority of Law* I explained some of the formal features of
pre-emptive reasons. My analysis has been criticised by Flathman in *The Practice
of Political Authority*, among others. It is not possible to reply to the criticism here.

peculiar to it and perhaps a few others, but are not characteristic of authorities in general. It might be thought, for
example, that the arbitrator is typical of adjudicative authorities, and that what might be called legislative authorities
differ from them in precisely these respects. Adjudicative
authorities, one might say, are precisely those in which the
role of the authority is to judge what are the reasons which
apply to its subjects and decide accordingly, i.e. their decisions are merely meant to declare what ought to be done
in any case.

A legislative authority on the other hand is one whose job
is to create new reasons for its subjects, i.e. reasons which
are new not merely in the sense of replacing other reasons
on which they depend, but in not purporting to replace any
reasons at all. If we understand 'legislative' and 'adjudicative' broadly, so the objection continues, all practical
authorities belong to at least one of these kinds.[1] It will be
conceded of course that legislative authorities act for reasons.
But theirs are reasons which apply to them and which do
not depend on, i.e. are not meant to reflect, reasons which
apply to their subjects. A military commander should order
his troops in the way best calculated to achieve victory at a
minimal cost. If he wisely orders his men to occupy a certain
hill it does not follow that they had reason to occupy that
hill even before they were ordered to do so. Parliament is to
distribute the burden of taxation in an equitable way, but it
does not follow that the citizens had any reason to pay tax
before the passing of the (just) tax law.

These are telling points. But the argument is by no means
over. First, even if not all legislative authorities share the
characteristics of dependence and pre-emptiveness we found
in the arbitrator's case, it is plain that some do. Consider,
for example, an Act of Parliament imposing on parents a
duty to maintain their young children. Parents have such a
duty independently of this Act, and only because they have

---

[1] This would be a very wide interpretation indeed. It would, for example, count
my instruction to my son to be back by midnight as legislative, and the policeman's
order to move on when a driver stops in a prohibited zone as adjudicative. But this
liberality does not affect the argument.

it is the Act justified. Parliament, of course, is not limited to
the enactment of laws where there is a prior obligation on
the subjects to behave in the required way. But there can be,
and perhaps there are, authorities which are so limited. Note
that the decrees of such a body will be binding even if they in
fact err as to what people's obligations are. The arbitrator's
decision is binding even if mistaken and so are the decrees
of our imagined legislator. Both are meant to decide on the
basis of dependent reasons and their decisions are therefore
pre-emptive.

The example shows that the objector's neat distinction
between adjudicative and legislative authorities is mistaken.
The mark of the adjudicator is simply that he is called upon
to decide what parties in dispute should have done or should
do in the circumstances of a particular case. Nevertheless,
the objector may well remain convinced that many legislative
authorities are not meant to act on dependent reasons and
that their directives are not pre-emptive. So let us consider
his examples with some care.

One simplifying assumption has to be explained before we
proceed. We have been concerned with the authoritative
imposition of duties. But authorities, even practical authorities, do much else besides. They can declare that a
certain day shall be a national holiday, that a certain organization shall have legal personality, that a person shall be
granted citizenship or shall be divorced or excommunicated,
that certain land shall be dedicated to the public, or that
some people shall have certain rights, and much else. Concentration on the imposition of duties does not, however,
distort our understanding of authority since all the other
functions authorities may have are ultimately explained by
reference to the imposition of duties. The possession of citizenship, for example, is important because it confers rights
(such as the right to vote in general elections) and duties
(such as the duty of loyalty). Rights themselves are grounds
for holding others to be duty bound to protect or promote
certain interests of the right-holder. Legal personality is the
capacity to have rights and duties. In every case the explanation of the normative effect of the exercise of authority
leads back, sometimes through very circuitous routes, to the

imposition of duties either by the authority itself or by some other persons. Therefore, while it is impossible to 'reduce' rights, status, etc., to duties, it is possible to explain 'authority' by explaining the sense in which authorities can impose duties.

One difficulty is that prising apart the imposition of duties from other effects of the exercise of authority is far from straightforward. Consider a tax law again. It not only imposes a duty to pay, but also sets up (not necessarily in the same statute) the machinery for collecting and distributing the money. When the imagined objector said that there was no reason to pay the money now due as tax before the tax law was passed he was of course right. But is this because there was then no machinery for collecting and distributing the money or because there was no authority-imposed duty to pay it?

For the first two years of the First World War there was no conscription in Britain, but there was machinery to recruit volunteers. So this may be the sort of case we are looking for, a case in which the effect of the duty can be separated from the effect of other aspects of authoritative action. In this case at any rate the conclusion is clear. By and large, those who approved of conscription when it came did so because they believed that it was everyone's duty to serve in the armed forces in any case. They would have denied that the conscription law imposed a completely new duty. It merely declared what people ought to have done. Because the doubters were bound, by the fact that they were subject to the authority of Parliament, to follow Parliament's judgment as to what their duties were, its Act is not merely dependent on those duties but also pre-empts them.

We are to imagine a situation in which the State provides all the services it currently provides, let us say roads and a sewerage system, free education and a free health service, social security and unemployment benefits and the like. They are provided by raising money from the public for a state-run charity, contributions to which are voluntary but which publishes guidelines for self-assessment for those who wish to use them. I hope it will be agreed that those who think that the tax law is justified do so partly because they believe that there is in the circumstances imagined a reason voluntarily to contribute a sum which is equivalent to a just tax.

Let us take stock of the argument so far. One thesis I am arguing for claims that authoritative reasons are pre-emptive: *the fact that an authority requires performance of an action is a reason for its performance which is not to be added to all other relevant reasons when assessing what to do, but should exclude and take the place of some of them.* It will be remembered that the thesis is only about legitimate authority. It is relevant for the explanation of the character of *de facto* authorities because every *de facto* authority either claims or is acknowledged by others to be a legitimate authority. But since not every authority is legitimate not every authoritative directive is a reason for action.

Furthermore, authoritative directives are not beyond challenge. First, they may be designed not finally to determine what is to be done in certain circumstances but merely to determine what ought to be done on the basis of certain considerations. For example, a directive may determine that from the economic point of view a certain action is required. It will then replace economic considerations but no others. Or the authority may direct that the final decision must be based on economic considerations only, thus replacing all but the economic factors. Even where an authoritative decision is meant finally to settle what is to be done it may be open to challenge on certain grounds, e.g. if an emergency occurs, or if the directive violates fundamental human rights, or if the authority acted arbitrarily. The non-excluded reasons and the grounds for challenging an authority's directives vary from case to case. They determine the conditions of legitimacy of the authority and the limits of its rightful power.

This point is worth emphasizing not only because of its importance in the developing argument to follow, but also because it marks the way in which my use of 'the limit of an authority's rightful power' differs from some common uses (though it conforms with others, including the legal usage). Sometimes authorities are understood to be limited by the kinds of acts which they can or cannot regulate (given some restrictive ways of classifying acts). In this book authorities are said to be limited also by the kinds of reasons on which they may or may not rely in making decisions and issuing directives, and by the kind of reasons their decisions can pre-empt.

The argument for the pre-emption thesis proceeds from another, which I shall call the dependence thesis. It says: *all authoritative directives should be based on reasons which already independently apply to the subjects of the directives and are relevant to their action in the cirumstances covered by the directive.* Such reasons I dubbed above 'dependent reasons'. The examples of conscription and taxation were intended to give the dependence thesis some plausibility, and in particular to disprove the suggestion that dependence is the mark of adjudication. But doubts are bound to linger and further clarifications are required to dispel them.

A few preliminary points. The dependence thesis does not claim that authorities always act for dependent reasons, but merely that they should do so. Ours is an attempt to explain the notion of legitimate authority through describing what one might call an ideal exercise of authority. Reality has a way of falling short of the ideal. We saw this regarding *de facto* authorities which are not legitimate. But naturally not even legitimate authorities always succeed, nor do they always try to live up to the ideal. It is nevertheless through their ideal functioning that they must be understood. For that is how they are supposed to function, that is how they publicly claim that they attempt to function, and, as we shall see below, that is the normal way to justify their authority (i.e. not by assuming that they always succeed in acting in the ideal way, but on the ground that they do so often enough to justify their power), and naturally authorities are judged and their performance evaluated by comparing them to the ideal.

Remember also that the thesis is not that authoritative determinations are binding only if they correctly reflect the reasons on which they depend. On the contrary, there is no point in having authorities unless their determinations are binding even if mistaken (though some mistakes may disqualify them). The whole point and purpose of authorities,

I shall argue below, is to pre-empt individual judgment on the merits of a case, and this will not be achieved if, in order to establish whether the authoritative determination is binding, individuals have to rely on their own judgment of the merits.

Nor does the thesis claim that authorities should always act in the interests of their subjects. Its claim is that their actions should reflect reasons which apply also to their subjects, but these need not be reasons advancing their interests. A military commander, for example, should put the defence of his country above the interests of his soldiers. He may therefore order them to act against their own interests. But then soldiers are supposed to put their country above their personal interests and but for this they would not have to obey their commander.

Much of the resistance to the dependence thesis comes from confusing it with a claim about what authorities do in fact, or with the view that requires authorities to act only in the interests of their subjects. But the most common confusion is between the dependence thesis and the no difference thesis, which was briefly discussed in the last chapter. The no difference thesis asserts that *the exercise of authority should make no difference to what its subjects ought to do*, for it ought to direct them to do what they ought to do in any event.[1] It may appear that the dependence thesis entails the no difference thesis, but this is not the case. There are at least three ways (others will be discussed in the next chapter) in which an authority acting correctly may make a difference to what its subjects ought to do, which are all consistent with the dependence thesis.

First, many aspects of every action we perform for a reason are not uniquely determined by reasons. I have a reason to buy a loaf of bread, but, let us assume, no reason to prefer a sliced loaf to an unsliced one or vice versa. Since I have a reason to buy a loaf of bread I have a reason to buy a sliced loaf, as well as a reason to buy an unsliced one. But I have no reason to get one rather than the other. Since there is no

---

[1] The no difference thesis is about what happens if authorities reach the right decision. Since their directives are binding even when mistaken, they do then make a difference.

other kind of bread, inevitably if I do as I have reason to and buy a loaf I will buy one or the other. That is, in acting on the best reasons I will also inevitably transcend reason and take a deliberate decision (e.g. to buy a sliced loaf) concerning some aspects of which reason is undetermined.

The same general considerations apply to directives issued by authorities. The legislator, for example, has reason to impose a certain tax. There are reasons showing that it is better to require that the tax due shall be paid either in quarterly or in monthly payments. These intervals are superior to all others. But while some reasons favour monthly payments and others favour quarterly ones, neither is sufficient to establish the superiority of doing it one way rather than the other. In this situation the authority may leave the choice to individuals. But sometimes there are decisive reasons against doing so. Then the authority has to decide for one of the two or more acceptable options.[1] When this happens the authoritative directive does make a difference. Without it individuals would have had a choice as to which of the acceptable solutions to adopt. The authority quite properly denies them the choice, and exercises it itself.

Second, as was mentioned in the last chapter, one important function of authoritative directives is to establish and help sustain conventions. Conventions are here understood in a narrow sense in which they are solutions to co-ordination problems, i.e. to situations in which the vast majority have sufficient reason to prefer to take that action which is (likely to be) taken by the vast majority. Where there is a co-ordination problem the issuing of an authoritative directive can supply the missing link in the argument. It makes it likely that a convention will be established to follow the authoritatively designated act. It is often the proper job of authorities to issue directives for this purpose. Such authoritative directives provide the subjects with reasons which they did not have before. They therefore make a difference to their practical deliberations, and serve to refute the no difference thesis.

---

[1] It would be a mistake to think of them as exactly tied options. All that is here assumed is that reasons are insufficient to establish the superiority of one option over the others.

It is true that once a useful co-ordinating convention is established every person has reason to adhere to it, a reason which is independent of the existence of the authority, a reason deriving entirely from the existence of the useful convention. The same is true where there is a good prospect that such a convention will emerge. The point of my argument is that sometimes authoritative intervention creates that prospect, and that it creates it because of its authoritativeness. Similarly, the existence of an authoritative directive may prevent or delay processes which, but for it, would have undermined the convention.

These cases are not only common, though hardly ever in the much over-simplified form we have considered, but also of some theoretical interest. Once the directive is issued, individuals have reasons to take the action it requires which they did not have before, because now there is ground to expect that a convention will be formed. But while this shows that the directive made a difference, it does not refute the dependence thesis. The authority took the action in order to help generate a convention. In so acting it acted for a dependent reason, for the assumption is that individuals have reason to wish for a convention and hence reason to take action to help form one. Every person in the group concerned has, before the directive is issued, a reason both to form a convention and to follow it once formed. This is the reason for which the legislation is adopted and it is, for the legislator, a dependent reason.[1]

Third, Prisoner's Dilemma type situations are another class of cases where authorities make a difference while conforming with the dependence thesis. In these cases while

---

[1] The importance of authorities for the generation and maintenance of conventions has led on occasion to ill-conceived attempts to explain the nature of authority exclusively by reference to conventions. Such accounts fail, as L. Green has shown in his 'The Authority of the State', a D.Phil. thesis approved by the University of Oxford 1984, to account for the pre-emptive force of authoritative directives. My account is consistent with Green's arguments on this point. The nature of authority is explained by the combination of the three theses we are discussing. Conventions are relevant only as one illustration of the non-equivalence of the dependence and the no difference theses. Conventions can arise in other ways and authorities can do other things. But one way of generating or protecting and stabilizing conventions is by authoritative intervention. Sometimes it is the best, or even the only feasible way. Even when it is not it is often a good way of generating conventions.

people have reason to act in a certain way, given the situation they are in, they also have reason to change the situation, though they are unable to do so by themselves. It is this feature, shared by cases where there are co-ordination problems, which enables authorities to make a difference while acting on dependent reasons. It should be remembered that many moral theories may land their adherents in Prisoner's Dilemma type situations. The problem does not arise merely through lack of moral fibre.[1]

Another source of doubt about the validity of the dependence thesis can be removed by eliminating an ambiguity in its formulation. It speaks of authoritative directives being based on or reflecting reasons which apply to their subjects in any case. This can be taken to mean that the one proper way for an authority to decide its actions is to ask itself what are the reasons which apply to its subjects and attempt to follow them. This is indeed a way of trying to meet the requirement of the dependence thesis. But it is not the only one, nor is it always the best. The dependence thesis does not exclude the authority from acting for other reasons which apply to it alone, and not to its subjects. All it requires is that its instructions will reflect the reasons which apply to its subjects, i.e. that they should require action which is justifiable by the reasons which apply to the subjects. Sometimes the best way to reach decisions which reflect the reasons which apply to the subjects is to adopt an indirect strategy and follow rules and considerations which do not themselves apply to the authority's subjects. Sometimes, in other words, one has to act for non-dependent reasons in order to maximize conformity to dependent reasons.

The clearest example of considerations which affect authoritative decisions but which do not apply to individuals acting on their own are considerations arising out of the needs and limitations of bureaucracies. Bureaucratic factors have to be considered alongside substantive considerations which do apply to the individual subjects of the law or any other

[1] For the relevance of Prisoner's Dilemmas to the study of authority see E. Ullman-Margalit, *The Emergence of Norms*, Oxford, 1980. For an analysis of the way Prisoner's Dilemmas arise within the bounds of various moral theories see D. Parfit, *Reasons and Persons*, Oxford, 1984.

authority. Bureaucracies, for example, are almost invariably forced to embrace a *de minimis* rule in order to be able to achieve their tasks where it really matters. The intrusion of the bureaucratic considerations is likely to lead to solutions which differ in many cases from those an individual should have adopted if left to himself. Reliance on such considerations is justified if and to the extent that they enable authorities to reach decisions which, when taken as a whole, better reflect the reasons which apply to the subjects. That is, an authority may rely on considerations which do not apply to its subjects when doing so reliably leads to decisions which approximate better than any which would have been reached by any other procedure, to those decisions best supported by reasons which apply to the subjects.

These considerations point to another way in which the no difference thesis distorts. Even while authoritative actions reflect the subjects' reasons, indeed in order that they should do so, they may well lead to different outcomes on particular occasions, and that without being in any way wrong or mistaken on those occasions.

I will return briefly to these considerations in the next chapter, where their importance in pointing to the source of doctrines of the authority of the State will appear. For the time being let me conclude by admitting that the considerations adumbrated in this section do not prove the dependence thesis. They adduce support for it mainly by removing misunderstandings and a few possible objections. Implicitly the argument appeals to our common understanding of the way authority should be exercised. The argument gains much strength by considering the case of theoretical authority, i.e. authority for believing in certain propositions. Nowadays it is not the fashion to talk of authorities in this context. Instead we have experts. But the notions are very similar, at least in all that matters to our concerns.

There is likely to be ready agreement that experts of all varieties are to give advice based on the very same reasons which should sway ordinary people who wish to form their minds independently. The expert's advantage is in his easy access to the evidence and in his better ability to grasp its significance. But the evidence on which he should base his advice to me is the same evidence on which it would have been appropriate for me to form my own judgment. It is possible that practical and theoretical authorities have little in common. But it is more likely that, while they provide reasons for different things, they share the same basic structure. If so, the fact that a dependence thesis is true of theoretical authorities is strong evidence to suppose that it holds for practical authorities as well.

3. The Justification of Authority

The dependence thesis, it will be remembered, is a moral thesis about the way authorities should use their powers. It is closely connected with a second moral thesis about the type of argument which could be used to establish the legitimacy of an authority. I shall call it *the normal justification thesis*. It claims that *the normal way to establish that a person has authority over another person involves showing that the alleged subject is likely better to comply with reasons which apply to him (other than the alleged authoritative directives) if he accepts the directives of the alleged authority as authoritatively binding and tries to follow them, rather than by trying to follow the reasons which apply to him directly.*

This way of justifying a claim that someone has legitimate authority, i.e. that those subject to his authority should acknowledge the authoritative force of his directives, is not the only one. It is, however, the normal one. Consider the case of a person whose reason for accepting his friend's advice is that the friend will be hurt if he does not. This may well be a perfectly good reason for accepting advice. But it is not the normal reason. It is regrettable that the friend will be hurt if his advice is not followed after it was given due consideration, or at least it is regrettable that he will be hurt to a degree which justifies this reaction. The friend himself does not intend his advice to be accepted for that reason, and is likely to be doubly hurt if he finds out that his advice was judged mistaken on its merits but was followed in order not to hurt him. The reason is that even when this is a good reason to accept advice it is not a reason to accept it as a piece of advice. It is a reason to accept it as a way of being kind to a friend.

The normal reason for accepting a piece of advice is that it is likely to be sound advice. The normal reason to offer advice is the very same. It will be clear that these judgments of normality are normative. But the very nature of advice can only be understood if we understand in what spirit it is meant to be offered and for what reasons it is meant to be taken. The explanation must leave room for deviant cases, for their existence is undeniable. But it must also draw the distinction between the deviant and the normal, for otherwise the very reason why the 'institution' exists and why deviant cases take the special form they do remains inexplicable.

The example of advice is close to the case of authority. Indeed some, though not all, advice is authoritative advice. It is, for example, sometimes justifiable to accept someone's authority in order not to hurt his feelings. Many grown-up people feel obliged by such considerations to continue to acknowledge the authority of their parents over them. But just as in the case of advice, and for the very same reasons, such grounds for recognizing the authority of another, even though sometimes good, are always deviant grounds.

Slightly different considerations show that some reasons for recognizing the authority of another are secondary. To call them secondary means that they are valid reasons only if they accompany other, primary, reasons which also conform to the normal justification thesis (whereas deviant reasons may validly replace the normal reasons). Accepting the authority or leadership of a person or an institution is, for example, a way of defining one's own identity as a member of a nation or some other group, though needless to say it is unlikely to be the only way any person will express his identification with such a group. Such a reason can be a perfectly valid reason, but only if there are other reasons which, in accord with the normal justification thesis, support the authority of that person. The secondary reasons help to meet the burden of proof required to establish a complete justification, i.e. they may suffice in conjunction with the primary reasons in circumstances in which the primary reasons alone will not be enough to establish the legitimacy of an authority. But reasons of identification and self-definition cannot by themselves establish the legitimacy of an authority.

Identification is a common and often proper ground for accepting authority. It is therefore important to establish the reasons why it is no more than a secondary justification dependent on the availability, at least to a certain degree, of another justification. Acceptance of an authority can be an act of identification with a group because it can be naturally regarded as expressing trust in the person or institution in authority and a willingness to share the fortunes of the group which are to a large extent determined by the authority.

But trust in the authority is trust that the authority is likely to discharge its duties properly. It therefore presupposes a principle which should govern its activities. Accepting the authority as a way of identifying with a group will be justified only if the trust is not altogether misplaced. Otherwise the odd situation may result that a person will quite properly express his identification with a group by supporting an institution which grossly betrays its duties to the group. For the same reasons one cannot properly express one's willingness to share the fortunes of a group by submitting to an authority which grossly betrays the trust it owes to the group. Identification with the group in such circumstances calls for the rejection of that authority.

The dependence and the normal justification theses are mutually reinforcing. If the normal and primary way of justifying the legitimacy of an authority is that it is more likely to act successfully on the reasons which apply to its subjects then it is hard to resist the dependence thesis. It merely claims that authorities should do that which they were appointed to do. Conversely, if the dependence thesis is accepted then the case for the normal justification thesis becomes very strong. It merely states that the normal and primary justification of any authority has to establish that it is qualified to follow with some degree of success the principles which should govern the decisions of all authorities. Together the two theses present a comprehensive view of the nature and role of legitimate authority. They articulate the service conception of the function of authorities, that is, the view that their role and primary normal function is to serve the governed. This, to repeat a point made earlier, does not mean that their sole role must be to further the interest of each or of all their subjects. It is to help them act on reasons which bind them.

It will be noticed that the normal justification thesis identifies the case that must normally be established to show that a person has authority. It is not a matter of showing that he is entitled to have authority, but that he has it, that he is in authority, with all the consequences which follow from this fact. The main objection to this point revolves round the feeling that a person can have authority, or be in authority only if his authority is recognized by some people, whose identity varies with the nature of his authority. The difficulty in assessing this point is that in most cases the normal justification cannot be established unless the putative authority enjoys some measure of recognition, and exercises power over its subjects. There is a strong case for holding that no political authority can be legitimate unless it is also a *de facto* authority. For the case for having any political authority rests to a large extent on its ability to solve co-ordination problems and extricate the population from Prisoner's Dilemma type situations.

These considerations explain why to say of someone that he is entitled to have authority means that he should be in a position of real power and then he will have legitimate authority. They may be sufficient to account for the feeling that as a matter of meaning, recognition is a condition of possession of legitimate authority. If I am right then this is not a matter of meaning, but of normative justification.

The normal justification thesis allows for deviant reasons. Apart from these it is meant to account for all the reasons there can be for accepting authorities. But a complete justification of authority has to do more than to provide valid reasons for its acceptance. It has also to establish that there are no reasons against its acceptance which defeat the reasons for the authority. Because the reasons against the acceptance of authority vary it is not possible to discover in advance how strong the reasons for acceptance of the authority need be to be sufficient.

Some reasons against the acceptance of authority pertain, with varying force, to many situations. One recurring kind of reason against accepting the authority of one person or institution is that there is another person or institution with a better claim to be recognized as an authority. The claim of the second is a reason against accepting the claim of the first only when the two authorities are incompatible, as are the claims of two governments to be legitimate governments of one country. Sometimes there are two compatible authorities whose powers overlap, as is the case with the authority of both parents over their children.

Another cluster of recurring considerations concerns the intrinsic desirability of people conducting their own life by their own lights. This obviously applies to some areas of life more than to others, to choice of friends more than to the choice of legal argument in a court case. The case for the validity of a claim to authority must include justificatory considerations sufficient to outweigh such counter-reasons. That is one reason why the case is hard to make. But if anarchists are right to think that it can never be made, this is for contingent reasons and not because of any inconsistency in the notion of a rational justification for authority, nor in the notion of authority over moral agents.

4. The Pre-emptive Thesis

From the dependence and normal justification theses it is but a short step to the pre-emption thesis. It turns on the general relation between the justification for a binding directive and its status as a reason for action, and more generally on the relation between rules as reasons for action and their justification. Consider the rule that, when being with one person and meeting another, one should introduce them to each other. The fact that this rule is a sound, valid or sensible rule is a reason for anyone to act in accordance with it. It is a sound rule because it facilitates social contact. But the fact that introducing people to each other in those circumstances facilitates social contacts is itself a reason for doing so. Do we then have two independent reasons for introducing people? Clearly not. When considering the weight or strength of the reasons for an action, the reasons for the rule cannot be added to the rule itself as additional reasons. We must count one or the other but not both. Authoritative directives are often rules, and even when they are not, because they lack the required generality, the same reasoning applies to them. Either the directive or the reasons for holding it to be binding should be counted but not both. To do otherwise is to be guilty of double counting.

This fact is a reflection of the role of rules in practical reasoning. They mediate between deeper-level considerations and concrete decisions. They provide an intermediate level of reasons to which one appeals in normal cases where a need for a decision arises. Reasons of that level can themselves be justified by reference to the deeper concerns on which they are based. The advantage of normally proceeding through the mediation of rules is enormous. It enables a person to consider and form an opinion on the general aspects of recurrent situations in advance of their occurence. It enables a person to achieve results which can be achieved only through an advance commitment to a whole series of actions, rather than by case to case examination.

More importantly, the practice allows the creation of a pluralistic culture. For it enables people to unite in support of some 'low or medium level' generalizations despite profound disagreements concerning their ultimate foundations, which some seek in religion, others in Marxism or in Liberalism, etc. I am not suggesting that the differences in the foundations do not lead to differences in practice. The point is that an orderly community can exist only if it shares many practices, and that in all modern pluralistic societies a great measure of toleration of vastly differing outlooks is made possible by the fact that many of them enable the vast majority of the population to accept common standards of conduct.

More directly relevant to our case is the fact that, through the acceptance of rules setting up authorities, people can entrust judgment as to what is to be done to another person or institution which will then be bound, in accordance with the dependence thesis, to exercise its best judgment primarily on the basis of the dependent reasons appropriate to the case. Thus the mediation of authorities may, where justified, improve people's compliance with practical and moral principles. This often enables them better to achieve the benefits that rules may bring as explained above, and other benefits besides.

These reflections on the mediating role of authoritative directives and of rules generally explain why they are reasons for actions. Ultimately, however, directives and rules derive their force from the considerations which justify them. That is, they do not add further weight to their justifying considerations. In any case in which one penetrates beyond the directives or the rules to their underlying justifications one has to discount the independent weight of the rule or the directive as a reason for action. Whatever force they have is completely exhausted by those underlying considerations. Contrariwise, whenever one takes a rule or a directive as a reason one cannot add to it as additional independent factors the reasons which justify it.

Hence the pre-emption thesis. Since the justification of the binding force of authoritative directives rests on dependent reasons, the reasons on which they depend are (to the extent that the directives are regarded simply as authoritative) replaced rather than added to by those directives. The service conception leads to the pre-emption thesis. Because authorities do not have the right to impose completely independent duties on people, because their directives should reflect dependent reasons which are binding on those people in any case, they have the right to replace people's own judgment on the merits of the case. Their directives pre-empt the force of at least some of the reasons which otherwise should have guided the actions of those people.[1]

---

[1] A. M. Honoré pointed out that even if an (informal) arbitration conluded in my favour, if I later become convinced that my original claim was mistaken I should acknowledge the claim of the other litigant rather than rely on the arbitrator's decision. Here it seems as if, contrary to the pre-emption thesis, the original reasons are not pre-empted by the arbitrator's decision. Nevertheless one's duty undergoes a complete change in such circumstances. I may rely on the arbitrator. I may say that we both agreed that our relations will be governed by his

The pre-emption thesis helps explain one additional re-spect in which the no difference thesis is wrong. The three respects surveyed in Section Two above depended on the difference that the existence of a legitimate authority makes to what one ought to do. The pre-emption thesis shows how its existence makes a difference to the reasons why one ought to do what one ought to do. In a sense this point is a trivially obvious one. If one ought to act because of an authoritative directive one's reasons are different than if one ought to perform the same act for other reasons. The non-trivial point I am making is that the difference is not in the presence of an additional reason for action, but in the existence of a pre-emptive reason. That is why what is validly required by a legitimate authority is one's duty, even where previously it was merely something one had sufficient reason to do. Authoritative directives make a difference in their ability to turn 'oughts' into duties.[1]

The pre-emption thesis will be readily accepted inasmuch as it concerns successful authoritative directives, i.e. those which correctly reflect the balance of reasons on which they depend. But, a common objection goes, the thesis cannot justify pre-empting reasons which the authority was meant to reflect correctly and failed to reflect. Successfully reflected reasons are those which show that the directive is valid. They are the justification for its binding force. Therefore, either they or the directive should be relied upon, but not both, that is not if relying on both means adding the weight of the directive to the force of the reasons justifying it when assessing the weight of the case for the directed action. Reasons that should have determined the authority's directive but failed to do so cannot be thought to belong to the jus-tification of the directive. On the contrary they tell against it. They are reasons for holding that it is not binding. The

decision, that I would have gone along with it had he made a mistake which harmed me. I would be rather ungenerous and unfriendly but nevertheless formally correct. The situation is the same as in cases of agreement. I buy a chest from you and a price is agreed. It then transpires that the chest is a valuable antique and the price I paid is ludicrously low. If I ought to pay a fair price for what I buy then I ought to come back and add to the agreed price.

[1] On the pre-emptive character of duties see my 'Promises and Obligations', *Law, Morality and Society*, ed. by P. M. S. Hacker and J. Raz, Oxford, 1977.

pre-emption thesis is wrong in claiming that they too are pre-empted.

So much for the objection. It fails because its premiss is false. Reasons which authoritative directives should, but fail to, reflect are none the less among the reasons which justify holding the directives binding. An authority is justified, according to the normal justification thesis, if it is more likely than its subjects to act correctly for the right reasons. That is how the subjects' reasons figure in the justification, both when they are correctly reflected in a particular directive and when they are not. If every time a directive is mistaken, i.e. every time it fails to reflect reason correctly, it were open to challenge as mistaken, the advantage gained by accepting the authority as a more reliable and successful guide to right reason would disappear. In trying to establish whether or not the directive correctly reflects right reason the subjects will be relying on their own judgments rather than on that of the authority, which, we are assuming, is more reliable.

These reflections suggest another objection to the preemption thesis. It says that in every case authoritative directives can be overridden or disregarded if they deviate much from the reasons which they are meant to reflect. It would not do, the objection continues, to say that the legitimate power of every authority is limited, and that one of the limitations is that it may not err much. For such a limitation defeats the pre-emption thesis since it requires every person in every case to consider the merits of the case before he can decide to accept an authoritative instruction.

The objection does not formally challenge the preemption thesis. It does not claim that the reasons which are supposed to be displaced by authoritative instructions are not replaced by them but should count as additional independent reasons alongside the instructions. Its effect is to deny that authoritative instructions can serve the mediating role assigned them above. That role is to enable people to act on non-ultimate reasons. It is to save them the need to refer to the very foundations of morality and practical reasoning generally in every case. But as the directives are binding only if they do not deviate much from right reason and as we should act on them only if they are binding, we always have to go back to fundamentals. We have to examine the reasons for and against the directive and judge whether it is justified in order to decide whether its mistake, if it is not justified, is large or small. The mediating role is unobtainable.

The failure of this objection stems from its confusion of a great mistake with a clear one. Consider a long addition of, say, some thirty numbers. One can make a very small mistake which is a very clear one, as when the sum is an integer whereas one and only one of the added numbers is a decimal fraction. On the other hand, the sum may be out by several thousands without the mistake being detectable except by laboriously going over the addition step by step. Even if legitimate authority is limited by the condition that its directives are not binding if clearly wrong, and I wish to express no opinion on whether it is so limited, it can play its mediating role. Establishing that something is clearly wrong does not require going through the underlying reasoning. It is not the case that the legitimate power of authorities is generally limited by the condition that it is defeated by significant mistakes which are not clear.

The pre-emption thesis depends on a distinction between jurisdictional and other mistakes. Most, if not all, authorities have limited powers. Mistakes which they make about factors which determine the limits of their jurisdiction render their decisions void. They are not binding as authoritative directives, though the circumstances of the case may require giving them some weight if, for example, others innocently have relied on them. Other mistakes do not affect the binding force of the directives. The pre-emption thesis claims that the factors about which the authority was wrong, and which are not jurisdictional factors, are pre-empted by the directive. The thesis would be pointless if most mistakes are jurisdictional or if in most cases it was particularly controversial and difficult to establish which are and which are not. But if this were so then most other accounts of authority would come to grief.

5. Objections

I will conclude this chapter by considering a few objections to the account of authority suggested above which challenge its general orientation. I shall start with a misunderstanding which the method of explanation adopted here is likely to give rise to among readers used to philosophical explanations of concepts such as authority being presented as accounts of the meanings of words.

Three theses were presented as part of an explanation of the concept of authority. They are supposed to advance our understanding of the concept by showing how authoritative action plays a special role in people's practical reasoning. But the theses are also normative ones. They instruct people how to take binding directives, and when to acknowledge that they are binding. The service conception is a normative doctrine about the conditions under which authority is legitimate and the manner in which authorities should conduct themselves. Is not that a confusion of conceptual analysis and normative argument? The answer is that there is an interdependence between conceptual and normative argument.

The philosophical explanation of authority is not an attempt to state the meaning of a word. It is a discussion of a concept which is deeply embedded in the philosophical and political traditions of our culture. The concept serves as an integral part of a whole mesh of ideas and beliefs, leading from one part of the net to another. There is not, nor has there ever been, complete agreement on all aspects of the concept's place and connections with other concepts. But there is, as part of our common culture, a good measure of agreement between any two people on many, though frequently not the same, points. Accounts of 'authority' attempt a double task. They are part of an attempt to make explicit elements of our common traditions: a highly prized activity in a culture which values self-awareness. At the same time such accounts take a position in the traditional debate about the precise connections between that and other concepts. They are partisan accounts furthering the cause of certain strands in the common tradition, by developing and producing new or newly recast arguments in their favour. The very activity is also an expression of faith in the tradition, of a willingness to understand oneself and the world in its terms and to carry on the argument, which in the area with which we are concerned is inescapably a normative argument, within the general framework defining the tradition. Faithfulness to the shape of common concepts is itself an act of normative significance.

Since this chapter is meant as a normative-explanatory account of the core notion of authority, it can be extended to explain reference to authority in various specific contexts. But such extensions are neither mechanical nor automatic. For example, the three theses apply in the most straightforward way to discourse of people being in authority or having authority over others. It is an account of authority relations between a legitimate authority and those subject to it. How does it help to understand discourse of someone being an authority? It is false that only a person in authority is an authority. There are various contexts in which we speak of a person or institution being an authority. Consider as an example cases where a person (but only exceptionally an institution) is said to be an authority on a certain matter, as in 'John is an authority on Chinese cooking' or 'Ruth is an authority on the stock exchange'. Neither John nor Ruth has authority over me, even though my Chinese cooking and my financial affairs will prosper if I follow their advice rather than trust my own judgment.

One may say that to be an authority on a certain matter is to be an authority about what to believe rather than about what to do. While generally true this does not solve the difficulty in the case of John and Ruth since each of them may claim to be both a theoretical and a practical authority. They do not have authority over me because the right way to treat their advice depends on my goals. If I want nothing but to prepare the best Chinese meal I can manage then I should just follow John's instructions. If I want to maximize my savings I should follow Ruth's advice. But if I wish to enjoy myself dabbling in cooking or in playing the stock exchange then I should try and form my own judgment. I should not yield to theirs unless I see its point and come to agree with them. Here the normal justification thesis establishes the credentials of John and Ruth as authorities in their fields. But whether or not there is a complete justification for me to regard their advice or instructions as guides to my conduct in the way I regard a binding authoritative directive depends on my other goals. In such cases while talking of a person as being an authority one refrains from talking of him as in authority over oneself, and avoids regarding his advice or instructions as binding, even when, given one's goals, one ought to treat it in exactly the same way as one treats a binding authoritative directive.

My proposed account of authority is not even an account of the meaning of the phrase 'X has authority over Y'. It is an account of legitimate authority, whereas the phrase is often used to refer to *de facto* authorities. There is no purely linguistic way of generally marking the intended use. As indicated above, the notion of a *de facto* authority depends on that of a legitimate authority since it implies not only actual power over people but, in the normal case, both that the person excercising that power claims to have legitimate authority and that he is acknowledged to have it by some people. In some unusual cases one is willing to apply the term when only one of these conditions obtains.

What is it to claim authority or to accept that someone has authority over one? It means to believe that one has legitimate authority, or that that person has authority over one. Here we encounter one of the main differences between normative-explanatory accounts such as the ones offered here of authority or the later account (in Chapter 7) of rights, and the purely linguistic explanations often advocated by analytic philosophers. A purely linguistic account of authority claims to yield a simple explanation of what people believe who believe that someone has legitimate authority. Had the above account been a linguistic account, an explanation of the meaning of 'legitimate authority', it would have followed that anyone who believes of a person that he has legitimate authority believes that that person satisfies the condition set by the justification thesis. This implication does not hold for a normative-explanatory account. In being normative it avows that it does not necessarily conform to everyone's notion of authority in all detail. It does claim to be an explanatory account in singling out important features of people's conception of authority. It helps explain what they believe in when they believe that a person has authority. But some people's beliefs may not conform to the account here given in all respects.

This is a key to the difference between linguistic and explanatory-normative accounts. The latter, while providing a crucial guide for the understanding of the way terms are used in different contexts, does not allow for a simple explanation based on substitutivity. This might have been a drawback of such accounts but for the fact that linguistic accounts understood in accord with the current consensus among analytic philosophers either are not possible or lack any philosophical interest. But that is a matter for an extensive argument which will have to wait another occasion.[1]

How can the account of authority here offered be thought to represent important strands in Western thought? If there is a common theme to liberal political theorizing on authority, it is that the legitimacy of authority rests on the duty to support and uphold just institutions, as, following Rawls, the duty is now usually called. But that duty is of course dependent on a prior understanding of which institutions are just. The account here offered is meant as a beginning of an answer to that question. Or rather it contributes by setting the question in a certain way. One has a duty to uphold and support authorities if they meet the conditions of the service conception as explained above.

Furthermore, the duty to uphold and support just institutions is, in some respects, wider than the duty which devolves on one as a result of the fact that someone has legitimate authority over one, in three different ways. First, there are just institutions which neither possess, nor claim to possess, any authority. Think of the British Council, or the BBC, for example. One owes them the duty to uphold and support them. But this has nothing to do with any issue concerning authority. Second, the duty involves more than a duty of obedience. One may be obligated to help fight opponents of the institution or help overcome obstacles to its successful operation in ways which one is not required

---

[1] For an incisive critique of much of the current consensus regarding language among analytic philosophers see G. Baker and P. M. S. Hacker, *Language, Sense and Nonsense*, Oxford, 1984.

by its laws to do. Third, the duty is owed to institutions which may have authority but only towards other people. For example, one may owe the duty to the just government of foreign countries. We must conclude, therefore, that the duty to support just institutions, where it has to do with just authorities, is parasitical on the normal justification thesis, and not an alternative to it. In other ways the duty to uphold and support just institutions is narrower than the duty corresponding to the right of a legitimate authority. One has a duty to obey those in authority over one even in circumstances in which disobedience does not imperil their existence or functioning.

To the extent that legitimate authorities have power over us, the pre-emption thesis governs our right attitude to them. The duty to uphold and support just institutions does not come into play. It is primarily an other-regarding duty. I have a duty to support just governments in foreign countries, even though they have no legitimate power over me. I have reason to support the authority of my neighbours over their children, etc. In other words, the duty to uphold and support just institutions comes into play when the conditions of legitimacy implied by the service conception of authority are satisfied. It then supplements the pre-emption thesis by showing that we should be concerned not merely to have the proper attitude to those in authority over us, but also to those in authority over others.

Finally, let us return to our starting point. What is wrong with regarding an authoritative directive as one additional prima facie reason for the action it directs, which supplements, rather than supplants, the other reasons for and against that action? The service conception establishes that the point of having authorities is that they are better at complying with the dependent reasons. Take a simplified situation. I regularly confront a decision, for example, whether or not to sell certain shares, in varying circumstances. Suppose that it is known that a financial expert reaches the 'right' decision (whatever that may be) in 20% more cases than I do when I do not rely on his advice. Should I not, when confronting such decisions, carry on as before but take his advice as a factor counting in favour of the decision he recommends?

Perhaps I should always take the case for his solution as being 20% stronger than it would otherwise appear to me to be. Perhaps some other, more complicated formula should be worked out. In any case would not the right course require me to give his advice prima facie rather than pre-emptive force? The answer is that it would not. In cases about which I know only that his performance is better than mine, letting his advice tilt the balance in favour of his solution will sometimes, depending on my rate of mistakes and the formula used, improve my performance. But I will continue to do less well than he does unless I let his judgment pre-empt mine.

Consider the case in a general way. Suppose I can identify a range of cases in which I am wrong more than the putative authority. Suppose I decide because of this to tilt the balance in all those cases in favour of its solution. That is, in every case I will first make up my own mind independently of the 'authority's' verdict, and then, in those cases in which my judgment differs from its, I will add a certain weight to the solution favoured by it, on the ground that it, the authority, knows better than I. This procedure will reverse my independent judgment in a certain proportion of the cases. Sometimes even after giving the argument favoured by the authority an extra weight it will not win. On other occasions the additional weight will make all the difference. How will I fare under this procedure? If, as we are assuming, there is no other relevant information available then we can expect that in the cases in which I endorse the authority's judgment my rate of mistakes declines and equals that of the authority. In the cases in which even now I contradict the authority's judgment the rate of my mistakes remains unchanged, i.e. greater than that of the authority. This shows that only by allowing the authority's judgment to pre-empt mine altogether will I succeed in improving my performance and bringing it to the level of the authority. Of course sometimes I do have additional information showing that the authority is better than me in some areas and not in others. This may be sufficient to show that it lacks authority over me in those other areas. The argument about the pre-emptiveness of authoritative decrees does not apply to such cases.

This way of reasoning is unrealistically simple even in the relatively straightforward circumstances of simple stock selling decisions. But it helps to illustrate the general lesson. If another's reasoning is usually better than mine, then comparing on each occasion our two sets of arguments may help me detect my mistake and mend my reasoning. It may help me more indirectly by alerting me to the fact that I may be wrong, and forcing me to reason again to double check my conclusion. But if neither is sufficient to bring my performance up to the level of the other person then my optimific course is to give his decision pre-emptive force. So long as this is done where improving the outcome is more important than deciding for oneself this acceptance of authority, far from being either irrational or an abdication of moral responsibility, is in fact the most rational course and the right way to discharge one's responsibilities.

4

The Authority of States

So far, even though we have kept an eye on the question of political authority, the discussion has been concerned with the wider notion of authority in general. In this chapter, while occasionally branching out to consider wider issues, the implications of the foregoing for the authority of states will be examined. The first section shows that the authority which states and governments claim cannot be based on the main argument for the justification of authority, i.e. that described by the normal justification thesis. Even reasonably just states claim more extensive authority than they are entitled to by that criterion. Sections 2 to 4 proceed to examine whether these limits of political authority can be extended by consent or in other ways. The final section of the chapter draws the emerging picture of the moral relations between the conscientious citizen and his state, assuming it to be reasonably just. It denies the existence of a general obligation to obey the law even in a reasonably just society, though it is argued that just governments may exist, and that in certain circumstances their existence is preferable to any alternative method of social organization. Throughout the discussion I refer interchangeably to the state, which is the political organization of a society, its government, the agent through which it acts, and the law, the vehicle through which much of its power is exercised. It is useful to avail ourselves of the general habit of personifying the law and talking of what it requires, permits, claims, authorizes, etc. The law requires, permits and claims what the organs of government, acting lawfully, and in particular the courts, say that it does.

1. The Normal Justification of Political Authority

The justification of authority, concluded the previous chapter, depends on one main argument, which may be extended and supported by a variety of secondary arguments. The main argument for the legitimacy of any authority is that in subjecting himself to it a person is more likely to act successfully for the reasons which apply to him than if he does not subject himself to its authority. For several reasons the normal justification thesis may seem to overlook some of the essential facts of political power. It therefore may be felt that the thesis cannot serve for the analysis of political authority. Before we proceed any further such doubts have to be dispelled.

The analysis of authority has concentrated exclusively on a one-to-one relation between an authority and a single person subject to it. Does not the fact that political authorities govern groups of people transform the picture? Does it not add to the reasons for which they have to act, and to the considerations which may justify their authority? It is an advantage of the analysis offered in the last chapter that it is capable of accounting for authority over a group on the basis of authority relations between individuals.

Suppose, for example, that what is commonly known as the general, or the community's, interest would be served by a certain public scheme such as compulsory education in mixed ability schools whose students are drawn from mixed social backgrounds. That may mean no more than that such a scheme may do more good than harm and that it would do more good than the obvious alternatives. This is not enough to show that anyone can have authority to introduce or enforce such a scheme. To have that authority over members of the community one has to show, among other conditions imposed by the normal justification thesis, at the very least that members of the community on whom the scheme will impose some burdens have reason to contribute their share to the maintenance of the scheme. Some of them will benefit by it. What of those who would not? The government has authority over them only if they have reason to contribute to a scheme which benefits others.

Suppose that they do. It is possible that they have a reason to do a little to promote such a scheme, whereas the government requires them to make much larger sacrifices. If so the requirement may be unjustified and the government may have no authority to impose it (see the next paragraph for the difference between these possibilities). One has, however, to be cautious here. It may be the case that such schemes cannot operate unless some people make a substantial sacrifice for them. If one had reason to contribute only a little to the scheme this might show that the scheme is unjustifiable since it requires greater sacrifice than can be justified. But sometimes when we say that every person is only required to sacrifice a little we mean that the antecedently expected sacrifice is small, i.e. that the odds that he will have to sacrifice a lot are small. But since the scheme is a good one, and since it is only viable if some people sacrifice a lot, it is a justified scheme, even though one may be called upon, according to fair procedures, to contribute much more than the antecedently expected sacrifice.

Reasoning along such lines is necessary to bridge the gap between the public and the private aspect of authority. It is not good enough to say that an authoritative measure is justified because it serves the public interest. If it is binding on individuals it has to be justified by considerations which bind them. Public authority is ultimately based on the moral duty which individuals owe their fellow humans.[1] Do these comments entail a total rejection of any doctrine of *raison d'état*, of the view that governments sometimes may, indeed should, act for reasons which are out of bounds to individuals? Not quite. It entails the subordination of political reasons to ordinary individual morality. If there are special political reasons then their use is justified to the extent that it enables individuals better to act for the ordinary reasons which apply to them. This may sometimes be the case. Sometimes, as was remarked above,[2] by relying on indirect strategic reasons one may achieve greater conformity with the underlying basic reasons than is possible through a direct attempt to pursue them. To the extent that this is so, there is room for a doctrine of reasons of state in political action.

The discussion of the previous paragraphs is, however,

---

[1] D. Gauthier has revived the Hobbesian argument that political authority and indeed morality generally can be founded on rational self-interest. As chs. 8 and 14 will make clear, the very notion of self-interest on which that argument is based is greatly flawed. See, e.g., D. Gauthier 'Morality and Advantage', *Philosophical Review*, 76 (1967), 460.

[2] See ch. 3, pp. 51–2.

misleading in one respect. It concentrates on an individual measure. Usually arguments for authority are general. They apply to the justification of the use of public power over a range of issues, for an extended period of time. But how general is political authority? What is the question to be asked when one wishes to determine the scope of the authority of law? Should it be, 'Has it authority in all matters?', or should one ask a separate question regarding its authority in matters of taxation, or perhaps one should inquire separately concerning its authority in matters of corporate taxation and personal taxation? How does our proposed account of authority deal with the generalized power of authority? It combines two features. On the one hand generality is built into the account: the normal justification of authority is that following it will enable its subjects better to conform with reason. One cannot establish that this is the case in one case without establishing that it is the case in all like cases. Authority is based on reason and reasons are general, therefore authority is essentially general.

On the other hand the thesis allows maximum flexibility in determining the scope of authority. It all depends on the person over whom authority is supposed to be exercised: his knowledge, strength of will, his reliability in various aspects of life, and on the government in question. These factors are relevant at two levels. First they determine whether an individual is better likely to conform to reason by following an authority or by following his own judgment independently of any authority. Second they determine under what circumstances he is likely to answer the first question correctly. Some people in some circumstances are more likely correctly to assess the argument for authority if put at one level of generality than at another. One has to assess that factor, and the importance of avoiding mistakes in such matters. One also has to take notice of the disadvantages to one's life of too obsessive a preoccupation with questions of the precise limits of authority. The importance of these considerations again will vary from person to person, and from one society to another. Finally, to the extent that political authority is justified by its ability to co-ordinate the activities of large populations, the vindication of its claim to

authority over any one individual may depend on its having
legitimate authority over the population at large.

Most common discussions of political authority presuppose existing political institutions and ask under what
conditions do institutions of that kind have legitimate authority. This begs many questions, and precludes many possibilities. It presupposes that either this government has all
the authority it claims over its population or it has none.
Here again we notice one of the special features of the account of the previous chapter. It allows for a very discriminating approach to the question. The government may
have only some of the of the authority it claims, it may have
more authority over one person than over another. The test
is as explained before: does following the authority's instructions improve conformity with reason? For every person the question has to be asked afresh, and for every one
it has to be asked in a manner which admits of various
qualifications. An expert pharmacologist may not be subject
to the authority of the government in matters of the safety
of drugs, an inhabitant of a little village by a river may
not be subject to its authority in matters of navigation and
conservation of the river by the banks of which he has spent
all his life.

These conclusions appear paradoxical. Ought not the
pharmacologist or the villager to obey the law, given that it
is a good law issued by a just government? I will postpone
consideration of the obligation to obey the law until the last
section of this chapter. For the time being let us remove two
other misunderstandings which make the above conclusion
appear paradoxical. First, it may appear as if the legitimacy
of an authority rests on its greater expertise. Are political
authorities to be equated with big Daddy who knows best?
Second, again the suspicion must creep back that the exclusive concentration on the individual blinds one to the real
business of government, which is to co-ordinate and control
large populations.

These doubts stem from a failure to appreciate the many
ways in which the communal character of political authorities affects their claim to legitimacy *vis-à-vis* each individual. Let us examine some of these points in brief. The

fact that political authorities rule over whole communities itself dictates some of the ways in which the question of the justification of such authorities should be formulated. Of the five most common reasons capable of establishing the legitimacy of an authority some are more appropriate to the political context than others. The five are:

1. The authority is wiser and therefore better able to establish how the individual should act.

2. It has a steadier will less likely to be tainted by bias, weakness or impetuosity, less likely to be diverted from right reason by temptations or pressures.

3. Direct individual action in an attempt to follow right reason is likely to be self-defeating. Individuals should follow an indirect strategy, guiding their action by one standard in order better to conform to another. And the best indirect strategy is to be guided by authority.

4. Deciding for oneself what to do causes anxiety, exhaustion, or involves costs in time or resources the avoidance of which by following authority does not have significant drawbacks, and is therefore justified. (This is a borderline case between normal and deviant justification, or rather it points to one of the many ambiguities in my formulation of the normal justification thesis.)

5. The authority is in a better position to achieve (if its legitimacy is acknowledged) what the individual has reason to but is in no position to achieve.

Though some of these reasons are currently out of fashion in discussions of political authority I believe they all have their role to play, though some are more important in some societies than in others. The last has for a long time been the argument most favoured by political theorists.

It is easy to see why so many people, from Hobbes onwards, have regarded the possession of *de facto* power, of actual effective power over the behaviour of people, as crucial to the possession of legitimate authority. If there is any range of activities in which those who possess great power clearly can do better than most people it is in co-ordinating the activities of many people. It seems plausible to suppose that unless a person enjoys or is soon likely to acquire effective power in a society he does not possess legitimate political authority over that society. He may deserve to have such authority. It may be better if he acquires it. He may even have a right to have it. But he does not as yet have it. One crucial condition which, in the case of political authorities governing sizeable societies, is necessary to establish their legitimacy, does not obtain. That is the ablity to co-ordinate the actions of members of the society in cases in which they have reason to co-ordinate their actions, and the ability to do so better than they can. That ability requires effective power over them. It is itself required for the fulfilment of the task we usually associate with political authority.

While effective power may be a necessary condition of political legitimacy it is not a sufficient condition. It is not in itself sufficient for legitimacy. The wicked governments we have known throughout history are evidence of this. They are unlikely to satisfy the test required by the main argument, i.e. that individuals were more likely to succeed in realizing that which reason required of them if subjected to the government concerned than if left to themselves.

Is political authority ever legitimate? In most contemporary societies the law is the only human institution claiming unlimited authority. Take the United Kingdom, for example. Parliament, according to English constitutional theory, can make and unmake any law, on any matter, and to any effect whatsoever. We know that some laws it may make will not be effective. They will be largely disregarded, or even lead to organized resistance. But we are not now concerned with the limits on the effective power of British political institutions. It is their claim to unlimited authority which is at stake here. Britain is a country without entrenched constitutional limits on the powers of its supreme regular legislator, Parliament. But things are much the same in countries with strong constitutional traditions. The American Congress's power to legislate may be limited by the Constitution, but the Constitution itself may be changed by law. Hence, even in the USA, the law claims unlimited authority.

Any conditional or qualified recognition of legitimacy will deny the law the authority it claims for itself. If you say 'one has an obligation to obey any law which does not violate fundamental human rights' you have denied that the law has the authority it claims for itself. This is not because the law does violate human rights. It may not. Nor because legal institutions intend to or will ever admit to violating human rights. They may not. It is because the law provides ways of changing the law and of adopting any law whatsoever, and it always claims authority for itself. That is, it claims unlimited authority, it claims that there is an obligation to obey it whatever its content may be.

Though politicians often claim that the authority the law claims for itself is justified, there has hardly been any political theorist in recent times who has shared this view. It is, however, often claimed that there is a qualified obligation to obey the law, based on the authority of governments in just regimes, for so long as they remain just. Such a qualified endorsement of the authority of the law falls short of acknowledging the authority the law claims for itself in two respects. First it denies it the right to impose certain obligations, denies that some laws if enacted will be binding. Thus, for example, they may deny that any government has authority to deprive people of their fundamental human rights. Secondly, it admits only a prima facie obligation to obey the law.

It is not that the law claims that one ought to obey the law come what may. There are many legal doctrines specifically designed to allow exceptions to legal requirements, doctrines such as self-defence, necessity, public policy, and the like. The point is that the law demands the right to define the permissible exceptions. Those who claim that the obligation to obey the law is prima facie only implicitly deny it that right. They maintain that there could be circumstances in which disobedience is justified even though the law itself does not admit that it is.

It is important to see that even this qualified recognition of authority, the recognition of the authority of just governments to impose prima facie obligations on their subjects, cannot be supported by the argument of the normal justification thesis. Again we have to take account of the flexible character of the argument of this thesis. People differ in

their knowledge, skills, strength of character and understanding. Since the main argument for authority depends on
such factors it is impossible to generalize and indicate an
area of government regulation which is better left to individuals. But regarding every person there are several such
areas. One person has wide and reliable knowledge of cars,
as well as an unimpeachable moral character. He may have
no reason to acknowledge the authority of the government
over him regarding the road worthiness of his car. Another
person, though lacking any special expertise, knows local
conditions well and has great insight into the needs of his
children. He may have no reason to acknowledge the government's authority over him regarding the conditions under
which parents may leave their children unattended by adults.

Notice that these examples do not depend on the law being
unjust. It may be a just law. It is based on reasons which
apply to its subjects. But because of the bureaucratic necessity to generalize and disregard distinctions too fine for
large-scale enforcement and administration, some people are
able to do better if they refuse to acknowledge the authority
of this law. We are forced to conclude that while the main
argument does confer qualified and partial authority on just
governments it invariably fails to justify the claims to authority which these governments make for themselves. The
people over whom governments have authority, the kind of
considerations which their instructions pre-empt and the
areas of activities over which they have authority are all, to
the extent that they are determined by the normal justification thesis, less extensive than the claims made by
governments and by the law. I have concentrated attention
on the undramatic failures of laws which are not unjust or
immoral authoritatively to bind everyone to whom they are
meant to apply. In doing so I did not of course mean to deny
that sometimes immoral or unjust laws are not authoritatively binding.

Remember that sometimes immoral or unjust laws may
be authoritatively binding, at least on some people. The
existence of the occasional bad law enacted by a just government does not by itself establish much. However just a
government may be, it is liable to pass undesirable and mor-

ally objectionable laws from time to time. This need not be due to any moral shortcoming in the government. Even assuming complete good will and unimpeachable moral convictions, inefficiency, ignorance and other ordinary facts of life will lead to objectionable laws being passed. Even so it may be that regarding each individual, he is less likely successfully to follow right reasons which apply to him anyway if left to himself than if he always obeys the directives of a just government including those which are morally reprehensible.

Can it be that governments have in such circumstances authority to pass immoral and unjust laws? The reason this conclusion is objectionable is because the locution 'X has authority to pass laws of kind X' indicates in most contexts that X has the authority to issue such laws in order to use it to make such laws. That is, it implies that part of the reason for his authority is that it be used in this way. Clearly it is not part of the reason for any government's authority that it should pass unjust or immoral laws. But one can have authority to do that which one ought not to do. I can delegate authority over my son to a baby-sitter instructing him to make sure my son is in bed by a certain time. If the baby-sitter orders my son to complete his home work after that time he is disregarding my instructions and his duty. But my son nevertheless has to obey him. He may, perhaps he should, complain to me. But since he was put in the charge of the baby-sitter he ought to obey even (some of) his misguided orders. This situation is very familiar from the law of agency. Agents often have authority to bind their principals in ways they should not they can act wrongly in the exercise of their authority without forfeiting it.

Governments may be acting within their authority when they act unjustly or immorally. But clearly some immoralities may be of a kind that no government has authority to commit. There may, in other words, be general limits to the authority of governments, limits restricting governmental powers over any of their subjects. The rest of this book is, in part, an exploration of one kind of such general limits. It examines the possibility that there are general restrictions on the authority of political institutions designed to protect individual liberty. But whether or not one can establish the existence of general limits to the authority of governments, the normal justification thesis invites a piece-meal approach to the question of the authority of govern-ments, which yields the conclusion that the extent of governmental authority varies from individual to individual, and is more limited than the authority governments claim for themselves in the case of most people.

The question we must now turn to is: can one of the subsidiary arguments for the justification of authority sup-plement the main argument and show that at least the autho-rity of relatively just governments is as wide as they claim it to be?

2. Consent

The long tradition that regards consent as either the foun-dation or a foundation of legitimate authority displays two separate strands of thought. One, deriving from Hobbes and Locke, regards the consent given as an expression of rational enlightened self-interest. Its approach is instrumental. One consents to the establishment of a political society and to its authority because of the benefits one will derive from its existence. The other approach, deriving from Rousseau, re-gards consent non-instrumentally. The consent is a consti-tutive element both of the condition of the person who gives it and of the society resulting from it, which is good in itself.[1]

In this section I will offer an analysis of consent. I will then show, in the next section, how the non-instrumental approach to consent allows for a natural extension of the scope of the legitimacy of an authority to some cases where there is no consent. 'Consent' means consent to a change in the normative situation of another—to a change in his rights and duties. It is sometimes expressed and is spoken of what is agreed. Consent is, however, narrower than agreement and is roughly equivalent to the performative sense of 'agree-

[1] Both types of consent arguments are based on actual consent and differ from the hypothetical consent theories recently made popular by John Rawls, which are a form of moral argument concerning the way a fair-minded person should reconcile his interests with those of others. Hypothetical consent theories tend to share the instrumental attitudes of the Hobbesian tradition.

ment'. One can agree *that* another has or should have a right, that is, believe that he has or should have it, or agree *to* give him a right. The first is a cognitive agreement, the second is a performative one.[1] By agreeing to give him a right one purports to confer it on him, or one promises to do so in the future (the expression is ambiguous).

Though consent, if valid, has normative consequences, and can only be explained through its purported normative consequences, it does not bear its normativeness on its face. The typical expressions using 'consent' are 'X consented to Y's doing . . .' or 'X consented to Y's being . . .'.[2] The second is completed by specifying a position or role the occupier of which possesses certain rights and duties, and which the consent purports to allow Y to occupy. For example, 'I consented to his being the leader'. The first kind of sentence is completed by specifying an action, and the consent purports to give Y a right to perform it. Less commonly, consent can be given to duties or requirements imposed on other people. For example, 'He consented to his son's being obliged to retake the examination.'

Consent is given by any behaviour (action or omission) undertaken in the belief that

1. it will change the normative situation of another;
2. it will do so because it is undertaken with such a belief;
3. it will be understood by its observers to be of this character.

The third condition characterizes consent as a (purportedly) public action. Consenting in one's heart is not a performative consent but a psychological state akin to coming to terms with. The core use of 'consent' is its use in the performative sense. It is explained by the combination of the first two

---

[1] Theories of hypothetical consent discuss not consent but cognitive agreement. It is the essence of consent that its actuality changes the normative situation. One may ask what one would have had to do had one consented. But this is in no way relevant to what one has to do given that one did not. What one would have believed in certain circumstances is equally immaterial to what one should now believe. But that one should have believed something in a hypothetical situation may and often is used as part of an argument to establish what one should now believe. See A. Woozley, *Law and Obedience*, London, 1979, pp. 93–7.

[2] Impersonal consent sentences are quantified sentences of the kind described: 'You consented to your dismissal' means 'You consented to being dismissed by whoever has authority to do so.'

conditions, and since it is a performative purporting to affect the rights or duties of another, it has to be public at least in intention.

Consenting is very similar to promising. Both purport to change the normative situation of another, and both purport to do so by voluntary acts undertaken in the belief that they have these normative consequences. Yet consenting and promising, while overlapping, are not the same. According to Simmons, consenting differs from promising in two ways:

First, consent in the strict sense is always given to the actions of other persons. Thus, I may consent to my daughter's marriage, to be governed by the decisions of the majority, or to my friend's handling my financial affairs. Promises, on the other hand, cannot, except in very special circumstances, ever be made concerning the actions of another person. Further, while both promises and consent generate special rights and obligations, the emphases in the two cases are different. The primary purpose of a promise is to undertake an obligation; the special rights which arise for the promisee are in a sense secondary. In giving consent to another's actions, however, our primary purpose is to authorise those actions and in so doing create for or accord to another a special right to act: the obligation generated on the consentor not to interfere with the exercise of this right takes, in this case, the secondary role.[1]

These are suggestive observations. But they are not quite right. One consents not only to actions but also to the holding of certain positions and to the imposition of duties and burdens. Promises quite often concern the actions of others: to consent to be governed by another is to promise to obey him; to consent to his joining the expedition is to promise to provide him with the facilities and the help made available to members of the expedition. Finally these examples in which to consent is to promise refute the suggestion that in one case the purpose is to confer rights and in the other to undertake an obligation.

Promising differs from consenting in two respects. Both establish promises to be a special case of consent. First, while promising always purports to impose obligations on the promisor, consenting does not always do so. Two cases of consent can be distinguished. In the first, consent does not

---

[1] A. Simmons, *Moral Principles and Political Obligation*, Princeton, 1979, p. 76.

purport to affect the agent's personal normative situation. The president may consent to a bill imposing a new tax or conferring certain rights. The commanding officer may consent to his soldiers' being assigned certain duties by another officer. The second kind of case includes those where the agent's personal normative position is affected by his consent, if it is valid, i.e. if it has its purported normative consequences. In the first type of case, but not necessarily in the second, the consent is a response to a proposal initiated by another. Consent can adversely affect the normative situation of the agent either by placing him under an obligation or by derogating from his rights. One can waive one's rights by consenting, but not by promising (except in the special case in which the very undertaking of an obligation to act in a certain way terminates one's right not to do so). Besides, sometimes a person's consent to a right or benefit is required for him to acquire that right or a benefit. Consent, in other words, differs from promises by being capable of investing the consentor with rights.

There are, therefore, three kinds of consent that do not impose obligations on the agent: first, where his personal situation is not affected by the consent; second, where his personal situation is favourably affected, for the consent is a condition of his possession of a right or of some other benefit; third, where his personal situation is adversely affected, but by waiving a right rather than by undertaking an obligation. It is worth noting, however, that consent to a political authority entails a promise to obey it (as well as perhaps an obligation to support it in other ways). It is an undertaking of an obligation.

Second, promises are made by acts intended to undertake obligations and confer rights. Only acts whose purpose is to realize this result are promises; not so consent. Acts undertaken for another purpose and not in order to consent can constitute consent if undertaken in the belief that they will confer a right or impose a duty and if the fact that they are undertaken with such a belief is the reason for them having this result. Typical examples are cases where one is given notice that everyone who enters a certain house, club, or park must abide by certain rules, obey a certain authority, or do so at his own risk.

Acts of consent are acts believed to change the normative situation because they are performed with that belief. They are performed by people who have certain beliefs about the normative consequences of their acts. In particular they believe that their beliefs make a difference to the consequences of their acts, that their acts impose duties, confer rights, grant permissions, and so on, in part because they believe that their acts do so. Consent, in other words, is an act purporting to change the normative situation. Not every act of consent succeeds in doing so, and those that succeed do so because they fall under reasons, not themselves created by consent, that show why acts of consent should, within certain limits, be a way of creating rights and duties. We cannot create reasons just by intending to do so and expressing that intention in action. Reasons precede the will. Though the latter can, within limits, create reasons, it can do so only when there is a non-will-based reason why it should. Admitting this, it might nevertheless be claimed that a person's consenting entails, as a matter of the meaning of 'consent', not only that he acted in the way I have described, but that his action has the purported normative consequences. Against this interpretation lies the evidence that we can and do say, when appropriate, things like 'Of course he consented to the operation, but that does not entitle you to perform it since he is just a child' (or he did not know how dangerous it is). I would, therefore, suggest that consent is to be explained by reference to its purported normative consequences only.

On what grounds is it ever justified to regard consent as having its purported normative consequences? In special circumstances there may be a variety of occasional reasons that make the consent valid. Most common, perhaps, are those cases where the person to whose rights the agent consented was misled, through the agent's fault, into believing that the consent was valid and acted reasonably on this belief to his detriment. The agent might, for example, be at fault if in the circumstances the consent could be taken as sufficient evidence that the agent has power to consent (i.e., that there were reasons for holding the consent valid) and the agent should have realized this. In such cases the agent's liability is to make good the detriment thus caused to the person to whose rights he consented. Occasionally this requires recognizing that the consent and the circumstances surrounding it create the rights it purported to create.[1]

It is clear that such a justification not only depends on very special circumstances but is essentially parasitic. It presupposes a reasonable belief in the existence of some other reasons for which consent is valid in some circumstances and the misled person's mistaken belief that these reasons apply to his case. Are there non-parasitic reasons that justify acknowledging the validity of consent in certain classes of cases?

One is tempted to say that consent is valid if one has a right that the normative consequences will not occur without one's consent. To say this is to say both too much and too little. It is saying too much in that the same normative consequences can sometimes be reached by different routes. For example, a person may consent to his child's staying the night with a friend only to find that his spouse has already allowed the child to do so. It is saying too little in that to ask for the reason for the validity of a consent to certain normative consequences is the same as to ask for the reason for recognizing a person as holding a certain right to bring about these consequences.

Many justifications of consent are instrumental. Were the consent to be valid then if the rights or duties consented to and their creation have good consequences, which outweigh the bad consequences to which their creation or existence lead, the validity of the consent is instrumentally justified. The most common type of instrumental argument relies, as a reason for recognizing the validity of consent, on the facts that the agent has the best information to judge whether it is best to create the right or not and that he is sufficiently motivated to act for the best. One such case is where the

---

[1] This case differs from the case in which the agent cognitively agreed, i.e. expressed a belief that a person has certain rights in a situation in which he should have known that the hearer may reasonably rely on the utterance to his detriment. The liability of the agent may be the same in both cases, but the reasons for it differ in detail.

consent, if effective, will not affect third parties, provided
that the agent is a normal adult able to judge his own interests
in the area involved and that the same is true of the person
receiving the right, assuming that he is able to refuse it if he
so wishes. Other cases are those where the agent's knowledge
and motivation can be surmised from the circumstances of
his life (parents or children) or where a special arrangement
is made to make sure of them (e.g., when legislators are
periodically elected, thus providing them with motives to
find out what are their electors' best interests and to satisfy
them, at least where the prestige, power, and lawful remuneration of their office are their only rewards and where
these rewards are themselves substantial).

Another common instrumental justification of consent
turns not on the benefits of consenting but on the benefit of
being able to consent. It is sometimes a way of endowing a
person with a responsibility that trains him to fulfil various
roles in the future, or that it is hoped will change his character for the better, or that endows its holder with prestige, or
that gives him a certain hold on other people and makes
them more likely to act in his interests.

There are no doubt other forms of instrumental justification, but these are the most common. In addition to them
and to other kinds of instrumental validation, consent can
be given non-instrumental validation in many contexts.
Through consenting a person attempts to fashion the shape
of his moral world. All too often moralists tend to regard a
person's moral life as the story of how he proves himself in
the face of moral demands imposed on him by chance and
circumstance. Crucial as this aspect is, it is but one side of a
person's moral history. The other side of the story evolves
around the person not as the object of demands imposed
from the outside, but as the creator of such demands addressed to himself. We are all to a considerable degree the
authors of our moral world. This theme will be further explored in Parts Four and Five of the book. A few brief
observations will suffice for present purposes.

Essentially, this view of people as each one partly creating
his own moral world is to be justified through arguments
concerning the nature of morality and moral knowledge.

These provide the framework within which generally valid considerations justify the specific ways through which people can impose moral demands upon themselves and can endow their lives with value or with moral significance. Broadly speaking, such considerations refer to two kinds of moral value. First, and most obviously, they depend on the value of some human relationships. The precise course of such relations and the detailed moral requirements they generate depend on the way individuals choose to develop them and the different normative implications with which they deliberately endow the relations. Consider, for example, the variety of morally permissible and even valuable courses that relations between children and their parents can take, and their different moral implications. With many relationships the case for self-creation is even stronger, since in them the fact that one chose to have a relationship of a certain kind and chose one's partner is part of what makes the relationship valuable. (Compare ideals of love of which this is true with those of which it is not.)

The second kind of moral value involved in the justification of different ways in which persons mould their moral world is the value of forming and pursuing projects that give shape and content to one's life. This is reflected in our admiration for people who have made something of their lives, sometimes against great odds, and in our somewhat disappointed judgment of those who merely drift through life.

Consenting often serves such projects and relationships instrumentally, but beyond that it is sometimes a constitutive element of relationships between people. There are relations that can be created by expressions of consent, and there are many in which such acts form or can form a component of their creation or perpetuation. A constituent element of projects and relations is the existence of consensual rights and obligations which express the persons' continued acknowledgement of the relations or the projects. Consenting to have one's mail opened by another, to be visited without prior arrangement, and to have another arrange aspects of one's plans or activities without prior consultation (e.g. accepting invitations in one's name) may or may not be justified by their instrumental value, but in any case they are taken in our culture as expressing the existence of certain attitudes, as in part constituting those attitudes. What actions express an attitude is largely a matter of social convention. Our conventions and those of other societies differ, but to the extent that they regard consent as expressing certain worthwhile relations, as a constituent element of such relations, they provide validation of the appropriate kinds of consent.

3. Consent as the Foundation of Authority

Turning to the relevance of consent to the obligation to obey the law, we will here be concerned not with the well-known problem that most citizens in any given society have not consented to the authority of their government, but with the prior question whether their consent, if given, would have been valid. The main lesson of the discussion of the previous section is that judgment on the validity of consent has to be discriminating. Consent may be valid in certain contexts or subject to certain conditions and invalid in other contexts and/or when the conditions are not met. From the fact that in some circumstances consent is valid, it does not follow that consent to the government's authority is valid. One has to examine closely what arguments can establish the validity of such consent.

Doubts about the validity of consent to political authority are sometimes expressed on the ground that citizens have no choice but to consent. Therefore, their consent is tainted by duress and is invalid. Such arguments show that the instrumental as well as the non-instrumental validations of consent depend on its being freely given. Duress that invalidates consent consists either of a credible threat to take substantial action against the agent or against a person or a cause that he values if he does not consent or in the taking of such actions against him or against persons or causes that he values with an offer to restore the situation if he does consent. Either way duress is always action designed to exert pressure in order to secure the consent. This explains why duress invalidates consent.

There is no harm in a person using his power to consent in order to avert a threat or to extricate himself or others from a dire situation. A person's power to confer rights on others by his consent does, however, expose him to blackmail and abuse. Given that, whatever the justification for giving him such power may be, it has nothing to do with encouraging blackmail, such action frustrates the purpose of validating the consent and is to be discouraged because of its undesirable consequences. If consent is invalidated by duress then duress may fail to achieve its aim. Hence, consent to a political authority secured by threats of legal penalties is not binding. But consent by a person in Hobbes's state of nature can be perfectly valid. The undesirable aspect of duress is not in the absence of choice but in the fact that it is engineered in order to extract the consent.

Consent to political authority, where given, is often free. It does not follow that it is binding. It is binding only if there are good reasons to enable people to subject themselves to political authorities by their consent. Can its validity ever be established by instrumental considerations alone? The conclusion of the first section was that a just government can exist even if its subjects are not bound by a general obligation to obey it. Therefore, consent cannot be justified as a necessary means to establish a just government. Moreover, to the extent that in order to establish or preserve a just government a qualified recognition of authority is necessary, such recognition in itself, independently of consent, is sufficient to establish a suitably qualified obligation to obey. The instrumental value of consent to the authority of just governments is to be seen as reinforcing other moral motives to support just institutions where those may fail due to human ignorance or weakness. Consent may produce the results that belief in other reasons should but may fail to produce. This is particularly valuable in the case of government officials. Their power to affect the public and the importance of public confidence in their loyalty give special importance to their fidelity to justified authority. Hence reinforcing this fidelity by consent is a valuable common practice in many countries. Consent, duly qualified, can play a subordinate but none the less valuable role in reinforcing independent obligations.

Against this undoubted benefit one has to set the likely bad consequences of recognizing the general and unqualified validity of consent to political authority. It may mislead people into obeying the law where, but for their consent, it would have been clear to them that it is better to disobey. An extreme example of this kind of distortion is provided by the scruples of many German generals about breaking their oath of loyalty. They took the oath, for the most part, in order to be able to pursue their chosen careers in the armed forces. Relying on the moral relevance of one's consent and exaggerating its moral significance is all the more tempting when doing so serves one's own interests. Denying such consent any validity, and educating people in that conviction, could prevent such distortions.

A second consideration against allowing consent to political authority general validity turns on the undesirability of allowing the validity of consent which binds for life, is open-ended, and affects wide-ranging aspects of a person's life. In these circumstances the presumption that the agent is a competent judge of what is best to do is very hard to maintain. Regarding political authorities, the most obvious danger is of a change of government or a change of circumstances which turns a reasonably just government into an unjust one. Human knowledge is as yet unable to predict such changes.

These costs of consent to political authority suggest that, on instrumental grounds, consent can only be held binding if it is so qualified that its effect is almost entirely confined to reinforcing independently existing obligations to obey. In other words one may validly consent to obey a government whose authority can be established in accordance with the normal justification thesis. Such a consent is binding, and is not trivial as it reinforces one's motivation to respect that government's authority. But it cannot be used as a way of endowing anyone with authority where that person had none.

Does non-instrumental justification relax the conditions under which consent to authority is binding? Relationships and personal projects are valuable only if they realize something of value. It is the autonomous achievement or pursuit of a goal or an activity of value which makes relationships and personal projects valuable. Hence, to the extent that consent is justified non-instrumentally as a constitutive element in a relationship between a citizen and his society, it is valid only if it exists between a citizen and a reasonably just society. I say a reasonably just society, rather than a reasonably just law, for consent to obey the law expresses an attitude not to the law but to the society whose law it is. It expresses an attitude to the law as an aspect of that society (which it can be only if the law is felt to express social conventions and outlook).

There are various attitudes towards society that consent to the authority of its laws can express. They can all be regarded as so many variations on a basic attitude of identification with the society, an attitude of belonging and of sharing in its collective life. Attitudes belonging to this family vary. They can be more or less intense. They may be associated with some features of society more than with others. They may, but need not, express themselves in one's attitude towards the law.

Rousseau's vision of the citizen's attitude toward his community is, of course, an example of an attitude of identification. It is, however, an extreme example. Identification includes much less intense and less exclusive attitudes. A person who finds value in identification need not be attracted by Rousseau's vision. He may prefer one of the milder varieties of this attitude. All that is necessarily involved is a sense of belonging that excludes indifference to the group as well as alienation from it.

That consent to be bound by the law is an expression of such an attitude of loyalty and identification (i.e. a sense of belonging) is a matter of fact.[1] As was noted, the forms in which relations and attitudes express themselves are largely

---

[1] I agree with J. L. Mackie's comment that respect for law can express not identification but some other attitudes, such as acknowledgement on the part of tourists that each country is entitled to regulate its own affairs in its own way. See Mackie, 'Obligations to Obey the Law', *Virginia Law Review* 67 (1981), 154. I have focused attention on identification with the society as being the most characteristic attitude thus expressed by citizens.

conventional. In many societies, the convention regarding consent assumes formalized and ritualistic forms, as with the requirements to give such formal consent upon assuming an important public office or when naturalizing. These are meant not merely, if at all, to serve a useful instrumental function, but also to be solemn, ritualized expressions of loyalty and identification. To say this, of course, does not mean that the consent is not binding on the agent. It is precisely because it is thought to be binding that it can serve as an expression of identification. For while the ways one expresses such attitudes and relationships are conventional, the means chosen by the convention are suitable for their role by virtue of some of their features. Undertaking an obligation to obey the law is an appropriate means of expressing identification with society, because it is a form of supporting social institutions, because it conveys a willingness to share in the common ways established in that society as expressed by its institutions, and because it expresses confidence in the reasonableness and good judgment of the government through one's willingness to take it on trust, as it were, that the law is just and that it should be complied with.[1]

I assume that consent to obey the laws of an unjust government is not a morally appropriate expression of identification with one's society. Either the society is, in such circumstances, alienated from its government and its laws or it is not. In the first case, identification with the law does not express identification with the society which is hostile to this law. In the second case one identifies oneself with the worst aspects of the society. Such an attitude cannot be morally valuable and cannot validate the consent. Noninstrumental validations of consent are, therefore, limited to consent to the authority of a reasonably just government. This condition is, as we saw above, weaker than that required by the main argument for the validation of authority. The main argument cannot validate wholesale the authority of even reasonably just governments. Nor can instrumental considerations validate consent to the authority of reasonably just governments. They do not extend the scope of authority covered by the main argument.

[1] See ch. 3, p. 55 above.

Noninstrumental considerations do that because they show consent itself to be independently valuable. Identification with one's community is, though not morally obligatory, a desirable state, at least if that community is reasonably just. Of course consent to obey the law is not a necessary condition of such an attitude. It can find expression in one's attitude to voluntary organizations, to the culture and traditions of the community, and in behaviour to its members when met in anonymous situations. Identification with the community is even consistent with hostility to its laws, if those are thought to be oppressive or unfair. All I have claimed is that consent to obey is recognized, and with reason, as one way of expressing such an attitude. That is enough to add to its value and regard it as valid, if the other conditions for the validity of consent are met.

These considerations adumbrate the argument for the secondary role of consent in the justification of authority. It is binding only if the conditions of the normal justification thesis are substantially met independently of the consent. But the non-instrumental argument shows that consent does extend the bounds of authority beyond what can be established without it. It is worth pointing out that it does so in accordance with the normal justification thesis. Where identification is a morally valuable attitude which can be expressed by binding oneself to the authority, one has a reason to do so which is served by consent to the authority. The whole point of the consent would be violated if, having given it, one proceeded to deny the binding force of the authority's directives. Therefore, it is necessary, once the consent has been given, to accord the authority's directives pre-emptive force in order to be able to express one's identification with one's society by consenting to the authority of its law. Since one has reason to express such an attitude in this way doing so enables one to conform to reasons which apply to one, which is the condition laid down by the normal justification thesis.

The argument establishes that by accepting that authority one follows reasons which apply to one anyway. The normal justification thesis states that accepting authority is justified only if it improves one's compliance with reason. This condition is met wherever there is value in people being able to express themselves in the way they choose, at least where acceptable alternatives present themselves. They may not have a reason to prefer one way of going about things to another, but the fact that they chose to do it in a particular way gives them a reason to prefer that way from now on. The issues raised by this point will loom large in Part Four, where the metaphor of people being part authors of their own moral world will be explained.

This argument brings out a further important point. It would be wrong to regard consent as a one-off act of identification. Since it gives one an additional reason to respect authoritative directives it affects all one's encounters with authority. Even if it does not lead one to obey authority more often than one would otherwise, it affects one's reasons and the significance of one's actions. Inasmuch as they are motivated by one's consent they become, in a small undramatic way, an expression of one's attitude to one's society. This point will become clearer when we consider the nature of respect for law in general.

4. Respect for Law

Consent theorists, correctly perceiving that consent to the authority of a reasonably just government does endow it with authority over the agent, and faced with the fact that few people actually consent to the authority of their government, have often tried to extend the notion of consent to cover more cases. Similar temptations overcame philosophers concerned with establishing a secure base for individual responsibility (e.g. as in estoppel and in various forms of vicarious liability, such as conspiracy, agency, authorization or complicity) or for exemption from liability (e.g. in doctrines about the assumption of risk). In many discussions of such issues consent is invoked and is understood to mean, roughly, the following: a person consents to an outcome if he performs an action which he believes to make that event more likely.

There is no denying that a person's beliefs about the likely consequences of his acts are relevant to his normative situation. But the reasons for that are in the general principle that people are responsible for the consequences of their actions. That is why if Jill knowingly leads Jim to expect that she will behave in a certain way she bears a responsibility to prevent harm to Jim as a result of this reliance, and so on.[1] Her duty is like the duty not to set fire to the forest which entails the duty to put out any fire one started. One reason why this principle in its most general form was not thought to provide the foundation of a general doctrine of consent and voluntary obligations is the widespread belief that 'causing' another to act is, at least in the matter of individual responsibility, unlike causing a natural event. This belief, expressed in the legal doctrine of *novus actus interruptus*, is that a person is reponsible for his own actions, and others are not responsible even if they induced his action by suggesting that there are reasons for it, or by behaving in ways which led him to form such a belief.

To be sure it was always recognized that in certain circumstances, such as those involving deceit, or an intention to cause harm or to exploit, one is responsible for inducing another to act. But only the paternalistic tendency to minimize the significance of action based on the agent's judgment of his situation led to the attempt to amalgamate all voluntary obligations into a generalized doctrine of duties arising out of responsibility for inducing others to act. Whatever one's view of the tendency which led to the attempt, the attempt was doomed. It essentially regards consent as existing whenever one's action brings about a natural event in the world or increases the likelihood of such an event. It leaves out the whole class of voluntary obligations where no such change occurs, such as promises which are not relied upon, nor expected to be relied upon.

Such cases may be relatively infrequent, but they remind us that the core notion of voluntary obligations is the knowing undertaking of an obligation. This is the reason why there is reliance when it occurs. Or at least that is why

---

[1] See D. N. MacCormick, *Essays in Social Democracy*, Oxford, 1982, ch. 10; and P. Atyiah, *Promises, Morals and Law*, Oxford, 1983, for two of several analyses of promising which attempt to reduce it to what is in effect nothing more than the general principle of personal responsiblity for one's actions.

reliance on a voluntary obligation is justified reliance, which the person having the obligation has to respect. Nothing here said denies that one reason for holding voluntary undertakings to be binding is to enable people to encourage reliance by committing themselves to a course of action. I am only insisting first that this need not be the only justification for the power (the normative power) to commit oneself, and second, that one encourages reliance through knowingly undertaking an obligation. And not, as some would have it, that one undertakes an obligation by inducing reliance.

The foregoing remarks apply directly to some of the inflationary accounts of voluntary obligations and of consent, and have to be adapted to meet the challenge presented by others.[1] The same strictures can also be adapted to apply to less inflationary accounts of consent. One particularly interesting example is Kleinig's conception of consent as 'an act in which one person tends to facilitate the initiative of another' in a manner which makes him a participant in that initiative who shares responsibility for it.[2]

Small insights turn into small fallacies in this account. For example, though normally consent is given in response to an initiative of another it need not be. I may go to my son's room and say to him: 'Since today is a special day you may play in my study while I work there.' I have given my consent to his being in my study, but on this occasion the initiative was mine. The example also serves to expose the major flaw in Kleinig's account. While participation and consent overlap, they do not coincide. My son and I do not participate in a game, nor in writing my paper. Do we participate in being in a room together? Nor do all who participate in a joint enterprise agree to its occurrence. It depends on whether participation is voluntary and on whether it was known to involve normative consequences.

---

[1] In particular my comments leave untouched the consent account of the assumption of risk. See, for example, B. Friedman's report to the Canadian Law Reform Commission which surveys the writing on the subject, and endorses an analysis of consent as a knowing action for the purpose of developing a legal doctrine concerning the assumption of risk. Here too, while not necessarily denying the merits of the account in other respects, I think it fails as an explanation of consent in leaving out of account its essence as a knowing authorisation.

[2] 'The Ethics of Consent', *Canadian Journal of Philosophy* suppl. vol. 1982, p. 91.

Kleinig is of course aware of this last point and considers further conditions required to establish the kind of participation which amounts to consent. But only conditions which are tantamount to the definition of consent given in Section One above would be adequate. Once they are included in the explanation participation drops out as an inessential part of many consent situations.

Kleinig's mistake is the familiar one. He fails to spot that the core element of consent is action in the belief that it changes the normative situation, and that the justification of the binding force of valid consents is the desirability of enabling people purposefully to change the normative situation in certain circumstances. He therefore confuses one common consequence of consent, i.e. that by consenting one becomes a participant in a joint enterprise, with its essence.

What we need, however, is not to stretch consent out of recognition but to examine whether the reasons that validate consent in general and consent to authority in particular cannot also be applied to some cases not involving consent. I think that they can.

Many people regard themselves as under the authority of the state. For reasons to be examined below this belief commonly expresses itself in a belief in a defeasible obligation to obey the law. With some, this view does not cohere with their other beliefs, and one cannot attribute to them belief in any coherent justification of their acceptance of an obligation to obey. Others think that the obligation is based on the sort of reasons that philosophers have adduced in support of an obligation to obey, which have been refuted by various writers in recent years,[1] and will be briefly considered below. There are others still who do not provide such fallacious arguments but regard the obligation as incumbent on them because they are citizens of the state or members of the society, because the government is their government or the law their law. Whether this is the way they express themselves does not matter so long as we can

[1] See R. P. Wolff, *In Defense of Anarchism*, New York, 1970; M. B. E. Smith 'Is There a Prima Facie Obligation to Obey the Law?', *Yale Law Journal* 82 (1973) 950; A. Woozley, *Law and Obedience*, London, 1979; A. Simmons, op. cit.; J. Raz, *The Authority of Law*, Oxford, 1979, ch. 12. For further explanation of the attitude of respect for law which is discussed below see Raz ibid., ch. 13.

establish that this is the substance of their view. Such views are often condemned as blind acceptance of authority without any reason. This is a mistake. They indicate that their holders identify with their society and hold themselves to be under an obligation to obey the law which they regard as expressing that attitude.

This attitude is not consent. It is probably not something initiated by any specific act or at any specific time. It is likely to be the product of a gradual process as lengthy as the process of acquiring a sense of belonging to a community and identifying with it. It need not, therefore, be related to any act performed in the belief that it has normative consequences. But in a reasonably just society this belief in an obligation to obey the law, this attitude of respect for law, is as valid as an obligation acquired through consent and for precisely the same reasons. It is instrumentally useful in the same way and it is an expression of the same worthwhile attitude of identification with the society. Therefore, people who share it have an obligation to obey the law that they acquire through their conduct of their own lives, as part authors of their own moral world.

Assuming that this kind of non-instrumental justification applies to consent and can provide a foundation for the authority of the state over those of its citizens who have consented to its authority, can the same argument be used to base authority on the attitude of respect? An obvious objection is that the attitude of respect is not regarded by those who display it as the source of their obligation. It is thought of as a requirement incumbent on citizens in virtue of the independently established authority of the state. The force of this point was recognized above. It was conceded that where the attitude of respect is based on false assumptions and on nothing else, and where it does not cohere with the person's other attitudes and beliefs, it cannot be the foundation of authority. But ill-articulated as many people's thoughts sometimes are in substance, they often amount to an assumption of semi-voluntary performative submission to an authority, because it is a morally worthwhile attitude to have.

Two features of the situation obscure its character. First,

because identification with one's community is morally worthwhile, and acceptance of the authority of the state an appropriate way (though not the only way) to express it, one may jump to the conclusion that one has an obligation to accept the authority of the state, or even that it has authority independently of such acceptance. Reflection on the analogous case of promises dispels this impression. There are times when making a certain promise (say to look after a friend's child if the friend dies before the child comes of age) are morally worthwhile but where one does not have an obligation to make them (remember that in this example too one may find other adequate ways to help one's friend). Certainly one is not under an obligation to look after the child if one did not promise to do so just because it would have been a good thing to promise.

Second, if the attitude of respect is itself the source of the legitimacy of the authority then it is a self-referential attitude. It respects the authority because it is legitimate, and it is legitimate because it is respected. One respects the authority which is founded on the very fact of being so respected. Again, self-reference, albeit of a slightly different character, is essential to the analyses of valid consent and of promising which are acts changing the normative situation because they are undertaken in the belief that they so change the normative situation.

5. The Political Obligation

Our conclusions are modest. They are so modest that some may find them disconcerting. Those who consent to the authority of reasonably just governments or respect their laws are subject to their authority and have an obligation to obey their laws. But not everyone does consent, nor do all have this attitude. Those who do not are not necessarily guilty of any wrongdoing. Obligations undertaken through consent or respect are voluntary or semi-voluntary obligations. They bind those who undertake them. Sometimes people have reason to undertake them, but only exceptionally does one do wrong in not undertaking them. As was noted above, however much one may value identification with one's community, since it can be expressed by other means than respect for law it cannot be a foundation of an obligation to respect the law, nor a basis for the general authority of governments over all their subjects.

Those who do not voluntarily or semi-voluntarily place themselves under the authority of relatively just governments are under a partial and qualified obligation to recognize the authority of such a government in their country. In particular its authority should be recognized to the extent necessary to enable it to secure goals, which individuals have reason to secure, for which social co-ordination is necessary or helpful, and where this is the most promising way of achieving them. Considerations of this kind would lead to a good deal of common authority, that is they would legitimate the authority of a government over all its subjects regarding a certain range of issues. Beyond that it will have authority regarding other issues which is based on other considerations, such as superior expertise, economy of effort, immunity from temptations and blackmail. These may affect large sections of the population in predominantly the same way. But here one may also expect a degree of individual variation. The authority of the state may be greater over some individuals than over others, depending on their personal circumstances. Indeed, it may vary for reasons which are in part a matter for individual decision and temperament. One person may wish to dedicate more of his time to other pursuits and therefore accept the authority of a reasonably just and competent government over a whole range of issues regarding which another may prefer to decide for himself, and be willing to invest the time and effort it takes to enable himself to decide wisely.

The normal exercise of political authority is by the making of laws and legally binding orders. That is why much of the discussion of the justification of political authority is undertaken by a consideration of the obligation to obey the law. The two questions are one if we understand the obligation to obey the law as an obligation to obey the law as it requires to be obeyed. This entails, as was pointed out above, that disobedience to a law is justified only if it is justified by an existing legal doctrine to that effect. The law recognizes,

through various defence doctrines and through the instruction to prosecutorial authorities to refrain from prosecution in certain cases where formally a person is guilty, that
disobedience to law is sometimes justified.[1] But an obligation
to obey the law as it is understood in political writings today
is a mere prima facie obligation. Such an obligation, usually
thought of as nothing more than a reason to obey, may be
based on reasons other than the authority of the law. It need
not import a recognition of authority.

When visiting a foreign country, for example, I may feel
that I have reason to obey its laws on the ground that if I do
not I may bring the reputation of my university into dis-
repute. This does not amount to a recognition of the authority of that government. It is consistent with denying its
authority and doing my best to overturn it, including inciting
its subjects to revolt against it. I will engage in these sub-
versive activities either only to the extent that they are
lawful, or where the risk to the reputation of my university
is overshadowed by the importance of my revolutionary activities. This is unlikely to be the case in my relations with
my hotel management, or in my relations with shopkeepers,
bus conductors and the like. It may well give me a reason to
break the law when encountering the secret police, when
coming up against censorship, or when confronting other
forms of injustice or repression.

Is there a prima facie obligation to obey the law which
transcends the limits of the state's authority? The most often
invoked argument to that effect relies on an obligation to
support and maintain just institutions. The argument can be
divided into two stages. First it is argued that where a state
is relatively just one ought to support and maintain it. This
leads to the second stage of the argument, to the effect that
disobeying the law undermines its authority, and is therefore
contrary to the obligation to support just institutions. It is
this second part of the argument which is flawed. It may
entail an obligation to obey certain of the more politically

---

[1] Not all defence doctrines recognize the existence of justifications of disobedience. Self-defence does, but the insanity defence establishes only an excuse.
Similarly discretion not to prosecute is sometime based on grounds irrelevant to
our purpose, e.g. that prosecution will cause widespread riots.

sensitive laws. But it is a melodramatic exaggeration to suppose that every breach of law endangers, by however small a degree, the survival of the government, or of law and order. Many acts of trespass, breaches of contract, violations of copyright, and so on, regrettable as some of them may be on other grounds, have no implications one way or another for the stability of the government and the law.

While the duty to support just institutions fails to establish an obligation to obey the law, it may well provide reasons to obey the law in circumstances where the law transcends the legitimate authority of the government. In many situations laws which violate human rights and oppress the population or sections of it cannot be broken without endangering the stability or even the very survival of relatively just institutions. It should also be noted that the obligation to support and maintain just institutions is likely to entail duties far above those of obedience to some laws. Lawful strikes may threaten the fabric of a society much more than many unlawful acts. So may demonstrations, mass boycotts of elections and suchlike political activities. The duty to support just institutions leads to a requirement of support in words and deeds, most commonly in a certain degree of political participation.

In spite of its importance, the duty to support and maintain just institutions fails to establish a general reason to obey even laws which the government is justified in making. Does not this failure undermine the very possibility of government, however just? It is important to remember that a government's power can and normally does quite properly extend to people who do not accept its authority. They are subject to its power partly because those who accept its authority are willing to obey its instructions, even when they affect people who do not accept its authority. In a rough and ready way we can divide the ways in which a government controls and influences people into three.

First, some accept its authority and obey its instructions because they are binding on them. Second, the government can and does manipulate the environment, physical, economic and social, in which people live. It constructs roads, flattens hills, digs canals, builds harbours, employs workers, contracts for services. In all these and similar ways a government can exercise power and control over people without attempting thereby to exercise authority over them. Finally, a government controls people by providing remedies for breaches of laws and for the violation of people's rights. People who are not subject to the authority of the law may then obey the rules for prudential reasons, or because even though they have no duty to obey, disobedience will do more harm than good.

It is worth pausing here momentarily to observe that such legally provided remedies can be morally justified even when applied to people who are not subject to the authority of the government and its laws. Consider for example the law of defamation. Assuming that it is what it should be, it does no more than incorporate into law a moral right existing independently of the law. The duty to compensate the defamed person is itself a moral duty. Enforcing such a duty against a person who refuses to pay damages is morally justified because it implements the moral rights of the defamed. One need not invoke the authority of the law over the defamer to justify such action. The law may not have authority over him. It makes no difference. The importance of the law in such matters is in creating a centre of power which makes it possible to enforce moral duties. It does so through the authority it exercises over government officials, and because the population at large is willing to see morality enforced, even in matters in which they are not subject to the authority of the government.

This point can be generalized. Imagine a relatively just government ruling over a relatively morally enlightened population. Such a government has authority over just about everyone in certain matters (those where individuals have reason to pursue goals requiring social cooperation which is more difficult to achieve in other ways) and various degrees of more extensive authority in varying measure over different people, either in virtue of other factors covered by the normal justification thesis or through voluntary submission by consent or respect. Because it enjoys this authority it is capable of affecting the fortunes of people beyond the scope of its authority in the two ways mentioned above. It manipulates the environment, and it is able to enforce moral duties on those who are inclined to disregard them. The fact that such action transcends its authority casts no doubt on its justifiability. In all such matters the government is in a position comparable to that of every private individual who can by his actions affect the fortunes of others over whom he has no authority, and who may, within limits, force people to obey their moral duty when they incline not to do so.

The misleadingly alarming appearance of our conclusions results from the fact that they show that where conformity is called for it is based only some of the time, and less often than is often imagined, on the legitimate authority of the government, and often on other considerations.

Theoretically the main conclusion of the foregoing discussion is in the emphasis on the separateness of the issues of (1) the authority of the state; (2) the scope of its justified power; (3) the obligation to support just institutions; (4) the obligation to obey the law. Interrelated as these four issues undoubtedly are, they do each bring into play independent considerations. In considering the core issue of the authority of the state the most important conclusion is in the relative independence of identification with one's community as a non-instrumental basis of authority, which is none the less subject to limits imposed by the normal justification thesis.

The puzzling aspect of our conclusions is in the refusal to give a yes or no answer to the question: is the authority of the government legitimate? We concluded that it is legitimate to various degrees regarding different people. We are used to thinking in such terms concerning tourists and temporary residents. It is time we applied the same reasoning to all. It is sometimes said that this is a novel view of the question, that until very recently all political theorists believed in a general obligation to obey the law.[1] But in fact the position here advocated is the traditional view which regards an obligation to obey as a result of a special relationship between an individual and his state. This was traditionally expressed in terms of some organic relationship between an individual and his community. Individualist theorists interpreted it as a social contract. Only in recent times have political theorists

[1] P. Soper, *A Theory of Law*, Cambridge Mass., 1984.

imagined that an obligation can be founded independently of such a relationship. The view supported in these chapters is closest to the traditional view emphasizing the so called organic relations between an individual and his community. The conclusion that the attitude of respect for law is not universal, if new, is a reflection of the way modern societies have developed, and is not a philosophical novelty.

II

ANTI-PERFECTIONISM

The stage is set for the examination of our main topic. Having established the kind of considerations which justify the setting up and guide the conduct of political authorities, we can now ask which of these protect individual freedom. That is, the first part explained the framework within which the normative examination of political authorities must be conducted. The rest of the book applies this framework to the consideration of the political protection and promotion of individual liberty.

In outlining the main features of a theory of authority much attention was given to the necessity of a piecemeal approach, allowing that just governments (and often unjust ones as well) have varying degrees of authority over different people. It remained an open question whether there are principled general limits to all political authorities. One interpretation of the value of political liberty is that it sets such limits to the power of governments. On this interpretation liberalism is the doctrine of limited government. Two important and influential doctrines which espouse this interpretation of liberalism are to be examined in this book. The better known one, that the power of governments is limited by human rights which they must respect, will be examined in Part Three. Part Two is devoted to the currently very popular anti-perfectionist doctrine.

It is natural to think of a limitation on the power of government as consisting in a delimitation of an area of individual activity into which governments may not step. Such conceptions of individual freedom as consisting in an inner sanctum immune from public interference will be briefly examined in Part Three of the book. The discussion of authority has already prepared us for the existence of boundaries of a different kind. This part is concerned with two forms of restriction both inspired by the same intuition, both seeking to capture one truth. One is the view that governments should be blind to the truth or falsity of moral ideals, or of conceptions of the good. That is, that neither the validity, cogency or truth of any conception of the good, nor the falsity, invalidity or stupidity of any other may be a reason for any governmental action. The other, related, view is that governments must be neutral regarding different people's conceptions of the good. That is, that governments must so conduct themselves that their actions will neither improve nor hinder the chances individuals have of living in accord with their conception of the good.

Both doctrines are inspired by the thought that people are autonomous moral agents who are to decide for themselves how to conduct their own lives and that governments are not moral judges with authority to force on them their conceptions of right and wrong. That is why anti-perfectionism is often regarded as being a doctrine of political freedom. When comparing theocratic states, communist or fascist states, and similar regimes with the liberal democracies of the West it appears plausible to maintain that the difference is not that the liberal states promote different ideals of the good, but that they promote none. Unlike illiberal states, which regard it as a primary function of the state to see to the moral character of society, liberal states shun such activities. They reject the idea that the state has a right to impose a conception of the good on its inhabitants, and this self-restraint forms the foundation of political liberty under liberal regimes.

Therefore, when anti-perfectionist principles are used to provide the foundation of a political theory they can be regarded as attempts to capture the core sense of the liberal ethos. Not all the supporters of the various principles of neutral political concern advance them as interpretations of liberalism, but their nature and the culture that produces them endow them with that character.

Since the distinction between neutrality and the exclusion of ideals is rarely drawn by supporters of either, the discussion in the next two chapters is closely interdependent. Though the spotlight will be on neutrality in Chapter Five, and on the exclusion of ideals in Chapter Six, many of the points made about one doctrine apply to the other as well, and no final conclusions concerning anti-perfectionism generally can be reached until both are examined. In examining both doctrines and their common source we shall come to realize the importance of coercion to this strand of liberal thought. For to the question of why governments are so limited a common answer, though not the only one, is that governments wield coercive power. The relevance of coercion will occupy much of Chapter Six.

5

Neutral Political Concern

'A state or government that claims. . . . [the citizen's] allegiance (as other individuals do not)', writes Robert Nozick, 'therefore scrupulously must be *neutral* between its citizens.'[1] Writers of an egalitarian liberal persuasion often join libertarian liberals in applauding the same sentiments, different though their interpretation of them usually is.

The anti-perfectionist principle claims that implementation and promotion of ideals of the good life, though worthy in themselves, are not a legitimate matter for governmental action. The doctrine of political neutrality seeks to implement it through a policy of neutrality. Government action should be neutral regarding ideals of the good life.[2] Such a doctrine is a doctrine of restraint. Doctrines of governmental restraint are those which deny the government's right to pursue certain valuable goals, or require it to maintain undisturbed a certain state of affairs, even though it could, if it were to try, improve it. As we shall see, many but not all liberal theories of political freedom are based on the endorsement of one or another of several principles of restraint, of which the principle of neutrality is one. Principles of restraint restrict the pursuit of good or valuable goals, they exclude action for valid, sound reasons for action, or they enjoin the government to preserve a state of affairs which there are good reasons to change. There is no need for a special principle to require action for good reasons, or to maintain valuable states of affairs. The doctrine of political neutrality is a doctrine of restraint for it advocates neutrality between valid and invalid ideals of the good. It does not

[1] R. Nozick, *Anarchy, State, and Utopia*, New York, 1974, p. 33 (italics in the original).

[2] This interpretation of the doctrine is silent on whether individual political action (voting in elections etc.) may rightly aim at the promotion of some conception of the good. Little attention has been paid to this as a separate issue in 'neutralist' writings.

demand that the government shall avoid promoting unacceptable ideals. Rather, it commands the government to
make sure that its actions do not help acceptable ideals more
than unacceptable ones, to see to it that its actions will not
hinder the cause of false ideals more than they do that of
true ones.

The fact that anti-perfectionism is based on restraint, on
not doing as much good as one can, lends it a slightly paradoxical air. But there is no denying its great intuitive appeal.
At the intuitive level anti-perfectionism responds to a widespread distrust of concentrated power and of bureaucracies.
Any political pursuit of ideals of the good is likely to be
botched and distorted. The best intentions and the wisest
council are likely to misfire if entrusted to the care of the
machinery of state action. Beyond that there is the deep-felt
conviction that it is not within the rights of any person to
use the machinery of state in order to force his conception
of the good life on other adult persons.

Later in the book we will consider alternative responses
based on these intuitions. Here the mention of but one example will suffice. A right of conscientious objection to military service, and perhaps to some other legal duties,
combines a political pursuit of goals which may be justified
by their contribution to a valid conception of the good with
a refusal to ram that conception down the throats of people
who are deeply opposed to it. In other words, one alternative
to anti-perfectionism is restrictions on the choice of means
through which perfectionist ideals are pursued. In a sense
anti-perfectionism is merely a more radical restriction of
the employment of means through which one may pursue
conceptions of the good. It denies the appropriateness of
using any political means to pursue such ends.

I will first examine the meaning of political neutrality
(Section One) and its possibility (Section Two). Consideration of some of the justifications advanced for it will
lead to casting doubts on its cogency. The argument will not
be concluded until the examination of the principle of the
exclusion of ideals from politics in the next chapter.

1. Forms of Neutrality

Nozick, in the quotation given above, writes of neutrality
between individuals. I referred to neutrality between ideals

or conceptions of the good. The two ideas are closely related. Discrimination between individuals consists in making it easier for some than for others to realize their ideals of the good. But it is important to distinguish between two principles of political neutrality:

Principles of Scope

A: Neutrality concerning each person's chances of implementing the ideal of the good he happens to have.
B: Neutrality as in A, but also regarding the likelihood that a person will adopt one conception of the good rather than another.

B is the more radical principle, and in the absence of any special reason to prefer A, and given that writers supporting neutrality say little that bears on the issue, I will assume that the doctrine of neutrality advocates neutrality as in B.

Another ambiguity concerns the level of neutrality. Is politics generally to be neutral between conceptions of the good, or does neutrality apply to the constitution only? The first, stricter, doctrine of neutrality allows that individuals may act to implement their ideals in their lives, and in the life of their community, but only to the extent that they can do so by non-political means. They may found voluntary associations, buy neighbourhoods and impose restrictive covenants on the use of properties in them, secure conditions of employment, endow charitable institutions, and promote their conception of the ideal community in many ways. Such activities, when successful, will make the pursuit of some ideals of the good easier, and that of others more difficult. But no planning regulation may be passed, no law affecting the education of the young or the use of the highway, and so on, which will make it easier to realize one conception of the good or more difficult to pursue another.

The second, less strict, doctrine allows the use of politics in the pursuit of ideals. It insists, however, that that will be done in a constitutional framework which allows everyone an equal chance to endorse any conception of the good and to realize it. The constitution is neutral. But the law is not necessarily so, and many people born today will find their chances to pursue different conceptions of the good affected by law as a result of the activities of our and previous generations. Again it seems best to assume the stricter doctrine as background for our discussion.

It is important to realize what is involved in talking of *principles* of neutrality. 'To be neutral. . . is to do one's best to help or to hinder the various parties concerned in an equal degree.'[1] This is the primary sense of neutrality, which I will call principled neutrality. In this sense one is neutral only if one can affect the fortunes of the parties and if one helps or hinders them to an equal degree and one does so because one believes that there are reasons for so acting which essentially depend on the fact that the action has an equal effect on the fortunes of the parties. One secondary sense of neutrality regards persons as neutral if they can affect the fortunes of the parties and if they affect the fortunes of all the parties equally regardless of their reasons for so doing. When 'neutral' is used in this sense I refer to it as by-product neutrality, for here neutrality may well be an accidental by-product of the agent's action and not its intended outcome.

Principles of neutrality state that there are reasons to be neutral. They are satisfied by any behaviour that affects the fortunes of the parties in equal degree (by-product neutrality). They are followed by people acting neutrally in a principled way, i.e., because they believe that there is a reason not to help or hinder one side more than the other. Our interest is in political theories that require neutrality, i.e., that are followed by acting neutrally in a principled way. Some theories may be such that behaviour that follows them is also neutral as a by-product. But those are of no special interest from our point of view.

Neutrality is sometimes conceived of as being necessarily at least prima facie desirable. If so, the principles of neutral political concern are at least prima facie valid. But the definition of neutrality adopted above is not committed to such

[1] A. Montefiore in the book he edited, *Neutrality and Impartiality*, Cambridge 1975, p. 5.

a view, which is rooted in the confused notion that to act neutrally is to act fairly. Montefiore gives a familiar example:

Two children may each appeal to their father to intervene. . . in some dispute between them. Their father may know that if he simply 'refuses to intervene' the older one, stronger and more resourceful, is bound to come out on top. . . In other words, the decision to remain neutral, according to the terms of our present definition, would amount to a decision to allow the naturally strong child to prevail. But this may look like a very odd form of neutrality to the weaker child.[1]

Does this show that the father would not be neutral if he remained aloof from the quarrel? Even if (and I do not accept this at all) neutrality could only be justified as a means to a fair contest, it should not be identified with action securing a fair contest. An attorney representing a client before a court helps to make the trial fair, but the attorney is not neutral. In his situation to act neutrally is to act unfairly. All that Montefiore's example shows is that there are circumstances in which it is unfair to act neutrally, where there are not even prima facie reasons to be neutral. The example is of a case where the father should not, not where he cannot, remain neutral. The question of the justification of neutral political concern invites moral and political argument and cannot be settled by the inherent appeal of neutrality as such.

Supporters of the doctrine of neutral political concern differ on many issues. But all of them endorse one or the other of the principles of political neutrality mentioned above and seek to implement it by some variant of the following principles of restraint which limit the political relevance of ideals of the good.

Interpretations of Political Neutrality

1. No political action may be undertaken or justified on the ground that it promotes an ideal of the good nor on the ground that it enables individuals to pursue an ideal of the good.
2. No political action may be undertaken if it makes a difference to the likelihood that a person will endorse one

[1] Ibid., p. 7.

conception of the good or another, or to his chances of realizing his conception of the good, unless other actions are undertaken which cancel out such effects.

3. One of the main goals of governmental authority, which is lexically prior to any other, is to ensure for all persons an equal ability to pursue in their lives and promote in their societies any ideal of the good of their choosing.

The first principle is offered by R. Nozick as an interpretation of neutrality. To the argument that his State is not neutral, for its political organization, its property and contract laws, favour the implementation of some conception of the good, Nozick replies:

Not every enforcement of a prohibition which differentially benefits people makes the state non-neutral. . . Would a prohibition against rape be non-neutral? It would, by hypothesis, differentially benefit people; but for potential rapists to complain that the prohibition was non-neutral between the sexes. . . would be absurd. There is an *independent* reason for prohibiting rape. . . That a prohibition thus independently justifiable works out to affect different people differently is no reason to condemn it as non-neutral, provided it was instituted or continues for (something like) the reasons which justify it. . . similarly with the prohibitions and enforcements of the minimal state.[1]

Nozick is certainly raising a point which supporters of the other versions of neutrality have to contend with. According to their interpretation of neutrality, he is implying, prohibiting rape is not neutral. But they have a ready answer to this challenge. Supporters of the third principle may claim that the reason rape is prohibited is that its perpetration deprives the raped of their chances to live according to their conception of the good. The limitation imposed on would-be rapists does no more than establish equal chances to pursue one's conception of the good. It limits people's ability to pursue some conceptions of the good, but only in order to equalize the opportunity to do so overall. Supporters of the second of the principles above will have a slightly different answer. Conceding that the prohibition of rape is itself non-neutral, they will then require the government to take action

[1] R. Nozick, *Anarchy, State, and Utopia*, pp. 272–3.

to compensate would-be rapists by improving their chances to realize other aspects of their conception of the good.

Notice that the thought that in principle a would-be rapist should be compensated for giving up the right to rape is implicit in the answer of the supporters of the third principle as well. They claim that the prohibition in fact merely equalizes people's ability to pursue their own conception of the good. If it turns out that this is not the case, if it is discovered that the prohibiton denies the would-be rapists more of a chance to pursue the good life than it gives their possible victims, then one may have to adjust other features of the political framework to make sure that this does not result in inequality of ability to pursue one's conception of the good. Many readers may join Nozick in regarding this as a *reductio ad absurdum* of the second and third principles stated above. We will return to their examination below. Whatever the force of Nozick's implied challenge to alternative interpretations of neutrality, the question remains whether his reply succeeds in its primary aim of defending his own.

Nozick's case rests on the view that so long as one is not acting for the reason that one's action will favour one of the parties or hinder the other, but for a valid independent reason, then one's neutrality is intact. If so then on the assumption, surely acceptable to Nozick as to most people, that the prospect of a profit is a valid reason for most commercial activities it follows that selling arms to one of the combatants for profit does not jeopardize one's neutrality. One is not free to deny that when one's action actually helps one of the parties then the profit is not a valid reason, for that is to abandon the case and adopt the view of neutrality espoused above according to which neutrality is determined by the consequences of one's action. Nozick's State is not neutral, and his principle (principle 1 above) is not a principle of neutrality, but it shares with the doctrine of neutrality an anti-perfectionist bias and will therefore be examined in the next chapter.

It may be thought that the same verdict applies to the third principle as well. Ensuring to all an equal ability to realize their conception of the good is more likely to require acting in a non-neutral way, acting to improve the ability of some at the expense of others. The principle is an anti-perfectionist principle but can it be regarded as a principle of neutrality? I think that this objection is mistaken and that the third principle is a principle of neutrality. I will call it the principle of comprehensive (political) neutrality to distinguish it from the second principle which will be called the principle of narrow (political) neutrality. We can best examine their character as two competing principles of neutrality in the context of objections to political neutrality the ground that it is impossible or even incoherent.

2. The Impossibility of Strict Political Neutrality

The most serious attempt to specify and defend a doctrine rather like our principle of comprehensive neutrality is that of J. Rawls. While our discussion in this chapter is of the doctrine of neutrality as such, Rawls' treatment of it will serve to illustrate the problems involved.

Rawls believes that principles chosen rationally but in ignorance of one's actual situation in society, one's natural endowments, and *one's conception of the good*, are bound to be neutral principles. He believes that under these conditions of choice, which he describes as the original position, there is only one set of principles which can be rationally chosen to govern a society enjoying favourable social and economic conditions. They are the principle of equal liberty, assuring everyone equal measure of an enumerated list of basic liberties (freedom of expression, religion, etc.) and the difference principle according to which everyone should enjoy equal allocation of the other primary goods (i.e. those desirable whatever one's conception of the good may be, e.g. wealth, income, opportunities, status) except in so far as deviation from strict equality would improve the prospects of the worst-off group in society. Rawls' theory deviates from comprehensive neutrality in requiring equal ability to pursue ideals of the good only in so far as that ability depends on the principle of equal liberty. For the rest, the difference principle allows deviations from an equal distribution of primary goods where the worst-off group will benefit from them. Finally, Rawls is only to a limited extent concerned with correcting inequalities in the ability to promote the good which are due to one's natural endowments (the difference principle is about social, not natural, primary goods).

T. Nagel has criticised Rawls' theory of justice on the ground that it purports to be neutral between different conceptions of the good, but is not. If Rawls' theory is based on a doctrine of neutrality it is a doctrine of comprehensive neutrality. Hence the relevance of the objection to our purpose. Nagel explains his position as follows:

It is a fundamental feature of Rawls' conception of the fairness of the original position that it should not permit the choice of principles of justice to depend on a particular conception of the good over which the parties may differ.

The construction does not, I think, accomplish this, and there are reasons to believe that it cannot be successfully carried out. Any hypothetical choice situation which requires agreement among the parties will have to impose strong restrictions on the grounds of choice, and these restrictions can be justified only in terms of a conception of the good. It is one of those cases in which there is no neutrality to be had, because neutrality needs as much justification as any other position. (pp. 8–9)[1]

The specific point that Nagel is making is that there is no way of justifying the conditions of choice in the original position except from the point of view of a certain conception of the good. But later on he makes it clear that this is so, at least in part, because the supposedly inevitable outcome of that choice is not really neutral:

The original position seems to presuppose not just a neutral theory of the good, but a liberal, individualistic conception according to which the best that can be wished for someone is the unimpeded pursuit of his own path, provided it does not interfere with the rights of others. The view is persuasively developed in the later portions of the book but without a sense of its controversial character.

Among different life plans of this general type the construction is neutral. But given that many conceptions of the good do not fit into the individualistic pattern, how can this be described as a fair choice situation for principles of justice? (p. 10)

[1] T. Nagel, 'Rawls on Justice', *Philosophical Review* 82 (1973) 220, reprinted in *Reading Rawls*, ed. N. Daniels, Oxford, 1975, to which all page references refer.

One should be careful not to misinterpret this point. Rawls often writes of individuals' conceptions of the good as if they are their views of the good life for themselves. But he is also aware that they may be conceptions of the good life for people generally and for society as a whole. Individuals may use their primary goods to promote non-individualistic conceptions of the good. To use Nagel's own words, individuals may use their primary goods to implement

views that hold a good life to be readily achievable only in certain well-defined types of social structure, or only in a society that works concertedly for the realization of certain higher human capacities and the suppression of baser ones, or only given certain types of economic relations among men. (p. 9)

The individualistic bias that Rawls is accused of by Nagel is not that he rules out such conceptions but that he is not neutral regarding them because he makes their successful pursuit more difficult than that of individualistic conceptions of the good. Nagel's reason for alleging the existence of the bias is that 'the primary goods are not equally valuable in pursuit of all conceptions of the good' (p. 9). They serve individualistic conceptions well enough but 'they are less useful in implementing' non-individualistic conceptions. This point is valid. Rawls is surprisingly brief and inexplicit on this issue. He seems to take assessment of wealth to be unproblematic.[1] If some market mechanism, actual or hypothetical, is assumed, the value of primary goods is the function of supply and demand where the demand is partly determined by the usefulness of the goods in the implementation of conceptions of the good which are actually pursued in that society and by the number of those pursuing different conceptions. Relative to any such evaluation of primary goods some conceptions of the good will be harder to implement, i.e., will require primary goods of greater value to realize, than others. These need not be non-individualistic conceptions. All conceptions involving the cultivation and satisfaction of the so-called expensive tastes are harder to satisfy, and the Rawlsian theory can be said to discriminate against them.

[1] J. Rawls, *A Theory of Justice*, Oxford, 1971, pp. 93-4.

Nonindividualistic conceptions are likely to be among the expensive tastes since their realization depends on the co-operation of others, and they will take some convincing to come round to the agent's point of view. Alternatively, it will take a lot of resources to buy their consent to his point of view. This consideration points to the fact that the very restrictions imposed on societies by the Rawlsian principles of justice make the implementation of some conceptions of the good more difficult and their pursuit by individuals less attractive than that of others. Furthermore, the implementation of some conceptions of the good is incompatible with the principles of justice and is ruled out altogether.

Neutrality, however, can be a matter of degree. One can deviate from complete neutrality to a greater or lesser extent. Can Rawls' principles be defended on the basis that they approximate complete neutrality better than any alternative? The argument remains to be made. Whatever our judgment of Rawls' principles on that account, at least if political neutrality is a coherent and desirable ideal then the impossibility of complete adherence to it need not undermine its force as a political doctrine. So let us turn to two arguments challenging the validity of the idea in a way which makes even approximation to complete neutrality a chimerical notion.

Neutrality is concerned only with the degree to which the parties are helped or hindered. It is silent concerning acts which neither help nor hinder. This may lead some to suppose that any attribution or commendation of neutrality assumes that whereas one is morally responsible (i.e., accountable) for what one does, one is not morally responsible for what one does not do, or some similar distinction. Those who reject this view may conclude that neutrality is impossible, or even incoherent. The conclusion is, however, unwarranted. No such assumption underlies the attributions of neutrality. Commendations of neutrality, while consistent with such a view, do not depend on it. They may be defended simply because in certain circumstances not helping is to be preferred to helping.

It is true, though, that valuing neutrality presupposes a distinction between not helping and hindering. Consider a country that has no commercial or other relations with either of two warring parties. This was true of Uruguay in relation to the war between Somalia and Ethiopia. It may nevertheless be true that such a country may have been able to establish links with either party. Would we say that Uruguay was not neutral unless the help that it could have and did not give Ethiopia was equal to the help that it could have and did not give Somalia? This will not be the case if, for example, Uruguay could have supplied the parties with a commodity that, though useful to both, was in short supply in one country but not in the other. Should we then say that Uruguay is not neutral unless it starts providing the country suffering from the shortage in that commodity? If by not helping it Uruguay is hindering it, then this conclusion is forced on us. But according to the common understanding of neutrality, Uruguay would have been breaking its neutrality if in the circumstances described it would have started supplying one of the paries with militarily useful materials after the outbreak of hostilities. It follows that the distinction between helping and hindering is crucial to an understanding of neutrality, as is the distinction between hindering and not helping. But it does not follow that this distinction is always of moral significance (neutrality is not always defensible). Nor does it follow that the distinction can always be drawn. Neutrality is possible in some cases, but it may be impossible in others.

A second argument designed to show that neutrality is chimerical claims that whether or not a person acts neutrally depends on the base line relative to which his behaviour is judged, and that there are always different base lines leading to conflicting judgments and no rational grounds to prefer one to the others. Imagine that the Reds are fighting the Blues. We have no commercial or other relations with the Blues, but we supply the Reds with essential food which helps them maintain their war effort. If we want to be neutral, should we continue normal supplies to the Reds or should they be discontinued? If we continue supplying the Reds, we will be helping them more than the Blues. If we discontinue supplies, we will be hindering the Reds more than the Blues. (I am assuming that even if similar supplies to the Blues will help them, continuing not to help them is not hindering them.) It may be said that this is just one of the cases where it is impossible to be neutral. Without confusing not helping and hindering, such cases cannot be multiplied. They form a special class where, in the circumstances of the case, not helping is hindering. But the case invites a more radical rebuttal. In it two standards of neutrality conflict.

The basic idea is simple. Neutrality is neutrality between parties in relation to some issue regarding which the success of one sets the other back. Various aspects of the parties' life, resources, and activities will be helpful to them in the conflict, but many of these are resources and activities that they will have possessed or engaged in or wished to possess or to engage in in any case, even if they did not take part in the contest. Some of the activities and resources are such that the parties engage or wish to engage in them or possess them only because of the conflict. We could therefore distinguish between comprehensive and narrow neutrality. Comprehensive neutrality consists in helping or hindering the parties in equal degree in all matters relevant to the conflict between them. Narrow neutrality consists in helping or hindering them to an equal degree in those activities and regarding those resources that they would wish neither to engage in nor to acquire but for the conflict.

'Neutrality' is used in ordinary discourse to indicate sometimes narrow and sometimes comprehensive neutrality. Sometimes various intermediate courses of conduct are seen as required by neutrality. This reflects the fact that several kinds of considerations may lead to different and incompatible policies all of which are commonly regarded as policies of neutrality, because all of them demonstrate an even-handed treatment of the parties either by not helping one more than the other, or by not helping one more than the other to take special measures to improve his position in the conflict, and so on. The difference between military equipment and food supplies illustrates the point. To be comprehensively neutral one should supply the Reds in our example neither with arms nor with food. But one is narrowly neutral even if one provides the Reds with normal food supplies. Arms on the other hand are needed specifically for military use, and continued supply of arms to one side is incompatible with neutrality.

Several subsidiary points require further argument. First, some arms are necessary for police action, some may be solicited and supplied in anticipation of a different possible conflict. This may show that unequal supply of arms can be compatible with narrow (though clearly not with comprehensive) neutrality. Second, some feel that no supply of arms to the combatants, however even-handed, is compatible with neutrality. My response is, in brief, that no-supply is not more neutral than even-handed supply. If it is thought to be preferable, this is for reasons having nothing to do with neutrality, such as a desire to bring the war to a speedy end or not to allow people to profit from wars. Third, my example assumed that we are regular suppliers of food to the Reds. This assures us that the continued supply is of normal quantities required anyway, but it also makes discontinuation of supply a positive harm rather than a refusal to help. Thus a person who has no regular trading relations with the parties can provide the Reds with their ordinary requirement of food while remaining narrowly neutral, or refuse to sell them anything that improves their position and be comprehensively neutral. We, being their regular suppliers, do not have the option of action that neither helps nor hinders. Finally, it may be claimed that real neutrality is comprehensive neutrality, narrow neutrality being compromised neutrality which is sometimes all that is possible. My point is merely that even if this is so, the fact remains that narrow neutrality is often all that is meant by 'neutrality'.

This brings us back, at long last, to the choice between the narrow and the comprehensive principles of neutrality broached in the last section. The conflict in which the state is supposed to be neutral is about the ability of people to choose and successfully pursue conceptions of the good (and these include ideals of the good society or world). It is therefore a comprehensive conflict. There is nothing outside it which can be useful for it but is not specifically necessary for it. The whole of life, so to speak, is involved in the pursuit of the good life. Can one be narrowly neutral in a comprehensive conflict?

Furthermore, within the range of duties which the State owes its citizens, failure to help is hinderance. If I owe a client a duty to increase the value of his investment portfolio then if I fail to take action which could enhance its value I am positively harming my client's interests. A surgeon who fails to take action to help the recovery of a patient prostrate in front of him in the operating theatre is hindering his recovery. So within the range of the state's responsibility to its subjects failing to help is hindering.

If the state is subjected to a requirement of comprehensive neutrality and if its duties to its citizens are very wide-ranging then the principle of comprehensive neutrality is a principle of neutrality indeed. On those assumptions the state can be neutral only if it creates conditions of equal opportunities for people to choose any conception of the good, with an equal prospect of realizing it. Egalitarian supporters of the neutrality principle such as Rawls endorse a variant on the principle of comprehensive neutrality. Libertarian supporters of neutral political concern gravitate towards the narrow principle. The difference is hardly surprising. It reflects the underlying, and all too often unexpressed, differing assumptions about the responsibilities of states and the limits of their authority. So much for clarifying the doctrine of neutrality. In evaluating its credentials our prime example will again be Rawls' theory.

3. Neutrality and the Social Role of Justice

Since in the original position no one knows his own moral ideals, his own conception of the good, Rawls concludes that no perfectionist standards will be adopted in it. The principles of justice adopted in the original position are neutral between different conceptions of the good. To vindicate Rawls' position one requires convincing reasons first for excluding moral and religious beliefs from the information available behind the veil of ignorance, and second for accepting that neutral or maximally neutral principles will be chosen in these circumstances. *A Theory of Justice* contains hardly any explicit argument for the exclusion of moral and religious beliefs from the original position. Such argument as there is turns on the need to secure unanimity, the need to have, in the original position, one viewpoint which can be the 'standpoint of one person selected at random' which excludes bargaining and guarantees unanimity. Therefore, only non-controversial information can be available. Otherwise there will be different standpoints defined by different informational bases, and it will be impossible to guarantee agreement. The obvious reply to this argument is that we need a reason to accept a decision reached behind *this* veil of ignorance, and the claim that no decision would be reached behind a differently constructed veil of ignorance is not such a reason unless it has already been shown, as it has not in fact, that we are bound by the results of *some* veil of ignorance, whatever it may be.

The argument showing that no moral ideal of the good will be chosen as a principle of justice in the original position is the argument that Rawls uses for rejecting perfectionist principles:

For while the persons in the original position take no interest in one another's interests, they know that they have (or may have) certain moral and religious interests and other cultural ends which they cannot put in jeopardy. Moreover, they are assumed to be committed to different conceptions of the good and they think that they are entitled to press their claims on one another to further their separate aims. The parties do not share a conception of the good by reference to which the fruition of their powers or even the satisfaction of their desires can be evaluated. They do not have an agreed criterion of perfection that can be used as a principle for choosing between instructions. To acknowledge any such standard would be, in effect, to accept a principle that might lead to a lesser religious or other liberty, if not to a loss of freedom altogether to advance many of one's spiritual ends. If the standard of excellence is reasonably clear, the parties have no way of knowing that their claims may not fall before the higher social goal of maximizing perfection. Thus it seems that the only understanding that the persons in the original position can reach is that everyone should have the greatest equal liberty consistent with a similar liberty for others. They cannot risk their freedom by authorizing a standard of value to define what is to be maximized by a teleological principle of justice. (pp. 327–8)

Rawls, however, claims more than this argument establishes. He claims not only that the parties to the original position will avoid choosing any particular perfectionist principle as a constituent of their doctrine of justice, but that they will not even accept a doctrine of justice including an agreed process for determining which perfectionist principle should be implemented in the state. Given their concern that only well-founded ideals of the good, and not any ideal one believes in, should be implemented, and given the general knowledge of human fallibility, it is not really surprising that the original position does not yield a commitment to any particular ideal. But it may yield an agreement to establish a constitutional framework most likely to lead to the pursuit of well-founded ideals, given the information available at any given time.[1] Ignorance of one's particular moral beliefs will not exclude this possibility, since the parties in the original position know that they have moral ideals. They accept, in other words, 'a natural duty' to pursue the best-founded moral ideal. This argument presupposes that moral ideals are based on rational considerations, and Rawls is anxious not to deny this: 'in making this argument,' he says, referring to the passage quoted above, 'I have not contended that the criteria of excellence lack a rational basis in everyday life' (p. 328).

An agreement on a method for choosing between perfectionist principles cannot be ruled out on the grounds that the methods of evaluating different ideals are themselves subject to evaluative controversy. They are not more controversial nor more evaluative than some of the psychological facts available to the parties, such as the Aristotelian prin-

---

[1] This point raises a wider issue of some importance to the evaluation of Rawls' procedure. Should one assume that the parties take notice in the original position of their own fallibility, and agree on constitutional arrangments that will be self-correcting if it turns out that the fundamental beliefs concerning human nature, on which their substantive principles of justice are based, turn out to be wrong, or not? One might think that they need not. We could always engage in the Rawlsian form of argument and apply it to the new information once it becomes available. This seems to be the way Rawls treats the problem (though he is sensitive to fallibility concerning applied principles (see pp. 195-7)). But quite apart from the fact that by this one assumes that in the original position the parties discount a general fact of human nature, namely its fallibility, this procedure will sanction non-adaptable constitutions—a highly counter-intuitive conclusion.

ciple and the considerations concerning self-respect on which the priority of liberty is based (cf. sections 65, 67, and 82). Nor has Rawls provided any argument to show that they are.

In his Dewey lectures Rawls regards the exclusion of beliefs about ideals of the good from the original position as part of an exclusion of all controversial information and forms of reasoning. Moral and religious disagreements are seen as endemic to a democratic society, and the validity of the Rawlsian conception of justice is limited to such a society.[1] The justification for excluding controversial truths from the original position lies in the social role of justice, which is 'to enable all members of society to make mutually acceptable to one another their shared institutions and basic arrangments, by citing what are publicly recognized as sufficient reasons.'[2] The interest of subjecting one's society and one's life to such principles of justice is assumed to be everyone's highest interest.[3]

It is of the utmost importance that the Rawlsian method of argument requiring unanimity behind the veil of ignorance should not be defended on the ground that otherwise the resulting principles would not be fair because unanimity is a condition of fairness, or by any other moral argument. Rather, the reason must be that principles not generated by the Rawlsian method will fail to fulfil the social role of a doctrine of justice.

The essential point is that a conception of justice fulfils its social role provided that citizens equally conscientious and sharing roughly the same beliefs find that, by affirming the framework of deliberation set up by it, they are normally led to a sufficient convergence of opinion. Thus a conception of justice is framed to meet the practical requirements of social life and to yield a public basis in the light of which citizens can justify to one another their common institutions. Such a conception need be only precise enough to achieve this result.[4]

Even if one accepts this view of the social role of a doctrine

[1] Rawls, 'Kantian Constructivism in Moral Theory', *Journal of Philosophy* 77 (1980) 540-2.
[2] Ibid., p. 517 and cf. p. 561.
[3] Ibid., p. 525.
[4] Ibid., p. 561.

of justice, and gives it the priority Rawls assigns to it, his conclusions are not supported by his arguments for at least three reasons.

First, even though different people differ in their conception of the good, it does not follow that in a given culture (and Rawls' theory claims validity only within our culture) there are no common elements in their varying conceptions of the good. Such common elements need not be excluded by the veil of ignorance since their presence does not jeopardize the social role of the doctrine of justice.

Second, in particular it is possible that there is a wide measure of agreement concerning the modes of reasoning by which ideals of the good are to be evaluated.

Third, and most important, is Rawls' blindness to the possibility that the social role of a doctrine of justice may be met by consensus concerning the second best, given that an ideal constitution is not feasible. Rawls assumes without argument that the social role can be fulfilled only by a perfect doctrine of justice, i.e., one which establishes a perfect government for his actual society. But there is no reason why the doctrine of justice actually reflected by the constitutional arrangements of a state may not be reached as a result of people realizing that their different ideals of the good, each leading to a different doctrine of justice, cannot be implemeted because of the widespread disagreement in society concerning their value. Each will then agree, as a second best, to a doctrine of justice to which all or nearly all members of society could agree (as a second best) if they argue rationally each from his different conception of the good provided they are united in ranking the need for a public conception of justice very highly in their order of priorities.

Some people may feel that Rawls' original position is already a description of a process of compromise, of settling for the second best. This, one may feel, is implied by the need to disregard one's conception of the good, thus jeopardizing one's chances of implementing it. When so regarded the objection will be rephrased: there is no reason to think that people who know they differ in their conceptions of the good but do not know how will reach a compromise, whereas those who also know how will not. In both cases one needs a common belief in the social role of justice and in its priority to be assured of a compromise. And in both cases if these conditions obtain some compromise will be reached, or at least there is a good chance that it will.

A doctrine of justice reached in this alternative way is likely to differ from Rawls' two principles. It will fulfil the social role of justice, but it will be agreed upon by a process of reasoning quite different from his. *First*, different ideals of the good far from being excluded will form the starting points of the argument about a doctrine of justice. *Second*, and as a result, supporters of different conceptions of the good will follow different routes in arguing for the doctrine of justice. There will be unanimity in the conclusion but (given the different starting points) no unanimity on the route to it. *Third*, the common feature of most routes will be the reliance on a rational reconstruction of a process of bargaining by which the common overriding goal of reaching an agreement leads the parties to compromise by accepting a less than perfect doctrine as the optimally realizable second best.

The resulting compromise will be fair by Rawls' own standards, in that each one of the parties conforms, while bargaining, to the principles of his morality. By the moral standards of some of the bargainers the claims of some of the others may be immoral. But this does not undermine the fairness of the outcome of the bargaining as long as all acknowledge the Rawlsian assumption of the overriding goal of achieving a common agreement concerning a doctrine of justice. This overriding goal entails that the best constitutional arrangements each person can reach while acting in conformity with his own moral ideals are morally valid, and since the commonly agreed upon arrangements are so regarded by everyone, they are morally binding on all.

For reasons which are fairly obvious this procedure of bargaining may in some societies lead to the endorsement of highly wicked principles as that society's doctrine of justice. This should be regarded as a *reductio ad absurdum* of the presupposition of Rawls' theory of justice and especially the assumption of the overriding goal to reach a doctrine of justice at whatever cost to one's conception of the good. I am not advocating the bargaining procedure described above. My purpose was merely to show that, though it is a perfectionist procedure, it is not ruled out by Rawls' arguments against perfectionism; and to suggest that the assumption that he relies upon against perfectionism leads to strongly counter-intuitive results.

4. From Neutrality to Pluralism

Rawls' Kantian constructivist approach to ethics suggest an argument for political neutrality which is in part independent of the one criticised above and which turns on autonomy:

> Kant held, I believe, that a person is acting autonomously when the principles of his action are chosen by him as the most adequate possible expression of his nature as a free and equal rational being. The principles he acts upon are not adopted because of his social position or natural endowments, or in view of the particular kind of society in which he lives or the specific things that he happens to want. To act on such principles is to act heteronomously. Now the veil of ignorance deprives the persons in the original position of the knowledge that would enable them to choose heteronomous principles.[1]

Rawls applies the Kantian insight only to the choice of the principles of justice. But it seems that if it is valid for that purpose, it must be valid for morality generally. In *A Theory of Justice* Rawls does not use the Kantian insight as an argument for the acceptability of his theory. He merely points out that his theory is consistent with it. But in 'Kantian Constructivism in Moral Theory' the Kantian insight is used to defend his theory against various criticisms by providing it with an epistemological foundation. Applied to moral considerations generally, the Kantian insight yields a new argument for excluding the parties' moral and religious beliefs behind the veil of ignorance. While not explicitly using this argument, Rawls comes close to doing so in saying that

> the parties in the original position do not agree on what the moral facts are, as if there already were such facts. It is not that, being

[1] Rawls, *A Theory of Justice*, p. 252.

situated impartially, they have a clear and undistorted view of a prior and independent moral order. Rather (for constructivism), there is no such order, and therefore no such facts apart from the procedure of construction as a whole; the facts are identified by the principles that result.[1]

In developing the Kantian insight along Rawlsian lines, several points must be borne in mind. *First*, the fundamental idea which enjoys universal validity is that morality is the free expression of a person's rational nature. The claim that principles chosen in the original position express this nature depends on a certain conception of the person which is among the deep common presuppositions of our culture but no more.[2] *Second*, Rawls is anxious to make clear that the choice of principles because they express human nature 'is not a so-called "radical" choice: that is, a choice not based on reasons. . . The notion of radical choice . . . finds no place in justice as fairness.'[3] Furthermore: 'The ideals of the person and of social cooperation. . . are not ideals that, at some moment in life, citizens are said simply to choose. One is to imagine that, for the most part, they find on examination that they hold these ideals, that they have taken them in part from the culture of their society.'[4] The conception of morality as an expression of the rational nature of people is consistent with the view that people's nature is socially determined, thus rendering the concrete manifestation of morality equally socially determined. *Third*, Rawls' conception of the person does not lead to unanimity of moral views.

Given this conception of morality, it is evident that the parties to the original position know nothing of their moral beliefs. They are not excluded, as is knowledge of the particular circumstances of each participant's life, in order to ensure that choice in the original position represents people's nature. They are in fact not excluded at all. The parties to

[1] Rawls, 'Kantian Constructivism and Moral Theory', p. 568.
[2] Cf. ibid., p. 520. It seems to me that Rawls is ambiguous on the crucial issue of whether the reflective equilibrium argument supports the fundamental Kantian insight or presupposes it. I assume here that there is a sense in which the latter is the case, though the full story is more complex and cannot be explored here.
[3] Ibid., p. 568.
[4] Ibid., pp. 568-9

the original position have no knowledge of their moral beliefs because they have as yet no moral beliefs and because whatever moral beliefs they should have depend on the outcome of their deliberations in the original position and cannot affect it. Thus extending the Kantian insight beyond political morality to morality as a whole explains the elimination of moral beliefs and ideals of the good from behind the veil of ignorance. But this argument by itself does not justify political neutrality. The argument for neutrality still rests on the further assumption that it is in people's highest interest to adopt principles fulfilling the social role of justice. Without its support we still have no reason to believe that any agreement will be reached behind the veil of ignorance. Rawls shows neither that this assumption follows from the Kantian insight nor that it leads to neutral political concern. The counter-argument of Section Four above still holds good.

This reconstruction of Rawls' argument for the doctrine of neutral political concern attempts to found it on the notion of autonomy through the notion of moral self-determination. The intuitive idea behind it seems to be this: since morality is an expression of one's rational nature, it is essentially self-determined. Given the social determination of the concept of a person and the absence of unanimity in the outcome of moral deliberation, the only proper course seems to be to endorse constitutional arrangements neutral between conceptions of the good in order to enable all individuals to develop and pursue their own conception of the good. Since no conception of the good which expresses the rational nature of the person upholding it is better than any other, the constitutional arrangements should be neutral between them. The role of the state is to enable all persons to express their nature and pursue their own autonomously conceived conception of the good and plan of life.

As noted, this intuitive idea relies on a plausible-looking but unfounded belief in the acceptance of a need for unanimously approved principles of justice as in everyone's highest interest. This is enough to reject it. Furthermore, this way of expressing the intuitive idea is unlikely to gain Rawls' approval. It advocates not neutral political concern as a principle of restraint but neutrality between those conceptions of the good which greatly value an autonomous development of one's life in accordance with one's rational nature. It is in fact not a doctrine of neutrality but of moral pluralism. Moral pluralism is often thought to necessitate neutral political concern. It will be the main task of Part Four of the book to explore the rationality of perfectionist moral pluralism, i.e. of pluralism of many forms of the good which are admitted to be so many valuable expressions of people's nature, but pluralism which allows that certain conceptions of the good are worthless and demeaning, and that political action may and should be taken to eradicate or at least curtail them. For the present all we need do is point to the logical gap between pluralism and neutrality.

Moral pluralism asserts the existence of a multitude of incompatible but morally valuable forms of life. It is coupled with an advocacy of autonomy. It naturally combines with the view that individuals should develop freely to find for themselves the form of the good which they wish to pursue in their life. Both combined lead to political conclusions which are in some ways akin to those of Rawls: political action should be concerned with providing individuals with the means by which they can develop, which enable them to choose and attempt to realize their own conception of the good. But there is nothing here which speaks for neutrality. For it is the goal of all political action to enable individuals to pursue valid conceptions of the good and to discourage evil or empty ones. Or at least that is the argument of Part Four. Our provisional conclusion can be no more than that Rawls and others arguing for neutrality in similar ways fail to establish their case, and that sometimes they assume too quick or simple a connection between neutrality and personal autonomy.

6

The Exclusion of Ideals

Rawls' advocacy of the doctrine of neutral political concern is the richest and most subtle of those offered in recent times. That is why much of the last chapter was concerned with his work. The discussion of the exclusion of ideals in the present chapter will similarly revolve round arguments advanced by Nozick. It will be preceded, however, by the examination of a simpler doctrine, political welfarism. It is worth remembering that this division of chapters is slightly misleading. It is based on the distinction between two anti-perfectionist doctrines, the exclusion of ideals and neutrality between ideals. But many of the arguments for one of the anti-perfectionist doctrines can be used to support the other. The most prominent advocates of anti-perfectionism have failed to distinguish between its neutralist and exclusionist forms.[1] So the rejection of neutrality in the preceding chapter is provisional only. For a final verdict we have to await the examination of the arguments for the exclusionary doctrine. Again we will start by briefly considering the meaning and coherence of the principle of the exclusion of ideals before proceeding to examine the arguments for it.

1. Preliminaries

So far we have avoided any clarification of what is meant by ideals or conceptions of the good. For the principle of neutral concern such clarification is not all that important. The easiest explanation is to say that conceptions of the good consist

[1] We noticed above that Nozick confused the two. It appears that Dworkin was not clear about the distinction either. He advocated neutrality in his article 'Liberalism' in *A Matter of Principle*, Cambridge Mass., 1985, first published in Hampshire (ed.): *Public and Private Morality*, Cambridge 1978) and then proceeded to advocate a form of the exclusion of ideals in 'Is There a Right to Pornography?' *Oxford Journal of Legal Studies*, 1 (1981), 177 (also reprinted in *A Matter of Principle*), without noticing the difference between the doctrines nor the fact that they conflict.

of the rest of morality (that is, all of it other than the principle of neutrality itself). Some advocates of neutrality may think it essential to understand the term in a more restricted sense. But even if it is understood in this all-encompassing way it makes the doctrine of neutrality a potent and intuitively appealing doctrine. Governments are, according to it, to be even-handed between all rival moralities. The principle of the exclusion of ideals does not enjoy this luxury. Unlike the principle of neutrality, it does not tell governments what to do. It merely forbids them to act for certain reasons. But can it really be that no moral reason can ever form a basis for governmental action? To be plausible the principle must be understood as presupposing some distinction within morality between that part called its conceptions of the good, which cannot be pursued politically, and the rest that can.

The ideals or conceptions of the good which are excluded from the political arena are to be broadly understood. Any judgment that an activity, way of life, or any aspect of it is either good or bad to any degree is a partial description of a conception of the good. So are statements on various aspects of the value of the organization of society, or any other judgments about the value of any state of society. The goodness of one's life may be enhanced by the fact that one lives in a society of a certain kind (devout, well-educated, prosperous etc.). So conceptions of the good encompass both private ideals (lots of leisure and sport, etc.) and societal conditions which contribute to them (general prosperity, general appreciation of the importance of physical activity, etc.).

Nor need conceptions of the good be exclusively or strongly based on moral considerations, if this term is understood in a narrow sense. The excellence of the life of a shepherd, living at close quarters with his animals, responding to the continuous changes in the natural world, proving his resolve and ingenuity in the face of many man-made and natural difficulties and crises, is not necessarily a moral excellence, in the narrow sense of that word. But the view that such a life displays these forms of excellence is part of a conception of the good. In this book 'moral' is used,

unless the contrary is indicated, in a very wide sense in which
it is roughly equivalent to 'evaluative'.

Excluding conceptions of the good from politics means,
at its simplest and most comprehensive, that the fact that
some conception of the good is true or valid or sound or
reasonable, etc., should never serve as a reason for any political action. Nor should the fact that a conception of the
good is false, invalid, unsound, unreasonable, etc. be allowed
to be a reason for a political action. Notice that the exclusion
is of the valid as well as of the invalid. Again, there is no
need for a principle instructing the government or anyone
else to base their actions on valid conceptions of the good
and to disregard invalid ones. It is the exclusion of both valid
and invalid, the prescription that political action should be
value-blind, which gives the principle its distinctive flavour.
It makes it a principle of restraint. The doctrine of the exclusion of ideals claims that government action should be
blind to all ideals of the good life, that implementation and
promotion of ideals of the good life, though worthy in itself,
is not a legitimate object of governmental action.

Naturally, supporters of the exclusion of ideals do not
wish to claim that governments may never act for moral
reasons. They allow, for example, that the fact that murder
is morally wrong is the reason (or at least part of the reason)
for making it an offence punishable by law. They draw a
distinction between two parts of morality. One, the doctrine
of the good, is out of bounds for governments. The other is
a proper, perhaps even the proper, basis for governmental
action: one view which has considerable currency holds
governments to be required to promote the goals that people
have, without discrimination based on their moral merit.
That is the view I dubbed political welfarism. Another divide which suggests itself is that between teleological and
deontological considerations, between the doctrines of the
good and of the right. According to it governments are to
base their measures on considerations of which actions are
right or wrong, but not on the grounds that some actions are
conducive to the good and others are not.

The notorious elusiveness of the distinction between the
right and the good did not deter Rawls, for in *A Theory of*

Justice the doctrine of neutrality incorporated in his conception of justice itself defines the distinction between the right and the good. The obscurity of the distinction is, however, an obstacle for those who wish to rely on an independently recognized distinction and employ it to provide a foundation for a doctrine of liberty. Nozick, who essentially limits governments to deontological considerations, avoided the problem by relying on a concept he introduced himself, that of side-constraints, which can be regarded as an explication of the idea of deontological considerations. Others have been much less explicit regarding the way they wish to divide morality into a part which is politically relevant, and a part which is not.

One possible doubt regarding the doctrine of the exclusion of ideals concerns the viability of such distinctions. I do not wish, however, to deny the possibility of drawing a coherent distinction between deontological and teleological considerations. The main argument of this chapter aims to cast doubt on whether the distinction justifies the conclusion that the good is out of bounds in politics. It tries to identify the reasons which lead people to embrace this form of anti-perfectionism, and to show that they are inadequate for the task.

Another, more general, prima facie argument will have to wait till later in the book. Even though deontological and teleological considerations are distinct they derive from a common moral core. Therefore, since the core moral concern should be politically promoted through the enforcement of some deontological constraints it seems plausible to hold that it should also be promoted by advancing the correct conception of the good as well. Since the two parts of morality are separate only at the superficial level, whereas at the fundamental level they both stem from a common source, there is a prima facie case for requiring political action to take notice of both.

2. Political Welfarism

Brian Barry identifies the doctrine of the exclusion of ideals as one important strand in liberalism:

Classical liberalism had other strands besides this one no doubt, but one was certainly the idea that the state is an instrument for satisfying the wants that men happen to have rather than a means of making good men (e.g. cultivating desirable wants or dispositions in its citizens).[1]

Barry, therefore, defines liberalism, for the purpose of his argument, as the view that ideal-regarding principles should not be used for prescribing the conduct of political actors. The definition identifies liberalism with the endorsement of a particular version of the doctrine of the exclusion of ideals by its use of Barry's previous distinction between want-and ideal-regarding principles:

Want-regarding principles. . . are principles which take as given the wants which people happen to have and concentrate attention entirely on the extent to which a certain policy will alter the overall amount of want-satisfaction or on the way in which the policy will affect the distribution among people of opportunities for satisfying wants. (p. 38)

I will regard the second half of the definition as referring to the distribution of actual satisfaction of desires rather than to the distribution of opportunities, though these may be an indicator of actual satisfaction: 'in order to evaluate the desirability of a state of affairs according to such principles, all the information we need is the amount and/or distribution among persons of want-satisfaction' (ibid.). Any non-want-regarding principle is ideal-regarding. Want-regarding theories are, therefore, instances of what A. Sen calls 'welfarism', i.e., the view that the goodness of a state of affairs depends ultimately on the set of individual utilities in that state.[2]

Not all welfarist theories are based on a principle of restraint. According to some, want-regarding considerations are the only ones relevant for the evaluation of any action. On this view, which I will call moral welfarism, there are no valid ideal-regarding principles and therefore to advocate

---

[1] B. Barry, *Political Argument*, London, 1963, p. 66. All page references to Barry are to this book. Barry has some effective criticism of his own against liberalism thus understood, which I shall not repeat here. As the following discussion will make clear, this statement of the liberal position by Barry is open to several interpretations only some of which lead to the doctrine of neutral political concern.

[2] A. Sen, 'Utilitarianism and Welfarism', *Journal of Philosophy*, 78 (1979), 463.

excluding them from political action is not to advocate restraint. Only those theorists who accept ideal-regarding
principles for determining the desirability of at least some
states of affairs and yet rely exclusively on want-regarding
principles in evaluating or advocating political action subscribe to the liberal precept as described by Barry above,
i.e., that it is not the business of the state to promote the
goodness of individuals. It should confine itself to the satisfaction of their desires. I shall dub 'political welfarism' the
kind of welfarist political theories that admit the validity of
some ideal-regarding principles but which confine their
force to non-political actions.

Political welfarism owes part of its popularity to a confusion between it and two quite distinct ideas. One is its
confusion with moral welfarism. The fact that moral welfarists who deny the validity of any ideal-regarding principles are not advocating restraint when they object to
reliance on ideal-regarding principles is often lost sight of.
Moral welfarists who, for example, object to the proscription
of so-called deviant sexual practices or of marijuana sometimes appeal to principles denying the state the right to
enforce 'private morality', whereas what they mean is the
denial of the state's right to enforce the wrong morality.
It is all too convenient for moral welfarists to assume the
mantle of political welfarists since this will serve their purpose just as well. But though their political results may be
identical, the two doctrines represent radically different
views of both morality and politics.

The other confusion is the belief that a commitment to
representative government commits one to political welfarism. 'Does not representative government mean an equal
chance for all to have their goals supported by the state? And
is not that the meaning of political welfarism?' The answer to
both questions is negative. The principles of representative
government guarantee some measure of control by the population over those in authority. They do not entail a commitment by the democratically constituted authorities to act
on welfarist considerations alone.

With these clarifications behind us, we can turn to an
evaluation of political welfarism. Want-satisfaction can be

supported as intrinsically good or as a means to some other good. Suppose a political welfarist holds it to be intrinsically good. He is then committed to the view that some intrinsic goods (want-satisfaction) may, while others (ideals in Barry's sense) may not, be pursued politically. He is committed, that is, to the view that certain means (political ones) may be used in pursuit of some goals but not of others. I shall take it for granted that, while possibly there are some ideals that cannot be promoted by political means and others that cannot be efficiently so promoted, it is not the case that no ideals can be efficiently pursued by political means. Such considerations cannot therefore be used to support a total ban on ideals from politics. After all, our hypothetical theorist is not proposing to ban the satisfaction of wants as a ground of political action, even though there are wants the satisfaction of which cannot, and others which cannot efficiently, be pursued by political means.

Are there grounds for believing that it is wrong to pursue politically any intrinsic goods other than the satisfaction of wants? It follows from the conclusion of the previous chapter that political welfarism is not neutral between ideals of the good since it clearly favours moral welfarism above all other views. But neutral or not, the main problem is to find any reason for supporting politically some elements of a conception of the good and not others that are admitted to be valid and valuable. I know of no attempts to answer the question which neither reduce themselves to an endorsement of moral welfarism nor rely on the false claim that one cannot promote ideals politically.

The difficulties with political welfarism, however, go deeper. Belief in ideal-regarding principles undermines the plausibility of regarding want-satisfaction as intrinsically good. People pursue goals and have desires for reasons. They believe that the objects of their desires or their pursuits are valuable (and sometimes that the pursuit itself is valuable not merely as a means to achieve its object). This reason-dependent character of goals and desires entails that any person who has a goal or a desire believes, if he has minimal understanding of their nature, that if he came to believe that there were no reasons to pursue the goal or the desire, he would no longer have them. Notice that belief in an appropriate reason is here merely made a necessary condition for the having of a goal or a desire. It is not assumed that one desires whatever one sees a reason for or whatever one holds to be valuable.[1]

A further consequence of the reason-dependent character of desires is that agents do not wish their desires satisfied if their belief in the existence of a reason for their desires is unfounded. One does not wish to have the medicine one desires to have if it does not have the medical properties that one believes to be the only reason for having it. People who wish the state to subsidize the arts do not wish it to do so if such subsidies will not help the development or propagation of the arts which they believe to be the only reason to subsidize them. One way in which 'wishing' is weaker than 'desiring' is that it is very close to 'believing that there is an undefeated reason for'.[2] Not wishing that what one desires will happen if one's belief in a reason for it is mistaken is no more than an acknowledgement of the reason-dependent character of desire. The desire is not itself a reason; it is merely an endorsement of a reason independent of it. This is true both of instrumental desires, i.e. desires based on a belief that their realization will serve other goals one has, and of what is desired for its own sake. I do not wish to have what I want for its intrinsic pleasure, if having it will not bring pleasure.[3]

[1] The point deserves a more detailed defence than is possible here. Let me note in brief that I am not supposing that deliberation on the nature of the reasons always accompanies the formation of desires nor that one always gives oneself an explicit account of such reasons. Akratic agents believe that the reason for their akratic behaviour is defeated by other reasons, but akratic action is undertaken for some reason that they believe in. Unconscious desires depend on conscious ones and are essentially redescriptions of them in ways that the agent may not use in accounting for his reasons for them.

[2] On the other hand wishing is stronger than desiring in being an overall judgment of the merits of the wished for, whereas a desire need be based on a partial evaluation of the desired only.

[3] Sometimes the fact that persons have desires changes the situation in a special way—the desires may acquire the character of a craving, i.e., they may as it were escape their control and dominate them quite independently of their beliefs about the appropriateness of the desires (though except in extreme pathological cases, the agents will continue to believe that they desire for a reason). In such cases they may acquire a new reason to satisfy their desires, i.e., to liberate themselves from their hold. But even in such cases it is not merely the fact that they desire that is

The point of this argument is that one does not wish one's desire satisfied if one's reason for the desire is mistaken even if one continues, through ignorance, to entertain the desire. One does not wish merely not to have mistaken desires; one also does not wish to have them satisfied. It is primarily the craving conception of desires that obscures this point by making the disappointment at a failure to satisfy one's desire appear like the suffering caused by a frustrated craving. In fact, the disappointment may be little more than belief that something for which there is a reason failed to happen. Where the fate of the desire largely depends on the personal performance of the agent, its failure is accompanied by disappointment at one's own incompetence, lack of good fortune, lack of support from others for one's plans, etc., and these do often constitute valid reasons for preventing the relevant kind of frustration. But it is enough to consider a desire to see one's party win the election (which leads one to vote for it) to see that not all desires lead to such reactions when frustrated.

If the observations on the reason-dependent character of desires are correct, even if they apply to some non-trivial categories of desires only, then want-satisfaction as such cannot be an intrinsic good. Those who deny the validity of all ideal-regarding principles may perhaps resist this conclusion. They may argue that it is based on the common existence of a second-order desire not to have one's false desires satisfied. They may proceed to claim that these second-order desires presuppose that some of the ideal-regarding reasons are valid reasons. They may concede that almost all people believe in some ideal-regarding principles and have second-order desires that their false ideal-based desires need not be satisfied. This second-order desire, however, relates to local mistakes, i.e. to mistakes concerning which ideal-regarding principles are valid, and to their consequences given the facts of the case. It does not apply to a case of a global mistake, i.e., where the mistake is a

their reason for wishing the desires to be satisfied. They may, e.g., be wrong in thinking that satisfying the desires is the best way to terminate their irrational craving and, unless they are akratic, they will wish the desires not to be satisfied if this is the case.

failure to see that *no* ideal-regarding principles are valid. If this is so, if people are guilty of the global mistake, then there is no reason to respect their second-order desire—or rather it does not apply in such circumstances. I do not wish to endorse this argument, but for the purpose of the present point we need not evaluate it. Suffice it to say that it is not available to political welfarists, for they accept the validity of some ideal-regarding principles.

It may be objected that all I have argued for is that people's desires are not their own reasons for pursuing the object of those desires. This need not mean that they are not reasons for others, who ought to help them. But the only reason for satisfying other people's desires is to help them, i.e., help them get what is good for them or what they want. The preceding argument shows that people do not wish their false desires satisfied, and that though in certain circumstances it is good for them to have them satisfied, this is by no means always the case. Hence want-satisfaction *qua* want-satisfaction is not intrinsically valuable, at least not if there are valid ideal-regarding principles.

Many who are tempted by political welfarism are influenced by a picture that depends on viewing want-satisfaction as instrumentally valued (whatever its intrinsic value may be). Even if the preceding argument is wrong, even if want-satisfaction is an intrinsic good, it is possible that it is its instrumental and not its intrinsic value that accounts for the view that want-regarding principles may, while ideal-regarding ones may not, guide political action.

The picture I have in mind is that of live and let live. People's lives are their own affairs. They may be moral or immoral, admirable or demeaning, and so on, but even when immoral they are none of the state's business, none of anyone's business except those whose lives they are. All that politics is concerned with is providing people with the means to pursue their own lives, i.e., with helping them satisfy their wants and realize their goals. The state should therefore act on welfarist grounds alone and shun all ideal-regarding principles. Attractive though this simplified picture is, it is riddled with ambiguities and difficulties, the solving of which transforms it in a radical way. One of these issues will be taken up now. The others will occupy us for the rest of this chapter and the next.

The live-and-let-live picture is ambiguous regarding the relevance of personal goals. Is it the state's duty to try and maximize their satisfaction, i.e., to make sure that people do succeed in leading the lives they have chosen, or should it make opportunities available to them that will enable them to try and lead the lives they have chosen?

The first interpretation is analogous to the one above. One does not help people to lead the lives they want to have by satisfying their false desires. People do not wish to have a life based on falsehood. The second interpretation requires the state, while avoiding any action designed to implement any conception of the good, to provide individuals with the means of pursuing their ideals of the good. But satisfying people's wants is not to be equated with providing them with the means of pursuing their ideals. Satisfying false wants concerning the means to one's ideals will not help in realizing them, and some useful means may not be wanted since the person does not realize their usefulness or fails to form rational plans concerning them.

The live-and-let-live picture leads us away from political welfarism and toward the suggestion that the state's concern is with the provision of adequate means for individuals to pursue their own ideals of the good.[1] This may be justified by invoking the value of autonomy, i.e. the view that the fact that a person controls aspects of his life, and determines their shape, gives his life value. Considerations of autonomy are central to the argument of Part Four of the book. They are also prominent in Nozick's version of the exclusion of

---

[1] Barry distinguishes between private-oriented and public-oriented wants. The first are those whose satisfaction materially impinges only upon the life of the person whose desires they are, or upon his or her family. Public-oriented wants are ones whose satisfaction affects a larger group (pp. 12–13; see also p. 63). Barry notes that public-oriented wants reflect people's ideals concerning the state of society and objects to giving them any weight as wants. They should be weighed according to the value of the ideals they express. My argument earlier in this section accords with this line of thought inasmuch as want-satisfaction is considered to be possibly of intrinsic value. But if the state's goal is to provide people with opportunities to pursue their own conception of the good, then public-oriented wants should count as well, though, as we have just seen, not in the sense that the state should strive to satisfy them, but in that it should provide opportunities for their pursuit as well as for the pursuit of private-oriented wants.

ideals. Since it is based on the distinction between teleological and deontological considerations it is in other respects far removed from political welfarism, and immune to the criticism here levelled against it. It is to Nozick's theory that we now turn.

3. Treating People as Ends

There are only individual people, different individual people with their own individual lives. Using one of these people for the benefit of others, uses him and benefits others. . . . To use a person in this way does not sufficiently respect and take account of the fact that he is a separate person, that his is the only life he has. *He* does not get some overbalancing good from his sacrifice, and no one is entitled to force this upon him—least of all a state or government that claims his allegiance. . . and that therefore scrupulously must be *neutral* between its citizens.[1]

These words of Nozick echo the Kantian injunction always to treat people as ends in themselves and never as means only. Nowhere again does he use the state's claim to allegiance as a reason for political neutrality. His argument amounts to an interpretation of the Kantian imperative. Nozick's interpretation relies on the notion of a side-constraint. Side-constraints are deontological constraints and will be examined in Chapter Eleven. Some preliminary explanation is necessary here to examine their use as principles of exclusion.

Side-constraints are agent-relative action reasons of an absolute or near absolute force. Let me explain[2]. Some reasons for action are based on the value of the outcome of those actions. Let us call these 'outcome reasons'. The reason for bringing injured people to hospital is (barring special circumstances) an outcome reason. Acting in this way will secure their health which, since it is a valued outcome, is also a reason for bringing it about. Some reasons, however, are based on the value of a particular (class of) agent(s) performing a certain action (including the bringing about by

[1] Nozick, *Anarchy, State, and Utopia*, p. 33.
[2] The explanation is adapted from the distinctions drawn by D. Parfit in 'Is Common Sense Morality Self Defeating?', *Journal of Philosophy*, 70 (1979), 533.

those agents of a certain outcome). I will call these action reasons. Parents have both an outcome and an action reason to show concern for the welfare of their children. The outcome reason is satisfied by the parents employing teachers and child minders. The action reason is satisfied only if parents personally involve themselves in the affairs of their children.

Some reasons are reasons for everyone. Everyone has reason to respect the rights of others, for example. Such reasons are agent-neutral. Other reasons are reasons for some people and not for others. Those are agent-relative reasons. A person who made a promise has an agent-relative reason to keep it, even though it may derive from an agent-neutral reason to keep one's promises. Both action and outcome reasons can be either agent-neutral or agent-relative.

The Kantian imperative is explicable only in terms of action reasons. The requirement is that people should personally treat people as ends, not that they shall secure for people the benfits which result from being so treated. (Are there such benefits?) But the imperative is open to an agent-neutral interpretation. Each person may be thought to have reason to help, or even make, others treat people as ends. It may be thought that the Kantian imperative is indifferent in a choice between treating others as ends oneself or treating them as means where doing so will make them treat others as ends, and where but for that action they would not have done so (for example, coercing a person not to coerce another).

Nozick rejects this interpretation of the Kantian imperative. He regards it as imposing side-constraints. A side-constraint is an agent-relative reasons of absolute or near absolute weight. It cannot be defeated by any other consideration or can only be defeated by a small number of enumerated considerations. Nozick explains:

The issue of whether a side-constraint view can be put in the form of the goal without-side-constraint view is a tricky one. One might think, for example, that each person could distinguish in his goal between *his* violating rights and someone else's doing it. Give the former infinite (negative) weight in his goal, and no amount of stopping others from violating rights can outweigh his violating someone's rights.[1]

Broadly speaking, Nozick believes in an agent-relative action reason against imposing sacrifices on individuals against their will. Nozick does not regard the prohibition as being as absolute and exceptionless as one would expect if it is to be an interpretation of the Kantian imperative. He allows for imposing sacrifices on people, even if there are no counterbalancing benefits for them (even though they are separate people and their lives are the only lives they have) in cases of self-defence. Moreover, Nozick goes a long way beyond self-defence by sanctioning the use of force by an organization not created by consent, if it could have been created by consent through the Invisible Hand mechanism. Perhaps an even more significant exception to the Nozickian version of the Kantian imperative is his principle of compensation that allows coercing some to reduce risks to others provided the former are adequately compensated.[2]

In fact, on occasion Nozick seems to suggest that imposing a sacrifice on a person does not offend against his version of the Kantian principle so long as he is compensated by receiving a counterbalancing good. So long as he is a net beneficiary from a transaction, could not one say that he was not treated merely as a means? Is it not true in such a case that his separateness and the fact that his life is the only one he has have been respected? And if so, can one not regard a whole series of mutually dependent transactions from some of which he stands to lose and from others to gain as one transaction since none will take place if the others do not? Such a series will be allowed if the initial expected balance of benefits and sacrifices is positive. The condition is met in many states, even in many illiberal states. Some people are perhaps net losers, but the initial expected balance may still be favourable to all.

These are genuine questions. They point to gaps in Nozick's argument and to ambiguities in his position which, if resolved in some ways, lead to conclusions far removed

---

[1] Nozick, *Anarchy, State, and Utopia*, p. 29 n. He regards such reformulations as inadequate but does not explain why.

[2] Ibid., pp. 78 ff.

from the spirit of *Anarchy, State, and Utopia*, though consistent with a certain interpretation of its premises.

Does the Kantian imperative in Nozick's interpretation
lead to political anti-perfectionism, and in particular does it
lead to a principle of the exclusion of ideals from politics?
Not without further and independent moral assumptions
(which Nozick does not defend). The crucial question is
whether coercion to comply with moral duties is consistent
with the Kantian imperative as interpreted by Nozick.
Nozick's view about self-defence suggests that it is but that
the duties not to infringe or put at risk others' rights are the
only moral duties there are. This pushes the question one
step back. What rights do people have? Do they, for example,
have a right that other members of their community contribute to the life of the community? Nozick's answer is
uncertain. He appears to deny the existence of such rights
but in principle excludes the justification of a theory of rights
from the book. What is clear is that it is neither the Kantian
imperative nor Nozick's interpretation of it which leads to
anti-perfectionism. If individuals have moral duties to contribute to other persons and to promote certain ideals, then
they are not being treated as means by being made to live
up to them.

4. Coercion and Autonomy

Nozick appears to claim that it is because the state acts
through coercion that it has to abjure perfectionism. It is
unobjectionable to win over another's clients in order to
benefit oneself, but one may not coerce them not to trade
with another. Is there anything about coercion or its political
use to justify anti-perfectionism?

Coercion is an evaluative term. While it has a fixed descriptive core, its meaning cannot be fully explained without
noting its moral significance. I will adopt the following definition of coercion.[1]

P coerces Q into not doing act A only if

---

[1] The first part of the definition is a modification of Nozick's in 'Coercion' in
Philosophy, Politics, and Society, ed. P. Laslett, W. G. Runciman, and Q. Skinner,
4th series, Oxford, 1972, pp. 104–6.

A (1) P communicates to Q that he intends to bring about or have brought about some consequence, C, if Q does A.

(2) P makes this communication intending Q to believe that he does so in order to get Q not to do A.

(3) That C will happen is, for Q, a reason of great weight for not doing A.

(4) Q believes that it is likely that P will bring about C if Q does A and that C would leave him worse off, having done A, than if he did not do A and P did not bring about C.

(5) Q does not do A.

(6) Part of Q's reason for not doing A is to avoid (or to lessen) the likelihood of C by making it less likely that P will bring it about.

B P's actions which conform to the conditions set out in *A* are prima facie wrong.

C The fact that Q acted under those circumstances is a reason for not blaming him for not doing A.

Only a communication meeting conditions *A*1–4 is a coercive threat. This definition is not an accurate explanation of the meaning of the expression in English for it disregards some of its uses. It concentrates on coercion by threats since this is the form of coercion relevant to political theory.[1] The definition's first, descriptive, part sets only necessary conditions for the application of the term. One's list of sufficient conditions as well as one's view of how evil the threatened consequence must be to count as a coercive threat depends on one's view of the evaluative significance of coercion. Conditions *B* and *C* are deliberately weak for there is no general agreement in the linguistic community on the precise evaluative significance of coercion. By some, or sometimes, it is held to render the coerced not responsible in the sense that the action is only nominally theirs, whereas in fact the coerced are being controlled by another in a way akin to physical compulsion. By others, or at other times, coercion

---

[1] In 'Threats, Offers, Law, Opinion, and Liberty' *American Philosophical Quarterly* 14 (1977) 265, P. Day mentions six coercive modes of influence: (1) forcing, (2) threatening, (3) extreme intimidation, (4) extreme temptation, (5) extreme domination, (6) extreme provocation.

is held to be no more than a mitigating circumstance. Whichever view one takes, it is not to be justified on linguistic or conceptual grounds but by the soundness of the moral theory of which it is a part.

I will briefly sketch a view of coercion based on assigning it the following evaluative role:

> B1. By issuing a coercive threat to another person one invades his autonomy.
>
> C1. The fact that a person acted under coercion is either a justification or a complete excuse for his action.

These principles state the evaluative significance of coercion regarding the acts of the coercer and the coerced respectively. They enable one to draw on one's views about autonomy, justification and excuses for determining what kinds of threats are (provided they meet conditions A1-4) coercive ones.

The following considerations begin to outline the reasons for the two principles. The descriptive meaning of coercion (conditions A1-6) is enough to explain some of the reasons for limiting coercion. Coercive threats differ from offers, for example, in that the former reduce the options available to the person to whom they are addressed whereas offers never worsen and often improve them.[1] Therefore, coercive threats are likely by themselves to change a person's situation significantly for the worse. Furthermore, it is normally more difficult to get people to act against their interests by making

---

[1] An offer creates an option its receiver may not have had before. It does not deprive the receiver of any options. A credible threat deprives the threatened person of the option of not acting as he or she is told to act and not suffering the threatened consequence. No new desirable options are created for the person. The traveller stopped by a highwayman gains the option of resisting the robber. But such an option is not a desirable one, i.e., it is one that people in normal circumstances would prefer not to have. A threatened consequence may be one that will happen anyway independently of the threat. If the threatened person knows of this, the threat is rendered ineffective, so that such cases will be rare and can be disregarded here. It is sometimes assumed that a person making an offer intends it to be taken up and that an offer gives an advantage or benefit. Neither is universally true. The person making the offer may be indifferent as to whether it will be accepted, or even hope that it will not (consider a polite offer to give a lift home to a person met at a party). An offer is more like a conditional promise: I undertake to do it if you want me to. Whether or not it is to one's advantage to be threatened, or to be made an offer, depends on whether or not it is in one's interest to have more or fewer options.

them an offer than by coercively threatening them (assuming that making the offers and the coercive threats are equally easy).

Finally, though coercion is sometimes meant to benefit the coerced person, we are only too familiar with the danger of exaggerating the degree to which people's well-being can be promoted in flat contradiction to their formed judgments and preferences. While offers may be made in order to induce people to act against their long-term interests, they themselves are in normal circumstances the best judges of that. Our concern is raised only if the person receiving an offer lacks the ability or knowledge to assess it or if there are reasons to regard the bargaining situation as unfair or inefficient. None of these considerations, however, explains why coercion is more suspect than other methods of encouraging people to act in ways deemed to be socially beneficial by making the alternative less attractive. Their main thrust is to cast doubt on the justification of widespread use of paternalistic coercion. Even in this area the differences between coercion and other paternalistic methods which these considerations reveal are merely in probabilities.

Two common views about coercion provide the clue to its normative significance. It is commonly said of the coerced that they were forced to do the coerced act and that they acted against their will. Such statements may appear paradoxical since the coerced prefer to comply with the threat and avoid the penalty. The coerced may regret the circumstances they are in, but so do many people who face hard unpleasant choices. This does not make us say that they acted against their will. Nor would it always justify saying that they were forced to act as they did. They had, as do the coerced, a genuine choice. The explanation lies in the character of the choice. Certain choices are forced or dictated choices. Certain choices (not necessarily the same) are made against one's will. I propose to identify the relevant choices by their normative consequences. This proposal is not to be justified as a piece of ordinary language analysis but on the grounds that while in accord with the core meaning of coercion it fruitfully ties it to sound moral principles.

A person is forced to act in a certain way if (1) he regrets the fact that he is in the circumstances he believes himself to be in and which are his reasons for acting as he does, and (2) his action is justified or excused. Notice that this definition allows that a person be forced to do what he wants to do anyway. The person being forced need not regret doing what he does. It is enough that he regrets the circumstances which make him do it. Furthermore, a person can desire (at one time) to be forced to do something that he believes he will not want to do at a later time. Likewise he can welcome being forced to do something which he wants to do but which his unwillingness to do is greater than his desire to do. In such cases the idea of being forced is pushed to its limits. The person being forced welcomes the fact that the choice is made easy for him, while regretting that his weakness, or some other circumstance, make him unable to choose for the right reasons.

The coerced person is forced to act as he did. Hence his action is either justified or excused. It is justified if the reasons for it, including the threat of harm if it is not undertaken, defeat the reasons against it, including the fact that undertaking it amounts to submitting to coercion which violates the agent's autonomy (as will be explained below). Not all forced actions are justified. A person may be forced to act immorally, as when a shipwrecked sea captain abandons many passengers to certain death in order to save the life of his only child.

Whether or not such action is excusable depends on further moral views the reasons for which have little to do with coercion. But since one's view of excusing principles affects one's willingness to acknowledge that people were coerced to act as they did, let me put forward a principle that I regard as reasonable, namely, that persons are excused where they acted in order to preserve the life they have or have embarked upon, provided only that their life is neither immoral nor not worth having.

Let the conditions necessary to enable a person to have the life he or she has or has set upon be called personal needs. Choices are dictated by personal needs if all but one non-trivial option will sacrifice a personal need and will make impossible the continuation of the life the agent has.[1] Personal needs are not necessarily the needs of survival. They are more like the needs for having a worthwhile life. For example, life may not be worthwhile, may not be morally possible, for parents who have betrayed their child. Therefore, persons threatened with the death of their child if they do not obey are, if this view is correct, faced with a choice dictated by personal needs: disobedience to the order of the child's kidnapper will make life morally impossible, will make the parents' life not worth living. Personal needs are, however, what is necessary to have the life one has or has set upon. Concert pianists may lose the life they have if their fingers are broken. A choice in which the pianist has only one option to avoid his fingers being broken is dictated by personal needs, even though the pianist is able to make a new life as a business consultant.[2]

Much more can and need be said to make the notion of a personal need clearer (and something more will be said in Chapter Fourteen), though nothing can make it precise enough to avoid difficult questions concerning many of its applications to particular cases. For present purposes, however, further elaboration is not required. My aim is merely to tie the notion of 'coercion' to a view about excuses. Let me repeat, however, that a choice is dictated by a personal need only if the need is to preserve neither a wicked life nor one not worth living. Hitler cannot be excused by claiming that he had to continue as he started or he would not have been able to pursue the life he had embarked upon.

In the light of all this, how serious need a threat be to be a coercive one? If it would justify a coerced action, its

[1] The reference to non-trivial options is needed since trivial options are always available. One can hand the money more or less slowly to the gunman who threatens, 'Your money or your life.'

[2] Whether or not an act is justified is an objective question, depending on how things were or could reasonably have been believed to be, rather than on the agent's beliefs. And this is true of moral as well as of other beliefs. The principle that personal needs excuse is similarly an objective one. Although to a degree persons make the life they have, what life they have made for themselves and whether this choice is dictated by personal need is an objective question. This is not to deny that other excusing principles may excuse those who erroneously believe that they are forced to act as they do. My only point is that they are neither forced nor coerced to take this action.

seriousness depends on the reasons against that action. If those are not very weighty, the threat need not be as serious as a threat to a personal need. It need only be of great weight to meet the linguistic convention concerning 'coercion' (condition $A3$ in the definition given above). A non-justifying threat, however, is a coercive one only if it excuses and it does so only if it is serious enough to create a choice dictated by personal needs.

Persons may be forced to act in a certain way by circumstances that are of nobody's making, or they may be forced by another's action which created the circumstances that forced them to act as they did. They are forced by another person only if they are forced by that person's action which was undertaken in order to force them to act as they did. One person may force another by changing the circumstances surrounding that other person's choice or by credibly threatening to do so if the other does not act in a certain way. Such forcing threats are coercive threats, and those who are forced by them are coerced to act as they did.

A person who forces another to act in a certain way, and therefore one who coerces another, makes him act against his will. He subjects the will of another to his own and thereby invades that person's autonomy. Let me explain. An autonomous agent or person is one who has the capacity to be or to become significantly autonomous at least to a minimal degree. Significant autonomy is a matter of degree. A person may be more or less autonomous. (Significantly) autonomous persons are those who can shape their life and determine its course. They are not merely rational agents who can choose between options after evaluating relevant information, but agents who can in addition adopt personal projects, develop relationships, and accept commitments to causes, through which their personal integrity and sense of dignity and self-respect are made concrete. In a word, significantly autonomous agents are part creators of their own moral world. Persons who are part creators of their own moral world have a commitment to projects, relationships, and causes which affects the kind of life that is for them worth living. It is not that they may not sacrifice projects or causes they are committed to for good reasons, but rather

that there are certain kinds of actions vis-à-vis their commitments which amount to betrayal, compromise their integrity, sacrifice their self-respect, and in extreme cases
render their life, i.e. the life they made for themselves,
worthless or even impossible (in a moral sense).

Much of the writing on autonomy focuses on an agent's
ability to form informed and effective judgments as a condition of autonomy. There can be no doubt of its importance.
But there are additional aspects to autonomy as (part)
authorship of one's life. One is relational: an autonomous
person is not subjected to the will of another. Another aspect
of autonomy concerns the quality of the options open to
agents. Their choices must not be dictated by personal
needs. One is a part author of one's world only if one is not
merely serving the will of another. Forcing persons, and
therefore coercing them, to act invades their autonomy because, first, the person who forces others directly intends
them to conform to his will. Subjecting others to his will is
either his end or his means to it. And, second, the coercer
aims at and succeeds in forcing others by restricting their
options.

All coercion invades autonomy by subjecting the will of
the coerced. Coercive threats which create a choice dictated
by personal needs, and most serious cases of coercion by the
state are of this kind, also invade autonomy by offending
against that aspect which concerns the quality of options.
The autonomous agent is one who is not always struggling
to maintain the minimum conditions of a worthwhile life.
The more one's choices are dictated by personal needs, the
less autonomous one becomes. Of course natural conditions
may also force people to make choices determined by the
need to secure the necessitites of a worthwhile life. And it
would be wrong to think that every such condition is in
any way regrettable. Autonomy is possible only within a
framework of constraints. The completely autonomous person is an impossibility. The ideal of the perfect existentialist
with no fixed biological and social nature who creates himself
as he goes along is an incoherent dream. An autonomous
personality can only develop and flourish against a background of biological and social constraints which fix some of

its human needs. Some choices are inevitably determined by those needs. Yet, harsh natural conditions can reduce the degree of autonomy of a person to a bare minimum just as effectively as systematic coercive intervention. Moreover, non-coercive interferences with a person's life and fortunes may also reduce his autonomy in the same way as coercive interventions do. The only differences are that *all* coercive interventions invade autonomy and they do so intentionally, whereas only *some* non-coercive interventions do so and usually as a by-product of their intended results. They are not direct assaults on the autonomy of persons.

These reflections on the moral significance of autonomy show that though coercion often, even usually, adversely affects people's well-being it does not deserve the special importance attributed to it in much of liberal political thought unless one holds personal autonomy to be of very great value. But even if one does it is easy to exaggerate the evils of coercion, in comparison with other evils or misfortunes which may fall to people in their life. Inasmuch as the liberal concern to limit coercion is a concern for the autonomy of persons, the liberal will also be anxious to secure natural and social conditions which enable individuals to develop an autonomous life. The liberal will seek to control the physical environment and to regulate the non-coercive effects that one person's acts have over others in order to secure an environment suitable for autonomous life. In pursuing such goals the liberal may be willing to use coercion.

Autonomy is a matter of degree. A single act of coercion of a not too serious nature makes little difference to a person's ability to lead an autonomous life. Of course coercion invades autonomy not only in its consequences but also in its intention. As such, it is normally an insult to the person's autonomy. He is being treated as a non-autonomous agent, an animal, a baby, or an imbecile. Often coercion is wrong primarily because it is an affront or an insult and not so much because of its more tangible consequences, which may not be very grave. In this respect, however, there is a significant difference between coercion by an ideal liberal state and coercion from most other sources. Since in-

dividuals are guaranteed adequate rights of political participation in the liberal state and since such a state is guided
by a public morality expressing concern for individual
autonomy, its coercive measures do not express an insult to
the autonomy of individuals. It is common knowledge that
they are motivated not by lack of respect for individual
autonomy but by concern for it. After all, coercion can be
genuinely for the good of the coerced and can even be sought
by them. These considerations do not, however, affect the
liberal concern to limit coercion in a non-ideal state.

5. On Some Underlying Intuitions

The spring from which anti-perfectionism flows is the feeling that foisting one's conception of the good on people
offends their dignity and does not treat them with respect.
R. Dworkin observes: 'The issue is at bottom . . . what is
the content of the respect that is necessary to dignity and
independence.'[1] Is one treating another with respect if one
treats him in accordance with sound moral principles, or
does respect for persons require ignoring morality (or parts
of it) in our relations with others? There can be little doubt
that stated in this way the question admits of only one
answer. One would be showing disrespect to another if one
ignored moral considerations in treating him. That was the
burden of the argument in Section 2 above. But perhaps
governments are the exception to this rule? Perhaps there
are moral considerations which show that governments can
respect persons only by ignoring certain moral dimensions?

The discussion of coercion established that the fact that
(some) governmental action is coercive, while profoundly
affecting the considerations which govern them, does not
justify the exclusion of ideals. As on previous occasions we
discover that the difficulty in finding cogent arguments does
not dispose of the question. A lingering doubt remains: have
we not overlooked some fundamental point?

Consider the following suggestion, endorsed by Dworkin:
'People have a right not to suffer disadvantage in the distribution of social goods and opportunities, including dis-

---

[1] R. Dworkin 'Liberalism', ibid., p. 143.

advantage in the liberties permitted to them by the criminal law, just on the ground that their officials or fellow citizens think that their opinions about the right way for them to lead their own lives are ignoble or wrong.'[1] This sounds like an anti-perfectionist right, but it is not. It excludes not ideals but the fact that people believe in them from serving as grounds for political actions. It serves in Dworkin's hands as a limit on the use of political welfarism, which he regards as the common or the proper method of justifying political action.[2] But it is possible that the appeal of anti-perfectionism is at least in part indirect. There is no way of acting, politically or otherwise, in pursuit of ideals except by relying on the judgment of some people as to which ideals are valid, and imposing it on others who disagree. Those whose views are imposed on the community do not regard the fact that they hold those views as a reason for their imposition on others who reject them. They maintain that their conception of the good is valid and that is the reason which justifies its imposition. But such action is constitutionally justified on the ground that the rulers, the majority, etc., chose to act in that way, regardless of the truth or soundness of their views.

The problem arises out of the apparent incongruity between the content-independent structure of authority, as analysed in Chapter 2 above, and the justification of authoritative action which should be content-dependent. Take a

---

[1] R. Dworkin, 'Is There a Right to Pornography?', ibid., p. 194

[2] It is not clear whether Dworkin himself regards the right as an anti-perfectionist principle. His 'Liberalism' explicitly supports anti-perfectionism. But nowhere does he expound or defend anti-perfectionist principles. In 'Is There a Right to Pornography?' p. 195 he is ambiguous on whether the right to moral independence is an anti-perfectionist right. In the main, however, his argument there seems to be a descendant of his earlier claim that external preferences should not be grounds for political action (see esp. 'What rights do we have?' in *Taking Rights Seriously*, London 1977). External preferences are preferences for the assignment of goods and opportunities to others. As Dworkin's argument in 'Is There a Right to Pornography?' makes clear, all the judgments which offend the right to moral independence are external preferences (though clearly not all external preferences are judgments about the values of another's life or projects). The right to moral independence, like its predecessor, the right not to have political action based on people's external preferences, is a restriction on political welfarism. It is stated by him to be a restriction on preference-satisfaction utilitarianism. But again his discussion makes clear that he regards this not as a moral theory but as the doctrine of political welfarism criticised in the previous chapter.

typical case. The authority with power to license drugs for public use approves of drugs on the ground that they are safe. It regards the safety of the drugs, and not its own beliefs about their safety, as proper ground for its action. It investigates each case in order to reach a conclusion which conforms to the facts and is willing to change its belief when it turns out to be at odds with the facts. At the same time it is inevitably the case that its decision is binding because it represents its bona fide belief, not because it is a sound decision. Mistaken decisions are equally binding. It would not be an authority if it did not have the power to err. It is therefore tempting to say that the reason for the authority's action is that it believes its action to be justified. That and not the actual justification of its action assures it of its binding force. When its decision is taken in pursuit of some ideal of the good it is the authority whose views are foisted on those who disagree with it. Any attempt to disguise this by saying that people are treated in accordance with sound moral principles overlooks the fact that what happens in real life is that some people are imposing their views on others who disagree with them.

Many confusions contribute to this chain of thought. First, at the conceptual level, it is not merely that authorities refer not to their belief that there are good reasons for their decisions but to the reasons themselves as grounds for action. While an authority's belief that a decision is based on sound considerations makes it binding even if it is not in fact sound, the reason for this is that acknowledging the validity of an authority's decision even if it is unsound is in fact more likely to lead to action supported by sound reason than any alternative method of deciding what to do.[1] In the terminology of two-level rule-based justifications, the authority's belief in the soundness of the decision brings the

---

[1] Belief that the decision is justified comes close to the bona fide condition of the legal validity of delegated legislation and of administrative action in Common Law jurisdictions. But my point depends on the justificatory argument supporting authority, as explained in Ch. 3, which need not be incorporated in formal legal conditions of validity. These require procedures for their implementation which may be counter-productive. Sometimes it is best to rely on the assumption that normally the bona fide condition will be met, and leave it to informal political pressures to reduce the risk of violations.

decision under a rule which is itself justified because it is likely to lead to action in accord with sound reason, and not because it leads to action conforming to the authority's view of right reason.

A danger of a second confusion is bound up with the argument from the possibility of mistake which is implicit in the chain of thought we are examining. Mistakes are always possible, as much when one is calculating the risk of a drought, or of future demand for steel, as in determining the requirements of freedom of religion. The endemic risk of mistakes and misjudgments affects decisions. It means that one must take account of the result of failure. Some courses of action, very advantageous if successful, lead to disasters if they fail. Others, perhaps leading to less advantageous results if they work, do not cause much harm if they fail. All this has to be taken into account. Just as in industrial design one may prefer a simple design which is unlikely to go wrong to a more powerful design which carries great risk of breakdown, so in political decisions one may lower one's sights to avoid risk of disasters. But the general effect of the risk of failure cannot lead to anti-perfectionism. It leads to general caution. The real issue is whether there is some special reason to fear failure or the consequences of failure when trying to promote conceptions of the good.

Nowhere in this book will general moral skepticism be discussed. General moral skepticism claims either that there never is a better moral reason for one action rather than another, or that one can never have good grounds for believing that one action is better supported by moral reason than another. If either of these claims is true then nothing in this book is of any value, nor is there room for any discussion of the morality of political action. Putting such general skepticism to one side, the question is: is there reason to think that one is more likely to be wrong about the character of the good life than about the sort of moral considerations which all agree should influence political action such as the right to life, to free expression, or free religious worship? I know of no such arguments. The argument in the rest of the book (starting in Chapter 8) showing that all aspects of morality derive from common sources refutes such a possibility.

The most deeply rooted confusion leading to the intuitive appeal of the anti-perfectionist is in the thought that anti-perfectionism is necessary to prevent people from imposing their favoured style of life on others. The confusion is both practical and moral. On the practical side it assumes that perfectionist action is aimed by one group at another, attempting to bring it to conform with its habits and way of life. This need not be the case. Perfectionist political action may be taken in support of social institutions which enjoy unanimous support in the community, in order to give them formal recognition, bring legal and administrative arrangements into line with them, facilitate their use by members of the community who wish to do so, and encourage the transmission of belief in their value to future generations. In many countries this is the significance of the legal recognition of monogamous marriage and prohibition of polygamy.

Furthermore, not all perfectionist action is a coercive imposition of a style of life. Much of it could be encouraging and facilitating action of the desired kind, or discouraging undesired modes of behaviour. Conferring honours on creative and performing artists, giving grants or loans to people who start community centres, taxing one kind of leisure activity, e.g., hunting, more heavily than others, are all cases in which political action in pursuit of conceptions of the good falls far short of the threatening popular image of imprisoning people who follow their religion, express their views in public, grow long hair, or consume harmless drugs.

Finally, the view we are discussing assumes a rigoristic moral outlook, that is one allowing for only one morally approved style of life. That is why it is suspected that if some people pursue a different style of life from that practised by those with political power they will be persecuted. Perfectionism is, however, compatible with moral pluralism, which allows that there are many morally valuable forms of life which are incompatible with each other. That possibility will be examined in detail in Part Five. If a plurality of incompatible, even rival, forms of life is valuable then perfectionism would not lead to the suppression of forms of life which are not practised by those in power.

Even if the anti-perfectionist worry about people imposing their conceptions of the good on others suffers from exaggeration for the reasons just described, is there not a simple argument supporting its conclusion? Perfectionism assumes that some people have greater insight into moral truth than others. But if one assumes that all stand an equal chance of erring in moral matters should we not let all adult persons conduct themselves by their own lights? Whatever else can be said about this argument one point is decisive. Supporting valuable forms of life is a social rather than an individual matter. Monogamy, assuming that it is the only morally valuable form of marriage, cannot be practised by an individual. It requires a culture which recognizes it, and which supports it through the public's attitude and through its formal institutions. Much more will be said on this point later in the book. The short summary is that perfectionist ideals require public action for their viability. Antiperfectionism in practice would lead not merely to a political stand-off from support for valuable conceptions of the good. It would undermine the chances of survival of many cherished aspects of our culture.

The sources of the appeal of anti-perfectionism are sound. It stems from concern for the dignity and integrity of individuals and a revulsion from letting one section of the community impose its favoured way of life on the rest. These concerns are real and important. They do not, however, justify anti-perfectionism. This part of the book must end with a negative conclusion. The exploration of the sources of anti-perfectionism in revealing genuine causes for concern does, however, point the way to the positive conclusions which will be developed in Part Five.

III

INDIVIDUALISTIC FREEDOM:
LIBERTY AND RIGHTS

This part concerns the view that the principles which protect individual liberty are principles asserting the existence of inviolable rights. By being bound to protect these rights governments are bound to respect individual freedom. That is, the freedom to which individuals are entitled is defined by their fundamental rights. Chapter Seven explains the nature of rights in general. Chapter Eight considers the possibility that rights provide the very foundation of morality. The arguments which refute that position also refute the right-based conception of freedom. They point to a relatively modest, though practically very important, role to rights in morality and politics. These conclusions are reinforced in Chapter Nine which evaluates the proposition that a fundamental right to equality is the basis of the liberal doctrine of liberty. Finally, Chapter Ten follows with a rough outline of the constitutional role of fundamental civil liberties.

7

The Nature of Rights

To prepare for the examination of doctrines which hold individual freedom to be based on rights, this chapter examines the nature of rights. It starts by a sketch of an account (Section 1), followed by an explanation of some of its technical points (Sections 2–5). Sections 6–8 touch on the philosophically significant aspects of the account: the capacity to have rights and the relations between rights, duties and interests. Finally Section 9 introduces the next chapter by considering the importance of rights, and raising the question whether rights can be morally fundamental.

1. Rights: The Main Features

One danger of prefacing a discussion of the importance of rights with a definition of the concept is that one may end with a definition according to which rights are not important, but which is not acceptable to those who claim that they are. An opposite danger is of proving their importance by calling anything of value a right. Both dangers result from the fact that a philosophical definition of 'a right', like those of coercion, authority and many other terms, is not an explanation of the ordinary meaning of a term. It follows the usage of writers on law, politics and morality who typically use the term to refer to a subclass of all the cases to which it can be applied with linguistic propriety.

Philosophical definitions of rights[1] attempt to capture the way the term is used in legal, political and moral writing and discourse. They both explain the existing tradition of moral and political debate and declare the author's intention of carrying on the debate within the boundaries of that tradition. At the same time they further that debate by sing-

---

[1] I refer of course to what philosophers most commonly do, whether they know it or not. I do not wish to deny that some understand their enterprise in other ways.

ling out certain features of rights, as traditionally understood, for special attention, on the grounds that they are
the features which best explain the role of rights in moral,
political, and legal discourse. It follows that while a philosophical definition may well be based on a particular moral
or political theory (the theory dictates which features of
rights, traditionally understood, best explain their role in
political, legal and moral discourse), it should not make that
theory the only one which recognizes rights.[1] To do so is to
try to win by verbal legislation. A successful philosophical
definition of rights illuminates a tradition of political and
moral discourse in which different theories offer incompatible views as to what rights there are and why. The
definition may advance the case of one such theory, but if
successful it explains and illuminates all. In this spirit I shall
first propose a definition of rights and then explain various
features of the definition and criticise some alternative
definitions.

Definition: 'X has a right' if and only if X can have rights,
and, other things being equal, an aspect of X's well-being
(his interest) is a sufficient reason for holding some other
person(s) to be under a duty.[2]

Capacity for possessing rights: An individual is capable of
having rights if and only if either his well-being is of ultimate
value or he is an 'artificial person' (e.g. a corporation).

Note that since 'a right' is a very general term, one rarely
asserts that someone has a right without specifying what
rights he has, just as one does not normally mention that a
person is subject to a duty without saying something more
about what duty it is. Sometimes one may state of another
that he has rights in order to indicate that he is the kind of

---

[1] Though a consideration of notions such as 'chastity', 'honour', 'chivalry' shows
that not all political or moral theories have room for all normative concepts. Some
theories may not recognize rights.

[2] The definition draws on several elements of analyses of rights which stem
from Bentham's beneficiary theory. It shares some features of R. M. Dworkin's
explanation in *Taking Rights Seriously*, London, 1977, p. 100 (but not of his better
known 'trump' theory), and has much in common with D. N. MacCormick's
'Rights in Legislation' in *Essays in Social Democracy*. Most of all I have been
influenced by K. Campbell's ideas in his 'The Concept of Rights', 1979, an Oxford
D.Phil. thesis.

creature who is capable of having rights. For example, one may say that slaves have (legal or moral) rights, or that partnerships have rights, or that foetuses have them. (Similarly one may say that monarchs have duties, etc.) The fact that assertions of rights *tout court* are rare does not invalidate the definition, nor does it detract from its value as the key to the explanation of all rights. It is true that there is much about statements of rights which cannot be learned from my definition alone. One needs to distinguish a right to perform an act from a right in an object, and that from a right to an object, and that from a right to a service or a facility, and that again from 'a right to. . .' where the dots stand for an abstract noun. A right to use the highway, for example, is a liberty right to use the highway or a right to have that liberty. A right in a car may be a right of ownership in the car, or some other right in it. Detailed explanations of rights are in part linguistic explanations (a right in a car differs from a right to a car) but in part they depend on political, legal or moral arguments (does a right to free speech include access to the mass media or to private premises?) The proposed definition is meant to be neutral concerning all such detailed questions. At the same time it aims to encapsulate the common core of all rights, and thus to help to explain their special role in practical thought.

The definition is of rights *simpliciter*. Some discourse of rights is of rights as viewed from the point of view of a certain system of thought, as when one compares Kantian rights with utilitarian rights. Prefixing an adjective to 'rights' is one way to indicate that the speaker does not necessarily accept the existence of the right and is merely considering the implications of a system of thought. (On other occasions such adjectives identify the contents of the rights, e.g. economic rights, or their source, e.g. promissory rights, or both.)

Rights are grounds of duties in others. The duties grounded in a right may be conditional.[1] Consider the duty of an employee to obey his employer's instructions con-

---

[1] Throughout I draw no distinction between duties and obligations. Nor will I indicate how to distinguish a future duty which will exist if a condition is satisfied (If . . . then one has a duty to . . .) from a presently existing conditional duty (One has a duty to . . . if . . .). I will assume that only conditional duties can be conditioned on the exercise of powers to impose them.

cerning the execution of his job. It is grounded in the employer's right to instruct his employees. But it is a
conditional duty, i.e. a duty (in matters connected with one's
employment) to perform an action if instructed by the employer to do so. When the condition which activates the duty
is an action of some person, and when the duty is conditional
on it because it is in the right-holder's interest to make that
person able to activate the duty at will, then the right confers
a power on the person on whose behaviour the duty
depends.[1] Thus the employer's right over the employees is
a ground for his power to instruct them. This power is one
aspect or one consequence of his right. But the very same
right also endows him with a power to delegate his authority
to others. It can, if he chooses to delegate authority, become
a source of a power in one of his subordinates. In that case
the employee will have a duty to obey the person in whom
power was vested and that duty as well as the power of the
delegated authority is grounded in the right of the employer.
To simplify I shall not dwell specifically on rights as the
grounds of powers.

2. Core and Derivative Rights

Some rights derive from others. Just as rights are grounds
for duties and powers so they can be for other rights. I shall
call a right which is grounded in another right a derivative
right. Non-derivative rights are core rights. The relation
between a derivative right and the core right (or any other
right) from which it derives is a justificatory one. The statement that the derivative right exists must be a conclusion of
a sound argument (non-redundantly) including a statement
entailing the existence of the core right. But not every right
thus entailed is a derivative one. The premisses must also
provide a justification for the existence of the derivative right
(and not merely evidence or even proof of its existence). To
do so their truth must be capable of being established with-

---

[1] For a clarification of the notion of a normative power cf. my *Practical Reasons
and Norms*, London, 1975, section 3.2. By extending the same reasoning rights can
be shown to be grounds of immunities and liberties: they are reasons for not
subjecting individuals to duties or to the power of others.

out relying on the truth of the conclusion. An example may illustrate the point.

Let us assume that I own a whole street because I bought (in separate transactions) all its houses. My ownership of a house in the street does not derive from my ownership of the street as a whole, even though the statement that I own a house in the street is entailed by the statement that I own the street. For in attempting to provide a normative justification for my rights I have to refer to the individual transactions by which I acquired the houses. Therefore my right in the street derives from my rights in the houses and not the other way round. Had I inherited the whole street from my grandfather the situation would have been reversed.

Without grasping the relation between core and derivative rights one is liable to fall into confusion. My right to walk on my hands is not directly based on an interest served either by my doing so or by others having duties not to stop me. It is based on my interest in being free to do as I wish, on which my general right to personal liberty is directly based. The right to walk on my hands is one instance of the general right to personal liberty. The right to personal liberty is the core right from which the other derives. Similarly my right to make the previous statement is a derivative of the core right of free speech, and my right to spoil the cigarette I am holding at the moment derives from my ownership in it, and so on. Often right-holders have a direct interest in that to which they have derivative rights. But those do not always ground their rights. A right is based on the interest which figures essentially in the justification of the statement that the right exists. The interest relates directly to the core right and indirectly to its derivatives. The relation of core and derivative rights is not that of entailment, but of the order of justification. The fact that a statement that everyone has a right to freedom of expression appears to entail the statement that everyone has a right to free political expression does not establish that the first is the core right and the second its derivative. It may well be that freedom of political speech is justified by considerations which do not apply to other kinds of speech. If it is also the case that, while separate in-dependent considerations justify freedom of commercial speech, and others still freedom of artistic expression, scientific and academic communications, etc., there are no general considerations which apply to all of the protected areas of speech, then the general right to freedom of expression is a derivative right. It is a mere generalization from the existence of several independent core rights.

Furthermore, a general right statement does not entail those statements of particular rights which are instances of it. I may have a right to free speech without having a right to libel people. In matters of libel, the right to free expression may be completely defeated by the interests of people in their reputation. I will return to this point later.

3. The Correlativity of Rights and Duties

It is sometimes argued that to every duty there is a corresponding right. It is evident from the proposed definition that there are no conceptual reasons for upholding such a view. Some moral theories may yield such a correlativity thesis as a result of their moral principles, but this possibility cannot be explored here.[1] A more popular thesis maintains that to every right there is a correlative duty. Since a right is a ground for duties there is a good deal of truth in this kind of correlativity thesis. Yet most of its common formulations are very misleading. R. Brandt's definition can serve as an example of many: 'X has an absolute right to enjoy, have or be secured in Y' means the same as 'It is someone's objective overall obligation to secure X in, or in the possession of, or in the enjoyment of Y, if X wishes it.'[2] He proceeds to define prima facie rights in terms of prima facie obligations. First, note that Brandt misleadingly suggests that to every right there corresponds one duty, that that duty is to guarantee the enjoyment or possession of the object of the right, and that it is conditional on the desire of the right-holder. All three points are mistaken. A right to education grounds a duty to provide educational opportunities to each individual, whether he wishes it or not. Many rights ground duties which fall short of securing their object, and they may

---

[1] It will be rejected in the next chapter. See also Ch. 10.
[2] Richard Brandt, *Ethical Theory*, Englewood Cliffs, NJ, 1959, p. 438.

ground many duties not one. A right to personal security does not require others to protect a person from all accident or injury. The right is, however, the foundation of several duties, such as the duty not to assault, rape or imprison the right-holder.

Secondly, and more importantly, Brandt fails to notice that the right is the ground of the duty. It is wrong to translate statements of rights into statements of 'the corresponding' duties. A right of one person is not a duty on another. It is the ground of a duty, ground which, if not counteracted by conflicting considerations, justifies holding that other person to have the duty.

Thirdly, there is no closed list of duties which correspond to the right. The existence of a right often leads to holding another to have a duty because of the existence of certain facts peculiar to the parties or general to the society in which they live. A change of circumstances may lead to the creation of new duties based on the old right. The right to political participation is not new, but only in modern states with their enormously complex bureaucracies does this right justify, as I think it does, a duty on the government to make public its plans and proposals before a decision on them is reached, as well as a duty to publish its reasons for a decision once reached (except in special categories of cases such as those involving defence secrets). This dynamic aspect of rights, their ability to create new duties, is fundamental to any understanding of their nature and function in practical thought. Unfortunately, most if not all formulations of the correlativity thesis disregard the dynamic aspect of rights. They all assume that a right can be exhaustively stated by stating those duties which it has already established.[1] This objection to the reduction of rights to duties does not rule out the possibility that 'A has a right to X' is reducible to 'There is a duty to secure A in X'. But since this duty can be based on grounds other than A's interest, the two statements are not equivalent.

4. Holding Individuals to be Under a Duty

The proposed definition states that if an individual has a right then a certain aspect of his well-being is a reason for

---

[1] Needless to say core rights can lead also to new derivative rights.

holding others to be under a duty. I used this phrase advisedly to preserve the ambiguity between saying that rights are a reason for judging a person to have a duty, and saying that they are reasons for imposing duties on him. They are in fact reasons of both kinds, but primarily of the first. Let me explain. Rights are (part of) the justification of many duties. They justify the view that people have those duties. But as has already been noted, they justify such a view only to the extent that there are no conflicting considerations of greater weight. Within certain institutional settings there are weighty reasons not so much against allowing rights to generate new duties as against allowing official action on the basis of new duties unless they are recognized by the appropriate institutions. Institutions such as universities, states, trade unions and football clubs are based on a concentration of power in certain bodies and a division of labour between officials whose duties are the execution of the institutions' policies and rules, and those who make and change those policies and rules. In such an institution it may be proper to say that rights are grounds not so much for judging that certain duties exist as for imposing them.

The right to political participation is a legal right in English law. But though in contemporary societies this right justifies holding the government to be under a duty to publicize its plans and the reasons for its decisions, there is no such legal duty on the government in English law. The duty is purely a moral duty. Nevertheless, the existence of a moral right to political participation, i.e. the fact that this right is given legal recognition and is already defended by some legal duties, is a ground for the authorized institutions (Parliament or the courts) to impose such a duty on government officials. If and when they do so, they will be making new law. But they will do so on the ground that this is justified and required by existing law. By the same token the legal right to political participation is a reason for investing people with a legal right to free information. It cannot be used to establish that they already have such a right.[1]

---

[1] These points are developed in my 'Legal Rights', *Oxford Journal of Legal Studies*, 4 (1984), 1, and 'The Internal Logic of the Law', *Materiali per Una Storia della Cultura Giuridica*, 14 (1984), 381.

5. Promises and Agreements

Some of the points made in the previous sections can be illustrated and clarified by using them to explain the rights involved in promises and agreements. These are two. There is the right to promise which a promisor must have if his promise is to be binding. And there is the right conferred on the promisee by the promise. I will examine them in that order.

The right to promise is based on the promisor's interest to be able to forge special bonds with other people.[1] The right is qualified. Not everyone has it. Small children and some mentally deranged people lack it. Furthermore, if it is not permissible to have bonds based on immorality, one's right to promise does not include the right to promise to perform immoral acts. The right to promise is no doubt further qualified. Since we are not here concerned with any of these qualifications I will from now on disregard them.

Those who assign sufficient importance to the interest people have in being able to impose on themselves obligations to other people as a means of creating special bonds with other people believe in a right to promise. But why is it a right? The interest on which it is based validates the promising principle, namely:

> If a person communicates an intention to undertake by that very act of communication a certain obligation then he has that obligation.

The promising principle establishes that if we promise we are obligated to act as we promised. It also establishes a present obligation to keep our promises, i.e. we are obligated to perform action X, if we promised to perform X. This is a conditional obligation. The condition is an act of the promisor and his obligation is conditional on his action because it is desirable that he should be able to bind himself if he so wishes. It follows that people's interest in being able to bind themselves is the basis of a power to promise which they

---

[1] I am here summarizing some of the points made in my 'Promises and Obligations', in P. M. S. Hacker and J. Raz (eds.), *Law, Morality and Society*, Oxford 1977; and in 'Promises in Morality and Law', *Harvard Law Review* 95 (1982) p. 916.

possess and of an obligation to keep promises they make. But neither the power nor the obligation point to a right to promise.

The right exists because the very same interest on which the power to promise and the duty to keep promises are based is also the ground for holding others to be subject to a duty not to interfere with one's promising. The duty requires one not to prevent a person from promising (e.g. by denying him the means of communicating an intention to undertake by that very communication an obligation, or by stopping others from receiving such communications). It also requires one not to force people to promise nor to induce them improperly to promise or not to promise. (Again I avoid examining the way these duties are qualified.) Violation of the duty not to interfere with a person's promising will frustrate his right to promise and the interest on which it is based, either by preventing the person from exercising his rights or by perverting the considerations on which he decides whether to promise or not. The fact that such interferences with the right are infrequent is reflected by the fact that the right to promise is rarely invoked in ordinary practical discourse. To conclude, the power to promise and the right to promise are distinct notions. But both stem from a common core, i.e. the interest of persons to be able to forge normative bonds with others. That is why they coexist, and one has the power to promise if and only if one has the right to do so.

The right to make a particular promise (e.g., to visit my aunt next weekend) is a derivative right of the general right to promise. One such derivative right is the right to make a conditional promise. Two kinds of conditional promises are of interest here:

First a promise made conditional on an action by the promisee (e.g., 'I will give you ten pounds if you give me the book').

Second (which is in fact a special case of the above), a promise made conditional on a promise to be given by the promisee (e.g., 'I will give you ten pounds if you promise to give me the book').

Whenever such a promise is made and the condition is fulfilled, there is an agreement between the promisor and the promisee. The right to make such promises is therefore a right to enter into agreements. There are other ways of making agreements but their analysis does not matter for our purpose.

So far we have discussed the right to promise. The right which the promise confers on the *promisee* does not derive from the right to promise which is a right of the *promisor*. Many writers on promises insist that the promised act must be or at least must be thought to be in the interest of the promisee. Elsewhere I have challenged this view and I will not return to the controversy here.[1] But it is interesting to relate this issue to the question of the promisee's right created by the promise.

One view regards the promisee's right under any particular promise as a core right based on his interest in the promised act (and the intention of the promisor to be obligated to perform the act). On this view, if there could be binding promises which do not benefit the promisee (and are not intended to do so) then there are promises which do not create rights in the promisee.

Such a consequence seems at odds with the conventions of discourse concerning promises. I therefore favour a second view (which complements the first) according to which each person has an interest that promises made to him will be kept. Of course, he might lose interest in the specific content of some promises, and keeping some of them may even work against his overall interest. But invariably he has a *pro tanto* interest that promises given to him be kept. This interest is the very one which is reflected in his right to promise. Namely, it is the interest to have voluntary special bonds with other people. We should remind ourselves that while the promisee may not be the initiator of the bond of which the promise is the whole or a part, he is not entirely passive either. It is always up to him to waive his right under the promise and thus terminate the binding force of the promise. It is this general interest which explains why every promise, and not only those performance of which is to the

---

[1] See 'Promises and Obligations', op. cit.

specific advantage of the promisee, creates a right in the promisee.

6. Capacity for Rights

The definition of rights does not itself settle the issue of who is capable of having rights beyond requiring that right-holders are creatures who have interests. What other features qualify a creature to be a potential right-holder is a question bound up with substantive moral issues. It cannot be fully debated here. But the special role of statements of rights in practical thought cannot be elucidated and the significance of the definition cannot be evaluated without a brief explanation of the conditions for the capacity for having rights.

There is little that needs be said here of the capacity of corporations and other 'artificial' persons to have rights. Whatever explains and accounts for the existence of such persons, who can act, be subject to duties, etc. also accounts for their capacity to have rights. Whether certain groups, such as families or nations, are artificial or natural persons is important for determining the conditions under which they may have rights. But we need not settle such matters here.

There is a view, which I shall call the reciprocity thesis, that only members of 'the same moral community' can have rights. This is narrowly interpreted when the same moral community is a community of interacting individuals whose obligations to each other are thought to derive from a social contract or to represent the outcome of a fair bargaining process or if morality is conceived of in some other way as a system for the mutual advantage of all members of the community. Wider conceptions of the moral community extend it to all moral agents and regard anyone who is subject to duties as being capable of rights.

The principle of capacity for rights stated at the beginning of the chapter is not committed to the reciprocity thesis but is consistent with it. Since by definition rights are nothing but grounds of duties, if duties observe a reciprocity condition and can be had only towards members of the (same) moral community then the same is true of rights. Alternatively, the reciprocity thesis obtains even if one can have duties towards non-members of the (same) moral community provided those are not based on the interests of the beneficiaries of those duties. For example, if my duties to (non-human) animals are based on considerations of my own character (I should not be a person who can tolerate causing pain, etc.) and not on the interests of animals, then animals do not have rights despite the fact that I have duties regarding them.

The merits of the reciprocity thesis will not be examined here. The problem to which the principle of capacity for rights is addressed is different. Often we ought to or even have duties to act in ways that benefit certain things, and often we ought so to act because of the benefit our action will bring those things. For example, I have a duty to water certain plants because I promised their owners to look after them while they are away on holiday. My gardener has a duty to look after my garden because his contract of employment says so. Some scientists have a duty to preserve certain rare species of plants because they are the only source of a medicine for a rare and fatal disease. In all these cases the people who have duties to act in certain ways have them because it benefits plants. Yet in none of them is it true that the plants have a right to the benefits. The reason is that in all these cases the benefit is to be conferred on a thing whose existence and prosperity are not of ultimate value.

Being of ultimate, i.e. non-derivative,[1] value is being intrinsically valuable, i.e. being valuable independently of one's instrumental value. Something is instrumentally valuable to the extent that it derives its value from the value of its consequences, or from the value of the consequences it is likely to have, or from the value of the consequences it can be used to produce. Having intrinsic value is being valuable even apart from one's instrumental value. But not everything which is intrinsically valuable is also of ultimate value.

Consider a man who has a deep attachment to his dog. I share many people's feeling that the relationship is valuable

---

[1] To say that something is of ultimate value is not to claim that one cannot justify the statement that that thing is valuable. It merely indicates that its value does not derive from its contribution to something else.

and the man's life as richer and better because of it. Many feel that the relationship is intrinsically valuable. Its value is not just that of a cause of a feeling of security and comfort in the man. Such feelings may be produced by tranquillizers. The relationship is not valued just as a tranquillizer. Its value is in its being a constitutive part of a valuable form of life. Those who share these views believe that the existence of the dog is intrinsically valuable. It is a logically necessary condition of the relationship and one which contributes to its value (it is the more valuable for being a relationship to a living—rather than a dead—dog). But so far as the story goes the intrinsic value of the dog is not ultimate for it derives from the dog's contribution to the well-being of the man. The man's well-being is here taken as the ultimate value. The dog non-instrumentally contributes to it. Hence his existence is intrinsically but derivatively valuable.

Some people are willing to go further and to hold that the value of the relationship between the man and the dog derives equally from its contribution to the well-being of the dog and that the dog's well-being is not merely derivatively important because of its contribution to the man's well-being. They hold it to be ultimately valuable. They regard the relationship between man and dog in the same way as they and most others regard a relationship between two persons.

My proposed principle of capacity for rights entails that those who regard the existence and well-being of (some) dogs as merely derivatively valuable (even if they believe them to be intrinsically valuable) are committed to the view that dogs can have no rights though we may have duties to protect or promote their well-being. For such people dogs have the same moral standing that many ascribe to works of art. Their existence is intrinsically valuable inasmuch as the appreciation of art is intrinsically valuable. But their value is derivative and not ultimate. It derives from their contribution to the well-being of persons.

It seems plausible to suppose that just as only those whose well-being is of ultimate value can have rights so only interests which are considered of ultimate value can be the basis of rights. But there are plenty of counter-examples demonstrating that some rights protect interests which are considered as of merely instrumental value. All the rights of corporations are justified by the need to protect the interests of these corporations but these are merely of instrumental value. The rights of journalists (however qualified) to protect their sources are normally justified by the interest of journalists in being able to collect information. But that interest is deemed to be worth protecting because it serves the public. That is, the journalists' interest is valued because of its usefulness to members of the public at large. The rights of priests, doctors and lawyers to preserve the confidentiality of their professional contacts are likewise justified ultimately by their value to members of the community at large.

Furthermore, some people, and this seems to be the general view of the English Common Law, regard the interests on which a right as fundamental as freedom of speech is based as instrumentally valuable. Scanlon[1] distinguishes between three kinds of interest on which the right of free speech is based: (1) speaker's interest, (2) audience interest, and (3) third party interest. Only the first is the interest of the right-holder, the interest of a person to be able to communicate with others. The second (the interest of persons that others will be free to communicate with them) and third (the interest of people to live in a society in which communication is free—even if they personally do not wish to communicate with others) are interests of people other than the right-holder in his right.

In the Common Law freedom of expression is regularly defended, where it is defended, on grounds of the public interest, that is on the interests of third parties. The right-holder's interest itself, conceived independently of its contribution to the public interest, is deemed insufficient to justify holding others to be subject to the extensive duties and disabilities commonly derived from the right of free speech.[2]

We must conclude that (apart from artificial persons) only

[1] See T. M. Scanlon, Jr., 'Freedom of Expression and Categories of Freedom', *University of Pittsburgh Law Review*, (1979), 519.

[2] Two typical English cases are A.-G. v Jonathan Cape Ltd. [1976] Q.B. 752; Home Office v Harman [1982] 1 All E.R. 532.

those whose well-being is intrinsically valuable can have rights. But that rights can be based on the instrumental value of the interests of such people.

7. *Rights and Interests*

According to the definition, rights-discourse indicates a kind of ground for a requirement of action. To say that a person ought to behave in a certain way is to assert a requirement for action without indicating its ground. To assert that an individual has a right is to indicate a ground for a requirement for action of a certain kind, i.e. that an aspect of his well-being is a ground for a duty on another person. The specific role of rights in practical thinking is, therefore, the grounding of duties in the interests of other beings.

Rights ground requirements for action in the interest of other beings. They therefore assume special importance in individualistic moral thinking. But belief in the existence of rights does not commit one to individualism. States, corporations and groups may be right-holders. Banks have legal and moral rights. Nations are commonly believed to have a right of self-determination, and so on.

Though rights are based on the interests of the right-holders, an individual may have rights which it is against his interest to have. A person may have property which is more trouble than it is worth. It may be in a person's interest to be imprisoned, even while he has a right to freedom. The explanation of this puzzle is that rights are vested in right-holders because they possess certain general characteristics: they are the beneficiaries of promises, nationals of a certain state, etc. Their rights serve their interests as persons with those characteristics, but they may be against their interests overall.

Some rights are held by persons as the agents, or organs of others. Thus company directors have rights as directors of the company. In such cases it is the interest of the principal which the right reflects. The same applies to rights held by persons *qua* guardians, trustees and the like.

The proposed definition of rights identified the interest on which the right is based as the reason for holding that

some persons have certain duties. Later on I referred to the
rights themselves as being the grounds for those duties. The
explanation is simple. The interests are part of the justification of the rights which are part of the justification of
the duties. Assertions of rights are typically intermediate
conclusions in arguments from ultimate values to duties.
They are, so to speak, points in the argument where many
considerations intersect and where the results of their conflicts are summarized to be used with additional premises
when need be. Such intermediate conclusions are used and
referred to as if they are themselves complete reasons. The
fact that practical arguments proceed through the mediation
of intermediate stages so that not every time a practical question arises does one refer to ultimate values for an answer is,
as we saw when discussing rules in Chapter Three, of crucial
importance in making social life possible, not only because it
saves time and tediousness, but primarily because it enables a
common culture to be formed round shared intermediate
conclusions, in spite of a great degree of haziness and disagreement concerning ultimate values.

For example, many who agree that people have a right to
promise will disagree with my view, expressed above, of the
interest on which it is based and will justify it only by reference to some other interests of the right-holders. The importance of intermediate steps like rights, duties, rules and
the like to a common culture explains and justifies the practice of referring to them as reasons in their own right, albeit
not ultimate reasons.

An interest is sufficient to base a right on if and only if
there is a sound argument of which the conclusion is that a
certain right exists and among its non-redundant premises
is a statement of some interest of the right-holder, the other
premises supplying grounds for attributing to it the required
importance, or for holding it to be relevant to a particular
person or class of persons so that they rather than others
are obligated to the right-holder. These premises must be
sufficient by themselves to entail that if there are no contrary
considerations then the individuals concerned have the right.
To these premises one needs to add others stating or establishing that these grounds are not altogether defeated by

conflicting reasons.[1] Together they establish the existence of the right.

One result of the fact that a right exists where the interests of the right-holders are sufficient to hold another to be obligated should be noted. Sometimes the fact that an action will serve someone's interest, while being a reason for doing it, is not sufficient to establish a duty to do it. Different moral theories differ on this point. Some utilitarian theories deny that there is a useful distinction between moral reasons for action and duties. Some moral views confine duties to matters affecting human needs, or human dignity, etc. Be that as it may, it is in principle possible that a person should not have a right that others shall act to promote a certain interest of his simply on account of the fact that while they should do so, while it is praiseworthy or virtuous of them if they do, they have no obligation so to act.

These considerations help to explain how it is that even if a person has a right, not everyone is necessarily under an obligation to do whatever will promote the interest on which it is based. Rights are held against certain persons. Some rights are held against the world at large, i.e. against all persons or against all with certain specified exceptions. Thus the right to personal security is the ground of a duty on everyone not to assault, imprison or rape a person. Other rights are held against certain persons in virtue of a special relation they have to the right-holder. Thus children have a right to be maintained by their parents. The reasons many rights are against some definite people are varied. Sometimes the interests on which they are based can be satisfied only by some people and not by others. For example, since contractual rights are based on an interest in being able to create special relations, they give rise to rights against other parties to the agreement as they are the only ones who can satisfy that interest on that occasion. In other cases, even though

---

[1] One case deserves special attention: if B's interest does not justify holding A to be under a duty to do X then B has no right that A shall do X even if A has a duty to do X based on the fact that the action will serve the interest of a class of individuals of whom B is one. Thus a government may have a duty to try to improve the standard of living of all its inhabitants of the country even though no single inhabitant has a right that the government shall try to improve his standard of living. This point will be developed in the next chapter.

many can satisfy the interests of the right-holder, these interests may be sufficient to establish a duty on some people and not on others.[1]

Just as rights may impose duties on some persons and not on others, so they can impose a duty to do certain things but not others. The right to life may impose a duty not to kill or endanger the life of another without imposing a duty to take whatever action is necessary to keep him alive. Which duties a right gives rise to depends partly on the basis of that right, on the considerations justifying its existence. It also depends on the absence of conflicting considerations. If conflicting considerations show that the basis of the would-be right is not enough to justify subjecting anyone to any duty, then the right does not exist. But often such conflicting considerations, while sufficient to show that some action cannot be required as a duty on the basis of the would-be right, do not affect the case for requiring other actions as a matter of duty. In such cases, the right exists, but it successfully grounds duties only for some of the actions which could promote the interest on which it is based.

8. Rights and Duties

Rights are the grounds of duties in the sense that one way of justifying holding a person to be subject to a duty is that this serves the interest on which another's right is based. Regarded from the opposite perspective the fact that rights are sufficient to ground duties limits the rights one has. Only where one's interest is a reason for another to behave in a way which protects or promotes it, and only when this reason has the peremptory character of a duty, and, finally, only when the duty is for conduct which makes a significant difference for the promotion or protection of that interest does the interest give rise to a right. Naturally there may be other grounds for not holding a person to be subject to such a duty. The definition requires that the right is a sufficient

[1] The fact that rights may be held against some persons only is compatible with the principle that everyone ought to respect everyone's rights. That principle asserts that all persons have a reason (not necessarily a conclusive one) to avoid action which will make it more difficult for those subject to duties towards right-holders to fulfil their obligations.

reason for a duty. Hence, as we saw, where the conflicting considerations altogether defeat the interests of the would-be right-holder, or when they weaken their force and no one could justifiably be held to be *obligated* on account of those interests, then there is no right. Where the conflicting considerations override those on which the right is based on some but not on all occasions, the general core right exists but the conflicting considerations may show that some of its possible derivations do not.

There is a necessary conflict between free speech on the one hand and the protection of people's reputation or the need to suppress criticism of the authorities in time of a major national emergency on the other. (I assume that in both cases the reasons for suppressing libellous or critical expression are also reasons for not holding individuals to have a duty to protect the freedom to express such views.) If in these circumstances the reasons against free expression override those in favour of free expression, then while it is true that one has a right to free expression, one does not have a right to libel or to criticise the government in an emergency. A general right is, therefore, only a prima facie ground for the existence of a particular right in circumstances to which it applies. Rights can conflict with other rights or with other duties, but if the conflicting considerations defeat the right they cannot be necessarily coextensive in their scope.[1]

These remarks help explain one sense in which rights ground duties. Two further points are, however, crucial to the understanding of the priority of rights to the duties which are based on them (and not all duties are based on rights). First, one may know of the existence of a right and of the reasons for it without knowing who is bound by duties based on it or what precisely are these duties. A person may know that every child has a right to education. He will, therefore, know that there are duties, conditional or unconditional, to provide children with education. But he may have no view

---

[1] Conflicts of rights are possible if conflicts of duties are. If considerations against requiring an action defeat the right-based reasons for requiring it on all the occasions to which they apply, then the right does not create a duty for that action. If, however, they defeat the right-based reasons on some occasions only, then the right-based reasons create a duty which is sometimes defeated.

on who has the duty. This question involves principles of responsibility. It is part of the function of such principles to determine the order of responsibility of different persons to the right-holder. Does the primary responsibility rest with the parents, with the community stepping in only if they cannot or will not meet their obligations? Or does the primary responsibility rest with the community? The issue is of great importance. If it is the parents' duty then there is no duty on the community to provide free education to all. And yet one may be in a position to assert that there is a right to education without knowing the solution to such a problem, or to whether the communal responsibility is local or national, whether it extends only to primary education or beyond and so on.

In a sense such ignorance shows that the person's knowledge of the precise content of the right to education is incomplete. But this merely means that he does not know all the implications of the right to education (given other true premisses). It does not mean that he does not understand the statement that every child has a right to education. Furthermore it is reflection on the right to education, its point and the reasons for it, which helps, together with other premisses, to establish such implications. If a duty is based on a right, on the other hand, then it trivially follows that one cannot know the reasons for it without knowing of the right (or without knowing that the interest which it protects is sufficient to be the ground of a duty—which is the definition of a right).

The second point to bear in mind is that the implications of a right, such as the right to education, and the duties it grounds, depend on additional premisses and these cannot in principle be wholly determined in advance. At least, if it is true in principle that the future cannot be entirely known in advance, then there may be future circumstances which were not predicted and which, given the right to education, give rise to a new duty which was not predicted in advance. Even if no such duty is unpredictable, the total implications of the right to education are in principle unpredictable. Because of this rights can be ascribed a dynamic character.

They are not merely the grounds of existing duties. With changing circumstances they can generate new duties.

9. *The Importance of Rights*

Let us recap. Rights ground duties. To say this is not to endorse the thesis that all duties derive from rights or that morality is right-based. It merely highlights the precedence of rights over some duties and the dynamic aspect of rights, their capacity to generate new duties with changing circumstances. Notice that because duties can be based on considerations other than someone's rights the statement (1) 'Children have a right to education' does not mean the same as statement (2) 'There is a duty to provide education for children.' (1) entails (2) but not the other way round. (1) informs us that the duty stated in (2) is based on the interests of the children. This information is not included in (2) itself.

The connection between rights and duties establishes that rights are special considerations, since duties are. But just as there are trivial duties so there are trivial rights. And not only derivative rights: core rights can also be of little consequence. The reason is the one remarked on in the first section of this chapter. Duties are special in the role they assume in practical reasoning. Their role cannot be captured by the usual weighing metaphor which applies to the evaluation of ordinary reasons. The have pre-emptive force. The point is seen clearly when we consider again the duty to obey a legitimate authority.[1] It is special since being pre-emptive it replaces rather than competes with (some of) the other reasons which apply in the circumstances. But the authority may have power over a trivial matter, and the importance of its directives relative to other considerations, those which they do not displace, need not be very great. It is not part of the very notion of a right that rights have great weight or importance. Some rights may be absolute, others may have little importance.

Are rights 'trumps', the expression given wide currency by Dworkin?[2] It all depends on what is meant by 'trumps'.

---

[1] This point is developed in my 'Promises and Obligations', op. cit..

[2] Dworkin, *Taking Rights Seriously*, London 1977, ch. 4. I have criticised Dwor-

Given that rights are based on people's interests it cannot be claimed that they are trumps in the sense of overriding other considerations based on individual interests. Moreover, in the discussion of collective rights in the next chapter we will see that collective or group rights represent the cumulative interests of many individuals who are members of the relevant groups. It follows that there is nothing essentially non-aggregative about rights. Nor are rights necessarily agent-relative considerations. Some rights and some duties are or may be agent-relative, but there is no reason to think that all are nor do I know of anyone who has argued that. Some people regard rights as the non-utilitarian component of morality. But one has to be at least a partial utilitarian to accept that. Furthermore, if one is a utilitarian at least in part one may well wish to argue that some rights are based on utilitarian considerations.[1]

Some have suggested that rights are distinctive in that, while being based on individual interests, they are given greater weight than is due to that interest.[2] But if rights are given greater weight than is warranted by the interest they protect considered in itself, this is presumably due to considerations which do not derive from concern for the wellbeing of the right-holder. Such considerations do exist. I may have a moral reason against killing a person who deserves to die, or who wishes me to kill him and whose suffering will make his death a blessing. But such reasons turn on my well-being or that of others. I may be the wrong person for the job, or I may refuse to defile my hands with his blood, or be a person whose life is committed to ways of

kin's account in 'Prof. Dworkin's Theory of Rights', *Political Studies*, 26 (1978) 123.

[1] See my argument to that effect in 'Hart on Moral Rights and Legal Duties', *Oxford Journal of Legal Studies*, 4 (1984), 123. The point has often been argued. See for another example, J. Gray 'Indirect Utility and Fundamental Human Rights' in E. F. Paul, F. D. Miller, Jr., J. Paul (eds.), *Human Rights*, Oxford 1984. For powerful, though ultimately unsuccessful, arguments that Utilitarianism is incompatible with rights see H. L. A. Hart, *Essays on Bentham*, ch. 4, Oxford, 1983; and D. Lyons, 'Utility and Rights', in J. Waldron (ed.), *Theories of Rights*, Oxford, 1985.

[2] This view is said by D. Regan, 'Glosses on Dworkin: Rights, Principles and Policies' in M. Cohen (ed.), *Dworkin and Contemporary Jurisprudence*, London 1984, to be the better interpretation of Dworkin's position. It is also apparently A. Sen's view. See his 'Rights and Agency', *Philosophy & Public Affairs*, 11 (1982), 3.

relating to other people which is inconsistent with killing, even a justified killing, or perhaps others may misinterpret my action with, given my position in life, undesirable consequences.

Many other, and more subtle, considerations may be adduced in such cases. They show that we have reasons to act in ways which benefit others, and reasons which depend on the fact that our action (or inaction) will benefit the other, but where the fundamental concern reflected in the reasons is not for the well-being of that other person. His well-being is merely instrumentally invoked. My definition of rights allows for such cases, provided that they amount to duties, and not merely to ordinary reasons for action. But it would be wrong to elevate them into a universal rule and claim that rights exist only when such considerations apply. Moreover, emphasizing the importance of these, generally marginal, factors obscures the fundamental role of rights in practical reasoning as representing concern for the interest of the right-holder sufficient to hold another subject to a duty.

Some will argue that the distinction between the interests of the (putative) right-holder and those of others misses a consideration which is central to the conception of rights as trumps. The duties one owes a right-holder derive from or express respect for him as a person. Rights, one may say, are based neither on the right-holders' interest, nor on that of others. Rather they express the right-holders' status as persons and the respect owed to them in recognition of that fact.

This may be a verbal disagreement. For it may be dissolved by responding that a person has an interest in being respected as a person. That shows that rights grounded in respect are based on interests. Whether or not the response dissolves the disagreement, it seems to me that people have such an interest. Yet logically it is a special kind of interest. It is not just one interest people have alongside others. Respecting a person consists in giving appropriate weight to his interest. The interest in being respected is but an element of the interest one has in one's interest. If respecting people is giving proper weight to their interests, then clearly we respect people by respecting their rights. But this is so precisely because their rights are based on their interests whose claim on us is sufficient to subject us to duties to respect them.[1] Since we respect others by giving proper weight to their interests, neither the duty of respect nor the interest in being respected can show that rights deserve greater weight than the interest they are based on.

Still, is it not open to argument that while respect for a person consists in giving due weight to his interest, the reasons for respecting him need not be to serve his interest? One may be duty-bound to respect a person just because one is a person oneself. Such a duty may defy consequentialist interpretation. On this interpretation it is not so much that rights have a force greater than the one justified by the interest they serve. At bottom their force is independent of that interest. That John's action will serve Judy's interest shows that it is an action which respects Judy. But John is obligated to perform it not in order to promote or defend Judy's interest. He may have a separate, independent reason to do that. The reason, the only one, on which Judy's right is based is that John, as a person, owes respect to all other persons.

Considerations of this kind do indeed exist, and will be discussed in the next chapter as well as in Part Four. They are what are traditionally known as deontological considerations. They have always been regarded, by those who believe in their validity, as establishing the existence of duties, rather than of rights. That attitude is captured and reflected in the explanation of rights advanced here. According to it rights must be based on the fact that the interest of the right holder is sufficient reason to hold another to be subject to a duty. The deontological view sketched above does not regard the interest of the alleged right-holder as the reason for the duty. It is, therefore, at best an argument for the existence of a duty with no corresponding right.

I believe that, whatever the general case for deontological

[1] The argument above disregards the possibility that personal autonomy is not to be counted among people's interests. The argument in Chs. 13 and 14 is designed to establish this point, among others. I do agree, however, that not everyone has an interest in personal autonomy. It is a cultural value, i.e. of value to people living in certain societies only. This denies the equation between respect for people and respect for personal autonomy. There is, however, no need to develop this point here.

duties, there are no good grounds for conceiving the duty of respect for persons along the lines suggested in the preceding two paragraphs. It is, as was indicated before, the duty to give due weight to the interests of persons. And it is grounded on the intrinsic desirability of the well-being of persons. To that extent it can give rise to rights: it serves as the basis of people's right that others shall give due weight to their interest. Being a very abstract right, nothing very concrete about how people should be treated follows from it without additional premisses. This explains why it is invoked not as a claim for any specific benefit, but as an assertion of status. To say 'I have a right to have my interest taken into account' is like saying 'I too am a person.' This may perhaps explain its 'deontological' flavour.

Not surprisingly, those who see rights as grounded on respect for persons deny that respect for persons consists in giving due weight to their interests. The reason is clear. Combining the claim that respect for persons consists in having due regard for their interests with the claim that rights rest on respect for persons leads to the conclusion that a person has a right that his interests will be duly respected. There is no apparent way by which this line of thought could explain the distinction between a person's interests which are protected by rights and those which are not. Instead, one may claim that respect for persons consists in respecting some of their interests only. In particular, it may be said, it consists in respecting their interest in being free to choose do and to live as they like. This may be thought to explain why some interests people have are not protected by rights. Rights protect not their interests generally but only their interest in freedom. The capacity to be free, to decide freely the course of their own lives, is what makes a person. Respecting people as people consists in giving due weight to their interest in having and exercising that capacity. On this view respect for people consists in respecting their interest to enjoy personal autonomy.

This argument calls for careful scrutiny. The claim, made above, that respecting people means giving proper weight to their interests is not a devious way to justify wholesale paternalism, at least not for those who believe in the value of personal autonomy. Since, as will be argued in Part Four, people's well-being is promoted by having an autonomous life, it is in their interest not to be subjected to the kind of oppressive paternalism which consists in running their lives for them allegedly in their own best interest. Therefore, the view that personal autonomy is an important element in people's well-being means that respect for people if under-stood as giving due consideration to all their interests leads to respect for their autonomy. It is true that on this view of respect it does not serve as a foundation of a theory of rights. But this is as it should be since one can, and people often do, show disrespect to others, including disrespect which amounts to denying their status as persons, by acts which do not violate rights. Each one of us can think of appropriate instances of insulting behaviour which illustrate the point.

It may be claimed that by defining rights as based on the well-being of individuals I have ruled out of court the view that morality is rights-based. By definition rights are not fundamental but derive from interests. If true this is a da-maging criticism. As explained in the first section the account of rights aims to make sense rather than nonsense of rival theories about the role of rights in morality. The view that rights are fundamental can, however, be explained in terms of the proposed definition.

All rights are based on interests. Some rights may be based on an interest in having those same rights.[1] No vicious circularity is involved in the claim that X has a certain right because it is his interest to have it. It is no more circular than the statement that Jack loves Jill because she needs his love. In many cases an individual's interest in a right does not justify holding him to have it unless it serves some other worth-while interest of his (or of others). My son's interest in a right to education justifies holding him to have it only because the right will serve his interest in education.

[1] One may think that one's right to X always derives from one's interest in X. If so then one's interest in having a right to X yields at best a right to have a right to X. It does not yield the right to X itself. This objection is based on a mis-understanding. While rights are based on interests of the right-holder, these need not be his interests in the object of the right. They can be any interests which can be served by the possession of the right. Since an interest in having a right can be served by having it, it can be the foundation of such a right.

If school places were saleable I would have had an interest in having a right to education even if further education were not in my interest. Such a right would serve my interest in my economic welfare since it would add to my disposable assets. Such an interest would not, of course justify holding me to have the right.

A right is a morally fundamental right if it is justified on the ground that it serves the right-holder's interest in having that right inasmuch as that interest is considered to be of ultimate value, i.e. inasmuch as the value of that interest does not derive from some other interest of the right-holder or of other persons.

Thus the proposed account of rights allows for the existence of fundamental moral rights. It has to be admitted though that it makes it unlikely that morality is rights-based. It is after all very unlikely that all moral considerations derive from people's interests in having rights. Are not their interests in avoiding starvation, in being adequately educated, and other similar interests of moral relevance as well? According to our account the special features of rights are their source in individual interest and their peremptory force, expressed in the fact that they are sufficient to hold people to be bound by duties. In these ways rights have a distinctive and important role in morality. But it is also a specialized role, not a comprehensive one. They contribute their share as a distinctive type of moral consideration, not as the foundation of all moral considerations. The next chapter points to some of the considerations omitted by those who concentrate on rights to the exclusion of all else.

8

Right-Based Moralities

Any moral theory allows for the existence of rights if it regards the interests of some individuals to be sufficient for holding others to be subject to duties. Some writers on morality and politics have suggested that rights are the foundation of political morality, or even morality generally. R. M. Dworkin has suggested that

political theories differ from one another. . . not simply in the particular goals, rights, and duties each sets out, but also in the way each connects the goals, rights, and duties it employs. It seems reasonable to suppose that any particular theory will give ultimate pride of place to just one of these concepts; it will take some overriding goal, or some set of fundamental rights, or some set of transcendent duties, as fundamental, and show other goals, rights, and duties as subordinate and derivative.[1]

Dworkin expressed the view that political morality is right-based. J. L. Mackie, adopting this classification, applied it to moral theories generally and claimed that morality is right-based (or rather that we should invent a morality which is).[2]

This chapter argues that neither morality nor political morality is right-based: that if morality has a foundation it includes duties, goals, virtues, etc. The argument presupposes certain moral views which will not here be defended. They introduce some of the main themes of the rest of this book: the rejection of moral individualism, and a moral outlook resting on the twin ideas of the constitutive role of a common culture on the one hand, and of individual action on the other hand, in the shaping of the moral world.

We are to envisage a moral theory the fundamental principles of which state that certain individuals have certain

[1] R. M. Dworkin, *Taking Rights Seriously*, p. 171.
[2] J. L. Mackie, 'Can There be a Right-Based Moral Theory?', *Midwest Studies in Philosophy*, 3 (1978), 350.

rights. They are its fundamental principles for, first, their justification does not presuppose any other moral principles, and, secondly, all valid moral views derive from them (with the addition of premises which do not by themselves yield any moral conclusions). Is any moral theory of this kind valid? Or, if you prefer, does a correct or sound morality have this structure? To simplify the discussion I will endorse right away the humanistic principle which claims that the explanation and justification of the goodness or badness of anything derives ultimately from its contribution, actual or possible, to human life and its quality.

Humanism, thus conceived, is not a moral theory. It merely sets a necessary condition for the acceptability of moral theories, a condition which can be satisfied by many different moral theories. Nor are all humanists committed to the view that all human life is of ultimate moral value. Their only commitment is that if some human life has no value or if some lives have more intrinsic value than others, this is in virtue of the quality of those lives. Many argue for a wider principle allowing ultimate value to all life, etc. But few claim that the humanistic principle is too wide. Since the conclusions argued for in this book will only be strengthened if the circle of ultimate value is wider, it will help secure the widest agreement to make the least demanding assumption and rest our argument entirely on the humanistic principle. Our goal is, therefore, to examine the plausibility of the view that morality is based on fundamental principles assigning rights to some or all human beings.[1]

1. Some Preliminary Doubts

The explanation of rights in the previous chapter seems congenial to a humanistic right-based approach to morality. It would fit well with a view which regards the interests of people as the only ultimate value. The protection and promotion of such human interests through the rights of people could be said to be what morality is all about. But is it? The purpose of this section is to introduce the doubts

[1] Whatever your views of the acceptability of the humanistic principle, they are unlikely to affect the validity of the arguments in this chapter.

which will be explored later in the chapter. It explains the respects in which right-based moralities are impoverished. A right-based morality is essentially a morality of rights and duties. Many moral views presuppose that there is more to morality than rights and duties and precepts which can be derived from them. Consider the following three examples.

(1) Though several moral philosophers use 'ought' and 'duty' interchangeably, many moral views presuppose a distinction between what one ought to do and what it is one's duty to do. The common view is that one ought to do that which one has a duty to do but one does not always have a duty to do that which one ought. Thus, while I ought to allow my neighbour who locked himself out of his house to use my phone, I have no duty to do so. On the other hand, since I have promised my neighbour to saw off a branch overhanging a corner of his garden this week, I have a duty, and therefore I ought, to do so. It is sometimes supposed that the difference is simply that there is greater reason to do that which one has a duty to do than to do that which one ought but has no duty to do. If this were so the difference between ought and duty would present no difficulty to the rights-theorists, for they may claim that they merely use 'duty' as equivalent to 'ought', and can use 'weighty duty' as equivalent to the normal 'duty'. The two examples above refute the suggestion that the difference between one's duties and what one simply ought to do is in the weight of the supporting reason since there is probably more reason to let my locked-out neighbour use my phone than to saw off the branch this week rather than next week. This is so even if one takes account of the harm my breaking my promise does to the reliability and credibility of promises between neighbours and in general. Duties are not reasons for action of a great weight. They are a special kind of requirement for action in the same way that authoritative instructions, while not necessarily more weighty than other reasons, have a special peremptory force.[1] Right-based moralities consist of rights and those special requirements which we call duties. They do not allow for the moral significance of ordinary

---

[1] This argument is developed in greater detail in my 'Promises and Obligations' in P. M. S. Hacker and J. Raz (eds.), *Law, Morality, and Society*.

reasons for action. It is easy to see that this point is deeply embedded in our understanding of rights and is not an arbitrary result of my definition of rights. Most people will agree, for example, that I ought to give other people information which it is in their interest to have. It is, however, generally thought that they have no right that I should do so and therefore that I have no duty to give them the information. Rights are tied to duties. Reasons for action which do not amount to duties escape the notice of a right-based morality.

(2) A second respect in which right-based moralities are impoverished is in not allowing for the moral significance of supererogation. Acts are supererogatory if their performance is praiseworthy and yet it is not morally wrong to omit them. There is no obligation to act in a supererogatory way. Indeed supererogation is identified with action beyond the call of duty.[1] Right-based moralities cannot account for the nature of supererogation and its role in moral life.

(3) Finally, right-based moralities cannot allow intrinsic moral value to virtue and the pursuit of excellence. Again the reason is much the same as before. None of the commonly recognized virtues and morally significant forms of excellence consists in discharging one's duties or being disposed to do so. Honesty is a virtue which is particularly closely tied to the duty not to deceive, and yet even it is not exhausted by compliance with the duty. The exemplary honest man is one who does more than his duty to make sure that his behaviour does not mislead others. He acts honestly out of certain motives and he holds certain appropriate beliefs regarding interpersonal communications and these display themselves in appropriate attitudes which he possesses.

Rights theorists may reply to all three examples that their views do not bar them from accommodating, in a derivative role, ordinary moral reasons for action, supererogation and moral excellence in their moral theories. This is true, but is no reply to the objections, which are not that right-based theories cannot make room for these notions at all, but rather

---

[1] Action beyond the call of duty is naturally not just any action one ought to do but has no duty to.

that they cannot allow them their true moral significance. Let me explain.

Any moral theory which allows for the existence of duties must allow for the existence of reasons which are not duties. This is a result of the fact that rights and duties are not transitive regarding the means which they require. Reasons for action transfer their force to the means by which their realization is facilitated. If I have a reason to bring you a glass of water then I have a reason to go to the kitchen to fetch a glass and fill it with water. But even if I have a duty to be in London at noon, it does not follow that I have a duty to take the 10 a.m. train, even though it will bring me to London at noon.[1] Rights are like duties in this respect. The fact that you have a right that I be in London at noon does not entail that you have a right that I shall take the 10 a.m. train. Needless to say, one has reason to take steps to discharge one's duties. Therefore, any moral theory which allows for the existence of duties must allow for the existence of ordinary reasons for duty-holders to take action to discharge their duties. Right-based theories allow for ordinary moral reasons of a derivative kind. This does not however avoid the objections which are that ordinary reasons are no less important and central to moral thinking than duties.

Similarly with virtue. Right-based theories can regard the cultivation of certain dispositions as instrumentally valuable if they predispose individuals to do their duty. They may even approve of individuals cultivating such dispositions for what they erroneously believe is their intrinsic value. Right-based theories (like utilitarian theories) cannot allow personal characteristics which are virtuous or morally praiseworthy to be judged intrinsically desirable and cultivated for their own sake. It is less clear to me what room there might be for supererogation within right-based theories. They can allow for a near relation, i.e. a special category of duties performance of which requires exceptional personal qualities such that their performance deserves praise and

[1] I leave it open whether or not one has a duty to do that which is both necessary and sufficient to comply with a duty. My claim is merely that one has no duty to do something because it is sufficient to comply with a duty. I do have reason to do that which is sufficient to follow a reason.

failure to discharge them, though wrong, is excusable. Despite this palliative, the objection remains that supererogation in its proper sense, which involves action beyond the call of duty, is not recognized in right-based theories.

The preceding discussion was meant to illustrate the ways in which right-based theories are impoverished. It has not established that the impoverishment involves any real moral loss. To show that is the aim of the rest of this chapter.

2. Rights and Individualism

Right-based moral theories are usually individualistic moral theories. There is as little agreement about the sense in which a moral outlook is or is not a form of individualism as there is on the sense of any other '-ism'. My explanation of moral individualism is therefore necessarily stipulative in part. My hope is that it captures an important element traditionally associated with individualism and a most important difference between humanistic moralities.[1] A moral theory will be said to be individualistic if it is a humanistic morality which does not recognize any intrinsic value in any collective good. In other words, individualistic moralities are humanistic moralities which hold that collective goods have instrumental value only.

Before we explore the connection between right-based moralities and individualism, here are a few further clarifications of the nature of moral individualism. A good is a public good in a certain society if and only if the distribution of its benefits in that society is not subject to voluntary control by anyone other than each potential beneficiary controlling his share of the benefits. I shall distinguish between contingent and inherent public goods. Water supply in a certain town may be a public good if the water pipe network does not allow for the switching-off of individual households. But it is only contingently a public good, as it is possible to change the supply system to enable control over distribution. Clean air is similarly a contingent public good. In this case we do not have the technology to control air distribution.

[1] For a survey of different notions of individualism see S. Lukes, *Individualism*, Oxford, 1973.

But the limitation of our technological ability in this respect is only a contingent one.

General beneficial features of a society are inherently public goods. It is a public good, and inherently so, that this society is a tolerant society, that it is an educated society, that it is infused with a sense of respect for human beings, etc. Living in a society with these characteristics is generally of benefit to individuals. These benefits are not to be confused with the benefit of having friends or acquaintances who are tolerant, educated, etc. One's friends can voluntarily control the distribution of the benefits of their friendship. The benefits I have in mind are the more diffuse ones deriving from the general character of the society to which one belongs. Different people benefit from the good qualities of the society to different degrees. But the degree to which they benefit depends on their character, interests, and dispositions, and cannot be directly controlled by others. (Usually they themselves have only partial and imperfect control over these factors.) Naturally one can exclude individuals from benefiting from such goods by excluding them from the society to which they pertain. But that does not affect the character of the goods as public goods which depends on non-exclusivity of enjoyment among members of the society in which they are public goods. I shall call inherent public goods 'collective goods'.

For obvious reasons economists have concerned themselves mostly with contingent public goods, and those are mostly of only instrumental value. Clean air is important for one's health and so on. If any public goods are intrinsically valuable then some of the collective goods are the most likely candidates. Commitment to a humanistic morality, however, often inclines people to believe that even collective goods can only be instrumentally valuable. Living in a tolerant society, for example, is thought to be good because it spares one the pain of petty-minded social persecution and the fear of it, and enables one to have a happier life by enabling one to develop freely one's inclinations and tastes. To suggest otherwise, to suggest that living in a tolerant society is good independently of its consequences, that it is intrinsically good is, in their opinion, to reject humanism, for it amounts

to asserting the intrinsic value of something which is not
human life or its quality.

   To understand why such misgivings are misplaced, and
to show that humanism is compatible with holding some
collective goods to be intrinsically valuable, we have to remind ourselves of, and to amplify, a few distinctions introduced in the previous chapter. Something is
instrumentally good if its value derives from the fact that
it makes certain consequences more likely, or that it can
contribute to producing certain consequences. Something is
intrinsically good or valuable if it is valuable independently
of the value of its actual or probable consequences, and not
on account of any consequences it can be used to produce or
to the production of which it can contribute causally. We
need to distinguish three different categories among the intrinsically valuable things. Those things are valuable in
themselves the existence of which is valuable irrespective of
what else exists. Things are constituent goods if they are
elements of what is good in itself which contribute to its
value, i.e. elements but for which a situation which is good
in itself would be less valuable. Both goods in themselves
and constituent goods are intrinsically good. So are ultimate
goods or values. The aspects of a good in itself which are
of ultimate value are those which explain and justify the
judgment that it is good in itself, and which are such that
their own value need not be explained or be justified by
reference to (their contribution to) other values. The relation
of ultimate values to intrinsic values which are not ultimate
is an explanatory or justificatory one. Ultimate values are
referred to in explaining the value of non-ultimate goods.

   The case of works of art, though they are not themselves
collective goods, will serve to explain the distinction and to
show that humanism is compatible with the view that some
collective goods have intrinsic value. Consider the value of
works of art not to their creator but to the public. No doubt
their value is many sided. Owning works of art could be a
sound investment, studying them could be a way of acquiring prestige or knowledge of human psychology, and so
on. Let us concentrate exclusively on their value to the public
as works of art (rather than as a means of acquiring prestige

or knowledge, etc.). One view of their value holds it to be intrinsic. Watching and contemplating works of art are valuable activities and a life which includes them is enriched because of them. If the life thus enriched is intrinsically good, then the existence of works of art is equally an intrinsic good. It is a constituent of the good which is a life including the experience of works of art. Let me refer to such a life as a life with art. The point is that one cannot experience works of art unless they exist. The value of the experience is in its being an experience of art. The experience cannot be explained except by reference to a belief in the existence of its object, and its value depends on the truth of that belief. On this view the existence of works of art is intrinsically valuable.

Such a view is compatible with humanism since the explanation of the intrinsic value of art is in its relation to the quality of life with art. A life with art is, we here assume for the sake of the example, a good in itself. The existence of works of art is a constituent good, and the quality of life with art which explains its value is the ultimate good. All three are intrinsic goods.

The value of art is interpreted differently by classical utilitarians, for example. They regard it as instrumentally valuable inasmuch as it may cause valuable sensations or emotions in an individual. The classical utilitarians interpret these sensations and emotions as being capable of being caused in some other way and therefore as only contingently connected with works of art, which are therefore merely instrumentally valuable.

The existence of works of art is not a collective good. My aim so far has been to show that humanism is consistent with holding that not only life and its quality are intrinsically valuable. Hence regarding collective goods as intrinsically valuable is compatible with a commitment to humanism. It is in principle also compatible with the view that morality is right-based. Nevertheless, right-based moral theories tend to be individualistic and to deny the intrinsic value of collective goods. The reason is not far to seek. Consider collective goods such as living in a beautiful town, which is economically prosperous, and in a society tolerant and cultured. Living in such an environment is in the interest of each of its inhabitants. It is more agreeable to live in such a society, whatever one's personal circumstances, than to live in one which lacks these attributes. But the fact that it is in my interest to live in such a society is not normally considered sufficient to establish that I have a right to live in such a society. The common view is that my interest that my society shall be of this character is a reason to develop it in such a direction, but that the existence of such a reason is not enough to show that I have a right that my society shall have this character.

This is explicable on the definition of rights offered above, according to which a right is a sufficient ground for holding another to have a duty. It is the common view that my interest in living in a prosperous, cultured, and tolerant society and in a beautiful environment is not enough to impose a duty on anyone to make my society and environment so. It does not follow that no one has such duties. I am inclined to say that the government has a duty to achieve all these goals or at least to try to do so. But its duty is not grounded in my interest alone. It is based on my interest and on the interests of everyone else, together with the fact that governments are special institutions whose proper functions and (normative) powers are limited.

Nothing in this section shows that right-based moralities must be individualistic. But its argument explains that it is not accidental that right-based theories have been and are likely to be individualistic. Given some widely accepted views of the kinds of consideration which establish one person's duty to another, it is unlikely that individuals have basic rights to collective goods. If, for example, others' duty to me is confined to not violating my integrity as a person and providing me with basic needs, then I have no right to collective goods for my interest in them is not among my basic needs for survival.

This example may, however, mislead. It may suggest that if some collective goods are intrinsically valuable then they are not of great importance, and that is why they fail to justify holding others to be duty-bound to satisfy them, or to do their best to satisfy them. This is far from the truth.

My interest in living in a prosperous, cultured, tolerant and beautiful environment is among my most important interests. It is more important than many aspects of my bodily integrity that others are duty bound to respect. The difference is that the maintenance of a collective good affects the life and imposes constraints on the activities of the bulk of the population, in matters which deeply affect them. It is difficult to imagine a successful argument imposing a duty to provide a collective good on the ground that it will serve the interests of one individual.

3. Autonomy and Rights

Is there anything wrong with moral individualism? Are any collective goods intrinsically desirable? I will suggest that some collective goods are intrinsically desirable if personal autonomy is intrinsically desirable. If this is so then right-based theories cannot account for the desirability of autonomy. This conclusion is of great interest to the contemporary debate, since some rights theories tend to emphasize the importance and value of personal autonomy. J. L. Mackie, for example, suggests that the fundamental right is, roughly speaking, a right to liberty: 'If we assume that, from the point of view of the morality we are constructing, what matters in human life is activity, but diverse activities determined by successive choices, we shall. . . take as central the right of persons progressively to choose how they live.'[1] Though he does not explicitly refer to autonomy, he seems to regard his invented morality as right-based because he maintains that only a right-based morality can express the fundamental value of autonomy.

The question of the relation between autonomy and rights transcends its relevance to the question whether morality is right-based. One common strand in liberal thought regards the promotion and protection of personal autonomy as the core of the liberal concern for liberty. This is also the view argued for in this book. Hence just as in Part Two we were concerned to show that personal autonomy does not lead to anti-perfectionism, so in this part we are concerned, among

[1] J. L. Mackie, op. cit., p. 355.

other issues, with the degree to which respect for personal autonomy rests on or is expressed in recognition of one or more fundamental rights.

For the purpose of the present argument only one aspect of the ideal of personal autonomy need concern us.[1] An autonomous person is part author of his own life. His life is, in part, of his own making. The autonomous person's life is marked not only by what it is but also by what it might have been and by the way it became what it is. A person is autonomous only if he has a variety of acceptable options available to him to choose from, and his life became as it is through his choice of some of these options. A person who has never had any significant choice, or was not aware of it, or never exercised choice in significant matters but simply drifted through life is not an autonomous person.

It should be clear from these observations that autonomy is here construed as a kind of achievement. To this sense of autonomy corresponds another, according to which it is the capacity to achieve the autonomous life. The discussion of autonomy in Chapter Six, for example, revolved mostly round autonomy as a capacity. In this sense a person is autonomous if he can become the author of his own life, i.e. if he can be autonomous in the first or primary sense. By the second sense of autonomy, a person is autonomous if the conditions of autonomous life obtain. Those are partly to do with the state of the individual concerned (that he is of sound mind, capable of rational thought and action, etc.) and partly to do with the circumstances of his life (especially that he has a sufficient range of significant options available to him at different stages of his life).

This distinction between an autonomous life as an achievement and a capacity for autonomy which is its pre-condition would not look quite the same to a supporter of a rights view of autonomy. He cannot claim that rights are justified because they protect autonomy. This would be to justify them instrumentally. He has to maintain that auto-nomy is constituted by rights and nothing else. The auto-nomous life is a life within unviolated rights. Unviolated rights create or protect opportunities. What one makes of

[1] It was encountered in Ch. 6 above, but for a full discussion see Ch. 13.

them is left undetermined by the sheer existence of the rights. Therefore, in terms of my distinction between autonomy as a capacity and as a successful use of it, the rights theorist would maintain that a capacity for autonomy guarantees that one's life is autonomous, e.g. that no use or neglect of that capacity can make the life of those who have it more or less autonomous. There are serious objections to this view. But their exploration will have to await Part Four. None of the arguments of this chapter depend on maintaining that autonomy is more than the life of a person with a certain capacity.

If having an autonomous life is an ultimate value, then having a sufficient range of acceptable options is of intrinsic value, for it is constitutive of an autonomous life that it is lived in circumstances where acceptable alternatives are present. The alternatives must be acceptable if the life is to be autonomous. As we saw in Chapter Six, a person whose every major decision was coerced, extracted from him by threats to his life, or by threats that would make the life he has or has embarked upon impossible, has not led an autonomous life. Similar considerations apply to a person who has spent his whole life fighting starvation and disease, and has had no opportunity to accomplish anything other than to stay alive. Only in Chapter Thirteen will we try to analyse what options are acceptable. All that concerns us here is that the ideal of personal autonomy (whose realization is clearly a matter of degree) requires not merely the presence of options but of acceptable ones.

The existence of many options consists in part in the existence of certain social conditions. One cannot have an option to be a barrister, a surgeon, or a psychiatrist in a society where those professions, and the institutions their existence presupposes, do not exist. While this will be readily acknowledged, it is sometimes overlooked that the same is true of the options of being an architect or of getting married. It is true that one need not live in a society at all to design buildings regularly, or to cohabit with another person. But doing so is not the same as being an architect or being married. An architect is one who belongs to a socially recognized profession. In many countries a homosexual can

cohabit with, but cannot be married to his homosexual partner, since to be married is to partake of a socially (and legally)
recognized and regulated type of relationship. Homosexuals
cannot do that if their society does not recognize and regulate
a pattern of relationship which could apply to them. They
can imitate some other recognized relationship. But essentially they have to develop their relations as they go along,
and do not have the option of benefiting from existing social
frameworks.

At least some of the social conditions which constitute
such options are collective goods. The existence of a society
with a legal profession or with recognized homosexual marriages is a collective good, for the distribution of its benefits is
not voluntarily controlled by anyone other than the potential
beneficiary. In a society where such opportunities exist and
make it possible for individuals to have an autonomous life,
their existence is intrinsically valuable. The ideal of personal
autonomy entails, therefore, that collective goods are at least
sometimes intrinsically valuable. I think that it entails much
more than that. Commonly accepted views about humans as
essentially social animals, and equally common views about
which options are worthwhile in life (for it is a condition of
a life being autonomous that the valuable options include an
adequate range of worthy opportunities) yield the conclusion
that many collective goods are intrinsically good. At the very
least living in a society, which is a collective good, is on this
view intrinsically good.

What conclusions is one to draw from these reflections
concerning the relation between rights and autonomy? In a
way the most important one is that the ideal of personal
autonomy is incompatible with moral individualism. Some
may proceed to claim that morality is nevertheless right-
based, but that since one of the fundamental rights is a right
to autonomy it follows that there are rights to collective
goods. Others may resist the idea that I have a right that my
society shall continue to exist and a right that it shall have
architects and surgeons and monogamous marriages. My
interest in being autonomous shows that it is in my interest
to live in a society where all those and many other options
are available. But it is not enough by itself to justify holding

others to be duty-bound to make sure that my society shall offer all these options. Given that the existence of these options is intrinsically valuable, they would conclude that morality includes fundamental values or ideals as well as fundamental rights.

More important is the conclusion that if autonomy is an ultimate value, then it affects wide-ranging aspects of social practices and institution. It is wrong to identify autonomy with right against coercion, for example, and to hold that right (i.e. the right against coercion) as defeating, because of the importance of personal autonomy, all, or almost all, other considerations. Many rights contribute to making autonomy possible, but no short list of concrete rights is sufficient for this purpose. The provision of many collective goods is constitutive of the very possibility of autonomy and it cannot be relegated to a subordinate role, compared with some alleged right against coercion, in the name of autonomy.

4. Collective Rights

Can our conclusions be avoided by admitting the existence of group or collective rights? Yassir Arafat, being a Palestinian, has an interest in Palestinian self-determination. At least in part that interest is based on a person's interest in living in a community which enables him to express in public and develop without repression those aspects of his personality which are bound up with his sense of identity as a member of his community. It is an interest of great importance to the well-being of very many people. Nevertheless, Arafat does not have a right to Palestinian self-determination. Self-determination is a typical collective good. Its satisfaction imposes far-reaching demands on the life of whole communities. Arafat's interest by itself does not justify imposing such far-reaching duties on so many other people. So he does not have it.

The right to Palestinian self-determination is at the moment flouted. Its recognition will demand considerable changes in the way of life, the future prospects and the habits of thought of many Israelis. But the fact that Arafat does not have a right to Palestinian self-determination does not depend on the existence of actual conflict and sacrifice. John Bull has no more right to British self-determination than Arafat has to Palestinian self-determination, even though Britain's self-determination is secure, and its perpetuation does not adversely affect anyone, or so I assume. A right is a ground for a duty of another. And a duty exists only if it would defeat certain conflicting considerations were they to exist. The absence of actual conflict is not enough to justify a claim of a right. For this reason one may indeed doubt the possibility of a justification for a fundamental individual right to a collective good.[1]

Whereas a person does not have a right to the self-determination of the community to which he belongs, nations do have such rights. The Palestinian people have a right to self-determination. Collective rights are typically rights to collective goods. Can morality be right-based, given that it is accepted that its foundation includes collective and not only individual rights?

A collective right exists when the following three conditions are met. First, it exists because an aspect of the interest of human beings justifies holding some person(s) to be subject to a duty. Second, the interests in question are the interests of individuals as members of a group in a public good and the right is a right to that public good because it serves their interest as members of the group. Thirdly, the interest of no single member of that group in that public good is sufficient by itself to justify holding another person to be subject to a duty.

The first condition is required for collective rights to be consistent with humanism. Rights, even collective rights, can only be there if they serve the interests of individuals. In that sense collective interests are a mere *façon de parler*. They are a way of referring to individual interests which arise out of the individuals' membership in communities. The other two conditions distinguish a collective right from a set of individual rights. The right to self-determination exemplifies the three features. It is valued because of the

---

[1] If the right is not fundamental then its justification may invoke the way in which respecting the interest of one person instrumentally serves the interest of others.

contribution of self-determination to the well-being of individual members of the group. Self-determination is not merely a public good but a collective one, and people's interest in it arises out of the fact that they are members of the group. Finally, though many individuals have an interest in the self-determination of their community, the interest of any one of them is an inadequate ground for holding others to be duty-bound to satisfy that interest. The right rests on the cumulative interests of many individuals. (This explains why though the existence of the interest does not depend on the size of the group, the existence of the right and its strength does.)

The same features are displayed by other collective rights. Consider, for example, the right of the British public to know how Britain was led into the Falkland war. It is a right for information to be made public, and therefore for a public good. It is held to be a collective right by those who think that it cannot be justified just on the basis of a single member of the public, but that it can be justified on the ground that the interests of many are at stake, and that they are their interests as members of a community in the way in which the community is run in their name, and for the running of which each one of them, as a member of the community, bears partial responsibility.

The notion of collective rights took root as an analogical extension of the more familiar idea of individual rights. But it is none the worse for that. In pointing to aspects of the personal sense of identity which are inextricably bound up with the existence of communities and their common culture, it recognizes the intrinsic value of some collective goods, and it frees rights discourse from its traditional association with moral individualism. But helpful as this is, it does not reinstate our shattered belief that morality is right-based. There are too many intrinsically valuable collective goods the value of which does not reside in their relevance to people's interests as members of communities. All the examples in the previous section are of this kind. All of them are collective goods to which no group has a collective right.

5. *Intrinsic Duties*

The considerations advanced above suggest that apart from some rights there are other values at the foundations of morality. In passing I have referred to the possibility that governments have duties which do not derive from the rights of individual human beings. The possibility that there are duties which do not correspond to any rights is allowed by the definition of rights, and is generally acknowledged by legal and political theorists. Yet the view that such duties must ultimately derive from fundamental rights or at least be based on the interests of people other than those subject to the duty has become sufficiently widespread that it is important to explain why it is rational to expect that there are fundamental moral duties which do not derive solely from the rights and interests of their potential beneficiaries, or which have no potential beneficiaries at all. I shall briefly discuss two cases purporting to show that some duties require non-instrumental justification, i.e. that their existence is of intrinsic, even if not necessarily of ultimate, value. They will also show that there are duties which do not derive from anyone's rights.

Both cases are designed to show how one particularly troublesome objection to the possibility of non-instrumental duties can be met. Let me, therefore, begin by stating the objection. Suppose it were said that people have a duty not to behave in a certain way because such behaviour is wicked or just plain morally wrong. The claim may then be made that that can be so only if there is some independent reason for objecting to that action. Otherwise there is no way of explaining why there is a duty to behave in this way rather than in any other. It would seem to follow that if an action is wrong because it is a breach of duty then there must be a reason (other than the fact that the action is wrong) to justify the existence of the duty. What can that reason be other than that the action infringes someone's rights or causes harm or that it jeopardizes some other value? If so, then the duty is instrumentally justified. In what way can this order of justification be avoided? How can the duty not to act in a certain way be justified by the wrongfulness of the action without proceeding to explain the wrongfulness of this action, rather than any other, by reference to the fact that it harms values or violates rights?

A first step towards meeting the objection is to suggest that there might be an instrumental reason to act in a certain way but one which does not establish a duty so to act. The instrumental reason establishes why one should act in this rather than in some other way, while non-instrumental considerations account for this being a duty. This suggestion is helpful, for while there are intrinsic duties which do not presuppose any instrumental reason for the duty-act (they are ceremonial or symbolic duties), often the justification of intrinsic duties includes an instrumental component. Let me turn to my two examples of intrinsic duties to illustrate this point. In explaining them I will say enough to show that they present requirements, reasons for action which are intrinsic and not based on rights. I will not show that these requirements amount to duties. I believe that the first of them does. But for the purpose at hand, i.e. for demonstrating the inadequacy of the rights approach, this additional argument is immaterial.

The first example assumes that there is a duty among friends which obliges a person to compensate his friend if his action has harmed the friend even though the harm was not caused through any fault of his. Normally our responsibility to make good harm we cause to others depends on fault or on special responsibility. Friends have a no-fault obligation to each other though normally it does not require full compensation. Evidently the fact that compensating someone is likely to benefit him is an instrumental reason for doing so. That reason is not enough to establish an obligation to compensate or else everyone will have an obligation to compensate for any loss or harm they cause. Yet this instrumental reason provides an essential component in the non-instrumental justification of the duty to compensate friends for harm done to them. The other elements in the justification turn on the nature of friendship.

Friendships entail a special concern for the welfare of the friend, concern for his welfare over and above the concern required of us towards other human beings generally. That concern manifests itself in many ways. But its expression is particularly urgent when we are the cause of harm to our friends. The urgency is not because then their need is greatest—it may not be. Nor is it because their need is our fault—for it need not be. The duty of friends which we are considering results from the natural cultural convention to regard unsolicited acts of compensation for harm one causes, even without fault, as particularly expressive of one's concern for the welfare of the compensated person (whether or not he is one's friend). Because such action expresses concern and because friendship is in part the expression of concern one has a duty to compensate one's friend for harm caused. Since friendship consists in part in such duties the existence of the duty is intrinsically valuable if the desirability of friendship itself is, as I shall assume without argument, intrinsic. By recognizing and respecting such duties towards another, as well as in other ways, one develops a friendship with another, and by denying them one undermines or ends friendships.[1]

For my second example, imagine that I own a Van Gogh painting. I therefore have a right to destroy it. I have an instrumental reason not to do so. I can sell it for a large sum. Furthermore many would derive great pleasure and enrichment if they could look at it. But no one has a right that I shall not destroy the painting. Nevertheless, while I owe no one a duty to preserve the painting I am under such a duty, at least in the weak sense that I ought to preserve it. The reason is that to destroy it and deny the duty is to do violence to art and to show oneself blind to one of the values which give life a meaning. The duty exists regardless of whether I profess to be a lover of art. If I do so profess then to violate the duty is to compromise my integrity. But everyone has a duty of respect towards the values which give meaning to human life, even to those on which one's life does not depend for its meaning. The moral conception I am relying on here is similar to the one underlying the previous example. One's respect for values does to a degree consist in action expressing it. Where such action is particularly apt

---

[1] On the non-instrumental relation between friendship and its normative constituents see further J. Raz, *The Authority of Law*, pp. 253–8.

and urgent there may be a duty which is then an intrinsic duty.

One common objection to such a line of argument is that while it is true that one ought to compensate one's friends and to preserve works of art there is no duty to do so. One ought to do so because of one's concern for one's friends and one's respect for art and not out of duty. But the objection is based on the wrong presupposition that if one has a duty one should comply with it because it is a duty. One may well have a duty to do something because of one's concern for a friend or one's respect for art.

6. Rights and Narrow Morality

The examples I used introduce themes which will be explored later on in the book. But even if my examples do not convince, I hope they make the view that there are intrinsic duties more plausible and less absurd or irrational. Sometimes a moral theory gains conviction because it seems to be the only one which is coherently statable. Whichever views we accept we always gain by being able to see them as just one of several alternative moral outlooks of various degrees of acceptability.

One objection which might be raised against the general way in which the argument about right-based moralities was conducted is that it misinterprets the general nature of morality, or at least that it overlooks the fact that rights are supposed by their proponents to be the foundations of morality in the narrow sense.[1]

Morality in the narrow sense is meant to include only all those principles which restrict the individual's pursuit of his personal goals and his advancement of his self-interest. It is not 'the art of life', i.e. the precepts instructing people how to live and what makes for a successful, meaningful, and worthwhile life. It is clear that right-based moralities can only be moralities in the narrow sense. An individual's rights do not provide him with reasons for action (though if he can

[1] On morality in the narrow sense see, e.g., G. J. Warnock, *The Object of Morality*, London, 1971, esp. chs. 2 and 5, and J. L. Mackie, *Ethics: Inventing Right and Wrong*, Harmondsworth, 1977, pp. 134–6.

expect his rights to be respected they inform him of some of his opportunities). It is implausible to assume that an individual can conduct his whole life on the basis of the sole motivation of respecting other people's rights. Nor is there any reason to commend such a mode of existence. It would be a life of total servitude to others. On the other hand, morality in the narrow sense may be right-based. Rights do exactly what morality is supposed to do: they set limits to the individual's pursuit of his own goals and interests. On the plausible assumption that the only valid grounds on which the free pursuit by people of their own lives can be restricted are the needs, interests, and preferences of other people, it becomes plausible to regard narrow morality as right-based.

We have reached here one of the fundamental divides between the right-based views and the outlook which informs all the preceding objections to the thought that morality is right-based. There is a fundamental objection to the very notion of morality in the narrow sense. Of course one may for convenience of exposition or other superficial purposes hive off any aspect of morality and discuss some of its problems separately. There can be no objection to that. The objection is to the notion that there is such a division at a fundamental level, that one can divide one's principles of action into those concerned with one's own personal goals and those concerned with others, in such a way that the principles are independent of each other. The mistake is to think that one can identify, say, the rights of others, while being completely ignorant of what values make a life meaningful and satisfying and what personal goals one has in life. Conversely, it is also a mistake to think that one can understand the values which can give a meaning to life and have personal goals and ideals while remaining ignorant of one's duties to others. There is no doubt a mutual independence at the superficial level. I need not decide whether to become a middle distance runner or a professional chess player before I understand my obligation to others. But by the time that is the main remaining problem about the kind of life I would like to have, all fundamental problems have already been settled.

It may be best to approach my objection to the conception of a narrow morality from the examples discussed earlier in this chapter. My duty not to destroy the Van Gogh is appropriate for inclusion in narrow morality for it is not based on my interests nor does it depend on the preservation of the painting being part of my personal goals. It can be seen as a potential limitation on my freedom to pursue self-interest or personal desires. And yet I have suggested earlier that the duty is not exclusively based on the interests of others. Those would establish a reason not to destroy the painting, but not an obligation not to do so. There is no way of analysing the respect due to art into two components, one representing a person's obligations to others concerning art, the other expressing the importance art has for his own personal tastes and interests. Consider a person who has no interest in the arts. Even he should respect them. Some will say that that requirement of respect is derived from the requirement to respect other persons, some of whom have an interest in art. But this is a partial and limited view. The general requirement of respecting art is one which people should regard not as a restriction on the pursuit of their personal goals, but as part of their general outlook on life. It is no mere internalization of a requirement based on the interests of others. It is part of the necessary process through which a person learns of the worthwhile options in life and through which he develops his own tastes and goals. It is also part of the process through which he relates to other people.

It is crucial for the development of normal personal re-lations that each person understands his own tastes and goals in ways which relate them to other people's goals and tastes. He must regard his own goals and tastes as valuable because they exemplify universal values or values which form part of a mosaic which in its entirety makes for valuable social life. He must, if he is to be capable of personal relations, find room for other people's values within that scheme. If I recognize an obligation to preserve the Van Gogh this is because I express thereby my recognition of the value of art and because through doing so I have come to recognize some of the worthwhile options, on which, even though I did not pursue them, my autonomy depends. By recognizing that very same value I also create the possibility of developing personal relations with other people, for those depend at the deepest level on a sharing of values.

Personal relations, on which we have just touched, are another area in which the boundary between morality in the narrow and wide sense is invisible. Personal friendships, marital relations, one's loyalty and sense of pride in one's workplace or one's country, are among the most valuable and rewarding aspects of many people's lives. Such relations are culturally determined forms of human interaction and it is through learning their value that one acquires a sense both of the possibilities of one's own life and of one's obligations to others. The two are aspects of one and the same conception of value. Consider one's sense of belonging to a certain country as a factor determining one's sense of identity and of the very same factor as requiring sacrifices in the interests of others. I do not deny that at times the two elements are separate. At times the obligation to one's country clearly conflicts with one's interests. In normal circumstances, however, one's relations to one's country help to shape one's interests, tastes, and goals. At all times one's obligations to one's country stem from the same source. Whether they are perceived as restrictions on one's freedom or as determining one's identity and interests they defy the division of morality into wide and narow components.

We have come full circle to a consideration of the intrinsic value of some collective goods. If collective goods such as membership in a society are intrinsically valuable, then it is to be expected that they provide the source both of personal goals and of obligations to others. The confrontational view of morality which pitches a person's own interests and goals as not only occasionally in conflict with his obligations to others but as deriving from independent and fundamentally different sources is essentially an individualistic conception. My objections to the view that morality is right-based derive from a sense of the inadequacy of the conception of morality in the narrow sense which itself is a reflection of the rejection of moral individualism.

9
Equality

Even if morality is not based on rights it may include rights in its foundations. At the very least some principles establishing rights, let us call them principles of entitlement, may be among the fundamental principles governing all political actions. One view holds that if not morality generally at least political morality is egalitarian, i.e. dominated, in a sense to be explained below, by a principle of equality. One version of this view holds that the fundamental egalitarian principle establishes a right to equality. You may wonder what relevance such views have to an essay on political freedom. The answer is that the alleged right to equality has been most suggestively put forward by some, in particular by R. M. Dworkin, as the definitive belief of political liberalism, or at least of any defensible version of it. Perhaps no less surprising is the fact that neither Marx nor Engels laid much store by equality. It is treated at any length only in *Anti-Duhring*, where it is regarded as a bourgeois political slogan of a definite content, i.e. that the bourgeoisie should share the rights and privileges of the first and second estates. It has no normative force, it signifies no moral or political ideal, but it can serve as a useful political slogan, claiming for the proletariat the rights and privileges of the bourgeoisie.

The charge that egalitarianism is formal and empty has since been repeated many times. Accordingly our first, and most space-consuming, task is to identify a sense of 'principles of equality' which is not merely formal and empty. We shall then briefly consider whether the egalitarian tradition in Western culture is egalitarian in that sense. Finally we shall ask whether egalitarianism is a plausible framework for an acceptable political morality.

1. The Problem

We assume a pre-analytical, a naive, ability to tell which theories are egalitarian. This is our ability to recognize theories as belonging to a certain historical tradition. We aim to account for the egalitarian character of these theories through the predominance within them of principles of a special kind. In other words we hope to explain the egalitarian character of theories through the egalitarian character of some important principles they contain. The first task is to find out which principles can be usefully regarded as principles of equality. I am using this qualified expression since in a sense all principles can be regarded as principles of equality simply in virtue of their generality. We are looking for principles which, first, are related to equality in a way absent in all other principles and, secondly, are capable of accounting for the egalitarian character of egalitarian theories. Finally, we are particularly concerned with the claim that there is a fundamental right to equality. Because of this we will pursue the argument by reference to principles which state rights. But the argument is of wider application. It is simple to reformulate all the examples and arguments excising all reference to rights, without affecting their force.

Principles which state (or confer) rights will be called principles of entitlement.[1] What sort of principle of entitlement confers a right to equality? Principles of entitlement can be either positive or negative. The general form of the positive principles is:

(1) All Fs are entitled to G.

The general form of the negative ones is:

(2) Being or not being an F is irrelevant to one's entitlement to G.

A positive principle asserts that certain fact (being an F) is (part of) a ground for a right, as well as identifying that right (as a right to G). A negative principle states that certain facts are not part of a ground for a right. Such principles are present in all theories, egalitarian and non-egalitarian alike. Which of them are principles of equality? Consider the following:

---

[1] Not every entitlement is a right. One is, for example, always entitled to do one's moral duty. One may have a duty to break the law without having a right to do so. Though of course, if it is a duty then it is right to do so. Cf. *The Authority of Law*, Ch. 14. But in this chapter I will disregard the discrepancies.

(3.1) All those who are equally F are entitled to equal G.

(3.2) All those who are equally F are equally entitled to G.

Corresponding formulae can easily be produced for negative principles. What is the significance of the mention of equality in (3.1) and (3.2)? Compare the following:

(1a) Human beings are entitled to education.

(3.1a) Those who are equally human are entitled to equal education.

(3.2a) Those who are equally human are equally entitled to education.

and

(1b) Intelligent people are entitled to university places.

(3.1b) Equally intelligent people are entitled to equal (comparable) university places.

(3.2b) Equally intelligent people are equally entitled to university places.

Inserting 'equally' in the specification of the ground, whether or not accompanied by a similar insertion in the statement of the consequence, suggests that the ground admits of degrees and that the degree to which one has the property which is the ground determines the degree to which one is entitled to the benefit, i.e. the strength of one's right to it (3.2a, 3.2b) or, the amount or quality of the benefit to which one is entitled (3.1a, 3.1b).

(3.1) and (3.2) are the general forms of principles couched in comparative terms where the degree to which one possess the quality which is the ground determines the strength of one's entitlement or its extent. (1), when interpreted narrowly to exclude (3.1) and (3.2), is the general form of principles couched in classificatory terms where the property, possession of which is the ground for the right, cannot be possessed in different degrees or where it does not matter to one's right to what degree it is possessed. Surely egalitarians and non-egalitarians may both wish to endorse principles of both kinds. They do not provide the clue to the identity of principles of equality.

Slightly different are statements of the following form:

(4.1) All Fs are entitled to equal G.
(4.2) All Fs are equally entitled to G.

These often amount to a combination of a positive and a negative principle: F is a ground for a right to G and nothing overrides it. For example, 'Every human being is equally entitled to education' may imply that no quality but that of being human is relevant to a right to education. Every moral and every political theory which claims either that it is a complete theory, or even merely that it is complete regarding some issue, contains a principle of equality in this sense. That is, it contains a closure principle stating that nothing else counts for the justification of moral or political action, or for action over education, etc.

Closure principles of this kind cannot therefore lend an egalitarian character to a theory. Yet it is hard to avoid the suspicion that some authors mean little else when they claim that their theories are egalitarian than that they are complete. R. M. Dworkin regards political morality as resting on one fundamental right of everyone to equal concern and respect.[1] This seems to mean that everyone has a right to concern and respect and that there is nothing else which may count in justifying political decisions. It is nothing but a closure principle to a political theory putting forward a right to concern and respect, and not a right to equality, as the foundation of all political morality.

In various contexts 'equal' and its cognates contribute variously to the sense of the expressions in which they appear. Some further cases will be examined in Sections 4 and 5 below. But for the most part its contribution does not help to uncover the peculiar quality of principles of equality we are looking for. This is not really surprising. All principles are statements of general reasons. As such they apply equally to all those who meet their conditions of application.

[1] See, for example, *A Matter of Principle*, London, 1985, Part 3. It can be further argued that statements to the effect that all are entitled to respect or to equal treatment, and the like by their common interpretations mean little more than that every person should count. They are affirmations of humanism, but neither say nor imply anything concerning the rights or duties that people have, how they should behave or how others should treat them.

Generality implies equality of application to a class. Adding 'equally' to the statement of the conditions or consequences of a principle does not necessarily turn it into one which has more to do with equality.

2. Equality as Universal Entitlement

The above argument does not establish much. It certainly does not establish that principles which are traditionally thought of as egalitarian have no properties related to our idea of equality which are unique to them. All I have argued for is that if there is such a quality it cannot be identified through the exclusive study of the use of 'equal' and like terms in the formulation of principles. Indeed, many principles commonly thought of as egalitarian (e.g. everyone has a right to free medicine or to education) are normally stated using no such expressions at all.

Some philosophers have suggested that egalitarian principles are principles of universal entitlement and principles entailed by them. In virtue of their generality all principles apply equally to classes of people. By the same token, however, they distinguish between those who meet their conditions of application and those who do not. Not so universal principles. Those apply to all and thus establish the equality of all with respect to the normative consequences they stipulate. No one is excluded. Who must be the subjects of a principle if it is to be universal? One suggestion may be that 'all' should include everything and the content of the principle be allowed to determine whether it is vacuously fulfilled in some cases. 'All are entitled to have their interests respected' would apply vacuously to stones because they have no interests. This suggestion would, however, allow too many principles to count as egalitarian principles. According to it, for example, 'All are entitled to have their property respected' is an egalitarian principle applying vacuously to those who have none.

Another suggestion is that a principle is universal if it applies to all moral subjects. But this characterization also allows too many principles to count as egalitarian ones. It too, for example, allows the property-respecting principle above to qualify as an egalitarian principle. So we must strengthen it by stipulating that to be universal the conditions of application of the principle should be such that it applies non-vacuously to every moral subject (at least during a certain period of his life and if he wants it to apply to him). Not everyone has property or can acquire it if he wants to. This definition is meant to guarantee that principles which qualify under it are truly universal, that every moral agent does in fact qualify under them to benefits and is not excluded except with his consent.

Even so not all universal principles can be regarded as egalitarian for though they all guarantee some benefit to all they do not entitle all to the same benefits: to each according to his intelligence, strength or beauty are all universal principles, provided that they entitle moral subjects to something, however little. Bentham's utilitarianism rests on a universal principle which applies to all moral subjects and prescribes equal respect for them all in the sense of considering each pleasure as intrinsically valuable and each pain as intrinsically bad regardless of whose pleasure or pain they are, and depending only on their intensity and duration. The inegalitarian consequences of this theory are so well known that it has become a paradigm case of a moral outlook denying the intrinsic value of equality. Universality may be a necessary condition for a principle to count as an egalitarian one (I shall later show that it is not), but it is not a sufficient qualification for egalitarian status.

3. Principles of Equal Distribution in Conflict

Perhaps (5.1) represents the characteristic form of principles of equality:

(5.1) If there are n Fs each is entitled to 1/n of all the G.

Comparing (5.1) with (1), 'All Fs are entitled to G', two questions present themselves: (a) Is (5.1) a distinct kind of principle? (b) Do principles of this form deserve the title of egalitarian principles? It cannot be claimed that whereas (1) determines that each F is entitled to a share of G it lacks any distributive aspect and does not determine the relative or absolute size of his share. Remember that (1) (as well as (5.1)) are assumed to be perspicacious statements of moral and political principles. That is, it is not merely that Fs are entitled to G but also that they are so entitled because they are Fs. Being an F is the ground of the entitlement. The ground of an entitlement determines its nature. If all Fs have an entitlement to G based on the same ground they have the same entitlement. Hence, if their entitlement is completely satisfied or respected they will in fact be receiving an equal amount of G each. This argument assumes that being an F is not a matter of degree (one cannot be more or less an F) or that if it is, the degree to which one is an F does not affect one's entitlement to G. In other cases principles of type (3.1) and (3.2) apply and they too have their distributional implications as we saw in Section 1 above.

Naturally, since every principle has merely a prima-facie force, it can happen that because of the operation of some other principles the all-things-considered entitlement to G of the Fs is not equal. But this is true of principles of type (5.1) as much as of those of type (1).

The situation is transformed in cases of scarcity, i.e., where it is impossible to satisfy all the justified claims to the full. Such situations give rise to conflicts of reasons, and principles of type (5.1) provide more determinate guidance as to their resolution than principles of type (1). Imagine that there are 2 Fs and 4 units of G and that each F is entitled to 3 units (his right will be completely satisfied if he has 3 units). Each F can have one G without denying the other anything he is entitled to. But they compete for the other two units. Each has a right to both and neither has a better claim than the other. So far as (1) is concerned, giving both units to one F or one unit each are equally good ways of distributing the two. (5.1) requires giving one each. Like (1), (5.1) is a principle of entitlement but it is also a principle of conflict. Let us separate these two elements in (5.1) and formulate a principle which is just a principle of conflict resolution:

(5.2) In scarcity each who has equal entitlement is entitled to an equal share.

The smallest unit is one which makes a difference. It need not coincide with any natural limit of divisibility. (Normally it will be one shoe rather than half a shoe.) When two have a right to one unit, and one right carries more weight than the other, then the principle of entitlement itself settles the conflict in favour of the weightier right. Thus principles of entitlement themselves determine the resolution of many conflicts. Sometimes, however, they judge two rights to be of equal or incommensurate weight. In such a case they do not dictate a preference for equal distribution or for any other distribution. Several distributions are consistent with them.[1] It may of course be that, all things considered, several possible distributions are equally good, i.e. that there are no other reasons to prefer one of them to the others. Or it may be that one of the distributions is preferable because it conforms better with some other principle. Some such principles are specifically tie-breaking principles. They presuppose some other reason for action and come into play when other conflicting reasons fail to yield a preference. These are principles of conflict and (5.2) is one of them.

Principles of the (5.2) variety are not merely a type distinct from other principles of entitlement, they also have a better claim to be regarded as principles of equality. They differ from ordinary principles of entitlement of type (1) in that the scope of the entitlement they stipulate depends on the actual number of people who qualify under them to the entitlement. Type (1) principles are not similarly affected. If all are entitled to a house then every person is entitled to a house regardless of the number of people who also qualify for a house under the principle. Naturally the number of qualifiers affects one's chances of having one's rights satisfied, but it does not affect the right itself. This difference explains why (5.2) is a form of a principle of equality in a

[1] To illustrate the point consider the following artificial example. F_1 and F_2 have an equal right to G. Let us say that the weight of each right (i.e. the score if it is completely satisfied) is 10, and that any partial satisfaction scores proportionately. That is, giving one of them half his entitlement gets 5, etc. Suppose that we have just enough G to satisfy one of them completely. Giving all the G to either of them will score 10, giving one of them 1/10 of the G will score 1, and giving the rest to the other will score 9. Giving each half the G will score 5 each. Any distribution will result in a score of 10.

sense that does not apply to type (1) principles—be they universal or not. Under type (1) principles each person's right is independent of that of other people. He has it because the reason for the right applies to him. Other people may or may not have the same right. If they do that is because there is in their case too a reason (the same one) to give them a right to G. When several people qualify under a principle the principle generates equality of rights, but that is entirely fortuitous. A person's right would be the same were he the only one to hold a right under the principle.

Principles of the (5.2) type, on the other hand, are designed to achieve equality. Each of their subjects' rights is adjusted according to the total number of those who qualify to make sure that each has a right to an equal share of the benefit. This feature can be present in principles which do not confer rights. In all cases its presence shows that equality is not only their result but is also their purpose. They are designed to achieve equality between their subjects with respect to their subject matter. They are (one kind of) principles of equality.

4. Egalitarian Principles

We identified one kind of egalitarian principles, the egalitarian conflict resolution. They are principles of equality because it is their purpose to ensure equality within their sphere of application. Equality is part of the ground on which such principles are based. The mark of their egalitarian character is their sensitivity to the number of people who qualify under them in the determination of the extent of the right they confer. (As well as the fact that they stipulate *equal* distribution between the qualifiers. A principle may stipulate distribution in different proportions among qualifiers.) This fact is typical of egalitarian principles of conflict. Egalitarian principles in the sense of principles whose ground is equality need not be principles of conflict and there may be other indications of their nature. One important kind of egalitarian principles is exemplified by (6):

(6) All Fs who do not have G have a right to G if some Fs have G.

Such principles, unlike principles of equal distribution in conflict, are not sensitive to the number of qualifiers. Instead they are sensitive to existing inequalities among members of the relevant group with respect to the relevant benefit. Ordinary principles of entitlement are indifferent to the existing distribution of their benefits. If all have a right to food, accommodation, education, etc. then their rights are the same regardless of whether they have no food, education etc. or but little or enough, or whether some have more than others. If the entitlement is based on need then each is entitled just to his needs. Unless the actual distribution of the benefit affects the nature or the extent of the need for it (which it may do) it is irrelevant to the right. Actual distribution determines whose rights have been satisfied and whose have not. It determines only the incidence of unsatisfied rights and their strength.

The sensitivity of (6)-type principles to existing distributions is the crucial pointer to their character as egalitarian principles. Being an F by itself does not qualify one to G. It is the actually existing inequality of distribution which creates the entitlement. The entitlement is designed to eliminate a specific kind of existing inequality. Such principles reflect the view that it is wrong or unjust for some Fs to have G while others have not. Such inequalities must be remedied. This can be done in one of two ways: either by depriving those Fs who have G of it, or by giving G to all the other Fs. So long as some Fs have the benefit while others are denied it the principle applies and the rest of the Fs have a right to G. If their right is satisfied the inequality is eliminated.

From now on I will regard (6)-type principles as the paradigmatic (strictly) egalitarian principles. (5.2)-type principles can for all practical purposes be regarded as a special case of (6). For every (5.2)-type principle one can formulate a logically equivalent (6)-type principle. There are other types of egalitarian principles.[1] But they can all be analysed as so many variants of type (6).

[1] There can be other kinds of principles sharing the essential features of (6), e.g. All Fs who do not have G have a right to it if some non-Fs have it. But (6) will serve here to illustrate the essential point.

Principles of equality do not in themselves give those Fs who happen to have the benefit a right to it. The mere accident of having a benefit is rarely thought a sufficient ground of title to it. Even conservative principles (in the sense of 'conservation' principles) usually rely on the harm deprivation will cause or on the likelihood that a re-distribution will be for the worse. Instead of achieving equal-ity by giving the benefit to those who lack it one can equally (in so far as egalitarian principles are concerned) achieve it by denying the benefit to those who have it, thus preventing the right under the principle from coming into being.

Egalitarian principles often lead to waste. If there is not enough of the benefit to go round then whatever of it we have should be wasted rather than given to, or allowed to be retained by, some. It is true that the principles themselves do not require waste, but often the only way to avoid vio-lating them is to create or allow waste. Needless to say we are here concerned with the egalitarian principles them-selves. There may be other principles proscribing waste which may have to be balanced against the egalitarian prin-ciples. It is only the effect of other principles which can explain our preference for giving the benefit to those who lack it to denying it to those who have it. This preference cannot be explained on the basis of the egalitarian principles themselves. The crucial point is that the egalitarian prin-ciples always permit waste as a way of satisfying them, and in quite common circumstances require it as the only way to satisfy them. To the extent that waste is avoided because of other principles, these are (potentially) conflicting prin-ciples. They are, to a degree, anti-egalitarian principles.

5. Rhetorical Egalitarianism

Some principles of entitlement, such as (5.2) and (6), are designed to promote equality as such. I will refer to such principles as 'strictly egalitarian' when wishing to dis-tinguish between them and other principles commonly re-garded as egalitarian. Theories dominated by them are strictly egalitarian theories. Much of the egalitarian tradition in western thought is strictly egalitarian. Yet it cannot be denied that equality is invoked on other grounds as well. Nor is it surprising. All principles of entitlement generate equality (in some respect) as an incidental by-product since all who have equal qualification under them have an equal right. Furthermore, some principles are naturally expressed using 'equality' or related terms, without having anything to do with egalitarianism. All closure principles (type (2) principles) are of this kind as well as principles (type (3)) where the qualification and the benefit admit of degrees, like 'Equally able people have a right to equal remuneration'.

Arguments and claims invoking equality but not relying on strictly egalitarian principles are rhetorical. This is not meant in a derogatory sense. It is simply that they are not claims designed to promote equality but rather to promote the cause of those who qualify under independently valid principles. They invoke equality sometimes to facilitate exposition (as in type (3) principles) and often to gain from the good name that 'equality' has in our culture. It was mentioned above that principles of equal respect or concern, etc., often amount to little more than an assertion that all human beings are moral subjects, to an assertion of humanism. Such principles can be expressed with equal ease without invoking equality. They are not designed to increase equality but to encourage recognition that the well-being of all human beings counts. If their resort to fashionable egalitarian formulations makes them more attractive, so much the better. The price we pay is in intellectual confusion since their egalitarian formulation is less perspicacious, i.e. less revealing of their true grounds, than some non-egalitarian formulations of the same principles: 'Being human is in itself sufficient ground for respect' is a more perspicacious rendering of 'All humans are entitled to equal respect'.

Rhetorical invocation of equality is appropriate to a variety of contexts. A parent who gives medicine to the healthy child and not to the sick one, or who deceives one of his children and not the others, is treating them unequally. A person who keeps his promises to one person and breaks his promises to another is, likewise, treating them unequally. But in all these cases the wrong is the same as where a parent has only one child whom he deceives, or to whom he denies the medicine when he is sick, or when a person always breaks his promises to all. Accusing a person of unequal treatment in these and many other contexts is permissible if he behaves wrongly or badly towards some while behaving properly towards others. To accuse him of unequal treatment, however, is not to identify the nature of the wrong: it could be any wrong and it is definitely not the wrong of creating or perpetuating inequalities. As my examples show the same wrong can exist in situations involving no inequality.

In these and in many other contexts in which equality is invoked it functions contextually rather than normatively. It indicates features of the situation in which the wrong is perpetrated which have nothing to do with the reasons for it being a wrong, nothing to do with the kind of wrong it is. This is not to say that such invocations of equality do not have useful argumentative functions. They are sometimes used *ad hominem*. 'You seem to acknowledge the force of the reason in one case so why do you deny it in the other? They also sometimes indicate that something can be done to improve things. Here I have in mind not so much charges of unequal treatment as of inequality in the way things are. Poverty may be no worse in a society where it afflicts only some than in a society where all are poor. It is bad or regrettable in both to the same degree and for the same reasons. The charge of inequality which can be levelled against only one of these societies is used here rhetorically. The wrong is poverty and its attendant suffering and degradation, not the inequality. But the inequality is an indication that there may be resources which can be used to remedy the situation. It is relevant to an argument about what can be done, as well as to arguments about responsibility for not doing enough to reduce the poverty.

I hope that these comments—and they are not meant to be exhaustive of the rhetorical use of equality—vindicate my claim that I am using 'rhetorical' literally and not pejoratively. The important point is that in all those cases the offence is other than inequality and the action to be taken is not designed to achieve equality but some other good.

6. Strict Egalitarianism

The previous section illustrated some of the rhetorical uses of 'equality', namely those where despite appearances the wrong to be righted is not inequality, where the ground or reason for action is not the maximization of equality. It is crucial not to confuse the point of these comments with another which is often voiced in criticism of egalitarianism. It is said to be empty because whatever the situation all are equal in some respect or another, and the only question is in what respect should people be equal, and anyway any equality in some respects means inequality in others.[1] All this is here presupposed. The point of the last section is not that we all promote equality in some respect or other but rather that insofar as we rely on principles which are not strictly egalitarian we do not promote equality as a goal at all, it is merely a by-product.

The purpose of the present section is to illustrate how in its core the egalitarian tradition in western culture can be reasonably interpreted as based on the dominating position of strictly egalitarian principles. The aim is to show that (6)-type principles, and others which are egalitarian in the same sense and can be regarded as variants of (6), are omnipresent in the main line of egalitarian theories, at least on some reasonable interpretations of these theories. Consider first the following principle:

(A) All are entitled to equal welfare.

Normal assertions of this sentence are best interpreted as implicit endorsement of two principles combined:

(1c) All are entitled to the maximum welfare there can be.
(6a) If some people are better off than others then those who are less well off are entitled to the extra benefits necessary to bring them to the level of welfare enjoyed by the better off.

The combined operation of both principles is (a) to favour securing as much welfare all round as possible; (b) when new benefits are created they should be allocated to the worst off (they have the stronger claim being supported by (1c) and

---

[1] This fact is fatal to most common versions of the view that the essence of egalitarianism is that equality needs no justification, only inequalities require justification.

(6a) whereas the better off are supported by (1c) only); (c) when new benefits cannot be produced the principles can be satisfied by transferring benefits to the less well off.

If (6a) is taken always to override (1c) when they conflict then the principles also require:

(d) When not enough benefits can be created or transferred some should be taken from the better off and wasted.

(e) Production of new benefits should not be undertaken and a lower level of welfare all round should be preferred if this is necessary to prevent creating or preserving inequalities of welfare.

Both are required to prevent violation of (6a). Needless to say different supporters of (A) assign different weights to its component principles. I have given it its most strongly egalitarian construction, the one which prefers equality over all else. Often theorists weaken their commitment to equality by allowing a degree of inequality for the sake of a higher level of welfare for some, all or many.

Many egalitarian principles conform to the same pattern: they are a combination of an ordinary principle of entitlement (type (1)) and a (6)-type principle controlling its application and dominating it totally or only relatively. Thus:

(B) All are entitled to equal opportunities

is normally understood as a combination of

(1d) All are entitled to all the opportunities there can be;

and

(6b) If some have more opportunities than others then those who have fewer are entitled to additional opportunities to bring them to the level of those who have more.

Some may query my interpretation of (A) and (B) on the ground that 'All are entitled to maximum welfare (or opportunities)' is an aggregative, not a distributive, principle and is not part of (A) or (B) but separate from them. This is a mistake. It is true that 'All are entitled to maximum welfare', etc., trivially entails that as many benefits as possible should be produced. This, which it is appropriate to name the principle of unlimited growth, is an aggregative principle but it is entirely unintelligible unless one assumes some distributive principle such as 'It is good that each person shall have as many benefits as possible'. Otherwise one would be maximizing the existence of an item which may be of no benefit to anyone, and in any case it would be maximized not because it is of benefit to anyone. Furthermore, (A) and (B) do not merely assert that if opportunities or other benefits are to be had at all they should be had in equal measure. They also assert that people are entitled to have them.

It cannot be proved that strictly egalitarian principles are embedded in all the core egalitarian views. All one can do is to provide some illustrations of the way principles commonly regarded as egalitarian, when analysed, are seen to include strictly egalitarian principles. Here is a further example:

> (7) Inequality in the distribution of G to Fs is justified only if it benefits all Fs (or alternatively: only if it benefits the least advantaged F).

(7) is but a weak version of a strictly egalitarian principle of the (6) variety. By (6) it follows that if someone has a certain benefit this fact by itself entitles others to the benefit. Hence it follows that none should have it unless all can have it. That giving the benefit to one is instrumental in providing it to all is but one way of satisfying the strictly egalitarian principle. (7) is a weak egalitarian principle for it does not insist that the benefit to be given to the person who has produced benefits for others shall not be greater than theirs.

> (C) Inequality in the distribution of any benefit is justified only if it benefits all.

Here a (7)-type principle is generalized to range over all benefits, and its sponsors usually give it absolute dominance so that it cannot be overridden by any other moral principle. A theory thus dominated by (C) may be only weakly egalitarian—tolerating as it does many inequalities—but it is egalitarian in the strict sense. Supporters of (C) usually interpret it to mean:

(1c) All are entitled to the maximum welfare there can be;

and

(6a) If some people are better off than others then those others are entitled to the extra benefits necessary to bring them to the level of the better off;

and

(D) When (1c) and (6a) are in conflict (6a) is overridden (i.e. inequalities are tolerated) provided all benefit to a certain degree in consequence.

In other words (C) is usually read as (A), plus a rule for resolving conflicts between the components of (A).

Moral theories are strictly egalitarian if they are dominated by strictly egalitarian principles. A theory is dominated by a (group of) principle(s) if and only if the principles are never or rarely overridden by other considerations and, secondly, they apply to the main cases to which the theory applies. The brief discussion above illustrates the plausibility of interpreting the western egalitarian tradition, especially in the twentieth century, as characterized by the dominance of strict egalitarian principles. The argument can and should be pursued in a much more systematic way. Yet ultimately the conclusions may well prove inconclusive. When confronting the problems of poverty and of denial of rights and opportunities in all societies one is rarely forced to choose between a pure humanistic concern for people and the strictly egalitarian point of view. Rhetorical egalitarian slogans are used by all, and serve to mask deep differences in the sources of one's concern for social improvement. To these we must now turn.

7. The Presuppositions of Egalitarianism

We are concerned with egalitarian principles which dominate moral or political theories at their foundations. There is no doubt that strictly egalitarian principles can often be instrumentally justified. They may diminish the occurrence of envy and hostility. They may help the creation of a team

spirit, encourage a positive attitude to one's workplace, and
so on. The prospect of such benefits can easily be exaggerated. It is true that inability to discriminate between cases
makes it impossible to generate certain negative attitudes
towards some of them, just as it denies one the opportunity
of developing positive attitudes towards some of them.
There are attitudes, both positive (love, friendship, admiration, respect for achievement, compassion for special
handicaps, etc.) and negative (envy, estrangement, fear and
aggression towards the different, the more successful, doubts
about one's own abilities and worth, etc.), which are associated with the perception of difference, i.e. which are
based on comparing different cases in a way which evaluates
them by their difference from others. But to the extent
that some of these attitudes are deeply rooted in the human
psyche, and social conditions only channel their expression, egalitarian devices are a wild goose chase after the
unachievable.

Yet within limited areas there is a place for instrumentally
justified egalitarian principles. One important instrumental
justification is captured by the slogan that justice must not
only be done, but be seen to be done. Political institutions
answerable to the public are often constrained by this very
fact to avoid action for reasons which cannot be adequately
explained in public. This sometimes justifies abiding by
egalitarian principles of limited scope. Beyond that, such
principles have symbolic or expressive functions in small
and intimate groups (as when one refuses an advantage because one's friend cannot share it) or with respect to positions of symbolic significance (the President should not
enjoy luxuries when the country is suffering great deprivations, etc.).

The undoubted validity of subsidiary egalitarian principles of limited scope does not in itself help either to confirm
or to refute the validity of strictly egalitarian moralities or
political theories. One extreme position can be quickly dismissed. Morality (or political morality) is not based just on
one or more principles of equality. It must contain other
principles concerning the well-being of people and the degree of our responsibility towards others. One reason for this

was noted before. Egalitarian principles would be indifferent between achieving equality through taking away from those who have and giving to those who have not. The implausibility of such a view points to the existence of additional fundamental principles which at least establish a preference for the non-wasteful option. Most would agree that they will do more. They will override the egalitarian principles in at least some circumstances in order to avoid waste when equality cannot be achieved in any other way.

The thought of a moral or political theory consisting entirely of egalitarian principles has other absurd consequences. The only intrinsic goods and ills such principles admit of are relational ones. If they constitute the entire foundation of morality then the happiness of a person does not matter except if there are other happy people. Nor is there any reason to avoid harming or hurting a person except on the ground that there are others who are unharmed and unhurt. The absurdity of this view is seen by the fact that we only have reason to care about inequalities in the distributions of *goods* and *ills*, that is of what is of value or disvalue for independent reasons. There is no reason to care about inequalities in the distribution of grains of sand, unless there is some other reason to wish to have or to avoid sand.

Even in egalitarian theories, we may conclude, while egalitarian principles dominate the others they are also secondary to the others. Their role is to supplement and control the application of these other principles. An egalitarian moral theory, i.e. one dominated by fundamental strict egalitarian principles, includes principles of entitlement (which are not particularly egalitarian) and egalitarian principles which control their application. But not every principle of entitlement can be sensibly regulated by an egalitarian principle, only non-diminishing and insatiable principles can.

The distinctions between what I shall call satiable and insatiable, and between diminishing and non-diminishing principles are of great importance. Satiable principles are marked by one feature: the demands the principles impose can be completely met. When they are completely met then whatever may happen and whatever might have happened the principles cannot be, nor could they have been, satisfied to a higher degree. An insatiable principle is one which it is always possible in principle to satisfy to a higher degree. Satiable principles are invariably also diminishing principles, i.e. according to them the more G an F has the weaker becomes the reason to give him more G. This property makes them diminishing principles.

Compare the following:

(E) Everyone should have as much pleasure as they can enjoy.

and

(F) Everyone's needs should be met.

It is reasonable to assume that (F) is satiable and diminishing whereas (E) is neither. That is, the greater a person's needs the greater the reason to satisfy them; and it is possible to meet a person's needs completely. On the other hand, a person can always have more pleasure, or a more intense pleasure, than he actually has. There is no supreme pleasure in the literal sense. Whatever pleasure you care to think about can be improved upon.

Diminishing principles are a subclass of comparative principles of type (3) which were discussed in Section 1 above. Some comparative principles make the strength of the reason depend on the degree to which one possesses the qualifying property (the more intelligent one is the more reason there is to give one education). Of these some have the further property that their partial satisfaction reduces one's qualification. These are the diminishing principles: 'Feed the hungry' is an example. The hungrier a person is the greater the reason to feed him. But once fed he becomes less hungry, and there is less reason to give him more food. In this, as in most cases of diminishing principles, there is a degree of deprivation beyond which a person cannot be helped. A person may have reached a degree of starvation at which his life can no longer be saved. This sets the limit to the application of such principles. It does not refute them.

As was noted satiable principles are also diminishing ones, that is, they include built-in indications of the relative strength of the reasons they state. The further one is from the point of satiation the stronger is one's right to the benefit conferred by the principle. Those whose unmet need for housing is greater have a stronger claim to be provided with housing. I am not sure whether there is a logical connection between the defining features of satiable and diminishing principles. But in all principles which have a serious claim for consideration the two go together.

Insatiable principles may also have a similar built-in weight-discounting measure. Even if they are inexhaustible and conformity with them is a matter of degree and is never complete, it is possible that the greater the conformity achieved the weaker becomes the reason to try for greater conformity. We can therefore distinguish between diminishing and non-diminishing insatiable principles. Whether a principle is a diminishing or a non-diminishing one depends on its underlying rationale. Principles commonly known as aggregative principles with no distributive implications are insatiable non-diminishing principles. Consider the principle:

(G′) Maximize wealth.

It would be ureasonable to interpret it as being indifferent between possessed and unpossessed wealth, between wealth hoarded in forgotten mountain caves and wealth actually possessed by people. It should be interpreted as saying: 'Maximize wealth for people.' This interpretation suggests itself because the only reason for having wealth is that it benefits people. So the underlying principle is more perspicaciously stated as:

(G) It is good if each has as much wealth as can be secured.

Consider one person, say Abigail. Ideally, this principle says, she should have all the wealth there can be, and the more the better. If Andrew also gets a share of the wealth it is because the same is true of him. The reason for giving him wealth is as good as the reason for giving it to her. So this single principle generates a conflict of reasons. There is reason to give all the wealth to each person, but naturally only one can in principle have all the wealth there can be. It does not follow that Andrew and Abigail should divide all the wealth equally between them. The principle is indifferent as to the distribution of wealth between the two. Any distribution will satisfy the principle to the same degree.

One way of seeing that the situation involves a conflict between the reasons for letting Abigail have the wealth and letting Andrew have it is by imagining a situation in which the same amount of wealth exists but only one of them is there to enjoy it. In this case whoever is there should get all the wealth there is.[1] Therefore, if there is nothing wrong in Andrew not getting all when Abigail is there this is because the same principle is also a reason to let her have the wealth. The two reasons conflict, but the principle is a non-diminishing one and provides no guidance as to the way the conflict is to be resolved. Any distribution will satisfy it. This is what is meant by saying that it is a purely aggregative principle.

Non-diminishing principles have the unacceptable consequences we encountered in Section 3, and which led to the introduction of egalitarian conflict-resolving principles. Imagine that Abigail's wealth measures £10,000 whereas Andrew has only £1,000 to his name. New wealth valued at £100 becomes available. Who should have it? The wealth-maximising principle tells us that there is equal reason to give it to each of them. Being a non-diminishing principle it disregards the existing disparity of wealth between them. It is indifferent as to who should get the extra wealth and thus it tolerates extreme inequalities.

This is the context which led to the growing appeal of strict egalitarianism. We noted at the outset that it plays no role in Marx's or Engels's thought. In part it owes its appeal to utilitarianism. Classical utilitarianism is based on a non-diminishing insatiable principle: 'Maximize the net amount of pleasure.' It shares all the features of the wealth-maximizing principle. It too is based on the value of pleasure to people. Distribution problems arise because of the conflict between different people's claims to have all the pleasure there can be. On the resolution of such conflicts the principle is silent. Classical utilitarianism is tantamount to (E):

---

[1] The principle is insatiable for it is always possible to increase the wealth available. The very notion of wealth may require more than a few people to be present, but this can be disregarded for the purpose of this example.

(E) Everyone should have as much pleasure as they can enjoy.

The reaction against the distributional consequences of this principle accounts for much of the appeal of strict egalitarianism. Those convinced of the soundness of classical utilitarianism in other respects felt that its one main failing is its disregard of the independent value of equality of net pleasure, and sought to supplement it with an egalitarian principle controlling the application of the basic utilitarian principle.

I shall not inquire whether there is indeed a sound case for regulating the operation of non-diminishing principles by their coupling with egalitarian principles. Instead I will suggest, in the next section, that insatiable non-diminishing principles are invalid, and therefore cannot be used to found a case for egalitarianism. If sound this constitutes a refutation of egalitarianism on the presupposition that there is no case for relying on egalitarian principles in combination with diminishing principles.

Is the presupposition true? Diminishing principles give more guidance in cases of conflict. If one is concerned with the alleviation of hunger rather than with the accumulation of wealth, then if Bess and Bert are equally hungry it makes no difference who gets a slice of bread. But if Bess had it and there is a second slice to be had then Bert should have that one, for now his hunger is worse than hers. This means that diminishing principles lead to an approximately equal distribution in any case. But the equality they give rise to is a by-product of their concern with the alleviation of hunger, and not a reflection of concern for equality. Is there any way of establishing whether there is an egalitarian principle at work in such cases, the existence of which is merely masked by the fact that its results are the same as those of the underlying hunger-preventing principle? Arguments for the existence of the invisible are always suspect, as well as intractable. The only way I know of dealing with the problem is to ask: why should one care about inequality in such a case? Why should one care that one person is more hungry than another? If the answer is that one cares because his hunger is worse, then this is captured by the hunger principle and is not an independent concern for equality.

Pure concern for equality may be expected to be separate from the independent recognition of the value of the matter in question (hunger in our example). It may be expected to serve as an independent source of value. We noted above that that does not happen. Equality is said to matter where it affects what is valued for independent reasons; it matters only because what is to be distributed is valuable for independent reasons. Principles of equality always depend on other principles determining the value of the benefits which the egalitarian principles regulate. If those other principles are satiable and diminishing does equality have any role to play? What does it add to the satiable, diminishing principle on which it depends? It may be expected to affect the weight one would assign to different reasons, thus affecting the resulting distributions.

This is the way I described its appeal above. It turns out that egalitarian principles do so in the case of non-diminishing principles but not in the case of diminishing ones. Do they have any role in regulating the operation of the latter? Only if they identify a source of concern which, even though it does not affect the outcome, improves our understanding of why the outcome is the right one. There is no way of conclusively proving that egalitarian principles fail to identify such a concern. But wherever one turns it is revealed that what makes us care about various inequalities is not the inequality but the concern identified by the underlying principle. It is the hunger of the hungry, the need of the needy, the suffering of the ill, and so on. The fact that they are worse off in the relevant respect than their neighbours is relevant. But it is relevant not as an independent evil of inequality. Its relevance is in showing that their hunger is greater, their need more pressing, their suffering more hurtful, and therefore our concern for the hungry, the needy, the suffering, and not our concern for equality, makes us give them the priority.

8. The Rejection of Egalitarianism

The exploration of the foundations of egalitarianism revealed that egalitarian theories are based on non-diminishing, usually insatiable principles the operation of which is subjected to egalitarian constraints. Viewed in this way strict egalitarianism is seen as a response to a perceived failure of non-diminishing principles. It is an attempt to analyse and remedy their shortcomings. Paradoxically this makes the fate of egalitarianism bound up with the fate of the principles it set out to remedy. If, while being right in judging non-diminishing principles to be deficient, strict egalitarianism failed to identify correctly the source of their deficiency, then egalitarianism itself is threatened. This is the ground for its rejection to be explained in this section. The rejection of egalitarianism is based on the rejection of its presupposition. The ideals at the foundation of morality and politics are all diminishing and satiable principles.

All I can do to support this sweeping conclusion is to show that one popular candidate for the status of a fundamental principle is satiable and diminishing. In doing that we will set a pattern of argument which can be applied, or so I claim, to show that any plausible principles of entitlement of a fundamental nature are satiable and diminishing. Let us stay with the concepts central to the utilitarian tradition. I interpreted classical utilitarianism as based on the pursuit of net pleasure, but its own proponents preferred to talk of the pursuit of happiness. Classical utilitarians misinterpreted happiness when they understood it to consist in net pleasure, i.e. in a balance of pleasure over pain. This, it has often been pointed out, impoverishes the concept. It also misconstrues a diminishing satiable principle as a non-diminishing insatiable one. The pursuit of pleasure is insatiable, and non-diminishing. The pursuit of happiness is diminishing and satiable. It is true that in some contexts (e.g., 'When I heard the news I was so happy') 'happy' is used to indicate a happy experience. In that use the pursuit of happiness is, like the pursuit of pleasure, insatiable and non-diminishing. But then happiness is not the accumulation of many happy experiences. When happiness is understood as a quality of a person's life or of periods of his life, the pursuit of happiness is diminishing and satiable.

Our concern for the suffering, the unhappy, the unfulfilled

is greater the greater their suffering or unhappiness. We have no reason to stop and ask whether the gap between this unhappy person and the rest of humanity is great to justify or to quantify our concern for him. His suffering or un-happiness matter in themselves, and the greater they are the more they matter. There may be many other equally unhappy, or unfulfilled, or suffering. It does not diminish the reason for helping that person, except inasmuch as it indicates that we have equal reason to be concerned with others.

The fact that the pursuit of happiness is a diminishing principle is in part explained by the satiability of happiness. Having had a happy childhood does not assure one of a happy adolescence. But a happy childhood, even if happy through the pleasures experienced during it only, can be perfectly happy. It can be so happy that adding pleasures to it would not make it happier.

Notice that the statement 'Since the ice-cream you had on the 17th of August last year gave you pleasure at the time, it follows that you would have been less happy last year had you not have it', is, barring special circumstances attending the consumption of that ice-cream, ludicrous. The same is true if you replace the pleasure of having an ice-cream cone with seeing Laurence Olivier in *Richard the Third*, and so on. There are pleasurable experiences which affect one's total happiness, but there are many more which do not. This is true of people who are not perfectly happy as well as of those who are.

In itself the point is compatible with insatiability, for it is compatible with saying that even though many pleasurable experiences are below the threshold which affects happiness, their accumulation does. Many more ice-creams on hot sum-mer days and good plays on cool winter nights may make one's life happier even if one more does not. If one's hap-piness is not complete this is true. But one can be perfectly happy in a way that no addition of pleasure, though welcome in itself, will increase or improve it. Be that as it may, the relative indifference of degrees of happiness to quantities of pleasure shows that there is a considerable indeterminacy in comparisons of happiness. Once a certain level of happiness is reached it becomes senseless to judge Carol, a mother suffering from the pains and pleasures common to that state, as well as pursuing an active and moderately successful career in medical research, either happier or less happy than Caroline, a dedicated career businesswoman, who is manager of a local branch of a bank, and has not yet abandoned hope of further promotion. The two are incommensurable.

Incommensurability will be discussed at some length later. It is relevant to our discussion for satiability does not mean that there is a point which is reached by all who get to the point of satiation (in the alleviation of hunger, the satisfaction of needs, or in happiness, etc.) so that they are all at precisely the same level in the relevant respect. All it implies is that there is no possibility of improving the position they reached. That condition is satisfied by complete incommensurability of happiness once a certain level of it is reached. While the remarks above do not prove the complete breakdown of comparability, they make it plausible to think that happiness is satiable.

One reason for failing to notice that happiness is satiable is the impression that if it were then there would be no reason for giving the perfectly happy person further pleasure or rewarding experiences. But that does not follow. Happines often involves capacity for pleasure, a sense of fun and an ability to appreciate rewarding experiences. A perfectly happy person has ambitions, pursuits, hobbies, etc. Like everyone else, he aspires to success in what he does. But success does not make him happier than he was, nor does failure make him unhappy, though disastrous failure does.

The satiability of the principle helps to explain why the pursuit of happiness is a diminishing principle. It indicates that the happier a person's life is the nearer it is to a state beyond which it cannot improve, at least not in happiness. That helps explain, we vaguely feel, why there is more reason to benefit those who are less happy than those who are more happy. In being further away from perfect happiness their lack is greater.

For those who accept the greatest happiness of the greatest number as the only fundamental moral principle, its diminishing character is all they need in order to reject egalitarianism. To the extent that other diminishing principles lie at the foundation of morality they equally leave no room for egalitarianism. It is hard to think of a fundamental principle which is non-diminishing.

10

Liberty and Rights

It is time to pull all the threads together and draw some general conclusions regarding the relationship between freedom and rights. It may appear that the two preceding chapters were myth-exploding, clarifying discussions. They exposed the fallacies of the adherence to equality as a fundamental value, and the inadequacies of rights as a foundation for morality or for political morality. In their course, however, much was established which leads to a clearer view of the role of rights in the protection of freedom. The first section of this chapter sums up and further defends the doubts whether the protection of liberty rests primarily on respect for individual rights. Section 2 proceeds to argue that the liberal tradition is not unequivocally individualistic, and that some of the typically liberal rights depend for their value on the existence of a certain public culture, which their protection serves to defend and promote. The third section presents a sketch of an alternative picture of the justification of providing entrenched constitutional protection for the typical liberal rights. According to this picture their role is not in articulating fundamental moral or political principles, nor in the protection of individualistic personal interests of absolute weight. It is to maintain and protect the fundamental moral and political culture of a community through specific institutional arrangements or political conventions.

1. Is Liberty Based on Rights?

Not surprisingly, few believe in the simple view that the doctrine of liberty consists in the justification of a right to liberty. Such a right, if it exists, cannot capture our concern for liberty because it is indiscriminate. It protects equally the liberty to eat green ice-creams and to religious worship.[1] Two avenues suggest themselves. The one proceeds to claim that political liberty consists in rights to certain basic liberties, such as freedom of expression, of political participation, of occupational choice, the freedom to establish a family by mutual agreement with a partner of one's choice, etc. The other seeks to establish an ideal of the free person. That ideal, often referred to as the ideal of the autonomous person, gives substance to the notion of worthwhile freedom. It allows discrimination between valuable and worthless or even detrimental freedoms, according to their contribution to the ideal of personal autonomy. It can then be asserted that political freedom is a right to personal autonomy.

The second avenue has the advantage of preserving the unity of the ideal of political freedom. If this ideal consists in a right to personal autonomy it may be manifested in so many derivative rights to basic liberties. They can then be seen to be united by a common concern for personal autonomy, which explains their pre-eminent status and determines what does and what does not belong with them. The first avenue, while possibly capable of justifying its list of basic liberties, is liable to provide disparate justifications for the varying liberties. The list of basic liberties is a matter of contention, but any list which is faithful to the Western liberal tradition will include widely diverse rights such as the right to be elected to parliament and the right to become a parent. Are both, when understood as core rights rather than as derived from another more fundamental right, motivated by a common core, a concern for liberty understood in a unitary, coherent way?

Further doubts about the cogency of the first avenue will emerge in the course of this chapter. In the main this book pursues the second course, but only half way. Its last part is dedicated to the political consequences of a doctrine of liberty based on an ideal of personal autonomy. But that ideal is not protected by a right to autonomy. The argument to that effect was set out in Chapter Eight. It rests on the fact

[1] Cf. the analogous point in the discussion of a presumption of liberty in chapter 1. The point is essentially that made by R. M. Dworkin in ch. 9 of *Taking Rights Seriously*.

that autonomy is possible only if various collective goods are available. The opportunity to form a family of one kind or another, to forge friendships, to pursue many of the skills, professions and occupations, to enjoy fiction, poetry, and the arts, to engage in many of the common leisure activities: these and others require an appropriate common culture to make them possible and valuable.

A right to autonomy can be had only if the interest of the right-holder justifies holding members of the society at large to be duty-bound to him to provide him with the social environment necessary to give him a chance to have an autonomous life. Assuming that the interest of one person cannot justify holding so many to be subject to potentially burdensome duties, regarding such fundamental aspects of their lives, it follows that there is no right to personal autonomy. Personal autonomy may be a moral ideal to be pursued by, among others, political action. It serves to justify and to reinforce various derivative rights which defend and promote limited aspects of personal autonomy. But in itself, in its full generality, it transcends what any individual has a right to. Put it another way: a person may be denied the chance to have an autonomous life, through the working of social institutions and by individual action, without any of his rights being overridden or violated.

One might say that this argument shows the force of the analysis of rights in Chapter Seven, on which it is based. It vindicates the observation made there that the analysis of moral concepts is itself a move in the argument about substantive moral conclusions. Can this strength turn into a weakness? Can one reject the analysis of rights precisely because it leads to such substantive moral conclusions, and replace it with another which will legitimate the claim that there is a right to autonomy? Such a move might be supported by the claim that my analysis is hanging by a thread. It requires that a right be justified by the service it does to the interest of the right-holder but it allows that the value placed on that interest may derive from its usefulness to others.

Contrast the case of the right of journalists to protect their sources and the right of self-determination. The journalist's interest is served by the right. But it would not deserve our respect, it would not have the weight it has, but for the fact that through protecting his interest one serves the interest of all in the free circulation of information which is of public interest. A Frenchman, on the other hand, does not have a right to the self-determination of the French nation even though it serves his interest. The fact that it serves his interest does not help it serve the interests of all the other Frenchmen. The right serves their interests severally, not by promoting the interests of their neighbours. Each Frenchman would benefit from the fact that the French enjoy the right even if none of the others were to benefit from it.

Is not that distinction too thin to bear the weight of such important conclusions? If it is admitted that a right may exist because it serves the interests of people other than the right-holder does it matter if their interests are served independently of or through the service that respect for the right renders to the interest of the right-holder? Fine as the distinction may be there is no way round it. Consider the consequences of dispensing with it. It will mean, for example, that each member of a nation has a right to the self-determination of the nation. It is his personal right. It will also mean that as each of us has an interest in an environment in which promises are kept and people do not deceive each other, I, as well as everyone else, have a right that you shall keep your promises and that you shall not deceive other people. Any wrong (of the appropriate kind) done to any one of us offends us all—as one might put it in a romantic moment. The fact that we do not hold people to have such rights shows that only if their own interest is sufficient to hold others bound by duties do they have such a right.

The interest of John in the actions which promote Mary's well-being is relevant if it is served through the fact that Mary's interest is thereby served. But it does not establish a separate right of John to such actions unless it is itself sufficient to justify the duty. Otherwise it becomes part of the case for Mary's right. If an interest of John, which is itself insufficient to establish any rights of his, is served by the actions which protect Mary's interests in a way which is independent of the benefit such acts bring her then it cannot be aggregated with Mary's interest to show that John too has a right.

To dispense with the condition that rights are based on the interests of the right-holder itself may appear at first as a heightening of moral sensitivity, or as an extension of fellow feeling. But it turns out to be a runaway inflation which debases the currency. It is not to be confused with the conceptually respectable, though morally dubious, claim that my interest that you shall not deceive your mother is indeed so great as to justify by itself, regardless of any other interests your promise-keeping will serve, holding you bound to do so. Were this true it would have established that I have such a right.

It is a concomitant of the view that analysing the terms of moral discourse is itself part of the moral argument, a taking of position in the moral debate, that the use and meaning of these terms change with changes in the climate of opinion. This happened to 'rights' as used in moral, legal and political writings. The analysis of Chapter Seven assigns the term a much wider sense than that allowed by most theorists some thirty or forty years ago.[1] The more liberal use of 'rights' notwithstanding, the concept preserves a special role in the moral and political spectrum. My analysis explains its uniqueness as a combination of two elements. First, rights have a special force which is expressed by the fact that they are grounds of duties, which are peremptory reasons for action. Second, rights express what is owed to the right-holder in virtue of the respect due to to his interest (albeit sometimes because of the benefits which may accrue to others if his interest is respected). If we waive the last condition we lose the distinctiveness of rights. The very point which those who favour the more extensive use of rights wish to make by insisting that individuals have a right to autonomy is thereby lost.

The special importance of rights is emphasized by moral

[1] Cf. D. D. Raphael (ed.), *Political Theory and the Rights of Man*, London, 1967; H. L. A. Hart 'Definition and Theory in Jurisprudence', *Essays in Jurisprudence*, and contrast his more recent statement on the subject in 'Legal Rights', in *Essays on Bentham*.

individualists who regard them as a protective shield against moral demands in the name of the well-being of others.[1] The idea of a right to personal autonomy, for example, is attractive partly because such a right establishes a limit to what can be demanded of an individual in the name of collective goals and of communal welfare. But if rights do not represent the special force of the interest of the right-holder then they cease to capture the idea of a protective shield against the claim of the well-being of others. The well-being of the community is then also a matter of rights, rights to a decent standard of living, to a fulfilling and enriching employment, to communal amenities, to the conservation of the environment, and so on. There is nothing wrong with any of these ideals. The point I am making is that if 'rights' comes to acquire such a weak meaning then it loses its ability to mark matters which are of special concern because of their importance to the right-holder, and which give the right-holder's interest special weight when it conflicts with other interests of other members of the community.

The argument of Chapter Eight did not rest on the definition of rights offered in the previous chapter. It rests on the belief, to be defended in the last part of the book, that personal autonomy depends on the persistence of collective goods, and therefore that the notion of an inherent general conflict between individual freedom and the needs of others is illusory. Though an individual's freedom, understood as personal autonomy, sometimes conflicts with the interests of others, it also depends on those interests and can be obtained only through collective goods which do not benefit anyone unless they benefit everyone. This fact, rather than any definition, undermines the individualist emphasis on the importance of rights.

2. The Collective Aspect of Liberal Rights

The liberal tradition was always ambivalent on the role and justification of fundamental rights. Some of the greatest liberal philosophers, such as J. S. Mill, whose analysis of

---

[1] The popularity of moral theories emphasizing the importance of rights led to attempts to assimilate them into a non-individualist perspective. See, e.g., Tom Campbell, *The Left and Rights*, London, 1983, and cf. S. Lukes' criticism of Marx's failure to do justice to rights in *Marxism and Morality*, Oxford, 1985.

rights is insightful and proved very influential, did not assign them a foundational role in their moral or political theory. Others, like Locke, did. It is true that rights loom large in some liberal writings, and when they do they are commonly pressed into service in the interest of an individualistic moral outlook. Liberal practical politics, however, is much more ambiguous. Many rights were advocated and fought for in the name of individual freedom. But this was done against a social background which secured collective goods without which those individual rights would not have served their avowed purpose. Unfortunately the existence of these collective goods was such a natural background that its contribution to securing the very ends which were supposed to be served by the rights was obscured, and all too often went unnoticed.

Religious toleration may have been defended in the name of individual conscience, but it served communal peace. More to my point, inasmuch as religion is and was a social institution embracing a community, its practices, rituals and common worship, the right to free religious worship, which stood at the cradle of liberalism, is in practice a right of communities to pursue their style of life or aspects of it, as well as a right of individuals to belong to respected communities. Thus while religious freedom was usually conceived of in terms of the interest of individuals, that interest and the ability to serve it rested in practice on the secure existence of a public good: the existence of religious communities within which people pursued the freedom that the right guaranteed them. Without the public good the right would not have had the significance it did have. Furthermore, the existence of the right to religious freedom served in fact to protect the public good. I venture to surmise that but for that it would not have acquired the importance that it did.

It is possible to argue that religious freedom deserves our respect and protection regardless of the accidental fact that in human history religions have been social institutions. My only point is that that would have been, despite the identity of its formal definition, a different right with vastly different implications. I for one find it difficult to know what importance it would have deserved in a world so different from our own. In any case the right which is so intimately tied to the early growth of liberal ideals was bound up with the existence of a public culture in which religion was a social institution. In interpreting the history of liberalism this fact is of great importance.

The right of conscientious objection, when recognized, was traditionally associated with religious objection to military service, and itself served to protect members of religious communities, as well as the communities of which they were members. Membership in a socially recognized community served as a test of sincerity. People enjoyed the right only if they shared the style of life of a known social group. Most commonly they enjoyed it only if they participated in the life of the group. It was unlikely that people would change their whole way of life just in order to avoid service. I am not expressing here any view regarding the rights and wrongs of extending the right to members of a recognized religion only. My purpose is merely to point to the non-individualistic elements in the right as traditionally recognized. Any genuinely individualistic conception of the right to conscientious objection encounters difficulties of establishing the genuineness of the objection which the traditionally communitarian approach to the right escaped.[1]

The struggle for the right of freedom of contract, and more generally for the freedom of all economic activity, was conducted against a background which set limits to the market which were taken for granted by almost all liberals. Citizenship was not up for sale. One's right to life could not be disposed of for money. Sexual services were not exchangeable against appointments to the civil service. Furthermore, not only was freedom of contract conceived to apply within vaguely defined bounds, its own value presupposed the existence of collective goods. There was great concern to establish the conditions which were deemed necessary for the optimal operation of a free market. As has

---

[1] In referring to the rights benefiting and protecting communities I do not mean only communities of people living in close proximity. Those living far apart may form a single community, known by its common and distinguishing traditions, practices and beliefs.

been often remarked, the free market is a normative social institution consisting not only in individual rights, but also in a network of practices and conventions relating to the conduct of negotiations, the communication of information, the avoidance of actions in restraint of trade, etc. The existence of that institution is a collective good. It benefits all who are subject to it and none of them can be excluded. The right to economic freedom, or the right to freedom of contract, does not exist in opposition to collective goods. Far from its purpose being to curtail the pursuit of collective goods, it presupposes and depends for its value on the existence of at least one collective good: the free market.

Much the same is true of other civil rights, be they traditional ones like freedom of speech or more modern ones like the right against discrimination. As was noted above, some aspects of freedom of speech cannot be explained at all except as protecting collective goods, i.e., preserving the character of the community as an open society. The freedom of the press illustrates the point. In most liberal democracies the press enjoys privileges not extended to ordinary individuals. Those include protection against action for libel or breach of privacy, access to information, priority in access to the courts or to Parliamentary sessions, special governmental briefings, and so on. They are sometimes enshrined in law, sometimes left to conventions. The justification of the special rights and privileges of the press are in its service to the community at large. The interest of individuals in living in an open society is not confined to those who desire to benefit from it as producers or consumers of information or opinion. It extends to all who live in that society, for they benefit from the participation of others in the free exchange of information and opinion.

What is true of freedom of the press is also true of many other aspects of freedom of speech. The precise boundaries of freedom of speech are notoriously controversial, but its core is and always was the protection of political speech and of the free exchange of information which is of public interest. It benefits all those who are subject to that political system. Thus while political theorists often highlight the protection for the individual dissident which it provides, in practice its primary role has been to provide a collective good, to protect the democratic character of the society.

It is significant that most rights against discrimination deal with discrimination on religious, ethnic and racial grounds, all of which are associated with membership of groups with their own distinctive culture. (They also include sexual discrimination, to which my comments do not apply.) Admitting that decisions adversely affecting individuals because of their race, religion or ethnic identity are very often wrong and unjust, it remains a puzzle which individualistic liberals find difficulty in solving why there is not a similar right against discrimination on grounds of height, one's sense of humour, etc. Decisions adversely affecting individuals because they are too tall, or lack a sense of humour, are as likely to be misguided and unjust as those based on religion or race. In part the answer does rest on pragmatic considerations. Race and religion are more common grounds of unjust discrimination. But at least in part the answer lies elsewhere. Discrimination on grounds of religion, nationality or race affects its victim in a more fundamental way. It distorts their ability to feel pride in membership in groups identification with which is an important element in their life.

It is true that these rights against discrimination are as helpful to those who wish to escape their ethnic, religious or racial identity as to those who identify with the group to which they belong. But my point is not that the right is meant to perpetuate the separateness of the group. The important point is that the right is meant to foster a public culture which enables people to take pride in their identity as members of such groups. Yet again we find that fundamental moral rights cannot be conceived as essentially in competition with collective goods. On examination either they are found to be an element in the protection of certain collective goods, or their value is found to depend on the existence of certain collective goods. To be sure, fundamental rights are often in competition with other collective goods, just as they may conflict with other rights. The aim of this section was not to suggest that such conflicts do not arise, nor to argue that when they do rights should always give way. The conclusion of this section is the more modest one: rights are not to be understood as inherently independent of collective goods, nor as essentially opposed to them. On the contrary, they both depend on and serve collective goods. Hence there is no general rule giving either rights or collective goods priority in cases of conflict.

3. An Alternative View of Constitutional Rights

The rejection of the view that individual liberty rests primarily on the existence of fundamental moral rights, while out of sympathy with an important individualistic strand in the liberal tradition, is not inherently at odds with that tradition which incorporates other strands which assign a humbler role to rights. Moreover, the insistence on the importance of civil rights is consistent with the rejection of moral individualism. The emerging view of morality is not one which denies rights a significant role. On the contrary, it is one in which rights play a central role as important ingredients in a mosaic of value-relations whose significance and implications cannot be spelled out except by reference to rights.

This way of viewing the role of rights does not assign them a privileged status in the moral firmament. It is inconsistent with any general thesis of the priority of rights over other considerations. Does it leave any room for the privileged position of civil rights in many constitutions? Or does it compel one to reject root and branch the doctrine of the constitutional protection of fundamental rights, and of their privileged position in international law? Every moral theory worthy of serious consideration allows for property and consensual rights, for rights of personal security and probably many more. These may well be fundamental rights in the sense that they are part of the deepest level of moral thought. It does not follow, of course, that they are either inalienable or of absolute or near absolute weight. The examination of such personal moral rights cannot and need not be pursued here. They are not specifically liberal rights. All humanist moralities tend to recognize them in one form or another. Our interest is in two other questions. First, are there specifically liberal human rights which also belong to the foundations of morality? Second, is there a fundamental moral case for the entrenchment of any rights, including the personal moral rights such as the right to personal security, in a rigid constitution, i.e. one which is immune from change in the normal political process?

The answer to the first of these questions was outlined above. It was there suggested that rights such as freedom of expression, association and assembly, freedom of the press, and of religion, the right to privacy and the right against discrimination rest on the importance of the interest of the right-holder which they serve. It was further suggested that the importance we attribute to the protection of those interests results from their service to the promotion and protection of a certain public culture. That culture is in turn valued for its contribution to the well-being of members of the community generally, and not only of the right-holders. The importance of liberal rights is in their service to the public good. That answer will be further reinforced through an examination of the second question to which we must now proceed. Why should the typically liberal rights, or any moral rights, be regarded as demanding special constitutional protection?

One view regards these rights as marking the boundary between the private and the public, between matters which are subject to political regulation and those which are, that is should be, beyond the reach of politics. The latter, designated as matters protected by constitutional rights, are left to individual decision and no political action may interfere with the sovereignty of individuals regarding them.[1] I doubt the cogency of this view, at least when applied to all constitutional rights. The doubt applies in particular to those rights, of which freedom of expression, privacy, freedom of religion, and the right against racial discrimination are examples, where one reason for affording special protection to individual interests is that thereby one also protects a collective good, an aspect of a public culture. The fact that

---

[1] The popularity of this picture is attested by the fact that it is shared by writers of such diverse views as R. Nozick (in *Anarchy, State and Utopia*) and R. M. Dworkin (in ch. 9 of *Taking Rights Seriously*).

those rights protect collective goods and are assigned their special importance because they do so is reason to think that they concern matters which are a legitimate subject of political action. The provision of public goods is a paradigm case of what governments are there for. This does not mean that they ought to be subjected to much or to any governmental intervention. It means that the reasons governing the degree of political intervention or of political restraint are contingent ones, depending on the conditions of particular societies at particular times.

If so, in what sense are they constitutional rights? Why should they be accorded a different status from any other moral rights, or from moral rights which merit legal protection? One may approach this question from the institutional angle. In general no questions concerning the appropriate institutions to implement moral and political principles are considered in this book. But given the widespread assumption that the special status of constitutional rights must be explained by their special moral force, it is worthwhile pointing out that there are well-known alternative arguments in favour of entrenched constitutional rights, namely arguments based on institutional considerations. In particular constitutional rights are devices for effecting a division of power between various branches of government.

The most visible fact about constitutional rights is that they are subjected to special institutional treatment. Matters which affect them are taken away from the exclusive control of ordinary legislative and administrative processes and subjected to the jurisdiction of the courts (or of special constitutional courts). The effect is that the current extent of, say, the legal right of free expression is a combined result of both legislation and judicial action, in circumstances in which the judiciary is acknowledged to have a right to modify the effect of legislative and governmental actions.

I should make it clear that the above remarks do not refer to the existence of written, entrenched bills of rights. They apply wherever there is a legal tradition which views the defence of civil rights as a special charge of the judiciary. This is the case in, for example, the United Kingdom, despite the absence of a written constitution or an entrenched bill of rights. It would be rash to assume that in countries with an entrenched constitution and a doctrine of judicial constitutional review the courts are necessarily more powerful or more active in controlling either the administration or the legislature than in countries lacking a written constitution. The English docrine of parliamentary sovereignty sometimes blinds people to the extent to which, through their powers to interpret Acts of Parliament, the courts can and not all that infrequently do exercise *de facto* judicial review over parliamentary legislation. Interpretative presumptions, such as a presumption that parliament does not intend to derogate from people's civil rights, are as powerful a tool in the hand of a judiciary keen on fulfilling a role in the protection of human rights as an entrenched bill of rights.[1] Much depends on the actual traditions and practices of the judiciary. The existence of a formal constitution may contribute to the formation and to the political defence of those traditions. But this depends on its use rather than on its existence.

At least some constitutional rights are primarily means of formal or informal institutional protection of collective goods. They protect these collective goods inasmuch as damage to them is caused by harming the interests of identifiable individuals. This explains why these aspects of the protection of collective goods are a matter of individual rights. Where harming an individual seriously jeopardizes the maintenance of a public good that harm is also a cause of a harm to the community. Therefore, there is in such cases an adequate instrumental justification for holding others to be subject to duties to refrain from such harm. It also explains why their protection can be entrusted to the hands of the judiciary. Courts are particularly suitable for dealing with disputes in which an individual has a special standing, and which relate to a limited, self-contained set of facts. They

---

[1] Presumptions, it will be remembered from ch. 1, are at home in institutional contexts. One of their roles is to justify decisions which will not be justified by the canons of reasons. The brief discussion that follows concentrates on the way the constitution is used to divert power to the courts. No comment is made on the existence of special provisions for amending the constitution, by parliamentary or other action. Their existence only serves to reinforce my conclusions.

are not particularly apt at dealing with issues determination of which depends on the way different alternatives affect whole communities over long periods.[1] Determining liability for an accident, rather than devising a pension scheme for the old, is their natural area of operation.

Why should one use constitutional rights as a means of dividing political power between the different organs of government? Why should they be used as part of a checks and balances mechanism? Many countries have found it expedient to provide different procedures for deciding different classes of issues. A common example is the creation of special procedures for changing the balance of powers between the states and the federal government in a federal state. Federal states distinguish between ordinary political action, which takes place within the existing framework of political institutions, and political action which changes that very framework. They tend to endorse special procedures for the second, procedures which have a built-in conservative bias in them, that is a bias which make constitutional changes more difficult to effect than ordinary political action.

In a similar way one may distinguish in every country between the basic political culture of that country, and its more detailed and transient arrangements. The basic political culture usually includes both ways of deciding political issues (such as a federal system) and some substantive principles concerning the rights and duties of governments and of individuals. The distinction between basic framework and transient regulation is one of degree, and is not susceptible to precise description. It does not coincide with any distinction of issues. Some aspects of the decision-making procedure belong to the transient part of the political arrangements of the country, others to its basic framework, etc. The distinction is one of stability and importance in the eyes of those who participate in the political process.

In the nature of things features of the basic political culture are less liable to change than its transient arrangements.

---

[1] None of the above is meant to deny that in certain countries during some periods courts are encouraged, or give themselves the courage to deal with the type of question they are not best suited to deal with.

It is sometimes advisable, and it is usually perceived to be advisable, to protect the stability of the basic political culture by institutional arrangements which isolate it to some extent from the pressures of day to day politics. This can be done by a two-chamber legislature with appropriate guidelines specifying the protection of the fundamentals of the political culture as part of the role of the second chamber. It can be done by the adoption of entrenched constitutions, or of presumptions of interpretation of legislative and administrative action which authorize the courts to modify their provisions inasmuch as they may affect basic aspects of the political culture. Constitutional rights contribute to this process. They are part of the institutional protection of the basic political culture of a society.

It is a commonplace of political life that entrenchment of a right in a special legislative or constitutional measure does not remove it from political strife. It merely leads to a greater role for the courts in determining the matter. The courts themselves are sensitive to political factors, and their decisions are based on political considerations. The slogan that the courts are, or should be, above politics is not necessarily wrong. It merely refers to a narrow conception of politics. The courts are, or at least they should be, above the rough and tumble of everyday political pressures. They should be relatively immune to passing fashions. In constitutional matters they may succeed in representing a lasting general consensus, even at times when prevailing trends disguise its existence from the majority of the public, and even in the face of a government whose reforming zeal blinds it to the need to preserve the fabric of the political culture. To the extent that the courts are able to act in these ways they fulfil an invaluable function in assuring society of the measure of continuity which is so essential to its well-being.

Continuity is not to be confused with stagnation. The special protection which the courts give to the constitution is not meant to stop it from changing. It is merely designed to make it change in response to different social processes from those which determine ordinary political change. In the wider sense of the political, the sense in which it encompasses all decisions by authoritative state organs, constitutional issues are, and should be, subject to change through the political process. The fact that the constitution affects the existence of the basic political culture, which is— if a good at all[1]—a collective good, is a prima facie reason for holding it to be a proper subject for political action, even though sometimes the only right political action is to take no action and to leave a certain area free from political interference.

The argument for the entrenchment of liberal constitutional rights derives therefore from several sources. First, there is the interest of the right-holder which the right serves. If its protection were not a valid reason for action then we would not be speaking of rights in these cases. But the interest of the right-holder in itself, in the case of many of the rights which were used as examples above, is insufficient to justify that degree of protection. It gets it because it is instrumentally useful to the preservation of a certain political culture, to the protection of various public or even collective goods. Finally, in various countries, due to their circumstances and to other features of their political institutions, the best way to ensure that people act as they should, i.e. that they show due respect for these interests, is by a division of labour which restricts the right of most people and of some political institutions to judge for themselves what precise duties those interests justify. The best way to secure the proper recognition for those interests is to confine the decision about their proper weight to a few specialist institutions, whose composition and mode of operation make them most suitable for the task.

This last point is, of course, common to the justification of all institutional rights. That is, it applies to the explanation of all legal rights, rights under the rules of voluntary associations, etc. All institutional rights are subject to the mediation of an authority whose task it is, in accordance with the dependance thesis, so to act that people will conform to reasons which apply to them better than if they were to

---

[1] In considering the position sketched in this section it is important to remember that its subject is the proper justification of the entrenchment of fundamental rights in societies where the legal system does give them proper weight. Nothing is here implied as to the proper response to a mildly or grossly unjust constitution.

decide independently of the authority's intervention. In those instances in which the authority attempts to secure behaviour which respects moral rights by giving them, say, legal recognition, the authoritative intervention puts a distance between the right and the interest it serves. One has a legal right because the authority declared that one has an interest which justifies holding others to be subject to duties. One has that legal right even if the authorities' declaration is mistaken. But the authority is a legitimate one, and the legal rights it decreed are (morally) valid, only if recognizing its decree is likely to improve one's conformity with right reason.

This gap between the interests justifying institutional rights and the institutional rights they justify, may have been misperceived by some. It may explain why some people were attracted to the view that rights, while serving interests, have force over and above that of the interests they serve. They thought that the weight of rights is greater. In fact rights should have precisely the force which the interest has. But being institutionalized one is not at liberty, assuming that the institution is based on legitimate authority, to act on one's own judgment as to the proper weight of the interest where it differs from that of the authority, for if one did one would be wrong more often than if one did not.

Fundamental liberal rights deserve special protection and recognition: that is, they are valid moral rights deserving legal-institutional protection over and above the normal legal protection, because they express values which should form a part of morally worthy political cultures; and they deserve such protection to the extent that the circumstances of the country concerned make it appropriate to create special procedures for the regulation of matters covered by those rights, for the preservation and the gradual development of these aspects of the political culture.[1]

[1] Our concern was with the rights the defence of which is one of the distinguishing marks of a liberal political morality. In part the same arguments can be extended to lay the foundations of an account of where and when it is right to give special constitutional protection to personal rights. Up to a point these differ from the typical liberal rights in being more individualistic. They are justified primarily by the protection they give to the interest of the right-holder which is intrinsically valuable, and not, or not to the same degree as are liberal rights, by their service to

This conclusion is not a theory of human rights. It is merely a statement of the perspective which should dominate such a theory. Is this the exclusive way in which fundamental rights should be understood? Every legal institution once it exists may be justifiably used on occasion for purposes which do not justify its creation or perpetuation. The practice of entrenching certain rights may sometimes be legitimately used to achieve incidental goals which do not belong the the justification of the practice itself. The hard question is whether the very existence of the practice of according preferred position to certain rights can be justified on additional grounds, independent of the considerations so far canvassed. One possible source of disquiet about the way the argument of this book has been developed so far is that it seems imbued with a strong consequentialist spirit and inimical to the view that there are absolute rights and duties based on non-consequentialist considerations. To the examination of this issue we must now turn.

---

a public culture. But they too are to be entrenched constitutional rights only in countries where the institutions likely to deal with the greatest success with the protection of these rights are the courts. That is, even in the case of these fundamental moral rights, their constitutional prominence, where justified, is due only in part to their moral importance. To a very large extent it is a matter of political expediency.

IV

SOCIETY AND VALUE

Several attempts to develop a doctrine of political freedom have been examined and found wanting. Their examination yielded a variety of leads, concerning, among others, coercion and our sensitivity to it, the nature of rights, the value of some collective goods, and the relation between wide and narrow morality. The last part of this book will pull them all together and draw some conclusions concerning the value of political freedom, and its proper role in our society. The view to be explained there is a familiar one. It is a perfectionist view of freedom, for it regards personal political freedom as an aspect of the good life. It is a view of freedom deriving from the value of personal autonomy and from value-pluralism. Freedom is valuable because it is, and to the extent that it is, a concomitant of the ideal of autonomous persons creating their own lives through progressive choices from a multiplicity of valuable options. The perception of freedom as constituted by the ideals of personal autonomy and value-pluralism is familiar and used to be very popular. It would not qualify as an interpretation of liberalism if it were not. But in recent times trends in moral philosophy which, to those who come under their influence, make it all but incomprehensible, have gathered force and extended their popularity. Theories of instrumental rationality and of consequentialist morality impose a regimented and impoverished range of concepts which are supposed to be the only ones used in practical thought. To be able to appreciate the traditional strand of liberal thought which rests on pluralism and autonomy it is necessary to shake free of the shackles imposed by those theories. This task belongs to Part Four. It raises some basic issues concerning practical rationality. In particular it provide a description of some aspects of personal well-being, aiming to show that practical thought is either non-consequentialist or consequentialist in an attenuated sense only, and that it depends on a balance between personal choice and social forms.

11
Consequentialism: an Introduction

There are two reasons for engaging in an extended discussion of the merits and failings of consequentialism. Utilitarianism, the only extensively explored consequentialist morality, has come to be identified in some circles with the growth of state intervention, and its ever increasing encroachment on individual freedom. It is true that utilitarianism stood at the cradle of English liberalism. But it is an abstract moral theory which may well, given different social circumstances, lead to anti-liberal conclusions. If so, and if utilitarianism is sound, then liberalism stands condemned as unsuitable for our day and age. Several liberal writers base their trust in liberalism on the rejection of utilitarianism and of consequentialist moralities in general. In particular, the rejection of consequentialism is sometimes associated with a rights-based liberalism. Thus the exploration of the controversy about the credentials of consequentialism is directly relevant to the project of this book.

Beyond this lies the fact that consequentialism or its rejection has far-reaching consequences for any moral or political argument. The implications of the conclusions to be reached here concerning the limits of consequentialism will reverberate through the arguments of the last part of the book.

There is, therefore, ample reason to confront the problem. The confrontation leads, in the next two chapters, to an examination of some aspects of our conception of value generally. Morality is thought to be concerned with the advancement of the well-being of individuals. The defence of pluralism and autonomy calls for an explanation of our notion of individual well-being. Only through examining these issues can we see clearly the degree to which consequentialism provides an adequate framework for morality. The present chapter does little more than set the scene.

1. Consequentialism: Some Common Themes

To reject consequentialism is not to claim that the consequences of an action are not among the reasons for or against its performance. It means that some valid reasons for action are not susceptible to a consequentialist interpretation, and therefore cannot be accommodated within a consequentialist theory of practical reason. This is, however, not as straightforward a matter as it seems. There is no one single idea which forms the core of consequentialism, none that is universally agreed upon to be an inescapable part of the consequentialist outlook. Talk of a rejection or a refutation of consequentialism has, therefore, to be understood in a qualified sense. All that those who criticise consequentialism can usually legitimately claim is the whittling away of several of the doctrines generally associated with it. I will list seven of the more common features associated with consequentialism. Some may wish to add to the list. Others may prefer to analyse consequentialism's leading ideas into different building blocks. Most consequentialists accept fewer than the listed features, but they disagree as to which to omit and which to add. The list is, however, a reasonably comprehensive enumeration of the ideas which were historically associated with consequentialism. Furthermore, this way of identifying the leading ideas helps with the argument that follows.

1. *Strict Consequentialism*: The only reasons for or against the performance of any action are the consequences that its performance or non-performance will or may have. The weight of reasons for and against an action is a function of the value of its consequences.

2. *Comparability*: All reasons are comparable in strength (or weight or importance—these terms will be used interchangeably). They and any of their combinations can be ranked by weight.

3. *Agent-Neutrality*: The evaluation of all possible consequences is agent-neutral. That is, the comparable value of any two states of affairs is the same from the point of view of all agents.

4. *Maximization*: An action is right if and only if its per-

formance maximizes value (or expected value), i.e. if and only if it has at least as high an (expected) value as any of the alternative actions open to the agent.

5. *Transparency*: Intrinsic values are transparent. That is, (i) the features of a state of affairs which make it intrinsically valuable are features which make it good for some agent or other, and (ii) a feature is intrinsically good only if, under normal conditions, the person (or other animal) for whom it is good is content with its presence and prefers it to its absence.

6. *Negative Responsibility I*: The foreseen consequences of an action and its intended consequences are equally relevant to its evaluation.

7. *Negative Responsibility II*: In evaluating an action the consequences of the agent's (possible and actual) omissions count for just as much as the consequences of his (possible and actual) commissions.

The last three features may be thought not to belong to a characterization of consequentialism. They concern not the structure of reasoning about what is best but the character of value and the conditions of responsibility. But their general acceptance by many consequentialists and the fact that many do not distinguish between them and other consequentialist features makes it useful to include them here.

Reflection on the term 'consequentialism' may make one feel that it is to be identified with the first of our features only. Most consequentialists agree, however, in abandoning this condition. They have sound reasons for doing so. The first condition leads to the denial that any action or omission can be intrinsically good or bad, except inasmuch as it is the consequence of some other action. Such a view cannot be sustained. Attempting to defend it leads to distorting our conception of agency. Is not destroying humanity intrinsically bad? To allow that it is and yet continue to hold to the first feature requires a denial that destroying humanity is a (possible) action. Only things like pressing buttons, or perhaps only moving muscles, or even only willing or forming intentions, will be allowed to count as possible actions. It is unlikely that, quite apart from the violence thus done to our understanding of agency, these desperate devices will succeed in saving the first condition. Even if one does not believe that only a good will is good in itself, one may accept that sometimes forming good intentions is intrinsically valuable.

These and similar problems induced many to abandon the first feature on our list by adopting a simple fiction, that of regarding the fact or the state of affairs that one performed an action as a consequence of one's performing it. This enabled some philosophers to maintain the appearance of a belief that only consequences count, while avoiding its substance. On occasion this fostered unnecessary verbal disagreement. Others endorsed reformulations of the first condition which achieve the same effect by different verbal means. But by and large it matters not whether one abandons the first condition in favour of a reformulation which allows that the intrinsic value of actions can be a reason for their performance or keeps it with the help of the simple fiction.

Another feature abandoned by many, though by no means all, consequentialists is maximization as described in the fourth principle above. Let me refer to it as naive maximization. The move away from it has been in two mutually compatible directions. One is towards the introduction of an independent distributive component, so that maximizing value, while a good in itself, which has to be pursued, other things being equal, has to compete with aims such as equalizing the distribution of value, improving the lot of the worse off, etc. Distributional principles can, however, be interpreted as concerned with the protection and promotion of certain relational states. They are then taken to presuppose the intrinsic goodness of relational states of equality of wealth, status, or whatever one is concerned to see distributed in the preferred pattern. Thus understood they are compatible with naive consequentialism. The second direction away from (naive) maximization is towards indirect maximization. The rightness of action is judged not by its expected value, but by its conformity to a rule of action which is itself judged as being the best of a range of alternatives determined by their ability effectively to serve as practical guides to action, and judged by whether faithful adherence to them, or whether the likely adherence to them, will achieve the best maximizing (and distributive) results.

More radically, it has been argued that sometimes, or even always, while one is permitted to act in the maximizing way, it is also permissible not to do so. Instead one may act in ways which promote a subclass of all desirable states of affairs, or which meet certain threshold conditions (they avoid worsening the situation, etc.).[1]

Many of those who declare themselves to have rejected consequentialism have concentrated primarily on criticizing agent-neutrality. Others have focused mainly on the doctrine of negative responsibility. The focus of the discussion in the next two chapters will be different. They concentrate on value-transparency and on comparability. It seems to me that many of the concerns which led people to embrace agent-relative principles are in fact fully met within an agent-neutral morality once it is realized how widespread is the breakdown of comparability, and how misconceived is the transparency thesis. I shall not, however, explore either the consequences of abandoning these principles for agent-neutrality nor their implications, which seem to be significant, for the debate about negative responsibility. To set the stage for the discussion of commensurability and value-transparency we will now turn to a review of some of the more powerful arguments which have been advanced against consequentialism.

2. Separateness of Persons: Trade Offs

Rawls was, to the best of my knowledge, the first to raise the objection that utilitarianism disregards the separateness of persons.[2] The aspect of utilitarianism he seems to object to concerns its balancing feature, i.e. its willingness to take from one person and give to another, depending on who will derive the greater net benefit from the allocation. This shows

---

[1] Both my 'Permission and Supererogation', *American Journal of Philosophy*, 12 (1975), 161, and S. Scheffler, *The Rejection of Consequentialism*, Oxford, 1983, support the case for permissions not to maximize in appropriate circumstances. M. Slote's *Common Sense Morality and Consequentialism*, London, 1985, advocates a form of threshold maximization.

[2] In *A Theory of Justice*, pp. 27, 29.

that the objection is not specifically against utilitarianism but is directed against a class of consequentialist theories, those which subscribe to the comparability and agent-neutrality assumptions, and do not add an independent distributive principle.

Yet it is not clear in what sense comparability and agent-neutrality disregard the separateness of persons. It is true that they require balancing the good of one person against that of another. But if the result is that the good of one person is sacrificed, it is sacrificed for the good of another. It is said that this equates a trade-off by giving a good to one person at the cost of depriving the same person of another good (e.g. he will get a refrigerator, but will lose his TV), with taking a good from one person in order to give it to another (taking one person's TV in order to give a refrigerator to another), without noticing that in the second case we trade across the boundaries between people. These boundaries, so the claim goes, drop out of the consequentialist reckoning.

To this the consequentialist can reply with justice that the fact that trade-offs are between persons is taken into account. The presentation of the two examples above made them appear misleadingly similar, and disguised a big difference between them. The value of, say, a refrigerator to a person depends on his general situation. In comparing the value of a refrigerator and of a TV to one person one takes his situation into account. Hence the comparison is mindful of the fact that either way he will have something. When judging the value of the goods to two people one determines the value of each of the goods to each person in light of that person's general situation. In their case it is a choice between something and nothing, and this would affect the consequences of the reallocation to them. So the fact that the trade-off is across personal boundaries is reflected in the way that the value of the goods is judged in the second example. It is calculated from the perspective of two people and not one, as in the first.

This reply seems to meet Rawls' principal objection. Some will feel that it is nevertheless inadequate. They will admit that this reply shows a formal difference between intrapersonal and inter-personal trade-offs which is captured by consequentialist reckoning. Yet they will contend that this difference does not account for all our intuitions about the difference between such trade-offs. The difficulty is that one can assess such intuitions only in the light of some theoretical account of their justification and of their place in practical thought. No such account is provided by Rawls. Perhaps his whole theory of justice is such an acount. But it is too remotely and indirectly related to the intuitions to serve as an explanation of their sources or as an assessment of their role or validity.

Nozick, however, seems to have additional reasons to support the charge that consequentialists disregard the separateness of persons. He invokes the 'Kantian principle that individuals are ends and not merely means; they may not be sacrificed or used for the achieving of other ends without their consent.'[1] This appears to block the possibility of imposing sacrifices on one person for the benefit of any other. A person may voluntarily make sacrifices for the sake of others. He may do so because he believes that that is morally the best thing to do. And he may be right in so thinking. Even so, no one is entitled to compel him to make the sacrifice. To do that is to treat him as a means to the end of benefiting another. That one may never (barring major catastrophes) do.

Why not? One may say that the Kantian principle is itself the answer. Nozick goes one step further in elucidating the scope of the principle. In particular, he indicates that it applies to autonomous creatures in the following sense: 'A person's shaping his life in accordance with some overall plan is his way of giving meaning to his life; only a person with the capacity to so shape his life can have or strive for meaningful life.'[2] Nozick indicates that it is to such persons that the Kantian principle applies, and that it applies to them because they are such persons.

The difficulty with Nozick's position is that any sacrifices such persons are compelled to make are in favour of other persons who are equally striving for a meaningful life. That

[1] *Anarchy, State and Utopia*, p. 31.
[2] Ibid., p. 50.

is presumably why it may be right, indeed obligatory, for an agent to sacrifice some of his interests, even his life, for the sake of another. But is he not then treating himself as a means for the end of protecting or promoting the interests of others? If Julia may so treat herself why cannot an outsider, say Rachel, treat her in the same way for the same reason? Why is Rachel not allowed to make Julia do what is morally right, on the ground that this would be to sacrifice Julia's interests for the sake of another, and thus to treat her as a means only, given that Julia herself is allowed, is indeed required, to treat herself as a means for the sake of others? Nozick's answer is of course that Rachel may get Julia to act against her (Julia's) own interest, so long as she gets Julia to behave in this way voluntarily. It is permissible, for example, to induce in a person desires which can only be satisfied by doing the morally decent thing. These can be induced by exploiting a person's envy of his successful neighbours, his weakness for sex, etc. But coercion, deceit and similar means are excluded as violating his rights. We do not find in this book, nor in any of Nozick's writings, much of an explanation as to why some means of getting people to act are allowed, while others are not.

The Kantian tradition suggests an answer which does not appear to be endorsed by Nozick. Perhaps the only way one is allowed to get another to perform or to avoid an action is by convincing him that that is the right way to act. According to this line of thought, the position of the agent himself is identical to that of the outsider. An agent who does what he ought for the wrong reasons is abusing himself, and is not obeying the moral law. At the same time inducing desires in another by exploiting a person's sexual appetite, or his envy of his neighbours, is wrong, even though it does not coerce him. One difficulty with such a position is that it provides immoral people with an immunity from outside restraint. It may be right to punish a murderer, for, according to Kantian principles, he deserves to be punished. But one cannot restrain him from murder, if he fails to be convinced of the evil character of his acts or intentions.

A simple way round that difficulty is to hold that the person who commits a moral wrong, or violates his moral duty, has thereby forfeited his rights, or some of his rights, against outside interference. This view radically transforms the whole picture. The limitations imposed on the way persons may be treated are now understood to be conditional on compliance with the moral law (or with parts of it). If so then the disagreement we identified between the consequentialist and the Kantian is largely dissolved. People should make sacrifices for the sake of others. If they do not do so voluntarily they are in the wrong, and the sacrifices may be forced on them. Neither will regard any moral violation, however petty, as justifying forfeiture of all the offender's rights. Neither will regard the offender as preserving all his rights intact whatever the offence. They may disagree about the details. But there is nothing in the consequentialist creed of the one nor in its rejection by the other to lead to such a disagreement.

Even though Nozick does not pursue the Kantian-inspired line of thought explained above, his view has to cope with the same charge of providing the would-be murderer with an immunity. His solution is rather like the simple solution just mentioned. He declares the murderer to have forfeited some of his rights through his actual or intended violation. The same applies to theft, trespass, etc. Nozick's theory does not entail, as it appears to do in the first quotation from him above, that a person cannot be compelled to sacrifice his interest in favour of that of another. He may be so compelled if that second person has a right that the first shall serve his interest, and therefore, the first has a duty to do so. It is the substantive theory of the moral responsibility of one person to another that determines how much of a person's interest we may compel him to sacrifice for the benefit of others. Nozick said enough to make it clear that he does not think that extant consequentialist theories contain an adequate account of responsibility to others. But he gave us little reason for sharing his judgment.

The argument so far did not, nor was it meant to, establish that there are no non-consequentialist implications to whatever valid content there is in the notion of separateness of persons. It merely showed that the Kantian maxim as invoked by Nozick does not reveal such implications, for it means no more than that one may not be compelled to sacrifice one's interest for the sake of another unless one has a moral duty to do so.

Perhaps we should make a fresh start by considering some of the sources for moral disquiet with consequentialism. One is disquiet about the comparability assumption on the ground that it leads to absurdities such as the approval of the murder of an innocent healthy person in order to obtain ice-cream. The value of one cone of ice-cream to one person will not justify murder, nor would the value of two cones for two people. But the more people there are the more value is secured by getting one cone for each of them. Consequentialist logic, so the argument goes, is committed to the view that at some point it will be justifiable, indeed required, to commit murder if that is the only way to get the ice-cream. The only escape route is to assign the life of an innocent person absolute weight, so that it will never be outweighed by any number of refreshing cones of ice-cream. Since similar chains of reasoning will lead one to assign infinite weight to grievous bodily harm, rape, the betrayal of friends and of one's country (if it is morally decent), and to much else, this escape route is equally unpalatable (to the consequentialist). It denies the possibility of trade-offs between any of those. The result is equivalent to abandoning consequentialism in all but name.

To overcome such objections it has been suggested[1] that benefits and harms should be classified into levels of urgency, so that each one belonging to one level shall be lexically prior to any combination of lower level benefits, while being subject to trade-offs against benefits belonging to its own level, and lexically inferior to higher level benefits. The suc-

---

[1] T. Scanlon, 'Preference and Urgency'. The outlandish character of the ice-cream example opens it to the charge that it is not a proper test of our moral intuitions. These, it may be claimed, can be relied upon only when they concern real life situations, which mine does not. Whatever the fate of this objection it can be by-passed by relying on real life examples. Consider the following simplified case adapted from one by Sen: a gang of ten bashers plans to beat up Ali. Donna can warn him, but is aware that though his pain will be five time as great as the satisfaction each of them will derive from the attack, given that there are ten bashers and one victim their total satisfaction is greater than his pain. Side effects can be evenly balanced in many cases. See Sen, 'Rights and Agency', *Philosophy & Public Affairs*, 11 (1982), 8–9.

cess of this device is in its ability to cope with all the difficulties of the sort mentioned, without generating new paradoxes of its own. It has been persuasively argued that that cannot be done, i.e. that many of our reasonable weighting decisions defy such a systematization.[1] Such arguments are, of course, merely persuasive. Greater imagination may defeat them. To strengthen their force we need an explanation of why our judgments defy such structuring, an explanation which will also validate those judgments, and remove the suspicion that they are merely the fruits of ignorance, irrationality, or moral insensitivity.

These doubts undermine belief in the availability of a correct consequentialist moral strategy, be it a maximizing one or not. They may also weaken one's faith in the comparability assumption which is presupposed by the search for a general moral strategy. In itself the undermining of the comparability assumption does little to illuminate the moral intuition about the separability of persons. The connection is through the content of those judgments which resist explanation consistent with comparability. They concern moral problems which, in their common manifestations both in peoples' actual experiences and in their imaginative thinking (shaped by history and fiction), concern balancing the interests of one person against another, rather than, as they may in principle, involve balancing different interests of a single person. They are cases of betraying a friend to make money, or to help the right party win the election in order to improve the lot of many; cases of victimizing an innocent person for the common good, i.e. for the welfare of many, and similar cases. It is the character of the intuitively picked examples which suggests that a correct explanation of the breakdown of comparability is connected with the features which led to the as yet obscure unease about the separability of persons.

3. Separateness of Persons: Agent-Neutrality

The challenge to comparability may explain one source of dissatisfaction with consequentialism, namely its handling

---

[1] J. Griffin, 'Are There Incommensurable Values', *Phil. & Public Affairs*, 7 (1977), 39.

of the balancing of people's interests. It is this source of discontent which encouraged a revival of interest in fundamental moral rights. Rights are grounds for duties on others, and duties are not just ordinary reasons to be aggregated and balanced in the ordinary way. Since rights are the grounds of duties, and not merely of ordinary reasons for action, they have peremptory force. This may suggest that they can do justice to the separability of persons in ways which consequentialism overlooks. We saw reason to doubt whether rights are the whole answer. They seem neither sufficient nor necessary for the purpose. But an analysis of the relations between separability and rights has to wait for an account of the intuitions about separability.

Whatever our ultimate verdict, it is evident that at least Nozick's reason for erecting rights as side-constraints derives from additional sources besides the doubts about comparability, if indeed these worried him at all.[1] The other intuition at work challenges agent-neutrality. Consider the moral prohibition on deceit. It is normally taken to mean that regarding each person, that person should not deceive. But this is an agent-relative interpretation. The consequentialist interpretation is that each person should so act that the number of deceits is as small as possible. The difference is made clear in a case in which Debbie is asked for information by Ellis, knowing that it will then be used to deceive two other people, each on a different occasion (and not necessarily by Ellis or through his fault). If the agent-relative interpretation is right Debbie should not deceive. She should, if there is no other way out, give away the correct information. On the agent-neutral interpretation this would be the wrong course of action. Debbie can, by deceiving, make it so that there will be only one deception rather than two. So that is what she should do. Our ordinary morality, so the argument goes, is agent-relative.

Before we go any further we should ward off one possible misunderstanding. One may say that the difference between those who believe that I should not deceive even if this is the only way to avoid two deceptions, and those who say that I should, is not of an agent-neutral v. an agent-relative

---

[1] The same is true of C. Fried's approach in *Right and Wrong*, Cambridge Mass,. 1978.

interpretation of the prohibition of deceit. Rather it has to do with whether one is concerned about the the person deceived, or about the act of deceiving. We followed Parfit[1] in distinguishing between action and outcome reasons. Action reasons are those where the value (be it instrumental or intrinsic) is in the performance of an action, i.e. where there is intrinsic value in certain agents performing actions of a certain kind. Outcome reasons are those where the value of the action is in its outcome or consequences (where neither the action itself nor the fact that it leads the same or other agents to perform some actions counts as an outcome).

It is tempting to think that if the reason for not deceiving is an outcome reason, that is if its purpose is to protect the potential victims of deception, then one should, other things being equal, deceive one person to save two from deception. If the reason is an action-reason then one should not, as that is one's way of avoiding the act of deceiving. A little reflection shows, however, that that is not what is at stake. The example is not one in which Ellis, or whoever is the would-be deceiver, will try to deceive the two victims whatever Debbie does. It is of a case where if deceived he will not even try to deceive them. (One may deceive him out of the opportunity to deceive.) Therefore those who take the reason to be an action reason would still think that Debbie should deceive, because that way that action reason is complied with to a higher degree. That way there will only be one act of deception, rather than two. If one thinks that Debbie should not deceive that is because one denies agent neutrality.[2]

Nozick's rights are side constraints, i.e. they are agent-relative reasons of absolute weight. Their absolute weight makes them appear counter-intuitive.[3] It seems safe to say that not all rights are side constraints, and perhaps, as was

---

[1] Cf. Parfit's *Reasons and Persons*, Oxford 1984, e.g. p. 104. These distinctions were introduced in ch. 6.

[2] Another unsuccessful attempt to avoid this conclusion is through relying on principles of responsibility which deny one's responsibility for consequences of one's action which are mediated in some ways by other people's choices. There is no doubt that in such cases the choosers are responsible. But does that absolve one of responsibility? Is not one responsible for a murder if one acted as a weapons consultant with the intention of bringing about the murder?

[3] See, e.g., Sen's construction of the Donna and Ali example in 'Rights and Agency', op. cit.

suggested in Chapter Seven, none are. But even so Nozick's theory attests to a widespread sense of unease with consequentialism. It not only reflects a sense of unease with the assumption of comparability. His side-constraint view of rights also demonstrates the allure of an agent-relative approach.

Nagel classifies agent-relative reasons into two categories, deontological restraints and personal goals, commitments, projects or relationships. Nozick's concern was with deontological restraints.[1] But one has to agree that people's ordinary practical judgment appears to display agent-relativity in connection with their own and other people's projects and relationships. That is, people normally agree that their own projects and relationships and those of other people are, when judged 'objectively', of comparable value. Yet they commonly maintain that sometimes one is entitled to pursue one's own goals, rather than promote the cause of other people's goals, even when doing the latter will have better consequences from an 'impartial' or 'objective' point of view.

One may well claim that these features of human judgment are so universal and inerradicable as to require no justification. But they are in need of an explanation. Furthermore, one needs a rebuttal of the possible consequentialist attempt to show that common judgment only appears, but in reality is not, inconsistent with agent neutrality. First, there is the familiar claim that since people are better at looking after their own projects than after those of others, it is best to inculcate in them a preference for their own projects and relationships. This indirect consequentialist strategy, (i.e. one which rejects direct maximization as described in our fourth listed feature) will admit ground-level agent-relativity, and justify it by higher level agent-neutral considerations, which make allowances for human nature.

This claim seems, however, to miss the point. It is precisely because people already care more about their own

[1] Though Nozick's ethical teachings in *Philosophical Explanations*, Oxford, 1981, cf. esp. pp. 294–300, suggest that he may agree with Nagel in holding projects and relationships to be equally agent-relative. For T. Nagel's classification see 'The Limits of Objectivity' in *The Tanner Lectures on Human Values*, vol. i, ed. S. McMurrin, Cambridge 1980, p. 120.

projects and relationships that they are better at looking after them. That is the feature to be explained. Why is it that human practical thought appears to be inescapably agent-relative? If it is indeed inevitable is it a manifestation of human imperfection? (Cannot one have the personal goal of promoting the goals of all without fear or favour? Will that too be agent-relative? Perhaps not, but it is no accident that that cannot be the main goal of more than a few.)

Secondly, and more seriously, the consequentialist will point out that all action reasons can only be satisfied by the person whose reasons they are. That is, if I have a reason to earn a living, my reason may be an outcome reason, a reason which is satisfied if I have enough for my needs. You can have that as your reason as well, that is you may have a reason to see to it that I have enough for my needs. But my reason may be, is often thought to be, an action reason. It may be a reason for me to earn a living by my own efforts. If so it is a reason which you cannot satisfy. All you can do is to help put me in a situation in which my efforts may bear fruit. Of course the reason may exclude even that possibility. My son has a reason to prepare his homework himself. This, much to my frustration, means not only that he himself should prepare it, but that he should do so unaided. Still, even here there are some forms of help (e.g. providing him with a quiet room) which are allowed.

The point the consequentialist is making is that some of what appears agent-relative is not. The appearance is simply a reflection of the fact that some reasons are action reasons. They should be given their agent-neutral weight by all. But since only some people can pursue them directly (i.e. actually satisfy them and not merely help others to do so), whereas outcome reasons can be directly pursued by all (in the normal case at any rate), those who can pursue them directly should, according to agent-neutral reasoning, dedicate a substantial proportion of their time to their pursuit. Projects, commitments and personal relations are (the source of) action reasons. That is why what appears agent-relative is agent-neutral, or at least is consistent with agent-neutrality.

Just as the earlier argument against Nozick's invocation of the Kantian maxim did not show that the moral views he is advocating are compatible with consequentialism, so the argument against Nagel's interpretation of personal projects and relationships is not meant to show that he is mistaken in claiming that they are irreconcilable with an agent-neutral view of practical reason. In both cases it seems likely that the authors do endorse non-consequentialist views, that they uphold the validity of moral views not susceptible to a consequentialist interpretation. Both my arguments rely on a similar strategy. They show that some of the constraints advocated by Nozick, and much of the partiality to one's own projects and relationships relied upon by Nagel, appear to be reconcilable with consequentialism. These authors did not point to a reason for thinking that all these cases are inconsistent with a consequentialist interpretation. This suggests that it is possible that where Nagel and Nozick endorse non-consequentialist moral views they are not backed by the intuitions which make their current statement of their position so appealing.

To illustrate this possibility consider the following passage by Nagel, in which he supports and illustrates the distinction between the agent-relative reason an agent has because he chooses to pursue a certain goal, and other agent-neutral reasons which are related to it.

Someone's having the freedom and the means in a general way to lead his life is not a good that can be appreciated only through the point of view of the particular sets of concerns and projects he has formed. It is a quite general good, like the goods of health, food, physical comfort, and life itself, and if agent-neutral value is going to be admitted at all, it will naturally attach to this. . . . This is not equivalent to assigning agent-neutral value to each person getting whatever he wants.[1]

Indeed not. But the reference to enabling people to develop projects and relationships, by providing them with the general means for doing so, suggests that the disagreement may be narrower than Nagel makes it appear. Many of the more important goals people adopt are important to them, at least in part, because they are things for *them* to do and to achieve. We want to be good parents, not only to have heal-

---

[1] Nagel, ibid., p. 124.

thy, well developed children. We want to cultivate friendships, not merely to be spontaneously loved and cherished
by others through no deeds of our own. We want to have
successful careers, not merely to have lots of money and a
reputation of success. We want to enjoy the games we play,
the books we read, the sights we see, the music we listen to,
not merely to be in a state of contentment one would be in if
one had all these pleasures (assuming that there is such a
state).

All these are action reasons. Their existence and prevalence among our goals, projects, relationships and commitments may give the appearance of agent relativity where
none exists. Nagel may have in mind further cases as well.
Consider Jane and Jerry, who both have the freedom and
the adequate means to develop their lives (which are insufficient to enable them to take their holidays in the Bahamas). Nagel may think that the fact that Jerry will enjoy
spending a week in the Bahamas is no reason at all for Jane
to give him a week there. If he also assumes at the same time
that if Jane will enjoy a holiday in the Bahamas she has a
reason to secure for herself the means for such a holiday,
then he is committed to a view which is incompatible with
agent neutrality. But it is doubtful whether that is a view
that Nagel holds. For he thinks that each of us 'has reason
to give significant weight to the simple sensory pleasures and
pain of others as well as to his own'.[2] He will admit that in
some sense there are non-sensory pleasures which are more
valuable than sensory ones—the pleasure of seeing again a
city one had a memorable experience in as a child compared
with the cool satisfying texture and taste of ice-cream. The
only reason he mentions for not extending the same treatment to non-sensory pains and pleasures is that they are
reasons for the agent because he wants them, and that is no
reason for anyone else.

This is a false premiss. It is not the case that non-sensory
pains and pleasures are reasons for the agent because he
wants them. Much of my pleasure in a holiday in the Bahamas will be non-sensory. It will be pleasure in knowing
how lucky I am to be there, relaxation from the tensions of

[2] Ibid., p. 121.

ordinary life, diversion from troublesome thoughts, and the like. I therefore have reason to take a holiday there. But I did not choose to be a person who will enjoy a holiday in the Bahamas. If Nagel does believe that there are no agent-neutral reasons in cases such as this or others where the reason is not an action reason, then he is committed to an agency-relative view of sound practical reasoning, but it is less clear that he has ordinary intuitions and common human experience on his side.

4. Separateness of Persons: Integrity

We need an explanation of the way projects and relationships figure in practical reasoning which, if it is to serve as an argument against consequentialism, ascribes to them special features, other than that they are action reasons. Bernard Williams offers such an explanation, and it suggests another way of interpreting our concern for the separateness of persons. Williams is criticising utilitarianism. But his point holds, if at all, against all consequentialists. He describes how a utilitarian, taking his own as well as everyone else's projects and interests into account, reaches a conclusion as to which action will maximize desirable outcomes. Then he raises the question, what if that action conflicts with the agent's own projects which are central to his life?

The point is not, as utilitarians may hasten to add, that if the project or attitude is that central to his life then to abandon it would be very disagreeable to him and great loss of utility will be involved. . . [O]nce he is prepared to look at it like that, the argument in any serious case is over anyway. The point is that he is identified with his actions as flowing from projects and attitudes which in some cases he takes seriously at the deepest level, as what his life is about. . . . It is absurd to demand of such a man, when the sums come in from the utility network. . . that he should just step aside from his own project and decision and acknowledge the decision which utilitarian calculation requires. It is to alienate him in a real sense from his actions and the source of his actions in his own convictions. It is to make him into a channel between the input of everyone's projects, including his own, and an output of optimific decision; but this is to neglect the extent to which his actions and his decisions have to be seen as the actions and decisions which flow from the projects and attitudes with which he is most closely identified. It is thus in the most literal sense an attack on his integrity.[1]

Nozick's concern for the separability of persons revolved round persons as impacted upon by others, as patients of others' actions. He wishes to limit the degree to which one may be compelled to make sacrifices for the sake of others, without limiting one's moral obligation voluntarily to make sacrifices for the sake of others. This led to concentration on the difference between the different ways of affecting other people's behaviour which appeared incapable of bearing the strain of his argument. Nagel shifted the weight of the anti-consequentialist argument from patient to agent. This is clearly so in the case of personal projects and relationships. But it is also true of his understanding of deontological constraints. Like Nozick he notices that 'deontological reasons have their full force against *your doing* something—not just against its happening'.[2] But unlike Nozick he correctly perceives that deontological reasons cannot get their agent-relative character from the interest they respect alone. That would lead to an agent-neutral reason (which may be an action reason). Their agent-relativity derives according to him from their concern with the agent.

Williams, like Nagel, finds the explanation of the agent relativity in the integrity of the agent. This provides a new and more promising attempt to account for the moral significance of the separateness of persons. One way in which Williams' account appears superior is that it involves a radically modified understanding of one's moral obligations towards others. The separateness of persons is not merely a limitation on the extent to which compliance with such obligations can be imposed on one from the outside, it is not merely a reflection of the moral relevance of coercion. Another promise held by Williams is the rejection of the view of separability of persons as a device to lighten the moral burden, to allow one an escape from moral rigorism.

[1] In J. J. C. Smart and B. Williams, *Utilitarianism; For and Against*, Cambridge, 1973, pp. 116–17.

[2] Nagel, ibid..

At the very start of the long quotation above he denies that that is a proper understanding of the problem. Instead what is at stake is gaining a correct perspective of the relationship between one's own projects and the moral requirements which arise independently of them. That perspective will not necessarily set a limit to required self-sacrifice. Sometimes there may be no other morally acceptable options than sacrificing one's life, and that may happen in circumstances not due to one's own previous immorality. The point is that when that is the case it is so because of considerations which chime in with one's integrity. Consequentialism is wrong not because it is rigoristic, but because it misperceives the relationship between morality and integrity.

The conclusions of this part of the book will be in line with Williams' views expressed above. And yet it has to be admitted that the quoted paragraph is deeply puzzling. To be sure, there are ways of dissociating from our own attitudes and projects which involve alienation and loss of integrity. But not every disengagement from ourselves is like that. We all sometimes do look at ourselves from the outside, and find the experience salutory. We often urge ourselves and others to do so more often. Consequentialism does indeed require a certain measure of dissociation. It requires us to conceive of ourselves as one person among many, whose claims on resources may conflict with other claims, who owes obligations to others, including obligations which are not of one's own choosing. Why is that an attack on integrity?

One might agree with Williams that if consequentialism stops us from having any other projects than maximizing desirable consequences then it attacks our integrity, denies the separability of persons, and leads to alienation. But he does not claim that. On the contrary, he points out that utilitarianism presupposes that people have other projects, besides that of maximizing everyone's happiness. Otherwise it will be empty.[1] The consequentialist merely asks of us that in comparing our projects and commitments with those of others we should not think that ours have a superior claim simply because they are ours. Some people would claim that that is the essence of morality. The idea seems to be built

[1] Williams, Ibid., pp. 110-13.

into the ideal-observer, original-position, universalizability, and other methods of moral reasoning, which between them account for deeply felt intuitions about the nature of morality. We require an account of why, this long moral tradition notwithstanding, that measure of disengagement from the personal point of view is an attack on our integrity. Is proceeding with one's projects only after making sure that they should not yield to other people's call on our time and resources inconsistent with identifying with our projects as what our life is about? Is it to treat ourselves as a channel in some impersonal decision procedure? And if it is, what room is there left for morality, any morality? Is not Williams' argument one which leads to the rejection not of utilitarianism alone but of any morality not based on the accident of the agent's own projects?

We should accept Nagel's remark that 'there can be good judgment without total justification. The fact that one cannot say why a certain decision is the correct one, given a particular balance of conflicting reasons, does not mean that the claim to correctness is meaningless. . . What makes this possible is *judgment* . . . which reveals itself over time in individual decisions rather than in the enunciation of general principles. . . in many cases it can be relied upon to take up the slack that remains beyond explicit rational argument.'[1] Even so one needs some argument for such judgment to take the slack from. Williams offers no alternative to the consequentialist way of impartially balancing the relative importance of various projects to those who have them.[2]

---

[1] T. Nagel, *Mortal Questions*, Cambridge, 1979, pp. 134–5.
[2] For a very sensitive account of how a consequentialist will set about such a task see J. Griffin, op. cit..

12

Personal Well-Being

1. Personal Goals

The previous chapter surveyed some intuitions and examined some arguments. The arguments were found wanting,
but one or two of them seemed promising. The intuitions
were not disproved, but neither did we gain much insight
into their sources or implications. It seemed at least possible
that all the valid intuitions can be absorbed into a consequentialist theory of practical reason. Our discussion will
remain bound by roughly the same intuitions. But we need
to make a fresh start on their explanation. We need to step
back from the arguments canvassed so far, in order to see
whether any reflections on the general features of values
and reasons for action will help us decide between them by
pointing to their roots in the structure of sound practical
reasoning.

Like all inquiries, this one starts in the middle. The
present section in particular will abound with undefended
assertions. They will be used to argue against consequentialism, at least in its common forms. But what
confidence can one have in them? A refutation of consequentialism has far-reaching consequences for morality.
But unlike the moralist who argues directly for the value of
certain actions, our inquiry concerns structural features of
practical reasoning. The intuitions I referred to matter not
as particular intuitions as to what is right in one case or
another. We automatically read them as instances of certain
general features of reasoning, which exemplify valid argument even while it is conceded that each of the chosen
examples may not in itself carry conviction.

Many of the claims made here are not a priori or conceptual truths. They describe, if true, general features of
human experience. Like Williams and Nagel I will assume
that pervasive and unshakeable features of human practical

thought need no justification, though they call for an explanation. The claim made for the undefended assertions that follow is that they are part of an explanation of such general features of practical thought. This claim is validated in part by their ability to account for what we call intuitions; in our case these are examples of the sort discussed in the previous chapter. In part the claim of these assertions to explain universal features of practical thought is validated by the fact that they mesh in with other explanations of practical thought, or of thought in general. In our case this partly depends on their ability to provide a foundation for some of the arguments put forward by Nagel and Williams. Finally, these assertions are validated in part by the absence of an alternative which is more successful in meeting the above two criteria. Since that is the route to validation the assertions made and not defended in this section gain some support from their use later on. But they must remain, so far as this chapter is concerned, unproved suggestions.

We shall be concerned with individual well-being. This concept captures one crucial evaluation of a person's life: how good or successful is it from his point of view? It is best understood by excluding what does not belong to it. It is not an evaluation of his contribution to the well-being of others, or to culture, or to the ecosystem, etc. The distinction should not be confused with a distinction between personal or 'prudential' reasons on the one hand, and moral or impersonal reasons of some other kind. Nor do we assume that a person's well-being is secured by pursuing 'prudential' reasons, or reasons of self-interest. When judging a person's well-being one is judging the success or failure of his life, not the means for that success or failure.

One can compare different states of a person, different periods of his life, and judge them to be better or worse for him. One can also compare them with what they might have been, with different ways in which his life might have developed and did not. Finally, one can compare various routes which are open to him, various ways in which his life may develop. These judgments may be formed by people other than that person himself, and their views may be closer to the mark than his. Often a person is better placed or more interested in forming an accurate judgment about his own well-being. But sometimes others are better placed and more impartial than he is. Notwithstanding this, it is generally the case that the value of various situations for a particular person depends to a large extent on his actual goals, as they are or will be throughout his life. The value to me of living near open country depends on whether among my pursuits there are any which make use of the country.

The main exceptions to this rule are biologically determined needs and desires. Perhaps all our needs, desires and goals are biologically determined to some degree. Perhaps none are entirely biologically determined. But they can be roughly placed on a scale by the degree to which they are so determined. For convenience I will assume a rough division into the biologically determined and the rest. The case for exception and nuance is easily made. Other things being equal, a person is better off when well fed, in moderate temperature, with sufficient sensory stimulation, in good health, etc., whether he adopts these as his goals or not. Sometimes a person's overall interest is in not having some or all of his biologically determined wants satisfied, but even then one does him some good (as well as a greater harm) by satisfying them. It is significant that normally people do want to satisfy their biologically determined urges and needs, but the benefits of their satisfaction do not depend on such desires. Indeed their satisfaction is normally beneficial even when it is not desired (though, as will be explained below, their contribution to the well-being of the person concerned may depend on their satisfaction being consonant with his comprehensive goals). Be that as it may, while there is no denying the importance of the biologically determined wants for the well-being of a person, it is clear that they are not the only determinants of that well-being. Much depends on his other goals, on whether he wants to be friends with someone, or to distance himself from another, to go camping in summer, to acquire a local reputation for hardheadedness, etc.

Some of these goals a person may have adopted deliberately, some he may have chosen. Others he may have drifted into, grown up with, never realized that anyone can fail to have them, etc. It makes no difference from our point of view which is which. What matters is that they are his goals, and I use the term broadly to cover his projects, plans, relationships, ambitions, commitments, and the like.[1] Since they are his goals he guides his actions towards them, they colour his perception of his environment and of the world at large, and they play a large part in his emotional responses and in his imaginative musings. They play, in other words, a conscious role in his life. They are not merely unknown forces, the existence of which is deduced or postulated by psychologists or social scientists because of their predictive value.

The reason I dwell on the function of a person's goals in determining his well-being is, in the first place, that goals which are not predominantly biologically determined have one important feature. One can normally do little to help a person, other than by helping him to achieve his goals, or by getting him to adopt goals that are better for him, or to abandon ones which are bad for him. That is, improving the well-being of a person can normally only be done through his goals. If they are bad for him the way to help him is to get him to change them, and not to frustrate their realization (except on the rare occasions when this is an adequate way of getting him to change them).

The point should not be exaggerated. One may save the life of another by stopping him from going to a football match that he is very keen on, where he would be killed in a football riot. But when we serve others' interests in ways which are independent of any service to their goals this is likely to be by advancing some biologically determined interest of theirs. What we normally cannot do is make someone who does not wish to see a Bogart film enjoy watching it

[1] In these initial clarifications 'goals' is used so broadly that if a person wants something then it is his goal to get it. But the result of these clarifications is that the term is used more in keeping with its ordinary implication of a longer-term objective. Goals are not necessarily desirable or desired for themselves. But they are nested in larger goals, or are larger goals themselves. At no point do I wish to suggest that the fact that a person wants something is in and by itself a reason for action either for him or for others. The use of 'goals' is, however, meant to preserve the ambivalence between the view that it is the fact that they are wanted and the view that it is what they are wanted for which makes them relevant to practical reason.

without also making him want to watch it. By way of contrast, we can benefit people by improving the room temperature, providing adequate sensory stimulation, etc., even while they continue to protest against such measures. The reason is conceptual, rather than empirical, though the conceptual connection is loose and allows certain exceptions. It rests on the fact that goals are adopted, or endorsed. They contribute to a person's well-being because they are his goals, they are what matters to him. Since I never wanted to be a concert violinist I am none the worse for not being one. Someone whose ambition it is or was to become a concert violinist is, other things being equal, worse off if he is not one than if he is.

One further characteristic of human goals has to be mentioned here. They are commonly nested within hierarchical structures. This fact eludes those studies of practical reasoning which concentrate on immediate goals, like 'I want a drink of water; so I have reason to get up, walk to the kitchen, turn the tap, etc.' These are salutary in showing the complexity of reasoning even in simple cases. But many of any person's goals are nested in his own complex goal structures. I am writing on this subject because I have reason to teach the subject to my students, because it is part of a plan for a book, and in order to clarify my own thoughts on the subject. Each of these three reasons is nested in larger projects of mine, sometimes splitting, sometimes merging into one. I teach, for example, to earn a living, but also in order to influence the way people think about certain issues. This last goal, but not the first, is also behind my plan to write a book, of which the chapter will be a part.

To be sure people also have isolated goals, reasons, or desires. These are often biologically determined, like a desire for a drink of water, or a need to go to the toilet. When they are not, and often even when they are, they are normally (obsessions being the exception) of relatively little weight. A person's important immediate goals are nested in larger projects. Moreover, the importance of the immediate goal depends primarily on the importance of the larger goal, and on the degree to which realization of the immediate goal is essential to the success of the larger one. The relevance of nestedness to the evaluation of the importance of goals means that to a large extent (the exception will be explained below) one does not measure the importance of an action by the number of goals it enables one to reach, but by its contribution to the highest goals it serves.

While the weight of a reason for an action does not correlate with the number of goals that action serves, it does, other things being equal, correspond to the comprehensiveness of the goal(s) the action serves. Other things being equal, if a goal permeates all aspects of one's life it, and actions serving it, are more important than if it affects only a short span of one's life or only a few aspects of it. I should underline the fact that this is only one dimension in the evaluation of goals. Besides, it is not a recommendation to embrace pervasive or life-encompassing goals. Some people do. Others are seized with horror at the very thought. I know of no reason to prefer one tendency to the other, though there are several against embracing either extreme. The only point made is that relative to each person, other things being equal, his more pervasive goals are more important to his well-being than his less pervasive ones. This too is a conceptual point. It is a result of the fact that in judging a person's well-being it is his life as a whole that one is judging. When we judge a person's well-being during a period of his life this leads us to take account of the possibility that that period might integrate in a generally successful life. If its character undermines the success of the life as a whole then it cannot be all that good in itself.

People may come to adopt goals in many different ways. Only some of them involve reasoning to any significant degree. When one reasons one's way out of one goal or into another one's reasoning will depend, in part, on some of one's existing goals. One may come to believe that a goal adhered to in the belief that it serves another does not in fact do so, or that one of one's goals impedes the realization of another, more important, goal, and so on. The goal(s) from which one reasons need not survive. One may abandon a goal on the ground that it is self-defeating, i.e. that all efforts to reach it get one further away from it. Nor need one always control lower goals by higher ones. The reverse can happen as well as when a person comes to realize that all his lower goals are better supported by values incompatible with one of his, hitherto, ultimate goals. Finally, people have second order goals, i.e. goals about what kind of goals they should have. They may want all their goals to be well integrated, to give their life a unity, to enable them to look at their past with pride, to enable them to remain spontaneous, and curious about new possibilities well into old age, etc.[1]

The above remarks are not meant to suggest that in practical reasoning anything goes so long as one ends with a consistent set of beliefs and goals. They merely illustrate the importance of the nestedness of goals in our practical reasoning. They are vindicated by the way people consider their own lives, as well as by their estimation of the well-being of others. They are incorporated into our concepts and reflected in our language and modes of reasoning. It may be worth reminding ourselves that while goals are what people guide their action by, they need not be capable of articulating their goals very precisely. Nagel's remarks concerning the exercise of judgment quoted above are to be taken as part of the background for the rest of our reflections.

2. Well-Being and Self-Interest

It is a consequence of the preceding observations that people's well-being is to a considerable extent a function of their non-biologically determined goals: goals which they have but could have avoided. To the extent that every person has reason to act in the interest of others his reasons derive from their goals. Barring the case of biological wants, one can help others only through their goals, i.e. either by leading them to change them, or by helping them satisfy them. Their goals will largely determine their welfare. Had they endorsed other goals they might have accomplished more in their lives, they might have contributed more to others, or to science.

---

[1] On the importance of second order goals see H. Frankfurt, 'Freedom of the Will and the Concept of a Person', *Journal of Philosophy*, 68 (1971), 5; and S. Blackburn, 'Truth Realism, and the Regulation of Theory' *Midwest Studies in Philosophy*, 5 (1980), and 'Rule Following and Moral Realism', in Holzman and Leich (eds.), *Wittgenstein: To Follow a Rule*, London, 1981.

But insofar as we are concerned exclusively with their well-being all this is largely irrelevant.

Of course we should, in many situations, help those whose life is of greater service to humanity. But that is, according to consequentialist thinking, because by helping them we help other people, those who will be helped by them, as well. Alternatively indirect consequentialism may find more circuitous reasons why helping the morally worthy is better. Nor would a consequentialist deny that one may like some people better than others, and like them because of their goals, because of the people they have become through the goals they pursued. This may be a legitimate consideration because by helping them we also serve ourselves. Again indirect consequentialists will have additional benefits to point to, such as the fact that preference for people with lovable character traits tends to encourage the cultivation of such traits to, in the long run, everyone's benefit. All these are legitimate consequentialist considerations but they all rely on reasons other than the well-being of the person concerned.

Our understanding of 'well-being' as the general term for evaluating success in life, so that the more successful the life the greater the well-being of the person whose life it is, seems to lend support to the transparency of values thesis (cf. p. 269). It may also appear to conflict with the argument concerning the reason-dependent character of goals advanced in Chapter Six. These appearances deceive through conflating well-being with another notion. I will use 'self-interest' to refer to the second.

Well-being is sometimes understood as a rough synonym of self-interest. The use of these notions reflects both moral convictions and beliefs about human motivation. According to some the two notions are indeed broadly interchangeable. While regarding 'interest' as roughly co-extensive with 'well-being', I shall follow a slightly different and narrower usage of 'self-interest'. In a nutshell, self-interest is largely a biological notion. Frustrating any of a person's biologically determined needs and desires is in itself against his self-interest, unless it instrumentally serves to improve the satisfaction of these needs and desires of his in the long run, or unless it prolongs his life, or protects him from danger. For anything which shortens a person's life is also against his self-interest. A person is held to have an interest in longevity, though there are various views on how much it counts as against physical suffering or debility.

Given the absence of a boundary between the biological and the cultural or conventional, one should not make too much of the proposition that self-interest is a biological concept. Success in self-serving pursuits advances one's self-interest as does contentment and satisfaction in any of one's pursuits. Contentment and satisfaction are part of any biologically defined notion of individual interest, as is witnessed by the fact that they play a part in our notion of the interest of even relatively primitive species of mammals. Self-serving pursuits are often assimilated to the biologically determined ones or to those which serve biologically determined needs. Therefore, success in self-serving pursuits and contentment and satisfaction are part of our notion of personal self-interest. Since it is in a person's self-interest to be content and satisfied, satisfaction with the way his affairs are conducted is in a person's self-interest. This may seem to bridge the gap between self-interest and well-being, which, as we saw, is concerned primarily with the success of our projects and goals. But it does not. There are four major differences between the two notions.

First, while both notions are sensitive to biological needs and desires, they are so in different ways. Self-interest is always adversely affected by the frustration of biological needs, and by the shortening of one's life. A person's well-being is not reduced by the shortening of his life, nor by frustrating his biological needs, when this is the means of or the accepted by-product of his pursuit of a valuable goal. A person who undergoes great deprivations in order to bring medical help to the victims of an epidemic is sacrificing his interest in favour of that of others, but his life is no less successful, rewarding or accomplished because of that.

It would, however, be wrong to move to the other extreme and maintain that the satisfaction of biologically determined needs contributes to one's well-being only if it helps the promotion of one's goals and projects. It is true that normally the pursuit of goals requires satisfaction of one's medium-range biological needs. (Though, often enough they come at the expense of one's long-term health and longevity interests.) Yet the value of biologically determined goals transcends their usefulness as means to other ends. At the very least they are also a precondition of one's ability rationally to adopt new goals and pursuits, and abandon existing ones. And that ability is of value independently of whether it is wanted or not.

Second, success and failure in the pursuit of our goals is in itself the major determinant of our well-being. It is true that the success of some of our goals, even those which are not biologically determined, promotes our self-interest, whereas their failure adversely affects it. But self-interest is indifferent to the fortunes of many other pursuits. The dividing lines between those goals whose success serves our self-interest and those which do not are far from clear, nor can they be generally applied to all our projects. Does a parent's success in advancing the prosperity of his child serve the self-interest of the parent? It certainly contributes to his well-being. His life is a better, more successful life as a result. He can take pride in his life because of his success in helping the interest of his child. But does it serve that aspect of his well-being which we identify as his self-interest? Or is it like his success in contributing to the anti-vivisectionist cause which also contributes to the success of his life and the pride he and others can take in it, but not through serving his self-interest?

I think that we have but rough and ready ways of delineating which aspects of a person's well-being concern his self-interest. Basically a person's self-interest, to the extent that it is served by the success of what he cares about, is served by success in those of his pursuits and relationships which he does not enter into to improve the well-being of others. This explanation is a negative one. It works by exclusion. Self-interest is what remains after subtracting from the wider notion of well-being success in those projects whose value (in the eye of the person in question) is their contribution to the well-being of others. This is no more than what we should expect given that we are discussing the aspect of self-interest which is determined by a person's pursuits.

Third, while people's success in other goals does not affect their self-interest, their contentment with their success does. People pursue goals in order to succeed in them. Since they care about their success, failure reflects adversely on their well-being, on the success of their life. This is so even if they neither know nor could be expected to know of the failure. Self-interest is unaffected by such factors. It is sensitive to a person's satisfaction with his own life. But not to whether that satisfaction or its absence is justified. This does not mean that the success of all his projects and goals makes a difference to the agent's well-being. What counts is how successful he was in pursuing them, how he managed in his pursuit of them. A person who actively campaigned to prevent the use of DDT may see its use actually increase in his lifetime, without this casting a shadow on his well-being. What matters from that point of view is the way he pursued his objectives and the contribution he made, relative to what could be expected, to his cause.

For the same reasons the success of the cause need not contribute to the success of his life, unless it results from the manner he conducted himself. That is also why wishing does not contribute to well-being. I am no better off if the people or causes whom I wish well prosper. Nor worse off if they languish. But a person who, whether or not by his own action, is protected from knowledge of the failure of his projects, so that he is content with his success, but his content is based on false beliefs, is nevertheless a failure. His self-interest is served by protecting him from that knowledge. His well-being, however, is compromised beyond repair. The second and third differences between well-being and self-interest contradict the thesis of the transparency of values. They will be further defended in the discussion of the reason-based character of goals below.

The fourth difference between well-being and self-interest is that a person's well-being depends on the value of his goals and pursuits. A person who spends all his time gambling has, other things being equal, less successful a life, even if he is a successful gambler, than a live stock farmer busily minding his farm. Their self-interest may be equally served by their activities, but their well-being is not. The reason is that they engage in what they do because they believe it to be a valuable, worthwhile activity (perhaps but not necessarily because of its value to others). They care about what they do on that basis. To the extent that their valuation is misguided it affects the success of their life.

What if the value of one person's goals and pursuits is less than that of another's, but neither of them is guilty of any mistake about their true value? If it turns out that each spent his life in activities which were as valuable as anything he could have done then, other things being equal, their lives are equally successful. That is another aspect of the subjectivity of the notion. It indicates the success of a person's life from his point of view, i.e. its intrinsic value rather than its instrumental value to others. Whenever we are given a choice we aspire to choose wisely, to make the best decision open to us in the circumstances. We can aspire to no less. But nor can we aspire to more. Nor can any more be asked of us. If a person does so successfully then his life is successful to the highest degree. That someone else could and did engage in more valuable pursuits, which the first person could not emulate for lack of ability or of opportunity, is irrelevant. We judge them more valuable because of their value to others. The second person's life was more valuable and more successful from that point of view. The impersonal value of activities and pursuits, i.e. their value judged independently of the fact that this agent does or can engage in them, is important from the agent's point of view, for each person wishes to engage in pursuits which are as valuable as any he can manage. In that he judges their value from the impersonal point of view. But since his aim is and can only be to do the best he can, achievements which are beyond him are irrelevant to a judgment of his personal well-being.[1]

---

[1] The akratic person does not want, in one sense, to do the best he can, since he acts intentionally against his own best judgment. But in doing so he fails to live up to his own aspirations, and his well-being suffers as a result.

It is crucial not to read too much into the characterization of reasons as 'impersonal'. It means that they are judged inasmuch as they are reasons to all, regardless of their desires or goals. For example, inasmuch as these activities are enjoyable, everyone has a reason to eat tasty delicacies, and to read good

3. Goals and Reasons

The last few paragraphs repeated claims made in Chapter Six, about the dependence of goals on reasons. To be sure we want to reach our goals, that is part of what it means for them to be our goals. But we are not stuck with our goals just because we have them. This is not a comment about our ability to change our goals. To a certain extent we can do so. We can deliberate on their merits, and if they are found wanting we can modify them. There is no denying that there are limits to our ability to change our goals, just as their are limits to our ability to kick our habits. My point is a more modest one. It is that taken one by one they present themselves as objects for our judgment. Unlike our habits, about which we may have not a good word to say, goals are supported by approving judgment. If I look for heroin because I cannot kick the habit then my wider goal is that of sparing myself intolerable or unnecessary suffering. It is not the same goal that a willing addict has. That our goals are objects of our judgment and that they are our goals only if we approve of them is also part of what it means for them to be our goals.

Both when a person chooses a goal and when he surveys the ones he has, he regards himself as looking for reasons for choosing one goal rather than another, and he holds himself to have the goals which he has for a reason. This last judgment has little or nothing to do with the way he came by these goals. It is about the way he holds them. This point is the same as the view often expressed that one must regard one's goals in a way which ascribes to them some desirability characteristics.[1] In the limiting case no reasoning of any complex kind will be forthcoming. The belief that the goal is valuable may amount to little more than that one would describe ones goals by expressions which ascribe desirability to them.

Two separate implications of the dependence of goals on

novels. Those who have made it one of their goals to study Saul Bellow in depth, or to become experts on Breton cuisine, have additional reasons for reading a new Bellow novel, or to visit a newly opened high quality Breton restaurant. The first are impersonal reasons. The second are personal ones.

[1] See G. E. M. Anscombe, *Intention*, Oxford, 1957.

reasons were relied on above. First, whatever we want for a reason we want to the extent that it serves that reason. If Jane wants to go to art school in order to improve her job prospects she wants to study there to the extent that doing so improves her job prospects. She may of course have other reasons besides, and they have to be added to complete the picture. The relevant reasons include all those she has in favour of attending the school, whether or not they are the ones which made her take the decision in the first place, and regardless of whether or not they are the major factors in her being at the school or what she would regard as pleasing side benefits of her studies in it. The conclusion which was drawn above was that being there does not serve her well-being if it does not improve her job prospects unless it serves some other aim she had or has come to embrace since going. Only inasmuch as attending the school serves her reasons is it something which she wants or cares about.

The point I am making is about the evaluation of the contribution of a person's project to the success of his life. It is not a psychological point. In our example we were not predicting how Jane will behave if she learns the truth. It may turn out that, unknown to her, she has developed a craving to be at art school which is beyond her control. This is relevant information indeed. But it is relevant because it points to goals she will come to acquire (to extend her general education by going to the school, or to go there in order to avoid the internal conflict that any reflection on the matter leads to, for example). In other words, psychological facts are relevant here because of their help in a normative evaluation, and not because the point itself is a psychological one.

The second implication was that the person has the goal on condition that his reason is a valid, valuable one. If it turns out that getting a job is not a good thing to do then Jane's well-being is not adversely affected by failing to get admitted to art school. Her pursuit of this goal was premissed on the belief that it is. She does not care for it, we are assuming, for any other reason. Her inability to reach her goal is a blessing in disguise if it is a valueless goal. She wants it because she believes it to be valuable, but she also wants not to have it if it is worthless.

But could it not be that her reasons are mere rational-
izations, that she would want to be there even if she becomes aware that they are false, and that she would just carry
on inventing flimsy unconvincing reasons for doing that
which she has no reason to do? Would one not say that in
that case she wants to go to art school, even though she has
no reason? If what she cares about matters then she clearly
cares about going to an art school. The next two chapters
will, I hope, clear me of the charge of underestimating the
role of desires and emotions in people's lives. It will be seen
that in the normal case they determine what one does; their
role is not only that of identifying reason's verdict and exe-
cuting it. It is much more a matter of determining what to
do where reason is powerless to decide. Rationalization, as
postulated in the example, is one of a large number of cases
of break down of normality, through a mismatch between
reality and one's conception of it. They present special problems which will not be discussed in this book.[1]

One reason for doubting the thesis defended above, i.e.,
that satisfaction of goals based on false reasons does not
contribute to one's well-being, is the ease with which we lose
sight of the significance of the interaction of the many goals
and concerns a person has. For example, people do not like
to fail in whatever they try, even if they realize that trying
was a mistake. Nor do they like to be rebuffed by others,
even when they know that the rebuff is for their own good.
Factors such as these seem to suggest that success in one's
goals promotes one's well-being, even when the reasons for
the goal do not support it, or are invalid. The mistake is
shown by isolating the interfering factors. Imagine that one's
goal does not come off for reasons which cannot be regarded
as a personal failure, nor as rebuff by others. Isolate in a
similar way other intruding factors. It then becomes easier

---

[1] Another apparent complication arises in the all too common cases in which a
person is doing for an invalid reason that which he has a good reason to do, but
one of which he is unaware. In fact these cases form no exception to the general
rule. Performing the action, say going to a concert, for the wrong reason, e.g. to
meet someone who will not in fact be there, will serve the good reason, e.g. enjoying
music, only if the person comes to adopt it as one of his goals. Therefore, such
cases are of interest only in being occasions in which people may come to adopt
new goals.

to see that non-satisfaction of goals which are based on bad reasons does not detract from one's well-being. This does not mean that people who have such goals do not suffer, But they suffer, their life is less successful, because they have false goals. They would not be any better off if their false goals were realized.

None of the above denies that people whose false goals fail feel disappointed and frustrated. All I am concerned to argue is that these frustrations are preferred by them to ignorant satisfaction. They fall in the category of unwelcome truths, which, hurtful as they are, people wish to have.[1] We are all aware that there are a large number of imaginable circumstances in which one would justifiably prefer not to be told unpalatable truths. Many of these cases are beside our point as they do not undermine the cogency of one's goals. Others which do could still be justifiable as temporary measures in special conditions. A person who systematically prefers not to know if the reasons for his goals are cogent or not shows that he is not really pursuing his goals for these reasons. He may be deceiving us or himself about his true reasons. Or he may be in some other pathological state. It is part of the very notion of having a reason for a goal that one's endorsement of the goals is conditional on the reason being a good one.

Arguments are sometimes advanced to the effect that while people have instrumental reasons for the goals they pursue as means to their ultimate ends, their only reason for the latter is that they want them. In its simplest form the argument runs foul of the fact that many of the goals which we described as nested in other goals are not means of getting to an ulterior end, but constitutive elements of it. Reformulated to meet this objection, the argument takes the form of the claim that the only reason one has for one's ultimate goals is that one wants them. Non-ultimate goals can be justified as means to or as constitutive elements of

---

[1] The dependence of well-being on absence of pain, disappointment, anxiety, frustration, and like emotions and feelings is often exaggerated. Anxiety, worry, disappointments, are an integral part of many valuable pursuits, relationships, careers, creative endeavours, etc. Therefore, if you like, their presence contributes to one's well-being inasmuch as the pursuits of which they are an essential part do so.

other goals. This view encompasses both a distortion and a truth.

People are indeed better able to find decisive reasons for small steps, for limited projects, than for comprehensive ones. It is easier to find decisive reasons for going home by one route or another, for buying a refrigerator or a dishwasher, and for decisions of a similar size, than for whether to read economics or law at university, whether to accept employment with a new employer in a new town or to stay where one is, and similarly large problems. Of course sometimes decisive reasons are available in the latter cases and fail to emerge in the small scale cases, but these do not change the general case. To the extent that one's ultimate goals tend, as they do, also to be one's most comprehensive goals it follows that in many cases one has no decisive reason for the goals one has which are independent of the fact that one has them. On the not very frequent occasions when one may choose between different goals which are not as yet one's own one may well not have a decisive reason to choose either way.

It does not follow that one's choice or judgment is not based on a reason. I may not have a reason to prefer going to medical school to going to law school. But if that is what I do then I do it because I believe that a medical education is important and worth while for it will, for example, enable me (1) to serve others, as well as (2) to have a satisfying career, and (3) to live and work in almost any country. 1 to 3 are my reasons, and the fact that I believe that I also have reasons for choosing a legal career which are no less worthy and important does not undermine the fact that when I choose medicine I choose it for the stated reasons. One can, and does, choose for a reason without believing that the reason is a better one than other reasons for alternative actions.[1] Ultimate comprehensive goals, no less than limited ones, are chosen (when they are chosen) and held for reasons.

[1] The will comes into play in various ways in supplementing these real or merely believed-in reasons for which people choose, or stick by their goals. In the simplest case it merely indicates that, having chosen the goal for what one takes to be good reasons, one is happy with the choice; one is willingly following that goal. At other times it may represent the opposite sentiment: since one pursued the goal for what seemed to be a good reason at the time, one is now stuck with it. That is one would

The claim that the reasons for preferring one comprehensive goal to another, other than the fact that one already has it, are often inconclusive is not an empirical claim.
There is no denying that some empirical factors point in the
same direction. In particular one's chances of success are
relevant to almost all evaluations of different projects, and
these are particularly hard to fathom when considering comprehensive goals, whether ultimate or not. But beyond such
reasons there are also conceptual obstacles to the comparative evaluation of comprehensive goals. Their exploration will be taken up in the next chapter, for it depends
on the breakdown of commensurability. We make a start on
that inquiry now by noticing another important feature of
comprehensive goals (ultimate or not), that is their dependence on the availability of social forms.

4. The Primacy of Action Reasons

Using 'goals', for the sake of brevity, to refer loosely to
whatever a person cares about, be it a relationship, his career,
a leisure activity, an interest in local history, a fascination
with children, the pleasure of drink or of good food, etc., is
not without dangers. There are more ways than I can think
of in which it may mislead. It may, for example, leave the
impression that I think that well-being concerns only a person's activities. In fact people's well-being is greatly affected
by what happens to them as well. My choice of term was,
however, deliberate. It was meant to emphasize that what
happens to a person affects his well-being largely through
the way it affects his active pursuits.

The one big exception is happenings which affect people's
biologically determined needs. An illness or an accident leading to a disability can affect one's well-being very
profoundly. So can a large inheritance, the bankruptcy of
one's employer, the award of the Booker Prize for literature,
etc. But these last events affect one only to the extent that

not have chosen that now if it were a fresh choice, but given the amount 'invested'
in the goal already it is now best to continue with it. For example: 'When I was
young I wanted to be a doctor, for medicine looked such a promising profession.
Now it's too late to change.' In both cases one's will in itself is not a reason at all.
But it can be. This topic will be considered in ch. 14.

they serve or do a disservice to goals one has, or lead one to change one's goals. To give but one example to illustrate the point. Does the failure of the local bus to turn up on time affect my life in any way? It all depends on my goals. If they are either served or frustrated by the event then it does. If they are left untouched by it, it does not. The same goes for anything which befalls one.

Another case which only seems to be an exception is that events which do not affect a person's goals but affect his ability or opportunity to have certain goals and pursue them successfully may also affect the success or value of his life. This issue will be discussed in the context of our examination of the ideal of personal autonomy.

This suggests that action reasons play the primary role in determining one's well-being. As a matter of general observation it is clear that many of a person's projects and goals provide him with action reasons; many are constituted by the endorsement of action reasons. When we think of what we can do for others we typically think of helping them reach or remain in a certain state. But a person forming plans for his life is likely to be equally, if not primarily, concerned with what to do, what he will do with himself, what he will make of himself, how he will conduct himself, and such questions. Our notion of a successful life is of a life well spent, of a life of achievement, of handicaps overcome, talents wisely used, of good judgment in the conduct of one's affairs, of warm and trusting relations with family and friends, stormy and enthusiastic involvement with other people, many hours spent having fun in good company, and so on. At the very least we can safely say that a large proportion of a person's goals are agency goals. They are normally goals others can help him reach, by providing the right environment, the right conditions. But they cannot reach them for him. Balancing one's own interests against those of others often means balancing pursuing goals oneself against providing conditions which help others with theirs.

One way to test the thesis of the primacy of action reasons is to think of a person who is entirely passive, and is continuously fed, cleaned, and pumped full with hash, so that he is perpetually content, and wants nothing but to stay in the same condition. It's a familiar imaginary horror. How do we rank the success of such a life? It is not the worst life one can have. It is simply not a life at all. It lacks activity, it lacks goals. To the extent that one is tempted to judge it more harshly than that and to regard it as a 'negative' life this is because of the wasted potentiality. It is a life which could have been and was not. We can isolate this feature by imagining that the human being concerned is mentally and physically affected in a way which rules out the possibility of a life with any kind of meaningful pursuit in it. Now it is just 'not really a life at all'. This does not preclude one from saying that it is better than human life. It is simply sufficiently unlike human life in the respects which matter that we regard it as only a degenerate case of human life. But clearly not being alive can be better than that life.

This in itself does not show, of course, that in an ordinary life there cannot be happenings which matter to the way it goes, to its success and value, and which do not derive that relevance from the goals and pursuits the agent has, or may have. But, or so is my thesis, barring those which affect biological needs there are no such happenings. This I will call the primacy of action reason. It may appear surprising at first blush. But I believe it to be deeply embedded in our conception of human life. Static, passive goals which people have turn out on examination to involve action reasons at their foundation. The desire to possess great power is essentially connected with the desire to wield it. For its possession is impossible, meaningless, unless it is a power exercised. (Deciding not to intervene is, it should be remembered, an exercise of power. It is not a decision which one who does not have power can take.) The desire to be loved is usually a desire to earn the love of others (or of another), at least through displaying one's lovable qualities. Very commonly it is also coupled with a desire to join in a loving relationship. The same goes for all other apparently passive goals.

5. Social Forms
In arguing about the nature of personal goals one is moving towards a conception of personal well-being, for it consists in large measure of the success of one's important pursuits.

The previous sections argued for three conditions of personal well-being.

(1) All but the biologically determined aspects of a person's well-being consist of the successful pursuit of goals which he has or should have. Beyond its biologically determined component a person's well-being can be promoted only through his willing acceptance of goals and pursuits.

(2) People adopt and pursue goals because they believe in their independent value, that is their value is believed to be at least in part independent of the fact that they were chosen and are pursued.

(3) Barring a person's biologically determined needs and desires his well-being depends, at the deepest level, on his action reasons and his success in following them.

Between them the three conditions steer a middle course between the subjectivist conception of welfare which endorses the condition of transparency (see p. 269 above) and a strong objective conception of well-being according to which whether a person is content in his situation or not has nothing to do with his well-being. Strong objectivists claim that when a person is well off he should be content. But they deny that he is not as well off as he might be if he is not content. The effect of the first two conditions is to affirm that though a person may be unaware of how well off he is, his willing engagement in his activities and pursuits is an essential ingredient of his prosperity.

The view to be defended in this section is that a person can have a comprehensive goal only if it is based on existing social forms, i.e. on forms of behaviour which are in fact widely practised in his society. Recall that a comprehensive goal is not a long-term goal. I may desire to visit Venice on my sixtieth birthday, and I may have been working to save for it ever since I was twenty-five. It is still not a comprehensive goal. To be that it itself (not merely its means) must have ramifications which pervade important dimensions of my life. This also entails that it does not consist merely of a repetition of one kind of activity. Going bell-ringing every Sunday is not a comprehensive goal in itself, but when it is conceived as a complex activity with social, sightseeing, architectural, and other interests and when it assumes a significance which pervades other times than those when one is actually on a bell-ringing outing, then it is a comprehensive goal.

Success in one's comprehensive goals is among the most important elements of one's well-being. Hence the present section argues in effect for the existence of a fourth condition of personal well-being.

(4) A person's well-being depends to a large extent on success in socially defined and determined pursuits and activities. (This condition reaffirms and expands the anti-individualistic argument of Chapter Eight.)

A comprehensive goal may be based on a social form in being a simple instance of it. An ordinary conventional marriage in our society can be used to illustrate what marriage is like. It exemplifies a widely shared social form, while being also an instance of a comprehensive goal of the people whose marriage it is, and who want it to be (or remain) a success. Many marriages, perhaps all, are not that conventional. They are based on a shared perception of a social form while deviating from it in some respects. They are deviations on a common theme, and they can typically be that because the social form itself recognizes the existence of variations, or even their importance. A couple may evolve an 'open' marriage even though this form is unknown to their society. But an open marriage is a relation combining elements of a conventional marriage and of a sexual pursuit which is kept free of emotional involvement. It is combination of elements of two socially recognizable forms. The thesis that comprehensive goals are inevitably based on socially existing forms is meant to be consistent with experimentation, and with variations on a common theme and the like. It is no more possible to delimit in advance the range of deviations which still count as based on a social form than it is to delimit the possible relations between the literal and the metaphorical use of an expression.

In talking of social forms I have in mind the public perception of common social forms of action, each of which has the internal richness and complexity which makes it into a possible comprehensive personal goal. Both the question of the degree to which the practice has to be shared, and the question of whether it has to be shared by one of the groups in the midst of which an individual lives, or of which he is a part, or if it is enough if it is a practice of a group he is familiar with, though not a member of, admit of no straightforward answer. Something more can be said on such issues when addressing particular goals: those of parenthood are likely to lead to different answers from those of leisure activities. But the reasons for the general thesis suggest that it is very much a matter of degree in most cases.

What are the reasons for the thesis? It is not a conventionalist thesis. It does not claim that whatever is practised with social approval is for that reason valuable. It says that the comprehensive goals a person finds valuable are based on social forms, whether or not these are socially approved social forms. In other words the thesis merely sets a limit to what comprehensive forms can be valuable for any person. They can be valuable only if they can be his goals and they can be his goals only if they are founded in social forms. I will mention reasons of two kinds for the thesis. The first shows that individual behaviour would not have the significance it has but for the existence of social forms. The second is to the effect that, even if the first were not the case, individuals would not have been able to acquire and maintain their goals except through continuous familiarity with the social forms.

First and most obviously, some comprehensive goals require social institutions for their very possibility. One cannot pursue a legal career except in a society governed by law, one cannot practise medicine except in a society in which such a practice is recognized. Notice that in principle one may be born into a society with no medical practice or knowledge endowed with an innate knowledge of medicine. One could then cure many diseases, but one could not be a medical doctor, of the kind we have in our society. It takes more than medical knowledge or curing powers to do that. A doctor participates in a complex social form, involving general recognition of a medical practice, its social organization, its status in society, its conventions about which matters are addressed to doctors and which not (there is no inherent logic to the practice of healthy people in our society consulting doctors about choice of contraceptives but not about choice of career), and its conventions about the suitable relations between doctors and their patients.

Therefore, the reasons we are considering are far-reaching indeed. Activities which do not appear to acquire their character from social forms in fact do so. Bird watching seems to be what any sighted person in the vicinity of birds can do. And so he can, except that that would not make him into a bird watcher. He can be that only in a society where this, or at least some other animal tracking activities, are recognized as leisure activities, and which furthermore shares certain attitudes to natural life generally. The point is that engaging in the same activities will play a different role, have a different significance in the life of the individual depending on social practices and attitudes to such activities. Much of the interest that people have in goals of these kinds is available to them because of the existence of suitable social forms. These comments explain why I prefer the phrase 'social forms' to the more familiar ones, such as 'social practices' or 'conventions'. These appear to be concerned exclusively with behaviour, and attitudes to behaviour. I mean social forms to consist of shared beliefs, folklore, high culture, collectively shared metaphors and imagination, and so on.

The second group of reasons for the thesis that one can only have comprehensive goals which are based on social forms does not depend on the fact that the significance of the goal is conditioned by the existence of an appropriate social form. Rather, taking that for granted, they point to the fact that an individual cannot acquire the goal by explicit deliberation. It can be acquired only by habituation. Consider again the relations between spouses, or parental behaviour. Such relations are dense, in the sense that they involve more than individuals, even those experienced in them, can explicitly describe. They involve for example ways of treating a tired and distressed friend. Each one of us reacts somewhat differently to different friends in the same

situation. This is in part a response to the personality of
the friends. But it is in part a reflection of conventions of
appropriate behaviour. Those distinguish between business
friends, personal friends, golfing friends, etc. They include
clues by which one judges the intensity or intimacy the relationship has reached, and these in turn determine what
reaction will be appropriate. All these we describe in-
adequately. They are adequately described only in fiction,
or in drama. But they are too dense to allow explicit description or learning, they can be learnt only by experience,
direct or derived (e.g. from fiction).

It is of course not only the learning which is not explicit.
Even once the patterns of behaviour have been learnt much,
indeed most, of our behaviour remains based on learnt
semi-automatic responses (i.e. ones which we can, usually
with some effort, suppress, but which we normally do not
deliberate on and which we are not explicitly aware of).
Often even where such responses can be deliberate they
should not be. They acquire their significance from the fact
that they are not. We value their spontaneity, their instinc-
tive, non-reflective immediacy.

Furthermore, often when the goal concerns interaction
between people, its very possibility depends on the partners
having correct expectations concerning the meaning of other
people's behaviour. The significance of a thousand tiny clues
of what is known as body language contribute, indeed are
often essential, to the success of the developing relationship.
All these are derived from the common culture, from the
shared social forms, and though they receive the individual
stamp of each person, their foundation in shared social forms
is continuing and lasting. Just as the eye continues to guide
the hand all the way to its target, and is not limited to
determining its original trajectory, so our continued awareness of the common culture continuously nourishes and directs our behaviour in pursuit of our goals.

It is not that a person cannot, through the development
of his own variations and combinations, transcend the social
form. People can, and sometimes do, do this, but inevitably
in such cases the distance they have travelled away from the
shared forms is, in these cases, the most significant aspect of

their situation. It more than anything else then determines the significance of their situation and its possibilities for those people.

6. The Inseparability of Morality and Well-Being

Morality is often contrasted with prudence as a body of principles restricting the pursuit of the agent's own interest for the sake of the interests of others. Morality judges the interests of all impartially. The agent's own interest counts in the balance as one among many. Prudence, on the other hand, reflects the agent's own interest exclusively. Others feature in it only inasmuch as they contribute to the agent's interest. The doctrine of the relations between morality and prudence is commonly understood to be about the relative weight one ought to assign them. Some say that there is no answer to that question. Morally speaking one ought to act morally and the agent's interest should guide his action only inasmuch as it affects moral considerations through being one of the many interests morality is about. Prudentially speaking, on the other hand, an agent should act in his own interest and other people's interests should count only inasmuch as they contribute to his own. On this view there is no higher point of view which enables one to adjudicate between morality and prudence.

Other doctrines seek to establish the priority of one point of view over the others. The Hobbesians, for example, seek to show that morality is a strategy for seeking one's long term advantage.[1] Others claim that pursuit of one's own interest presupposes the binding force of morality, or commits one to uphold moral principles which are therefore superior to prudence when they conflict.[2] Particularly popular are views which suggest that while it is always admirable to prefer morality to prudence, it is permissible to prefer

[1] The most forceful advocacy of a subtle Hobbesian approach comes from D. Gauthier. See, e.g., 'Morality and Advantage', in J. Raz (ed.), *Practical Reasoning*, Oxford, 1978; 'Reason and Maximization', *Canadian Journal of Philosophy*, 4 (1975), 411, 'Thomas Hobbes: Moral Theorist', *Journal of Philosophy*, 76 (1979), 547.

[2] A. Gewirth's *Reason and Morality*, Chicago, 1978, is a powerful example of this kind.

prudence to moral considerations except where the latter impose moral duties. Other compromises introduce weighting into the process: it is morally permissible for an agent to give greater weight to his own interest than to moral considerations, but where moral considerations are very pressing they should take precedence over the agent's interest.

Though they are not always presented in this way, agent-relative conceptions of morality can be seen as attempts to develop a *moral* doctrine about the relations between morality and the agent's interest which escapes the trite dichotomy in which morality requires placing moral considerations above self-interested ones whereas prudence requires the opposite. Agent-relative moralities give a larger role to the agent's interest within morality. They advocate moralities which allow people to put their own interest first within certain bounds.[1] To a considerable extent the legitimate concerns which led people to advocate agent-relative moralities seem to me to be accounted for by a realization of the importance of action reasons for individual well-being, the degree to which people define the parameters of their own well-being through their own actions, and the existence of pervasive incommensurability. We will return to this point in the next chapter. But these considerations do not solve the problem of the relations between morality and prudence. They leave one puzzled as to how to avoid giving priority to one over the other, or how to justify a 'compromise' position assigning a limited role to each of the two rival points of view.

The most penetrating statement of the difficulty that the conventional and the consequentialist views of morality pose to any attempt to find room for the agent's own point of view is Williams' passage, which was quoted in the previous chapter:

The point is not. . . that if the project or attitude is that central to his life then to abandon it would be very disagreeable to him. . . [O]nce he is prepared to look at it like that, the argument in any serious case is over anyway. The point is that he is identified with

[1] Charles Fried's *Right and Wrong*, Cambridge Mass., 1978, and S. Scheffler's *The Refutation of Consequentialism*, Oxford, 1983, are clearest in seeing agent relativity as a matter of striking the right balance between morality and self-interest.

his actions as flowing from projects and attitudes which in some cases he takes seriously at the deepest level. . . . It is absurd to demand of such a man. . . that he should just step aside from his own projects and decisions and acknowledge the decision which utilitarian calculation requires. It is to alienate him in a real sense from his actions and the source of his actions in his own convictions.[1]

This passage was generally interpreted as pointing towards agent-relativity. It was taken to criticise agent-neutral moralities. I think that its lesson is different and deeper. It points to a problem that cannot be solved except by radically revising one's notions of morality and of personal interest in a way which denies that they represent two separately comprehensible points of view. If so, then the problem of their relations is transformed in a way which solves Williams' problem. (It should be admitted that on that interpretation the dramatic nature of Williams' example is immaterial to his case, and is merely useful from the literary point of view.)

Both the popular and the philosophically fashionable pictures of human beings accept an asymmetry between people's concern for their own interest and their concern to do what is morally right. Somehow their concern for their own interest is secure and natural. Sometimes it is held to be a conceptual truth that people are motivated to pursue their own interest. Their willingness to do the moral thing is more precarious. It is the result of socialization which harnesses their self-interested instincts. Or, if morality is held to be, or to be served by, a natural inclination, it is thought of as a weaker force, easily overwhelmed by one's self-serving instincts. It is a very misleading picture. To unravel its mistakes we need to take another look at the notion of self-interest.

It is a much misunderstood truism that every person has reason to look after his own interest. Two misinterpretations abound. One regards the truism as a simple fact about human nature, that all human beings are egoists by nature. The

---

[1] *Utilitarianism: For and Against*, pp. 116–17. I am sorry to say that Williams himself fails to derive the lesson to be recommended below from his own insight. See his *Ethics and The Limits of Philosophy*, London 1985.

other regards the truism as a tautology. One's interest is to
have whatever one wants to have. Since desiring something
is a reason to have it one has reason to have what one desires,
i.e. one has reason to pursue one's interest. Both views were
stated in a rough and ready way. Both have been developed
into two whole families of sophisticated theories. The human
nature view was elaborated by various theories about the
contribution of egoism and altruism to human make-up, and
the way in which the first may develop into the second; the
tautology interpretation by defining self-interest in terms of
a subclass of one's desires only (rational desires, etc.). Both
interpretations hold some truth and much which is false.
Each helps expose the fallacy of the other.

The distinction between well-being and self-interest helps
to clarify matters. The tautology thesis is plainly false if read
to mean that self-interest, in the sense identified in Section
2 above, is necessarily desired by all people. Clearly there
are people who do not wish to live, or who do not wish to
avoid injury, etc. If it is the case that people generally wish
to pursue their self-interest this can only be a factual generalization. Supporters of the tautology thesis clearly identify self-interest with the notion we called 'well-being'. As
we saw, well-being is largely determined by one's projects,
by what one cares about. To that extent it is tautological that
our pursuits serve our well-being. But it is neither tautological nor true that we pursue our well-being. That is, it is
false that we pursue our goals, which define our well-being,
because they are our goals. We pursue them because they
are, as we believe, worth pursuing. In other words, those
who support the tautology thesis are right inasmuch as they
are in the vicinity of a true tautology: The success of our
pursuits promotes our well-being. Yet they fail to identify
the right tautology when they claim that we necessarily pursue our well-being, if this is taken to represent our goal or
concern, our reason for having the goals we have.

The mistake of the tautology thesis is in assuming that
wanting something is a reason for action. As was argued
above we want what we want for reasons and, barring special
circumstances, we try to achieve what we want for the same
reasons. We further saw that when we are wrong in our

estimation of the reasons for our goals and relationships it is not in our interest to succeed in them. It is then also possible to say that though in a sense we want to succeed in them, in another sense we do not. They are our goals, but only under a false description. Under their true descriptions they are not what we want.[1]

Much the same can be said about the thesis that it is an empirical fact that people pursue their interest. It is not a plain fact that we pursue our well-being. On the one hand, it is tautological that success in our pursuits serves our well-being. On the other hand, it is false that we pursue our goals because their pursuit serves our well-being. Nor is it an empirical fact that we pursue our self-interest. Often our pursuits lead us to sacrifice our self-interest in the pursuit of goals we care most about. All that can be said is that people tend to pursue their medium-range biological needs.

Most regrettable is the fact that the common discussions of the agent's own interest which pitch it against his moral duties tend to concentrate on self-interest rather than on well-being. Their well-being, and not their self-interest, matters most both morally and to people themselves. Therefore, the relation between an agent's well-being and morality is the real issue. The notion of self-interest is thus demoted to a secondary place. The important notion is the wider one of well-being. For many diverse purposes it may be useful to discuss self-interest, rather than well-being. But the very distinction between well-being and self-interest is, and can be, no more than a rough and ready discrimination. It breaks down if too much is made of it. One point of breakdown, to give an example, is very familiar. Sometimes we wish to advance the well-being of another without serving the causes he cares about. Joan does not love the people John loves but she loves him and wishes to help him but not them. To start with it may seem that her course is clearly charted. She

---

[1] These remarks are much over-simplified. In particular they leave out the fact that by becoming aware of our mistake we may find alternative reasons for continuing with the same goals, e.g. that it will be rather painful to change, or that our goal possesses other laudable features. Others concerned with our well-being should not regard the existence of false desires as reason for their satisfaction. But they should regard the fact that we would remain attached to our goals, even if our mistake is exposed, as such a reason.

should advance John's self-interest, but not help him with his altruistic pursuits. Very soon we discover the futility of this advice. For one thing John's life may be so intertwined with that of some of the people he loves that it is meaningless to say that their prosperity does not serve his self-interest. For another, his non-self-interested goals may be his main preoccupation at this particular period in his life. Joan cannot do much to help him except by helping him with them.

What really matters to people is all that we group under their well-being. This includes more, it may include much more, than their self-interest. It may also include less. Here is our clue to the relationship between morality and well-being. If there is an inherent or a fundamental conflict between well-being and morality, if morality is indeed the limiting of the pursuit of well-being in the interest of others, then the projects and interests that people develop and care about must have an inherent or natural tendency to conflict with the interests of others. There is no denying that such conflicts happen all too often. It is also true that some environmental and social conditions make it unlikely that the biologicallydetermined needs of all will be met and that some of these tend to lead people into conflict in their attempt to satisfy those needs. But I know of no reason to regard the existence of pervasive conflicts as conceptually or naturally inescapable. Occasional conflict between well-being and morality is endemic. But so are conflicts between different aspects of one's well-being.

On the contrary we have reason to think that conflicts between morality and the agent's well-being, albeit inevitable, are only accidental and occasional. Given that the well-being of the agent is in the successful pursuit of valuable goals, and that value depends on social forms, it is of the essence of value that it contributes to the constitution of the agent's personal well-being just as much as it defines moral objectives. The source of value is one for the individual and the community. It is one and the same from the individual and from the moral point of view. Individuals define the contours of their own lives by drawing on the communal pool of values. These will, in well-ordered societies, contribute indiscriminately both to their self-interest and to other aspects of their well-being. They also define the field of moral values. There is but one source for morality and for personal well-being.

It is important not to go overboard and read the above as suggesting an inevitable identity of moral and personal concerns. All I argue for is that individuals inevitably derive the goals by which they constitute their lives from the stock of social forms available to them, and the feasible variations on it. If those social forms are morally valid, if they enshrine sound moral conceptions, then it is easy for people generally to find themselves with, and to choose for themselves, goals which lead to a rough coincidence in their own lives of moral and personal concerns. In their careers, personal relations and other interests they will be engaged on activities which serve themselves and others at the same time. By being teachers, production workers, drivers, public servants, loyal friends and family people, loyal to their communities, nature loving, and so on, they will be pursuing their own goals, enhancing their own well-being, and also serving their communities, and generally living in a morally worthy way.

The dependence of well-being on personal goals, and the dependence of these on social forms, guarantees the essential identity of people's responsiveness to their own well-being and to morality, *provided those social forms are morally sound.* There is no guarantee that some individuals will not find it impossible to adjust and will turn to immoral forms of life. It merely follows that their well-being will suffer as well. They may well be trapped in their own fate, unable to escape their own immoral ways. But then, in such a society, success in their own lives will escape them as well. Their well-being depends on their ability to make sense in their own lives of the, by our assumption morally sound, social forms of their society. We are assuming that they are immoral through their inability to do so, and this amounts to the undermining of their own well-being. Apart from these cases, and the occasional conflict in the life of any person between morality and self-interest, the main source of deviation between morality and a person's concern for his own well-being arises where the social forms availbale to him in his society are morally wicked, as when a young person grows up in an area where membership in a racist group is the social norm. Such cases do arise. They arise all too often. But they are neither conceptual nor natural necessities or strong tendencies.

Some may agree with all that was said so far and yet feel that the main problem was merely swept under the carpet in the concession that there are occasional conflicts between the agent's well-being and the well-being of others. That is indeed the main problem, and its consideration is not to be dismissed glibly by a few comments here. All that this argument is designed to establish is that the resolution of such conflicts is to be found in values which are both the foundation of the agent's own well-being and the reasons which compel respect for the well-being of others. He must remain faithful to these values, and be guided by them in such conflicts, or else his own well-being will be compromised, and not only that of others. These remarks deny that there is a logical difference between a conflict of reasons which affect only the well-being of the agent, and such a conflict where the well-being of the agent is in conflict with that of others. Both types of conflict are rooted in values on which the well-being of the agent is founded, and their resolution depends on the guidance which these same values provide. But there is nothing here to imply that there is always one correct resolution to conflicts of reasons. Where there is no resolution, or where more than one resolution is correct, different people may act differently while none acts against reason. But these matters cannot be explored here.

Who then is the moral person? What is the proper relationship between self-interest and moral concern? At a superficial level one is inclined to say that he is a person among whose pursuits there are many non-self-interested ones, and whose self-interested goals do not conflict, except occasionally, with the well-being of others. This, though true, takes the divide between one's self-interest and the other aspects of one's well-being too seriously. A better answer is that the morally good person is he whose prosperity is so intertwined with the pursuit of goals which advance intrinsic values and the well-being of others that it is impossible to separate his personal well-being from his moral concerns.

13

Incommensurability

The previous chapter argued for six main conclusions. *First*, to a large degree the well-being of a person is determined by his goals. Whether what he does or what happens to him is good for him or not depends to a considerable extent on what goals he has. *Second*, important goals form nested structures. They are comprehensive goals in which are embedded as constituent parts more limited goals. *Third*, goals are held for reasons, and those normally are not (at least not exclusively) the will of the agent but the value of his goals. *Fourth*, comprehensive goals are based on social forms. *Fifth*, other than one's biologically determined needs personal well-being depends primarily on action reasons. *Sixth*, morality and personal well-being are not two independent and mutually conflicting systems of values, and there is no essential tendency in their demands, or the reasons for action that they generate, to conflict. While the first and the fifth of these conclusions explain the allure of the fifth feature of consequentialism, the thesis of the transparency of values, the third and fourth conclusions establish the falsity of this thesis. The present chapter aims to refute the second feature of consequentialism, its belief in comparability. The conclusions of the previous chapter, it will be argued, entail that both values and valuables are to a large degree incommensurable.

The task divides into three. First, the notion of incommensurability has to be explained and shown to be a credible, useful concept. Second, the existence of a widespread belief in pervasive incommensurability between significant options has to be established. Third, that belief has to be explained in a way which brings out the value of incommensurabilities, the impact they have on people's well-being.

1. The Concept

One difficulty in arguing for incommensurability is in finding conceptual room for it. What could it mean? Given any
two values, say liberty and equality, could it fail to be the
case that either liberty is more important than equality, or it
is less important, or that liberty and equality are equal in
importance? Is there a fourth possibility? Of course, this way
of describing the problem is very misleading. We are not
looking for another judgment of the relative importance of
two valuable options. Rather we are looking for failure of
comparability (I will use 'incomparable' and 'incommensurate' interchangeably). This provides the clue for a
simple definition of incommensurability.

> A and B are incommensurate if it is neither true that
> one is better than the other nor true that they are of equal
> value.[1]

People might say: But what else can two options be? If
neither is better than the other, surely their value must be
the same. Sometimes comparative judgments of importance
are implicitly understood to be between independent values.
In such cases it may be far from clear what comparison is
meant. Is it a question about the comparative value of complete freedom and absolute equality? If so it is possible that
comparing liberty and equality is meaningless. It makes
sense to talk of the relative weight of options one can at least
in principle choose between. It makes no sense to talk of
choosing between perfect liberty and absolute equality. As
long as one is a person one has some liberty. Nor is it clear
what could be meant by 'a situation of total inequality', in
whatever respect one cares to think of. Similarly, one cannot
be equal to another in all respects, without being that other,
nor can one be free to do everything. Certain freedoms consist in part of a degree of unfreedom (being married *is*, in
part, not having the freedom to seek other partners). All one
can do, this argument runs, is to compare different combinations of liberty and equality, for we can have a choice
between such packages. But to say that it makes no sense to

---

[1] Incommensurability is so defined that only what is valuable (or of negative
value) can fail to be comparable in value with another valuable.

compare liberty and equality in themselves is not to admit incommensurability, for judgments of incommensurability deny the truth and not the meaningfulness of judgments of commensurability.

If, on the other hand, comparisons of the value of liberty and equality are meant to be comparisons of types of options then it is clear that they are incommensurable. That is, the class of all liberty-enhancing options may be incommensurate with the class of all food-providing options. This simply means that it is not the case that whatever one's circumstances any food-providing option is better than any liberty-enhancing one, nor is the opposite true. At the same time it is not the case that, whatever the circumstances, any option of the one kind is of equal value to any option of the other kind. One would expect type incommensurability to be true of all or at least most natural types. But the incommensurability we are interested in is that of individual options. Is there conceptual room for it?

Assume that we start with two options, A and B, of which the first is the better one. Gradually improve B and reduce the value of A. There must, it seems, come a point where they are equal in value. Clearly this argument is based on confusion. It presupposes, for example, that degrees of improvement are infinitely divisible. Only then is there any reason to expect that one option would be level with the other before it surpasses it. Of course, the disappearance of the point of equality does not yield incommensurability. It means that one jumped by too much and now B is better than A. So even if one assumes that what determines the value of different options is not indefinitely divisible, and that as a result precise equality cannot always be achieved, there is still no room for incommensurability. It means only that there might come a point when the smallest conceivable improvement in the value of the lesser option makes it more valuable than the other one. There is no equality, but nor is there incommensurability.

The conceivability of incommensurability has to be established in two steps. First, one must give it an interpretation which explains in what way incommensurability differs from equality of value. The definition leaves one with the uncomfortable suspicion that they are merely different names for the same thing. Secondly, one must provide some account of how that conceptual possibility might be realized. Otherwise the suspicion that, though the definition is clear enough, there is a conceptual impediment to the existence of incommensurabilities is bound to linger.

To begin with, however, let us note that the definition allows for two distinct types of incommensurability. *First*, there is the case in which it is false that of A and B either one is better than the other or they are of equal value. *Second*, there is the case in which this statement is neither true nor false.

I shall refer to the second as *indeterminacy* of value. For the most part when talking of incommensurability I shall have the first case only in mind. So far as I can see indeterminacy of value is an undoubted result of the general indeterminacy of language, which is itself a consequence of the indeterminacy of action and intention. Its importance lies in its general relevance to the understanding of language and of action. I am not aware of any very significant implications it has for practical thought. Except for the occasional incidental reference I will therefore disregard it from now on.

Let me start with the explanation of the difference between equality of value and incommensurability. One way of bringing out the difference is by saying that if two options are incommensurate then reason has no judgment to make concerning their relative value. Saying that they are of equal value is passing a judgment about their relative value, whereas saying that they are incommensurate is not. I shall return to this contrast later; but first let us mention another way of stating the difference.

Incommensurability implies (subject to a reservation to be entered below) that an option may be better than one of two incommensurate options without being better than the other. In this respect incommensurability is unlike equality. What is better than one of two equal options is necessarily better than the other. We can illustrate the idea by looking at another concept with a similar structure, that of resemblance. John Mackie explains:

[C]onsiderations may be imperfectly commensurable, so that neither of the opposing cases is stronger than the other, and yet they are not finely balanced. Consider the analogous question about three brothers: Is Peter more like James than he is like John? There may be an objectively right and determinable answer to this question, but again there may not. It may be that the only correct reply is that Peter is more like James in some ways, and more like John in others, and that there is no objective reason for putting more weight on the former points of resemblance than on the latter, or vice versa. While we might say that Peter's likeness to James is equal to his likeness to John . . . this does not mean that any slight additional resemblance to either would decide the issue; hence it does not mean that this equality expresses an improbably exact balance.[1]

The test of incommensurability is failure of transitivity. *Two valuable options are incommensurable if (1) neither is better than the other, and (2) there is (or could be) another option which is better than one but is not better than the other.*

This failure of transitivity is of great importance, for so many assume that if A is not worse than B and C is better than A it follows that C is better than B. This is a *non sequitur*. In the study of people's actual valuations of different options, reliance on transitivity of this kind often leads the researcher to find either irrationality, or hidden preferences which restore transitivity, where neither exists. Revealed preferences are a very incomplete and misleading clue to people's valuations. These can be accurately gauged only if one takes account of people's own reasons for different valuations (a delicate task which is in principle incapable of completion, as it is impossible completely and exhaustively to describe a person's set of values at any given time). Their reasons may reveal belief in incommensurability without betraying irrationality.

We have here a simple way of determining whether two options are incommensurate given that it is known that neither is better than the other. If it is possible for one of them to be improved without thereby becoming better than the other, or if there can be another option which is better than the one but not better than the other, then the two original

[1] J. L. Mackie, 'The Third Theory of Law', *Philolophy & Public Affairs*, 7 (1977–8), 9.

options are incommensurate. I shall call this feature the *mark
of incommensurability*. But remember that it is not its definition. While being, for most purposes, perfectly sufficient
as a test of incomparability, it is not in fact a necessary
condition of incomparability. It would have been a necessary
condition had value been indefinitely divisible, i.e. had it
been the case that between any two options which are not
equal in value there is another (possible) option better than
the one and worse than the other. But most values may well
be discrete. If for one option to be better than the other it is
necessarily the case that it is possible to perceive (in some
appropriate sense of this word) the difference in their value
then most values seem to be discrete. Be that as it may, if
value is discrete then two options may be incommensurate
even when they do not display the mark of incommensurability. That is it may be the case that neither of
them is better than the other nor are they of equal value, and
yet any conceivable option which is better than the one is
better than the other. The same could be the case for any
option worse than one of them. This shows that the mark of
incommensurability should not be confused with its meaning. But it does not diminish its utility as a mark, a test of
incommensurability which is likely to be adequate for all our
purposes.

   Given this account of the difference between incomparability and equality, let us proceed to the second
stage and ask whether we have any reason to think that
incommensurability is at all possible. The most important
source of incomparability is 'incomplete' definition of the
contribution of criteria to a value. This is most obvious
where a value is a function of several criteria, so that a good
novelist, for example, might be judged by his humour, his
insight, his imaginativeness and his ability to plot. It is possible that our weighting of the different criteria does not
establish a complete ranking of all possible combinations. In
this example the different criteria are themselves evaluative
ones. It is valuable to have insight, as well as to be able to
invent plots, to be imaginative, etc. Incomparability can also
exist if the value depends on a multiplicity of purely descriptive criteria.

There are at least two other sources of incomparability. First, indeterminacy results from vagueness and the absence of sharp boundaries which infect language generally and therefore apply to value measured by a single criterion as well. These apply even in cases in which a single descriptive criterion determines the value of options. Suppose one is judging how good a sign post is by its visibility. Its visibility depends, let us simplify, on its size only. The bigger it is the more visible it is, until it reaches a certain point beyond which its visibility declines (since it fills the horizon and is no longer easily seen as a single object). There is likely to be a range of sizes regarding which it will be neither true nor false both that different signs are of equal visibility and that one is more visible than the other.

Second, value is often determined by the probability that the option will produce certain effects. Judgments of probability are infected by considerable incommensurabilities of their own. These are contagious and are transmitted to the value of the relevant options. They do not depend on multi-criteria evaluations.

There is a strong temptation to think of incommensurability as an imperfection, an incompleteness. Why don't we develop the function from the different features to the overall valuation until it is complete and eliminate thereby all incommensurability? The mistake in this thought is that it assumes that there is a true value behind the ranking of options, and that the ranking is a kind of technique for measuring this value. It is true of course that when we express a judgment about the value of options we strive to identify what is true independently of our valuation. But the ranking which determines the relative value of options is not a way of getting at some deeper truth, it constitutes the value of the options. Values may change, but such a change is not a discovery of a deeper truth. It is simply a change of value. Therefore, where there is incommensurability it is the ultimate truth. There is nothing further behind it, nor is it a sign of an imperfection.

Mackie emphasized marginal, small-scale incommensurabilities. It may readily be agreed that small pockets of incommensurability abound. That is, it may be agreed that people's judgments of value are not very fine, so that most options are surrounded by margins of incommensurability. I value a walk in the park this afternoon more than reading a book at home. But one can successively change the odds, making the park a little windier, the book accompanied by a glass of port, until one would say that neither is better than the other. At this point it is almost always possible to imagine a small but definite improvement in one option which will not be sufficient to make the improved option better than the other. Imagine that I am indifferent as between a walk in the park and a book with a glass of Scotch at home. It is possible that though I will definitely prefer (*a*) the book with a glass of port to (*b*) the book with Scotch, I am indifferent as between either and (*c*) a walk in the park. This establishes that I regard (*a*) and (*c*) as incommensurate. It seems plausible that normally people's valuation of options allows for marginal incommensurability of this sort. Furthermore, it seems plausible that they are not always wrong when their evaluations are incommensurable, i.e. that marginal incommensurability is a feature of sound practical reasoning generally.

Marginal incommensurability creates bounded areas of incommensurability, pockets of breakdown of comparability which may be regarded as no threat to the consequentialist position. Once you make one option not merely definitely and perceptibly, but also significantly better than the other it becomes better. These cases pose a theoretical puzzle for the consequentialist who has to adjust his assumptions to cope with them, but they need not undermine his substantive beliefs about the way people should behave, since they are marginal cases, bounded by the test of significance. The real question is whether there are cases of significant incommensurabilities.

2. *Incommensurability and Rough Equality*

There are plenty of insignificant incommensurabilities. Here are two cups, one of coffee and one of tea. As it happens (*a*) neither is of greater value to me than the other; (*b*) warming the cup of tea a little will improve its value; and (*c*) the improved cup of tea will be neither better nor worse than the cup of coffee. Hence the two cups are incommensurate in value. What could be more trivial than that?

The very possibility of significant incommensurabilities appears to be mysterious. Some people say that the only significant failure of comparisons is of a different kind altogether, i.e. it is a case in which two options cannot be compared in any way. This *radical incomparability* excludes even the possibility of judging that of two options neither is better nor are they of equal value. That judgment is itself, I take the claim to be, a comparison of their value ending with a negative conclusion. Radical incomparability does not leave any room for any comparisons whatsoever, not even negative ones.

This seems to be a confusion. It mistakes the meaning of incomparability as we have been using the expression. Statements of incommensurability, i.e., statements that of two options neither is better nor are they of equal value, do not compare the value of options. They are denials that their values are comparable. Incommensurability is not yet another valuation of the relative merits of two options alongside such valuations as having greater value or having equal value. It is a rejection of the applicability of such judgments to the options in question.

That having been said, it is true that we can distinguish the narrow meaning of incommensurability, i.e. that it is false that one of the options is better and false that they are of equal value, from the broader meaning of the term which does leave room for another kind of failure of comparability, the one we called *indeterminacy*. The radical incomparability I vaguely described above seems to be nothing other than indeterminacy. But far from being the only true and radical case of breakdown of comparability, completely different from our insignificant incommensurabilities, indeterminacy seems to be a less dramatic case of wide incommensurability. I adverted to vagueness and indeterminacy of language as sources of indeterminacy of value-judgment. It was not my intention to suggest that such indeterminacy is trivial or unimportant in people's lives. It may profoundly affect lives which are caught in its web. But it seems to me that the issues of its significance are the same, and trail the general issues of the significance of narrow incommensurability. From the point of view of the explanation of practical thought it does not represent any special important issues.

Just as it is misleading to aspire to some deeper true incommensurability, more profound than the notion we have in mind, so it is misleading to dismiss the significance of incommensurability of our kind on the ground that it simply means *rough equality*. If A and B are roughly equal then the difference in their value is not great. A may be better than B and yet be also roughly equal to it. This is not a trivial point. To establish rough equality one needs, it would seem, some way of measuring the difference in value and establishing that it is not great. This is easiest when distances between options are susceptible to cardinal measurement. Clearly not all options are susceptible to this, and none of those which are incommensurate are. Can rough equality consist merely in certain ranking relations? It is arguable, for example, that if every possible option that is better than A is also better than B and every possible option that is worse than A is worse than B and vice versa, then A and B are roughly of equal value. This condition can be met even if A and B are not of the same value provided there is some conceptual or principled impossibility of indefinite divisibility. It could then be the case that A is better than B, or vice versa. But it could also be that they are incommensurable, and still roughly of equal value.

Considerations to be advanced in a moment suggest that this condition is insufficient to establish rough equality of value. In any case the condition is clearly inadequate for its task. It fails, for example, to identify as insignificant the difference in the value of the cups of tea and coffee we started with. In fact it fails to discover rough equality among any options which meet the test of the mark of incommensurability. It is the mark of incommensurability that it fails, that there are possible options better than A and yet not better than B, or vice versa. Only incommensurabilities which cannot be identified by this test turn out to be between roughly equal options.

But can the two cups of our example really be of roughly

equal value? I said that it seems as if rough equality presupposes an ability to establish that the gap between the
value of the two options is not great. It presupposes, in other
words, or seems to, a comparative judgment of the value of
the two options. But did we not say that incommensurability
is defined as the denial that such comparisons are true of
the options concerned? If so then by definition incommensurability is incompatible with rough equality. But
then the two cups are not of roughly the same value.

Something has gone seriously wrong. It seems that we
have been looking at the wrong kind of criterion for rough
equality. It seems that there are criteria which have nothing
or little to do with the ranking of the options concerned. Let
us make a fresh start and accept that two options are of
roughly equal value if one is right to be indifferent between
them, i.e. if little depends on which is chosen, if it does not
matter which one chooses. Perhaps this condition obtains
sometimes even among incommensurabilities.

Indeed the new test seems to reverse the situation. It now
seems that all incommensurables are necessarily roughly
equal in value. The argument is simple:

(1) Two options are roughly equal if and only if it does not
    matter which one is chosen, if it is right to be indifferent
    between them.
(2) What rightly makes one care about which option to
    choose is that one is better supported by reason than
    the other.
(3) There is no reason to prefer either of two in-
    commensurable options.
    Therefore, all incommensurables are of roughly equal
    value.

Since I approve of the new test, subject to a clarification
to be made in a minute, the only way to avoid the conclusion
is to challenge the second premiss. It appears solid. Is not
the existence of a reason to prefer one option to the other
what makes the choice significant? Do we not say that if the
options are of equal value then it does not matter which one
is chosen? But on reflection it turns out that (2) is false, and
owes its intuitive appeal to a confusion between it and:

(2¹) What rightly makes one care about which option to choose is that each is supported by weighty, and very different reasons.

Let us take as our example the case of a person who has to choose between two options. The one will irrevocably commit him to a career in law, the other will irrevocably commit him to a career as a clarinettist. He is equally suited for both, and he stands an equal chance of success in both. It seems to me that this is the sort of decision that anyone facing it quite rightly cares a lot about. It is a choice that one ought not be indifferent to, or unconcerned about. To be indifferent to this kind of choice is not to have a proper respect for oneself.[1]

Furthermore, I can be certain of all I have just written while not knowing whether or not either the legal or the musical option is better than the other. Assume, for example, that neither is better than the other. It hardly needs arguing that in that case they are incommensurable. The suggestion that they are of exactly the same value cannot be entertained seriously. One would still be greatly and rightly concerned about the choice. It is one of major significance for one's life. The example shows that we can judge the importance of the reasons for two options without judging their relative importance. This is hardly surprising. As was pointed out in the last chapter, the more comprehensive an option is, i.e. the more aspects of one's life it affects, the more important it is, other things being equal. It follows that incommensurable options can be of roughly equal value. But that they need not be. The choice between them can be the most momentous choice one will ever face.[2]

Three clarifications may help to bolster the argument.

---

[1] It will be noticed that I declined to follow the oft repeated advice to separate issues of the logic or structure of value from substantive questions of what is valuable. I doubt whether there is any sharp or significant divide between questions of rationality, of the structure of comprehensible practical thought, and substantive evaluative issues, such as the nature of individual well-being, what makes a person better off.

[2] The ability to classify two options into one class of value, e.g. determining that each is quite valuable but not very valuable, does not establish rough equality of value. It all depends on how significant the differences are between options in one class. They may be very great indeed, as are the differences between all options which have a positive value.

First, notice that not only the importance of the reasons for the options, but also the degree to which they differ, determine the significance of the choice. Suppose one's choice is between a post with Slaughter & May and one with Freshfields. Each is as comprehensive a choice as the one in our previous example. But, different as those much respected firms of solicitors are, the differences between the reasons for the options pale into insignificance compared with the ones in the other example. Consequently the choice itself is much less momentous, even though, precisely because the reasons are more of a kind, one of the options is much more likely to be a better one than in our other case.

Second, the significance of a choice turns out to have little or nothing to do with the fact that one option is better than the other. Brown bread is definitely better than white. But the choice can hardly be deemed to be a very significant one. One does not care much which one chooses. Premiss (2) above is altogether wrong. It follows that if there are no significant choices between options of exactly equal value that is because there are no options of equal value among those supported by weighty and very different reasons. This seems to me correct. But that is another story.

Third, we have discovered that there are two different notions of rough equality of value. The one presupposes a measure of value to establish that the options are close in value. The other depends on the significance of the choice between the options. The first does not apply to incommensurable options since by definition one cannot measure the gap in value between them. The second does apply. It reveals that some of these options are of roughly the same value while others are not. The difference between the significant and the trivial breakdown of comparability is not a difference in meanings of incommensurability, but in the significance of the choice between different incommensurable options.

The puzzle we began with was: how can incommensurability be anything other than trivial? It attests to the indeterminacy of reason. Where the considerations for and against two alternatives are incommensurate, reason is indeterminate. It provides no better case for one alternative than for the other. Since it follows that there is no reason to shun one of the alternatives in favour of the other, we are in a sense free to choose which course to follow. That sense of freedom is special, and may be misleading. It is unlike the situation where one course of action is as good as the other. It is indifferent which action we take. They are equally good and equally bad. Incomparability does not ensure equality of merit and demerit. It does not mean indifference. It marks the inability of reason to guide our action, not the insignificance of our choice.[1]

How can that be? We are not concerned with the inability of reason to guarantee that we are guided by it. Our perennial ability to act irrationally is not in question here. Nor are we questioning the fact that many aspects of every action are not in fact guided by reason. Those aspects of an action which constitute a person's style are an obvious example. Normally one does not reason about one's body posture, manner of movement or speech, and the like. But all these can become subject to reasoning. One may, as an actor might, plan carefully every aspect of one's gait and demeanour. Incommensurability speaks not of what does escape reason but of what must elude it. This too is unremarkable if what eludes it is insignificant. We are unperturbed by the pervasiveness of insignificant incommensurabilities of the kind instanced in Section 1 because they apply to insignificant choices. It does not matter whether I stay at home to read a book or go for a walk in the park if there is no reason to prefer one course of action to the other.

We sought the explanation in the consequences of the choice. The consequences may transform the nature of a person's project, or change the relations between him and the people closest to him. When a choice between two incommensurate alternatives has such far-reaching consequences it is a significant choice, even though reason fails to provide complete guidance. It is a mistake to think that if the consequences are momentous they will translate into

[1] To be precise there are reasons for (and against) each of the incommensurate options, and these may be enough to determine their ranking as against other options. But in the choice between the incommensurate options reason is unable to provide any guidance.

reasons for one action or the other which will make the choice determined. For one thing, the consequences may be of a kind that should not guide one's action (as when one should act out of friendship and fellow feeling and not on the ground that one's help and support will be appreciated and reciprocated). For another, even where they guide one's choice they may fail to determine its outcome. The choice between looking after an aged parent and getting married in order to have a family of one's own is momentous in its consequences. It should be informed by knowledge of these consequences. And yet they may well fail to yield a determined outcome, a definite right or wrong, wise or foolish decision.

3. Denying Comparability

The argument so far was meant to cut through the conceptual fog and to establish the possibility of significant incommensurablity. It did little to demonstrate its existence or to explain why it arises, and what if any positive role it plays in our practical thought. Before we tackle these tasks (in the next section) it would be helpful to reflect on another aspect of the methods employed to establish what is the comparative value of options in the eyes of people. These reflections yield a brief, abstract argument for the existence of significant incommensurabilities.

In a lifetime an individual passes judgment on the relative value of a large number of alternative options, but they are inevitably a small proportion of all possible comparative judgments. Theories which provide general recipes for comparing values, when they are not victims of the illusion that revealed preferences provide the clue to their problem, begin by establishing people's actual judgments on the relative value of options, and extrapolate principles which can be applied generally and without restriction to any pair of alternatives. Unrestricted generality is built into the theory-forming process as a theoretical desideratum. The question of incommensurability is begged without argument. Suppose we give it a fair hearing. What can be said in favour of significant incommensurability?

To start with, having abandoned the methodological preference for unrestricted generality, we are free to take seriously the fact that people not only form judgments of the
comparative merit of some options but also deny the comparability of others. Not surprisingly in a given culture these
reactions tend to be widely shared. It is common to deny,
for example, that the comprehensive goals discussed in the
previous chapter are comparable in value. People are likely
to refuse to pronounce on the comparative value of a career
in teaching and in dentistry. They deny the comparability
of playing a musical instrument and cycling to visit old
churches as pastimes, etc. Such judgments of incomparability may be expressed in a variety of ways. We
should not be surprised if as often as saying that such options
are incomparable people will simply refuse to compare them,
or will say that there is nothing to choose between them, or
will express ignorance as to their comparative value, etc.
Their true meaning can be established in the ways described
in the previous sections. If people's evaluations can form a
foundation for a general theory of comparative value judgments, perhaps people's refusal to evaluate could provide a
pointer to the existence of one class of significant incommensurability. Simple non-valuations may be significant
as well. But they may also be accidental. Refusals to evaluate
must be significant.

Their significance is, however, problematic. One may
point out, first, that while people reject the thought of comparing the value of various options when the question is
raised in the abstract, they do make decisions about trade-
offs when the issue is forced on them by the circumstances
of their lives. Second, even while refusing to make comparisons, people are engaged in choices that imply such comparisons. For example, one may refuse to admit the
comparability of married life in modest circumstances with
life as a rich single person while preferring cohabitation to
marriage for tax or similar reasons, and agreeing to part with
one's partner in order to go abroad and make money for
several months. Could not one combine these valuations
of the symbolic significance of the marriage bond with the
valuation of the worth of actual companionship and, with

the addition of other similar indicators, conclude what value that person, his protestations to the contrary not-withstanding, really does assign to his marriage?

The problem with pursuing this suggestion and trying to work out the comparative value people assign to options that they refuse to compare is that it leaves out of account the refusal to compare values itself. It bypasses and ignores it. To do so is to falsify people's judgments of comparative value. One retort is that the refusal is not ignored. While it is denied relevance to the valuation of the options one is refusing to compare, it is given its proper and separate place as being a negative valuation of the activity of comparing values. If Judy refuses to judge whether she values her friendship with John more or less than she values $1,000,000, she nevertheless does regard it as worth either more or less or precisely the same as $1,000,000, but she also values not thinking about this question. Hence her refusal to compare.

Judy's reply is that she does not mind taking time off and answering the question about the comparative value of her friendship and the money. All she meant is that they are incommensurate, and that is the answer. There is no thought she refuses to entertain. Only an a priori commitment to commensurability can lead one to misrepresent her belief in the incommensurability of two options as a negative valu-ation of a third option. Later on we will see that an emotional response to attempts to press on one comparisons of in-commensurable options is a natural and justifiable con-comitant of some judgments of incommensurability, as is the reply that one of the incommensurable options 'is not an option one would even consider' as an alternative to the other. But neither fact can be equated with putting a negative value to the activity of thinking about the question. Those thoughts are pointless and annoying. But the annoyance and feelings of pointlessness are not to be equated with judg-ments of incommensurability. They are sometimes absent, as in most cool philosophical discussions, while the judg-ments which normally trigger them remain.

The defender of commensurability may remain un-impressed by his inability to explain refusals to compare value. He will say that whatever the explanation it is not that the person who denies that two options are comparable really finds them incommensurate. He will rely again on the two reasons mentioned above. First, when a choice is forced on the person he will prefer one option to the other, and his choice is not arbitrary. It may well, for example, be predictable. Second, one is able to extrapolate his relative evaluation of the options he refuses to compare on the basis of other comparative judgments he is happy to make. The very person who denies that one can measure the value of friendship in money or in other commodities is often willing to sacrifice a friendship for a job which takes him to a different part of the country. The same person may well decline the offer of the job for the sake of which he will sacrifice a friendship if an opportunity for an equally well-paid job arises in his own town. So he is in effect trading a friendship for money, and by extrapolation its rough monetary value can be established.

Both reasons are, however, illegitimate. The second, extrapolation, relies on transitivity and commensurability. It therefore begs the question. Our analysis of incommensurability does, at the same time, block the consequentialist first move. The ability and willingness to choose does not depend on valuing the chosen option more than the rejected one. One is able to choose when the two are of exactly the same value, as well as when they are incommensurate. The fact of the choice does not reveal why it was made. The chooser may even have chosen the less valued option, as in cases of weakness of the will. Nor is the fact that the choice is not arbitrary sufficient to establish that it was done because the chooser values the chosen option over its alternative. The choice is not arbitrary in one or both of two respects. First it may be based on a reason. Though the reason is incommensurate with the reason for the alternative it shows the value of that option and when that option is chosen it is chosen because of its value. Second, the choice may be in character. The chooser is the kind of person who would choose thus in the prevailing circumstances. But far from his non-arbitrary choice necessarily reflecting his valuation, it may even run contrary to it, as it does if he is prone to weakness of the will in certain circumstances.[1]

There is a further difficulty which the supporter of commensurability must face, and it brings us to the heart of the matter. His tests for assigning judgments of comparative value to people must satisfy the condition that their application does not change those people's judgment of comparative value. It will be conceded that often when people are forced to choose between what they hold to be incommensurable options they will at the time of choosing or subsequently come to hold views concerning the comparative value of these options. But do these views reflect their previous beliefs, or are they new beliefs acquired under the impact of the forced choice? If one takes seriously the early sincere refusal to compare the value of the different options then one must conclude that the test changed these people's valuations rather than revealed them. The normal assumption to the contrary is based on the a priori methodological commitment to commensurability.

Saying that two options are incommensurate does not preclude choice. Rational action is action for (what the agent takes to be) an undefeated reason. It is not necessarily action for a reason which defeats all others. We are, it is essential to remember, inquiring into the structure of practical reasoning, i.e. of the ways people conceive of themselves and their options and judge them. Psychological or other theories may explain, even predict, people's choices on some of the occasions in which they find their options to be incommensurate. This is compatible with widespread incommensurability. While the agent's reasoning figures in many explanations of behaviour there are other factors which also play a part.

Often a mounting pressure to choose leads to the formation of a judgment of comparative value. The agent will come to think that one option is better than another. But this, far from revealing the agent's antecedent view of the comparative value of the options, indicates a change in his judgment. Sometimes those changes are dramatic and far-

---

[1] To claim that actions which are in character reveal unconscious valuation is to misunderstand the role of valuation in a person's life. Cf. above p. 291.

reaching. Having made certain agonizing choices we feel that
we will never be the same again. We often refer to loss of
innocence on such occasions. To a certain extent this is
part of everyone's growing up. We learn to confront choices
which are 'part of life'. The occurrence of such changes of
valuations in growing up shows that they need not be, and
mostly are not, very dramatic. They are part of a continuous
process of revaluation which we undergo throughout life.
But not all incommensurabilities are eliminated in this way.
Many remain, and some of them play a special positive role
in our lives.

4. The Incomparability of Comprehensive Goals

People have certain biologically determined needs. Most of
them do not essentially involve meaningful relations with
another person, though many become, in most cultures, the
foundations of such relations. Though the satisfaction of
these needs to a certain level of adequacy is necessary for
people's well-being it is not sufficient. All except those who
live in circumstances of the most severe deprivation, have
aspirations, projects and preoccupations which far transcend
the satisfaction of the bare biologically determined needs.
Certain aspirations are of such value that those who do not
share them are impoverished by that alone, however successful they are in the pursuits in which they actually engage.
I will be concerned exclusively with these aspects of personal
well-being.

In the previous chapter it was argued that people endorse
their pursuits, relationships, and all they care about for
reasons. That is, that they have them because of their belief in
their value. Now I wish to suggest that in many cases those
reasons are indeterminate in the following sense: but for the
fact that the project, pursuit or relationship is one the person
concerned is already engaged in, if he is, the reasons for him
to be engaged in it are incommensurate with reasons for him
to engage in some other projects, pursuits, or relationships,
which are incompatible with those he has.

There are two aspects to the proposition. First, the value
of many pursuits to people other than the agent, their value

to society, cannot be compared with the value of many alternative pursuits. Second, their value to the agent, their contribution to his well-being, cannot be compared with that of many others. Some pursuits are of value to society, either instrumentally or intrinsically, more than others. Which is more valuable varies with the circumstances of a particular society. There are times when a career as a medical practitioner does more good than a career in medical research. There are times when the reverse is the case. But in many circumstances such judgments regarding certain options are out of place. Both pursuits are valuable, but it makes no sense to say that one is more valuable than the other nor that they are of equal value. Most of the time this will be true of medical research and medical practice, as well as of a career as a book illustrator or a pig farmer, or an electrical engineer, or a product designer for a manufacturer of household goods, etc.

It is customary to concede that often we do not know which pursuit is more valuable to society, but it is always one or the other or they are of equal value. Our ignorance is due to incomplete information. This response is all the more plausible since often it is indeed the case that ignorance alone stops us from discovering which pursuit is the more valuable to others in the circumstances. But if the contribution of various events to the agent's well-being is incommensurate it is hard to avoid the conclusion that so is their contribution to the well-being of others.

Suppose one compares the option of a career in law with a career in teaching. Suppose, to simplify, that if one were a teacher one would encourage some pupils to become (successful) solicitors who would otherwise have become (successful) general practitioners, and that that is all the significant difference one's becoming a teacher would make to others. If one became a solicitor, we will again assume for the sake of simplicity, one would prevent the dismissal of several employees of the Central Electricity Generating Board, who, had they been dismissed, would have started a small business as contractors for electrical jobs. If the well-being of the pupils under the one scenario is incommensurate with their well-being under the alternative scenario, and if the same is true of the electrical engineers, then the value of the two options (teaching or the law) to others is incommensurate.

So it all depends on the incomparability of the value of the options to the well-being of the agent. Let us start by considering personal relationships. Consider the comparative value of an attachment to a sibling, built on the traditions and memories nurtured since childhood, with a committed and intimate relationship based on common leisure pursuits and many weekends and annual holidays spent together. Each relationship has its own colour, its own feel. They are valuable but not in any comparable way.

It is easy to see that all these cases are cases where the relationships or pursuits are not of exactly equal value. One need only conceive of a way of improving one option which will leave it non-comparable with the alternative. Imagine that the relationship with a sibling we have just considered is improved if the two live in the same neighbourhood. Is it then better or more valuable than the other kind of friendship we envisaged? My point is not a skeptical one. There is no denying that some pursuits are more valuable than others. It is also sometimes the case that our inability to judge the comparative merit of various pursuits is due to incomplete information. But often it is not. Often there is no information (I mean no true information, as opposed to imagining possible circumstances) which could settle the issue. The alternatives are simply incommensurate.

One further factor should be mentioned. Success in one's pursuits is important to personal well-being. Some people are incapable of succeeding in some options. It is better to be a successful accountant than a dentist constantly struggling with a sense of inadequacy in one's profession. It is better to be a spontaneous and lively nurse, feeling at ease in one's job, than a teacher fighting a sense of estrangement from one's pupils or one's school. There are many dimensions and aspects to success and they all help in judging the relevant value of options. Career decisions are among those which are greatly influenced by considerations of the prospect of success. One major criterion in such choices is the satisfaction of the pursuit, which is closely allied with success in it, and its attendant rewards. We often feel that any hesitation and doubts we have stem from incomplete information regarding these factors. Since the relevant information is always in short supply the feeling is not surprising. If many of the important options open to people are incommensurate it is natural that deliberation concentrates on what is or may be commensurate. Even if these factors do not yield a unique verdict in favour of one option and against all others, they are the only ones which can influence reason, the only proper matter for reasoning.

But it is a mistake to concentrate on the way people make such choices. Many of our major pursuits and relationships are not chosen after deliberation. Some of them are generally felt to be ill-suited for deliberate choice. This is the common view of people's concern and love for their parents or siblings, to give but one example. It is wrong, according to general consensus, to choose whether to be a devoted child by one's chances of success. One should simply do one's best to succeed, taking obstacles as a challenge rather than as proof that one need not try.

In any case our concern is with judgments of value, which may be those of a third party, or of the agent himself in retrospect. (Strictly speaking our question is: disregarding the fact that these projects are or are not ones which were voluntarily pursued by these people is it possible to compare the success of their lives? But the proviso does not matter. It affects, as we will shortly see, the value of one's life. But it does not re-establish general commensurability.)

When we compare the lives of two people, with very different styles of life, who were each moderately successful and contented in whatever they did (family, career, other interests) the only ground for judging that one had a better life than the other is if one style of life is intrinsically better than the other. It is often not the case that one person's well-being was greater, less or equal than that of another. They are simply incommensurate. We lack any grounds for judging a career as a graphic designer to be intrinsically better or worse for those engaged in it than a career as a livestock farmer or a gliding instructor, assuming that they are likely to be equally successful and content in them. Nor do we have any grounds for judging bird-watching a better or worse leisure interest than an interest in science fiction, etc. In all such cases, and they are very numerous indeed, the only reason to prefer one option to another from the point of view of the agent's well-being, is his chance of succeeding in the different pursuits. When these are indeterminate, so are his options.

The preceding is an appeal to familiar ways of thinking of and evaluating people's lives rather than an argument for their correctness. Yet again what we need is not an argument justifying such ways of thinking. There is no need, nor any way, to justify pervasive features of human thought. But there is a need for an explanation which makes them intelligible. Part of the explanation we already possess, or at least we have a beginning of it. The dependence of value on social forms makes the brute existence of incomparabilities no more than one would expect. It is crucial to avoid the misleading picture of there being something, enigmatically known as 'value', the quantity of which is increased by people having rewarding friendships, enriching occupations, etc. There are only people, with their relationships, careers, interests, etc. Some of them are more valuable than others. But just as the existence of valuable options depends on social forms so, up to a point, their comparative merits depend on social conventions. In practical thought, as we already had occasion to notice, sometimes truth depends on belief. While a person's belief that his goal is valuable does not make it so, the social conventions regarding the relative value of options do in part determine their value. Social conventions are contingent and finite. They are exhaustible, and are bound to leave plenty of room for incommensurability.

But the value of a pursuit or relationship to a person does not depend entirely on its abstract value. We saw, for example, that it also depends on the likelihood that that person will be successful in them. Could one not protest that I have so far disregarded the main factor, that is whether the pursuit or relationship is in that person's interest or not? Surely they are all to be judged by their contribution to that person, by the way or the degree to which they serve his self-interest, or his well-being, if one prefers this term. Appealing as this thought may be, it is guilty of presupposing the existence of something definite: 'self-interest', which everything else may serve or harm. This picture holds regarding a person's biologically determined needs (and is therefore tempting when thinking of 'self-interest', a notion which accords biological needs a particularly major role). While our biologically determined needs are largely determined by factors independent of our actions, these actions may affect the satisfaction or frustration of such needs. But the picture breaks down when one goes beyond the biologically determined to other aspects of a person's well-being.

Here our well-being depends on our actions to a much greater degree. We do not suffer from an unsuccessful love affair unless we engage in a love affair. I am better off if I am a good teacher, and worse off if I am a bad one. But I am not worse off because I cannot sing, since singing plays no role in my life. It could have been otherwise, but it is not. The point should not be exaggerated. It is not the claim that everything which affects our well-being is a result of our action. I can easily be captured by somebody who will torture me unless I sing in tune. And torture me he will. My point is simply that the fact that we care about one thing rather than another determines to a considerable degree what is in our interest and what is not. Therefore we cannot rank options by their contribution to our well-being. The conditions of our well-being, we might say, were not yet created. They are determined by our choices, and therefore they can guide our choices only to a limited extent. In large measure the direction is the other way: our choices determine our well-being. At that stage indeterminacy reigns, for many of the options are incommensurate, and reason cannot advise us how to choose between options which are incommensurate, except to tell us to avoid those we are unlikely to succeed in.

5. Constitutive Incommensurabilities

Some of the examples of incommensurability mentioned in passing earlier in the chapter are attended by special features and are a part of complex attitudes which make them a distinct type of incommensurability to be called 'constitutive incommensurabilities'. First, If A and B are incomparable options of this kind then if an agent is in a situation in which option A is his and B can be obtained by forgoing A he will normally refuse to do so. Similarly if B is his he will not exchange it for A. Agents tend to remain in the position they are in. Second, they obtain between options which have special significance for people's ability successfully to engage in certain pursuits or relationships: the refusal to trade one option for the other is a condition of the agent's ability successfully to pursue one of his goals. Finally, it is typical, where options of this kind are involved, for agents to regard the very thought that they may be comparable in value as abhorrent. There are many gradations of lesser or greater reluctance to undertake such comparisons. But for almost every person there are comparisons he will feel indignant if asked to make, and which he will, in normal circumstances, emphatically refuse to make.

One may say that the special context of these incommensurabilities is that belief in their existence contributes to an attitude which is a barrier to exchange. The fact that two options cannot be compared is viewed as an obstacle to trade-offs. The barrier is not absolute. It is as if trade-offs involve a heavy price. The very willingness to exchange such incomparables has grave consequences to the life of that agent. It undermines his ability to succeed in certain pursuits. One such case is that of some parents who maintain that there is no way in which the value of having children can be compared with money, material position, status or prestige, etc. (I deliberately hedge and refer to the attitude of some such parents, since others may have perhaps superficially similar attitudes which none the less differ fundamentally from the one I will use as an example of this kind of incommensurability.) For such parents, having children and having money cannot be compared in value. Moreover, they will be indignant at the suggestion that such a comparison is possible. Finally, they will refuse to contemplate even the possibility of such an exchange.

At this point one may begin to suspect that the appearance of judgments of incomparability I am relying on is due to a simple ambiguity. Is it not the case that examples like this trigger, not judgments that the options cannot be compared, but rather a specific comparison, namely that one option is better than the other to a degree which puts it beyond compare. Keeping one's child is better than any amount of money, or anything that money can buy. I do not doubt that many do indeed hold that view. But my example concerns the others, those for whom it is equally unacceptable to buy a child as to sell one. For them it is not the case that having a child is worth more than any sum of money. If it were then they would not object to buying children when they want them.

Can one meet this point by a finer description of the two options? In the one case the question is whether or not to give away a child one has in exchange for money or other goods. In the other the question is whether to get a child and give away money or other goods. It is possible that keeping a child one has is best, having the money is second best and getting a child one does not have is the least attractive possibility. That valuation will explain why one neither buys nor sells children. This does not even seem to be a credible account of many people's attitudes. It distorts the views of many who say that having children is more important than having money but that they are not a commodity which has a price in money or in other commodities. They deny that having money is more important than getting a child. Their lives will confirm their belief. They will forgo promotion, take a cut in their income, undertake expensive medical treatment in order to have children.

Perhaps what they object to is a naked exchange of children for money or other commodities. Their value-ranking may be the following: avoiding naked exchanges of children for commodities is best. Having children is second best. Having money or other commodities is third best. This will show that they put having children above having money. But they regard what I called naked exchanges of children and money as worst. I should admit to the obvious, namely that people's attitudes on these matters even when apparently similar do differ in detail to a considerable degree. The interpretation I am about to give may not reflect everyone's attitudes. There are many nuances not mentioned here at all. It may even be that some hold to the ranking mentioned: having children is better than having money, but naked exchanges are worst of all. I doubt, however, whether many people feel that for the following reason.

For many, having children does not have a money price because exchanging them for money, whether buying or selling, is inconsistent with a proper appreciation of the value of parenthood. In a way which calls for an explanation, both their rejection of the idea that having children has a price and their refusal even to contemplate such exchanges are part of their respect for parenthood, an expression of the very high value which they place on having children. Since the value of not exchanging children for money derives from the value of having children it is misleading and distorting to say that of these two they value having children less. These remarks merely deepen the mystery. How can one both refuse, for good reasons, to exchange children for money and vice versa and deny that there is a price for having children?

There is no doubt that the choices of people who have these attitudes are consistent with certain ways of ranking the options. My argument does not depend on denying that. My claim is the more elusive one that the rankings which are consistent with these views and treat all options as commensurate do not represent people's actual valuations. But the argument is incomplete until an alternative explanation is seen to be possible. Presenting it requires some background.

I will argue that significant social forms, which delineate the basic shape of the projects and relationships which constitute human well-being, depend on a combination of incommensurability with a total refusal even to consider exchanging one incommensurate option for another. The argument relates to social forms as we know them. It will not show that others, not committed to incommensurability, are inconceivable. But it will establish that a society based on them will be radically different from any society known to us.

Many people, to give an example of a familiar kind, will leave their spouses for a month to do a job they do not like in order to earn some money. And yet they will not agree to leave the spouse for the same month for an offer of money, even a significantly larger sum of money. They will feel indignant that someone supposes that they are willing to trade the company of their spouse for money from a stranger. The point is not that everyone reacts like this, but that it is a fairly typical reaction, and that it exemplifies reactions in many other situations. The explanation of such reactions is familiar. First, people are sensitive to the motives behind various offers, and to their symbolic singificance. They may, for example, accept money if they believe that it is offered out of genuine willing friendship, but not otherwise. Second, certain actions have a symbolic significance.

It is easy, however, to misinterpet such situations. Parting with one's spouse for a job, one is tempted to say, also means that in fact there is a price put on the company of one's spouse. But it does not have this symbolic significance and therefore is not perceived as equally objectionable. This is a distorted view of the situation, a misunderstanding of the character of symbolic action. An action has symbolic significance in virtue of social conventions which determine its meaning.[1] Its symbolic significance transcends an action's 'real' impact in the world. Hence actions which are otherwise similar may differ in their meaning.

This is not to say that symbolic meaning is entirely conventional. In various ways many symbolic acts are suitable vehicles of their meaning. In our example, the symbolic significance of the fact that one cannot trade companionship for naked money but one can for a job is that while companionship is not up for sale, it is but one ingredient in a complex pattern of life including work. It competes with those other ingredients in legitimate ways which allow individuals to strike their own balance between them. But this freedom is limited and there are balances which indicate lack of concern for the spouse, lack of loyalty to the relationship. Sometimes over-dedication to one's job, over-concern to earn money by one's job, etc., are also inconsistent with proper relations with a spouse. All this and much besides is indicated by the symbolic significance of taking money for

---

[1] Though to a limited extent private conventions can create private symbols.

not seeing someone. Money exchanges are the mark of liquidity, of easy, fast exchangeability. Because of this they are natural candidates for certain symbolic messages. But only those familiar with the conventions can understand their meaning.

A symbolic action, in other words, illuminates, for those who understand it, the nature of the choices they have in matters far beyond that action itself, choices which involve, in our example, many aspects of their relations with their spouses. Symbolic actions can have such significance since they depend on conventions. The very relationship between spouses depends, as was explained in the previous chapter, on the existence of social conventions. These conventions are constitutive of the relationship. They determine its typical contours. They do this partly by assigning symbolic meaning to certain modes of behaviour.

The most crucial fact about the kind of symbolic actions we are examining is now visible: *what has symbolic significance is the very judgment that companionship is incommensurable with money*. That holding that an action has a certain value can be self-verifying, can be the source of the action's value may seem, at first blush, surprising. But a little reflection shows that this is part and parcel of the symbolic, and therefore conventional, character of the value. We know that not everyone is capable of having friends, or any relationships involving companionship. The capacity to have such relations involves interest in other people, empathy with them, and other psychological attributes. It also involves certain evaluative beliefs. Only those who realize that having a spouse or a friend is a relationship which carries distinctive obligations are capable of having such relations. Part of that capacity is the recognition of the symbolic significance of certain actions. Which acts give offence, and which ones are expressions of affection or of the existence of a special bond, for example, is often a matter of the symbolic significance of various actions.

As was remarked above, an act's symbolic significance necessarily depends (at least in part) on its conventional meaning. As conventions are constituted by the attitudes of those who adhere to them, the fact that to be capable of relationships involving companionship I must share the relevant conventions tends to reinforce their existence. So much is familiar ground. My claim regarding incommensurability is that belief in incommensurability is itself a qualification for having certain relations. The attitude of mind which constitutes such a belief is analogous to attitudes such as respect for the other person, which are commonly accepted as prerequisites for a capacity for these relations. Here we encounter another aspect of our lives which the picture of practical life associated with acceptance of commensurability distorts. It assumes that valuing an option is one thing and believing that one does is another and is logically independent of one's valuation. In fact when it comes to symbolic values the two tend to merge (though not to a degree which makes self-deception or mistakes about one's own beliefs impossible).

Its convention-dependent character means that symbolic significance is in the eye of the beholder. If he does not perceive it it does not have that value for him. This does not mean that he can disregard symbolic reasons with impunity. Two situations have to be distinguished. A person may believe that holding there to be a price for companionship is incompatible with having a loving relations with one's spouse and still he may come to view his relations with his spouse as having a price. He is then disloyal, and he damages his relations with his spouse, perhaps even irretrievably so. On the other hand he may not believe that it has that significance. He may believe that everything has its price and so does his relationship with his spouse. In such a case he never had the relations with his spouse of which belief in incommensurability is a symbolic constituent. He may or may not have tried and succeeded in forging an alternative relationship, which is a variant on the conventional one. That is not the issue. All that is relevant for our argument is the fact that if he does not believe that the action has that symbolic meaning then it does not have it for him, with the result that the opportunity to have a certain kind of relationship with his spouse is denied him.[1]

---

[1] All such examples require much filling in to stand up to examination. Cf. my discussion of friendship in *The Authority of Law*, Essay 12.

Here lies the explanation of why constitutive in-commensurabilities look like value rankings. It is a mis-leading appearance which besets all constitutive elements of any normative institution. As H. L. A. Hart has pointed out,[1] there is no legal prohibition against making an un-witnessed will. It is simply invalid. It is a constitutive ele-ment of the legal institution of bequest that one has the normative power to bequeath one's belongings only in writ-ing and in front of two witnesses. This often leads to the mistaken belief that one may not make an unattested will. The truth is that the action is perfectly legal. It is merely incapable of achieving the transfer of property after death. Those who wish to achieve it had better get their wills attested. The same confusion can arise outside the law. Many people believe that promises of young children regarding the medium or long-term future are not binding.[2] It is wrong to identify this with a prohibition on making or receiving such promises. The contrary is the case. Making promises about conduct in the more remote future is one way in which children develop a sense of responsibility, a capacity to think ahead and plan, etc.

Certain judgments about the non-comparability of certain options and certain attitudes to the exchangeability of op-tions are constitutive of relations with friends, spouses, pa-rents, etc. Only those who hold the view that friendship is neither better nor worse than money, but is simply not comparable to money or other commodities are *capable* of having friends. Similarly only those who would not even consider exchanges of money for friendship are capable of having friends. This is a reasoned attitude. It is based on the recognition that it constitutes a condition for a capacity for friendship. Since it is a reasoned preference for one option over another it looks like a ranking, like judging friendship to be more valuable than money. But if it were so then it would amount to a condemnation of those who forgo the possibility of friendship for money as people who act wrongly and against reason. Some may take this attitude. But others (most of us, on reflection) do not. They regard

[1] *The Concept of Law*, pp. 27 ff.
[2] For the reasons set out in Ch. 4.

such people as one regards people who neglected their musical abilities and lost their sensitivity to music in order to be better able to pursue some other goals. Such people have made their choice among the valuable options of life, and their choice disables them from pursuing certain avenues. Those, for example, whose single-minded pursuit of a career led them to put a price on any human association lost the capacity for friendship. They are similarly incapacitated, but they did not, just by doing so, act against reason. Their career, say in politics, may be fulfilling and idealistic. Their life is impoverished in certain respects, but enriched in others. Our judgment of them is no different from our judgment of people who lost their ability to form close and exclusive personal ties through joining a monastic order.

People who say, 'For me money is more important than friends' are neither mistaken nor do they commit a wrong. They are simply incapable of having friends. Their belief disqualifies them from being true friends. They may be aware of this, people like that often are. They may either pride themselves on or regret the fact that they are incapable of having friends, or just accept it as a plain fact. So long as they are aware of the fact there is no mistake that they commit. Just as people who are incapable of great acts of heroism are neither ignorant nor in the wrong, they are merely limited in certain ways, so people who fail to see that personal relations cannot be valued in terms of commodities are limited. They are incapable of having the deeper kinds of personal relations.

6. Loyalty and Commitment

Constitutive incommensurabilities are not merely cases where reasons run out. They mark areas which are out of bounds for anyone interested in the personal relations and the pursuits of which they are constitutive. Here failure of commensurability is a success. It is impoverishing to compare the value of a marriage with an increase in salary. It diminishes one's potentiality as a human being to put a value on one's friendship in terms of improved living conditions. In these cases incommensurabilities are not just part of the inevitabilities of life. They are part of the building blocks of valuable pursuits and relationships.

The main significance of such incommensurabilities is in making possible the pursuits and relationships of which they are a constitutive part. In so contributing to the shape of many pursuits and relationships they also add to the foundations of duties of loyalty. We must briefly examine this connection in order to solve the last part of the jigsaw. Is it not wrong to give up a friendship for money? And if it is can the choice be between incommensurables?

All social forms involve ways of being true to the project or to the relationship which they define. Quite apart from the question whether one is a good parent, child, spouse, friend, employee, citizen, stamp-collector, music lover, and so on, there is the question of whether one is true to one's relationships or pursuits. One may be bad in pursuing them in a large number of ways. One may be clumsy, neglectful, thoughtless, of bad judgment, misconceiving one's role or duty, and so on. And with all that one may be true to one's pursuits or relationships. Contrariwise, one may do a lot of good as a parent, spouse, employee, music lover, etc., while being false to one's pursuit or relationship. Indeed people have been known to betray their friends or their employers in the interest of those friends. Many a soap opera has capitalized on the idea of the lover who is disloyal in order to break the relationship because he realizes, correctly, that that is in the best interest of his loved one. Such cases may show that being false to one's pursuit or relationship is, sometimes, justified. But even a justified betrayal is a betrayal.

The fact that pursuits and relationships can be betrayed shows that loyalty is a distinctive virtue. It is one which is relatively independent of success in the pursuit or the relationship. It does not indicate how good one is in the pursuit or the relationship. It shows that one is truly engaged in them. Loyalty is related to but is distinct from commitment. There are degrees of commitment. They are in part degrees of dedication and in part degrees of involvement, that is degrees to which the relationship or pursuit matters to one's overall well-being. One may say that loyalty is the minimum required commitment. But that reverses the relation of the two notions. Only if one is engaged in a pursuit or a relationship can one be loyal or disloyal to it, or in it. Only citizens can betray their country, only parents can betray their children. Commitment is a way of being or getting engaged. It signifies that one is engaged as a predictable result of one's own conduct in a pursuit or a relationship. That is not the same as being loyal to it, though the fact that one is disloyal may make the pursuit or relationship impossible. Gross betrayal normally does. One has to be committed in order to be able to be true or false, loyal or disloyal.

Being true to pursuits and relations is being engaged in them according to their terms. Many pursuits and relations are voluntary ones. Even those who are engaged in them may abandon them without doing anything wrong. Legitimate ways of detaching oneself from them do involve the adoption of behaviour and value-judgments which are incompatible with the pursuits or relations which are being abandoned. These are cases where one pays the price, which is the loss of the pursuit, but is willing to do so. Even voluntary pursuits and relations may not, however, be abandoned any way one likes. There are conventions which prohibit certain ways of abandoning them. Some conventions protect the interests of others involved in the pursuits or relations. But some define what a person of integrity may or may not be. Violation of these conventions is a betrayal of the relationship or the pursuit. It compromises one's integrity. Loyalty to one's pursuits and relationships is a condition of integrity. A person of integrity is loyal to his commitments. In normal circumstances disloyalty not only ends a particular pursuit or relationship, but undermines one's ability to engage in relations or pursuits of this kind altogether.[1]

Constitutive incommensurabilities play their part in con-

---

[1] There is another way of failing to engage, which is inconstancy. The inconstant changes relations in ways which are, taken separately, unexceptional but which given his predilection for them show a defect of character. The disloyal destroys his engagements in ways which are intrinsically bad, even if they are sometimes justified in the circumstances. Perpetual disloyalty is, like inconstancy, a defect in one's ability to engage in pursuits and relationships. Both may affect one type of relationships or pursuits only, or take a more general form.

ventions of fidelity to relationships and pursuits. Being engaged in a pursuit or a relationship includes belief that certain options are not comparable in value. Abandoning such beliefs is therefore one way of abandoning the pursuit. Regarding a particular relationship as a proper subject for an exchange damages or even destroys it. Regarding a class of relationships as comparable in value with other options with which they are by their constitutive conventions incomparable, makes one unfit for, incapable of having, relations of that kind. Such changes of view are not wrong in themselves. They do however have weighty consequences. They limit one's life and restrict one's potential for the future. Thereby they affect one's well-being even when not involving wrongful behaviour.

But conventions establishing constitutive incommensurabilities also feature in the definition of the duties of loyalty. In certain circumstances putting a value on an option in a way which is inconsistent with the pursuit amounts to a betrayal, or to disloyalty. Such valuations and actions which are based on them are not only destructive of the relations or pursuits with which they are inconsistent, they not merely undermine one's ability to engage in such pursuits or relations in general, they are also wrong in themselves. In those circumstances incommensurability forms the foundation of duties. But even then the effect of the incommensurability itself, as a condition of a capacity for relations and pursuits, is separate from that of the duties of loyalty with which it, like other constitutive elements of relations and pursuits, is involved in appropriate circumstances. As was pointed out above, belief in the incomparability of the options is constitutive of the capacity to engage in the pursuit, and is therefore shared by all who have the capacity, whether or not they are actually engaged in the pursuit. The duties of loyalty, on the other hand, apply only to those who are so engaged. Only they can either conform with or violate them. Hence they should not be confused with the conventions of constitutive incommensurabilities on which they are based.

So much for the arguments for the existence of constitutive incommensurabilities. It did not establish that they must exist for human life to be possible, nor did it establish that they should exist according to sound moral principles. It comes close to doing the latter. If these incommensurabilities are as pervasive a feature of life in our culture as was here suggested, then life according to commensurate principles will be radically different from our own. It is a mistake to think of it as life in our society and culture differing from our present existence only in being more thoroughly rational. It will involve a radical change in our society and culture.

In *The Communist Manifesto* Marx and Engels wrote: 'The bourgeoisie, . . . has put an end to all feudal, patriarchal, idyllic relations . . . It has resolved personal worth into exchange value, and in place of the numberless indefeasible chartered freedoms, has set up that single, unconscionable freedom—Free Trade.'[1] They were wrong. Liberal capitalist culture merely replaced some social forms with others. But they were not altogether wrong. Much liberal capitalist economics and ethics advanced what Marx and Engels rightly viewed with horror as an ideal. It was, and is, put forward as an ideal of rationality. I have argued that if it is an ideal it is a moral ideal, an advocacy of a different culture, of different social forms.

7. Moral Dilemmas

General commensurability is a common assumption of most consequentialists. But need it be? And in any case does its failure help the qualms about consequentialism expressed by writers such as Williams, Nagel and Nozick? The implicit claim running through the argument was that if there are pervasive incommensurabilities then consequentialism is to be rejected. This may look a strange claim. After all nothing was said to show that anything other than the consequences of one's actions counts. Furthermore, the argument revolved round the personal well-being of an agent. It has, it may be alleged, no bearing on consequentialism when this is understood as a type of moral theory.

[1] The *Communist Manifesto*, quoted from R. Tucker (ed.), *The Marx–Engels Reader*, New York, 1972, p. 475.

First let me repeat a point made at the beginning of our discussion of consequentialism (in Chapter Eleven). There is no feature of practical reasoning which can be identified as the core or essential doctrine of consequentialism. Every single one of the features listed there as the most common marks of consequentialism was rejected by some consequentialist theories. Therefore, the arguments of the last two chapters can only claim to modify or to weaken the consequetialist element in our understanding of practical reasoning.

Widespread significant incommensurability undermines consequentialism obliquely. It allows that there are pockets of commensurability within which maximization, or alternative reasoning strategies, reign supreme. Some such pockets may be of considerable importance. Besides there are fragments of reasoning based on maximization which form components of many practical arguments. But widespread incommensurabilities put paid to the hope of developing a general system or technology of calculation for practical reasoning. Some consequentialists and some of their critics may find these conclusions respectively reassuring or disappointing. They may say that the argument for widespread incommensurability remains within essentially a consequentialist frame of reference.

The argument of this book does not touch the most radical attempt to refute consequentialism. That denies that morality, even the action-guiding part of it, can be based on a comparison of the relative value of different states of affairs.[1] Yet it seems to me that the kinds of failure of comparability which were discussed in the last chapter may offer a clue to some of the concerns of the anti-consequentialists. The most straightforward case is that of inter-personal comparisons of well-being. Traditional arguments purporting to establish that such comparisons are either meaningless or unknowable are addressed to difficulties in comparing states of different people. But if it is often impossible to compare in value two

[1] P. Foot, *Morality and Objectivity*, ed. T. Honderich, London, 1985, denied the meaningfulness of such unrestricted comparisons. A. Muller, 'Radical Subjectivity: Morality v. Utilitarianism', *Ratio*, 19 (1977), 115 challenged the possibility of giving a formulation of moral principles in these terms. See also J. M. Finnis, *Fundamentals of Ethics*, Oxford, 1984, p. 119.

states or two possible careers of one person then it is plain
that for the very same reasons it is impossible to compare
the well-being of different people who follow those two incommensurate states or careers. This opens the possibility
of explaining why it is equally implausible to say that inter-
personal comparisons are never possible and that they are
always possible, at least in principle. They are possible precisely in those cases where it is possible to compare the value
of two options or courses of events for one and the same
person. But as we saw such possibilities are often
unavailable.

Exploration of all these issues is out of place in this book.
But let me briefly discuss another point of contact with anti-
consequentialist concerns: the problem of moral dilemmas.
Most, if not all, the cases used as examples of moral dilemmas are cases of a choice between evils. They are cases
of being in a situation in which whatever one does either one
will wrong people, or one will fail in some binding duty
(possibly a duty to help).[1] They divide into two classes.
Some are said to be cases in which one of the agent's options
is clearly the better one, or at least involves the lesser evil.
In such cases there is a right course of action. One would be
in the wrong if one failed to take the right action. Nevertheless, it is claimed, performing the right action does not
mean that one does not do a wrong. Harming another or
failing one's duty in the imagined circumstances is a wrong
even if it is, on balance, the best and the only right thing to
do. The second type of case is different. In it there is no
right or best action. All the avenues which are open to one
are wrong. Whatever one does one would be doing evil or
wronging another.

Incommensurability may help in the explanation of both
cases. Its implications for the second case appear more obvious. If all the agent's options involve wronging others or
just doing evil and if none of them is the lesser evil then
there is no action that is the right action for him to do. It is
easy to misconceive the importance of this point. It is true

---

[1] The fact that all the agent's options will lead to a situation which is worse than
the one existing before his action is neither necessary nor sufficient to establish that
he is in a dilemma. All this shows is that his situation is unfortunate.

that this is not a case where the agent will fail in performing the right action, not a case in which his act will be worse than some other option open to him. It would therefore be misleading simply to say that the agent is bound to act wrongly. This suggests that there is an evaluation of the comparative merit of the options, where none exists. Still, linguistic usage is flexible, and often 'I acted wrongly' conveys no more than 'I performed a wrongful act'. In any case, it is of the essence of dilemmas that those facing them have no morally acceptable option. It is question-begging to assume that a person can only do wrong by failing to perform a better act which he could have done. Anyone asserting the existence of dilemmas of the second kind is denying precisely that. The claim that there are such dilemmas is a claim that one can do wrong in other situations as well. Incommensurability shows that there is conceptual room for a notion of wrongdoing which does not involve failing to take a better action available to one.

It is impossible to warn often enough that from the impossibility of comparing the degree of badness of two options it does not follow that they are bad to the same degree. Such equality of evils is not a real possibility where the options differ from each other in a significant way. It is to be found only when one chooses not only between evils but between two forms of exactly the same evil. This happens when one's only choice is between the use of two similar poisons, etc. The relevance of such situations is merely in reminding us that in a sense moral dilemmas arise even when one has no choice at all.

If it were possible that an agent were in a situation in which there were only one action which he could not but do, and if it were an evil action, then he would find himself in the same moral bind as in a moral dilemma. However, there is no action without choice. The choice makes it an action. It does not account for its being a dilemma. It is a dilemma because one cannot escape performing a wrong. The agent who is aware of his situation will in most cases be tormented by it and is likely to find it hard to bring himself to decide what to do. But that is one, and not the most important, of the consequences of choice among significantly different and incomparable options. One is as likely to experience a difficulty in choosing between two very attractive options if they are very unlike each other and incommensurate. Witness the difficulties which people experience in trying to choose between developing a friendship with one or the other of two people they are attracted to, or in career choices. On the other hand, if in a moral dilemma the two bad options are very much alike the difficulty of choice will not be experienced. What then remains is the realization that one is doomed to perform an evil act or one which wrongs another.[1]

The challenge facing the case for the existence of dilemmas is obvious. Dilemmas must be distinguished from three situations with which they may be confused. First, there are cases in which all the options facing an agent are unpalatable. He has to choose between travelling by air, of which he is terrified and which he finds unpleasant, and losing an attractive job. Or, a factory owner may have to choose between letting down his father or letting down his workers. In many cases we face a choice of evils. Few of them show anything other than that the world is not specifically made to suit our purposes. Are dilemmas simply cases in which sensitive, the unkind will say squeamish, people face unpalatable choices?

Second, there is no doubt that an action which may be wrong in some circumstances is right in others. It is generally wrong to kill or to deceive. But it is right to kill a murderer intent on killing others if that is the only way to foil his murderous plan. It is generally wrong to deceive, but it is right to deceive a would-be murderer if doing so will frustrate his design and save his victim. In such cases the agent is not choosing between two wrongs. He is in a situation in which it is right to do what is normally wrong. It may be, it normally is, regrettable that such circumstances arise, but they do not show that one is wronging another or performing

---

[1] Literally 'moral dilemma' means a situation in which one is at a loss what to choose and where the choice turns on moral considerations. But in philosophical writings on the subject it came to signify a kind of a moral Hobson's choice of a dramatic nature such as the choice between killing one's crying baby or letting the Nazis discover and murder a large number of hiding refugees, or abandoning one's ailing mother to join the resistance or failing in one's duty to one's country to look after one's mother. I will follow the custom of concentrating on the nature of the choice rather than on the indecision to which it leads.

an evil act. Does the case for the existence of dilemmas depend on confusing a choice between options which are normally wrong with a choice between options which are wrong in the actual circumstances of the case?

Finally, sometimes people land themselves through their own fault in a situation in which the best option open to them is one which is normally wrong. Sometimes they are judged blameworthy for what they do when they have no choice as an indirect way of blaming them for what they did when they had the choice. If there are dilemmas they must be distinguishable from these cases, or at least from this interpretation of these cases.

Incommensurability provides a way of distinguishing between dilemmas (of the second kind) and all three types of case. They all presuppose commensurability. They are attempts to dissolve the appearance of dilemmas by explaining to us that there is a better and a worse, a right and a wrong action in cases which appear to be cases of dilemmas and then explaining away the appearance of a dilemma as due to other factors. None of these explanations applies to a choice between incommensurate evils. When faced with two wrongful actions which cannot be compared we lack the overall verdict of which is best, or which is right in the circumstances. Whatever one does one does a wrong, or performs an evil act. Incommensurability establishes conceptual room for the notion of doing evil or wronging another without either failure to perform a better action which was available or a justification for the action which shows that it is all right in the circumstances. This kind of logical room falls short of establishing the possibility of dilemmas. It does not give moral meaning to that possibility. To do so one has to show the place of dilemmas in morality, to show how they fit in with, are an integral and inevitable part of, the rest of morality. One has to show why the fact that an agent is faced with options none of which is better or worse than the others does not justify his choice of one of them, whatever it may be.

The short answer is that the moral significance of wrong doing, which is common to wronging others or doing evil when faced with a moral dilemma and to 'ordinary' wrong doing, is personal failure and damage to the agent's well-being. What makes dramatic dilemmas dramatic is the destruction they bring to the agent's own life. This fact is bound to escape the notice of those who regard morality as a system of social engineering. For them judgments of right and wrong conduct are means of manoeuvring people to behave in a certain way by means of social pressure or the internalization of norms of conduct. Viewed in that way, since the purpose of moral judgment is to get people to avoid some actions in favour of others, there can be no wrong action without a choice.

More surprisingly, even many who regard morality as primarily concerned with the agent's conduct of his own life fail to see the possibility of wrongdoing in the absence of choice. Morality, and reason in general, they might say, at least inasmuch as they are concerned with conduct, rather than character, are all about directing the agent's choices. Where there is no choice there are no directions to be given. It may be misleading in such cases to say that the agent did the right thing, but equally misleading to say that he took an evil or a wrong action. Both judgments are misleading in suggesting that there was a choice, i.e. a choice between better and worse options. Where none exists it makes no sense to judge the action.

This argument puts the cart before the horse. If reason guides choices it does so by pointing to the value of different courses of action and of their consequences. Only because they have this or that value should they be chosen or avoided. The value of actions is, generally speaking, independent of whether or not they are or can be chosen. This statement must be doubly qualified straight away. The value of some actions depends on the spirit in which, or on the reasons for which, they are undertaken. In that respect the value of those actions is not entirely independent of whether they are chosen. Secondly, inasmuch as morality and reason have to do with the conduct of people's lives it is arguable that what cannot in principle be done cannot in principle have any value, either good or bad. Likewise, what cannot in principle be avoided cannot have a value except inasmuch as it contributes to avoidable aspects of life.[1] My argument concerns only dilemmas between what is avoidable in principle but cannot be avoided in particular conditions.

Given that the value of an action is in general independent of the ability to choose it in particular circumstances, to complain that it does not have a negative value because one cannot avoid it or a positive one because one cannot choose it is to commit the unforgivable sin of irrational optimism, i.e. of believing that not only can one always do what is best in the circumstances (which is in itself doubtful) but that whatever the circumstances, the possibilities they offer the agent determine what is valuable and what is not. Nobody I know is guilty of this sin. But many are willing to believe that while it is possible that one's circumstances will present one only with poor choices they cannot be so bad as to leave one with no option but to do wrong. The explanation offered for that belief is that judging that in every situation there is at least one option which is not wrong is not judging the value of the option, but rather offering advice about its eligibility compared with the others. There is no denying that many judgments do precisely that. The point is that where an agent is faced with only two options and they are incommensurable that kind of judgment is out of the question. One cannot compare the value of the options, one can only judge their value each one on its own. If each involves wrongdoing then there is no escaping the conclusion that whatever the agent does he will do wrong.

To summarize the argument so far: the moral character of an action as wrong or evil serves as a guide to the agent, as a reason for his action, because reasons for action follow the value of what they are reasons for. That value is there independently of one's ability to choose or to avoid it on this particular occasion. When an evil action is unavoidable it is still evil. It is evil, ultimately, because of what it does to the well-being of the agent and of others. It does the same even when the only way to avoid it is to perform another evil action.

[1] These remarks are in line with Ruth Marcus 'Moral Dilemmas and Consistency', *Journal of Philosophy*, 77 (1980), 121, and R. Chisholm, e.g. in 'Practical Reason and the Logic of Requirement', J. Raz (ed.) *Practical Reasoning*, Oxford 1978.

This argument takes us beyond dilemmas which involve incommensurabilities and opens the way to an explanation of the first kind of dilemmas. They are those which involve a choice between a lesser and a greater evil, where it is right to do the lesser evil and wrong to do anything else, and where one may yet claim that one did a wrong even while doing the right thing. In other words, they are cases where the fact that one's best option involves wrong doing does not erase the wrongful character of the action. They are moral dilemmas because they are cases in which the act which is morally required of one is wrongful. Those who think of the moral character of actions purely in term of the guidance they give agents will find this description incomprehensible. Those who remember that guidance depends on the value of the action will see the possibility that in certain regrettable circumstances one may be morally guided towards an action which is wrongful, and its wrongfulness is not negated by its being the best of what is available. It is yet again a situation where the act will damage the agent's well-being, and often that of others as well. In that it is a wrongful act even as the agent has no morally acceptable way of escaping it.

To avoid any possible misunderstanding let it be repeated that the claim here made is not that the action is wrongful because it adversely affects the agent's well-being. Rather it adversely affects his well-being because it is wrongful. The relevance of pointing out its consequences to his well-being is to counter the objection that saying of an action one cannot escape that it is wrongful is idle and confusing talk. It is a bad action but being the best in the circumstances there can be nothing one may convey except confusion by saying that it is wrongful. To this charge the answer was that there is a difference between performing a bad action where the circumstances not only make its performance unavoidable but erase its character as wrongful, and those cases when they do not. In the second kind of case only do the dire consequences to the agent's well-being follow the action. (People who are not in this situation may mistakenly think that they are. They may for no good reason regard their actions as having sealed their fate, and condemned them to abjure any close relations, any possibility of meaningful life.)

Several important questions remain to be considered. In particular, why does an action which is inevitable affect the agent's well-being when this is understood as the success of his life? If it does why does it have moral colouring? Failure in a piano competition may undermine a pianist's well-being. But it has no moral connotations. Can the inevitable be morally significant? All these questions ultimately come to this: what sort of consequences to the agent's well-being can flow from his immorality? Does not morality affect the fate of others, while prudence alone matters to the agent's own well-being?

The answers are implicit in the analysis of personal well-being and of its relation to morality offered in Chapter Twelve. Disregarding yet again the important class of biologically determined needs, the success of a person's life depends on the success of his pursuits and relationships. This depends in part on his success in achieving his goals, and in part on the value of these goals. If he fails to achieve his goals his life is, at least to a certain extent, a failure. The shape of his goals is not entirely up to him. They are so many variations on the social forms available to him. Therein lies the possibility of tragic choices, i.e. choices under circumstances in which whatever a person does he would irreparably damage one of the projects or relationships which he pursued and which shape his life. It may even be a choice which will make it impossible for him to have a life worth living. Such dilemmas are moral dilemmas when the goals they involve are among those where the demands of morality and the conditions of the person's own well-being coincide.

V

FREEDOM AND POLITICS

The traditional autonomy-oriented conception of individual freedom, of which the views defended in this book are a variant, leads to a 'moralistic' doctrine of political freedom, i.e. one based on the moral value of individual liberty. Part Four, partial and incomplete though its argument was, laid the required moral foundations for this conception. It outlined the features of a theory of value necessary for an adequate defence of political liberty. They provide the foundation for the examination in Chapter Fourteen of personal autonomy and of value-pluralism. Between them these two doctrines define the view of personal freedom which is defended in this book, and provide it with a basis in the moral outlook explained above. Finally, Chapter Fifteen outlines the implications for political action of this conception of pluralism. In many ways the argument seeks merely to reestablish some of the basic tenets of Millean liberalism. Chapter Fifteen proposes a reinterpretation of Mill's harm principle, and points to the ways in which it has to be transcended. Personal freedom, when understood as presupposing value-pluralism and as expressing itself in personal autonomy, can and should be promoted by political action. The interpretation of the political protection of freedom as purely a doctrine of limited government finds no support here. But with all that, respect for liberty imposes on governments the sort of constraints advocated by the reinterpreted harm principle. It should form part of the doctrine of liberty.

14

Autonomy and Pluralism

1. Personal Autonomy

1.1 *The relation between autonomy and the capacity for it.* The fact that our self-interest, and more generally, what counts towards our well-being, is to a considerable extent determined by our own actions, does not presuppose free or deliberate choice of options. To be sure our well-being is not served by projects we are coerced into unless we come willingly to embrace them. But not everything we willingly embrace is something we have freely or deliberately chosen from among various alternatives open to us. The relationship between children and their parents is an obvious example. Notwithstanding the fact that it can, and sometimes does, go badly wrong, it is a relationship most people willingly embrace but do not freely choose. It is a relationship people are committed to and care deeply about. But it is not one which most of them have ever confronted in their own minds as an object of choice.

In western industrial societies a particular conception of individual well-being has acquired considerable popularity. It is the ideal of personal autonomy. It transcends the conceptual point that personal well-being is partly determined by success in willingly endorsed pursuits and holds the free choice of goals and relations as an essential ingredient of individual well-being. The ruling idea behind the ideal of personal autonomy is that people should make their own lives. The autonomous person is a (part) author of his own life. The ideal of personal autonomy is the vision of people controlling, to some degree, their own destiny, fashioning it through successive decisions throughout their lives.

It is an ideal particularly suited to the conditions of the industrial age and its aftermath with their fast changing technologies and free movement of labour. They call for an ability to cope with changing technological, economic and social conditions, for an ability to adjust, to acquire new skills, to move from one subculture to another, to come to terms with new scientific and moral views.[1] Its suitability for our conditions and the deep roots it has by now acquired in our culture contribute to a powerful case for this ideal. But it would be wrong to identify the ideal with the ability to cope with the shifting dunes of modern society. Autonomy is an ideal of self-creation. There were autonomous people in many past periods, whether or not they themselves or others around them thought of this as an ideal way of being.[2]

The autonomous person is part author of his life. The image this metaphor is meant to conjure up is not that of the regimented, compulsive person who decides when young what life to have and spends the rest of it living it out according to plan. In the words of J. L. Mackie 'there is not one goal but indefinitely many diverse goals, and . . . they are the objects of progressive (not once-for-all or conclusive) choices.'[3] As Mackie's comment reminds us, the ideal of personal autonomy is not to be identified with the ideal of giving one's life a unity. An autonomous person's well-being consists in the successful pursuits of self-chosen goals and relationships. Like all people's, his will also be nested goals, with the more comprehensive ones being, other things being equal, the more important ones. None of this tells us anything which is specific to the ideal of autonomy. It does not

[1] See D. Riesman, *The Lonely Crowd*, New York, 1950, for an understanding of autonomy as the capacity to cope with these conditions.

[2] Personal autonomy, which is a particular ideal of individual well-being should not be confused with the only very indirectly related notion of moral autonomy. The latter originates with Kantian idea that morality consists of self-enacted principles: 'The will is therefore not merely subject to the law, but is so subject that it must be considered as also making the law for itself and precisely on this account as first of all subject of the law (of which it can regard itself as the author).' (Fundamental Principles of the Metaphysic of Morals, tr. H. J. Paton, London, 1956, pp. 98–9.) In Kant's though not in all other versions, authorship reduced itself to a vanishing point as it allowed only one set of principles which people can rationally legislate and they are the same for all. Nobody can escape their rule simply by being irrational and refusing to accept them. Personal autonomy, by contrast, is essentially about the freedom of persons to choose their own lives. Moral autonomy both in the Kantian and in other versions is a doctrine about the nature of morality. Personal autonomy is no more than one specific moral ideal which, if valid, is one element in a moral doctrine.

[3] J. L. Mackie, 'Can There Be a Right-Based Moral Theory?', *Midwest Studies in Philosophy*, 3 (1978), 354–5.

require an attempt to impose any special unity on one's life. The autonomous life may consist of diverse and heterogeneous pursuits. And a person who frequently changes his tastes can be as autonomous as one who never shakes off his adolescent preferences.

Autonomy is opposed to a life of coerced choices. It contrasts with a life of no choices, or of drifting through life without ever exercising one's capacity to choose. Evidently the autonomous life calls for a certain degree of self-awareness. To choose one must be aware of one's options. If these are to include changes in pervasive aspects of one's life, as they must if the person is to count as an autonomous person, then the autonomous person must be aware of his life as stretching over time. He must be capable of understanding how various choices will have considerable and lasting impact on his life. He may always prefer to avoid long-term commitments. But he must be aware of their availability. This has led to some over-intellectualized conceptions of personal autonomy. I know of nothing wrong with the intellectual life, just as I know of nothing wrong with people who consciously endow their lives with great unity. But the ideal of personal autonomy is meant to be wider and compatible with other styles of life, including those which are very unintellectual.

I have spoken of the ideal of autonomy as a life freely chosen. It is a life which is here primarily judged as autonomous or not, and it is so judged by its history. As was noted before[1] the autonomous life is discerned not by what there is in it but by how it came to be. It is discerned, if you like, by what it might have been and by why it is not other than what it is. But autonomy is often conceived as the condition of a person who has a certain ability. E. Beardsley, for example, characterizes it as the power to determine which acts to perform and which experiences to have. She regards the power as including the power to choose and the power to bring about what one has chosen.[2]

---

[1] See Ch. 7 above.

[2] E. L. Beardsley, 'Privacy: Autonomy and Selective Disclosure' Nomos XIII: Privacy, ed. J. R. Pennock and J. W. Chapman, 1971, p. 57. I found S. I. Benn's distinction between autonomy and autarchy particularly valuable. See his 'Free-

There is no doubt that one needs certain abilities to lead an autonomous life. The question is whether the possession of these abilities is valuable because they are necessary for the autonomous life, which is the source of their value, or whether what matters ultimately from the moral point of view is the possession of the abilities as such.

It is hard to conceive of an argument that possession of a capacity is valuable even though its exercise is devoid of value. Ascetic and disciplinarian moralities are an example. They value the possession of power because of the value of giving up its exercise, or for the discipline and will-power that doing so instils. Barring such extreme moralities or exceptional circumstances belief in the value of a capacity commits one to the value of some cases of its exercise. The opposite view, i.e. that it is valuable to possess an ability even though none of its uses is valuable, is too far fetched. It seems very implausible, however, to suppose that while whenever one possesses an ability some of its possible uses are valuable, this is entirely coincidental. The only reasonable supposition is that either its use makes its possession valuable or the other way round. But as one can have an ability without exercising it, if its possession is the root of value then there is no reason for it to affect the value of its exercise. On the other hand, one cannot exercise an ability one does not possess. If the value of one is the ground for the value of the other it must, therefore, be the value of the exercise which endows the capacity with what it is worth.

The ideal of autonomy is that of the autonomous life. The capacity for autonomy is a secondary sense of 'autonomy'. I am using 'capacity' in a very wide sense. Perhaps it is better called the 'conditions of autonomy'. I will use both expressions on occasion. The conditions of autonomy are complex and consist of three distinct components: appropriate mental abilities, an adequate range of options, and independence.

If a person is to be maker or author of his own life then he must have the mental abilities to form intentions of a sufficiently complex kind, and plan their execution. These

dom, Autonomy and the Concept of a Person', *Proceedings of the Aristotelian Society* (1976), 116.

include minimum rationality, the ability to comprehend the means required to realize his goals, the mental faculties necessary to plan actions, etc. For a person to enjoy an autonomous life he must actually use these faculties to choose what life to have. There must in other words be adequate options available for him to choose from. Finally, his choice must be free from coercion and manipulation by others, he must be independent. All three conditions, mental abilities, adequacy of options, and independence admit of degree. Autonomy in both its primary and secondary senses is a matter of degree. One's life may be more or less autonomous. I will say a little more on these conditions below before turning in the next section to examine the normative character of the autonomous life.

1.2 *The Adequacy of Options* No one can control all aspects of his life. How much control is required for the life to be autonomous, and what counts as an adequate exercise of control (as opposed to being forced by circumstances, or deceived by one's own ignorance, or governed by one's weaknesses) is an enormously difficult problem. Fortunately for us, though its solution is required in order to formulate policies to implement the autonomy-based doctrine of political freedom to be developed in the next chapter, it is not required in order to appreciate the structure of the ideal of toleration, which is our sole concern. All that has to be accepted is that to be autonomous a person must not only be given a choice but he must be given an adequate range of choices. A person whose every decision is extracted from him by coercion is not an autonomous person. Nor is a person autonomous if he is paralysed and therefore cannot take advantage of the options which are offered to him. We will need to examine some of the criteria of adequacy for available options. But we do not require for the purposes of the present argument a general doctrine of the adequacy of options.

Consider the following two imaginary cases:

The Man in the Pit. A person falls down a pit and remains there for the rest of his life, unable to climb out or to summon help. There is just enough ready food to keep him alive without (after he gets used to it) any suffering. He can do nothing much, not even move much. His choices are confined to whether to eat now or a little later, whether to sleep now or a little later, whether to scratch his left ear or not.

The Hounded Woman. A person finds herself on a small desert island. She shares the island with a fierce carnivorous animal which perpetually hunts for her. Her mental stamina, her intellectual ingenuity, her will power and her physical resources are taxed to their limits by her struggle to remain alive. She never has a chance to do or even to think of anything other than how to escape from the beast.

Neither the Man in the Pit nor the Hounded Woman enjoys an autonomous life. The reason is that though they both have choices neither has an adequate range of options to choose from. They present two extremes of failure of adequacy of choice. The one has only trivial options to choose from. His options are all short-term and negligible in their significance and effects. The other person's predicament is the opposite one. All her choices are potentially horrendous in their consequences. If she ever puts one foot wrong she will be devoured by the beast.

The criteria of the adequacy of the options available to a person must meet several distinct concerns. They should include options with long term pervasive consequences as well as short term options of little consequence, and a fair spread in between. We should be able both to choose long term commitments or projects and to develop lasting relationships and be able to develop and pursue them by means which we choose from time to time. It is intolerable that we should have no influence over the choice of our occupation or of our friends. But it is equally unacceptable that we should not be able to decide on trivia such as when to wash or when to comb our hair. This aspect of the requirement of adequate choice is necessary to make sure that our control extends to all aspects of our lives. This is clearly required by the basic idea of being the author of one's life.[1]

---

[1] One other aspect of the problem of adequacy of options has to be noted here in order to avoid a common misunderstanding. People usually control their lives not by deciding once and for all what to do for the rest of their lives. Rather they take successive decisions, with the later ones sometimes reversing earlier decisions, sometimes further implementing them, and often dealing with matters unaffected by the earlier decisions. The question arises, to what extent does autonomy require

Another consideration concerning adequacy relates to the variety of options available. Clearly not number but variety matters. A choice between hundreds of identical and identically situated houses is no choice, compared with a choice between a town flat and a suburban house, for example. Some of the capacities with which the human species is genetically endowed come coupled with innate drives for their use. We have innate drives to move around, to exercise our bodies, to stimulate our senses, to engage our imagination and our affection, to occupy our mind. To a considerable degree culture and civilization consist in training and channelling these innate drives. To be autonomous and to have an autonomous life, a person must have options which enable him to sustain throughout his life activities which, taken together, exercise all the capacities human beings have an innate drive to exercise, as well as to decline to develop any of them.

This formulation, far too abstract to serve as a direct guide to social policy, needs further elaboration. It needs, for example, to be cashed in terms of the options available in a particular society. It is however a virtue of the formulated test that it is not culture-bound. It points to the way in which the options available in different cultures can be evaluated and compared.

The test of variety helps draw the line between autonomy and another ideal it is often confused with: self-realization. Self-realization consists in the development to their full extent of all, or all the valuable capacities a person possesses. The autonomous person is the one who makes his own life and he may choose the path of self-realization or reject it. Nor is autonomy a precondition of self-realization, for one can stumble into a life of self-realization or be manipulated into it or reach it in some other way which is inconsistent with autonomy. One cannot deny this last claim on the ground that one of the capacities one has to develop is that of choosing one's own life. For this and any other capacity

the continuous possibility of choice throughout one's life. Given that every decision, at least once implemented, closes options previously open to one (it may also open up new options) the question of whether, and when, one's own decisions may limit one's autonomy raises tricky issues.

can be developed by simulation and deceit, i.e. by misleading the person to believe that he controls his destiny. In any case autonomy is at best one of many elements which contribute to self-realization and it does not enjoy any special importance compared with many of the others. The autonomous person must have options which will enable him to develop all his abilities, as well as to concentrate on some of them. One is not autonomous if one cannot choose a life of self-realization, nor is one autonomous if one cannot reject this ideal.

The Hounded Woman has to a considerable extent adequate variety. We can further develop her story to provide her with medium and long-term options all dominated by her one overpowering need and desire to escape being devoured by the beast. It is true that even so she does not fully meet our conditions because she cannot avoid using all her faculties. She has no option to develop into an unimaginative athlete, nor to become a physically weak but very imaginative person. But we say that she does not have this choice because a choice between survival and death is no choice from our perspective (and we need not deny that she may be very grateful that at least she was left this choice). An adequate range of options must therefore meet an additional separate condition. For most of the time the choice should not be dominated by the need to protect the life one has. A choice is dominated by that need if all options except one will make the continuation of the life one has rather unlikely.

We are now in a position better to understand this obscure description, and I shall briefly recapitulate some of the points made before (especially in Chapter Six). Since people's well-being depends to a considerable extent on the projects and relationships around which their lives revolve, frustrating their successful pursuit undermines people's well-being. To the extent that much of a person's life depends on one comprehensive goal, forcing him into a choice where all but one option would involve sacrificing this goal is an attempt to coerce him. His choice is dominated by the need to preserve the life he has. He may freely choose to sacrifice that life and that may be the only right choice open to him. But whenever one is forced into a coerced choice, even if yielding to it is not justified it is excused by the fact that the agent's life is put in the balance. This was the point of the example in which a pianist is threatened that his fingers will be crushed unless he complies with instructions. The explanation we now have of the dependence of people's well-being on their goals explains the metaphorical sense of 'the life one has or has embarked upon'. Like all aspects of well-being the notion is fuzzy for well-being admits many degrees, which are mirrored in degrees of damage to it.

But the general dependence of people's well-being on their projects does not in itself justify the normative claims made about coercion in Chapter Six. Since a person may survive the loss of the life he embarked upon and find an alternative life in which he may thrive (and the successful breakdown of many marriages is a case in point), should not that factor be taken into account? It would show that coercing a person need not be as bad as was stated. Sometimes he can resist the coercion, pay the consequences, and start on another successful project. Nor would one always be excused in succumbing to a threat which is dominated by the need to protect the life one has. The normative principles put forward in Chapter Six relied on the value of personal autonomy. They presupposed that the success of a person's life is judged not only by the success of his projects but also by how he came to have them. The contribution of autonomy to a person's life explains why coercion is the evil it is, and why it provides an excuse to those who yield to it.

1.3 *Independence*. Coercion diminishes a person's options. It is sometimes supposed that that provides a full explanation of why it invades autonomy. It reduces the coerced person's options below adequacy. But it need not. One may be coerced not to pursue one option while being left with plenty of others to choose from. Furthermore, loss of options through coercion is deemed to be a greater loss of autonomy than a similar loss brought about by other means. That is why slaves are thought to lack autonomy even if they enjoy a range of options which, were they free, would have been deemed sufficient. Manipulation, unlike coercion, does not interfere with a person's options. Instead it perverts the way that person reaches decisions, forms preferences or adopts goals. It too is an invasion of autonomy whose severity exceeds the importance of the distortion it causes.

Coercion and manipulation draw our attention to a separate dimension of the conditions of personal autonomy: independence. It cannot be reduced to any of the others. It attests to the fact that autonomy is in part a social ideal. It designates one aspect of the proper relations between people. Coercion and manipulation subject the will of one person to that of another. That violates his independence and is inconsistent with his autonomy. This explains why coercion and manipulation are intentional actions: they would not amount to a subjecting of the will of another person if they were not. The invasions of autonomy which they mark are not due only to their consequences. They violate autonomy because of the kind of treatment of others that they are.

It is commonplace to say that by coercing or manipulating a person one treats him as an object rather than as an autonomous person. But how can that be so even if the consequences of one's coercion are negligible? Our discussion in the previous two chapters points to the answer. The natural fact that coercion and manipulation reduce options or distort normal processes of decision and the formation of preferences has become the basis of a social convention loading them with meaning regardless of their actual consequences. They have acquired a symbolic meaning expressing disregard or even contempt for the coerced or manipulated people. As we saw in our earlier discussion in Chapter Six, such conventions are not exceptionless. There is nothing wrong with coercion used to stop one from stepping into the road and under a car. Such exceptions only reinforce the argument for the conventional and symbolic or expressive character of the prohibition against coercion and manipulation, at least to the extent that it transcends the severity of the actual consequences of these actions.

2. Autonomy and Value

2.1 *Aiming at the good.* Autonomy requires that many morally acceptable options be available to a person. 'Our conception of Freedom', rightly observe Benn and Weinstein, 'is bounded by our notions of what might be worthwhile.'[1] This is an additional aspect of the test of adequacy of the available options. It is of great importance to the connection between autonomy and freedom.

I shall use a rather artificial and extreme example to bring out the point. Imagine a person who can pursue an occupation of his choice but at the price of committing murder for each option he rejects. First he has to choose whether to become an electrician. He can refuse provided he kills one person. Then he is offered a career in dentistry, which again he is free to refuse if he kills another person, and so on. Like the person facing the proverbial gunman demanding 'your money or your life', who is acting freely if he defies the threat and risks his life, the person in our dilemma is acting freely if he agrees to murder in order to become a dentist, rather than an electrician. If he does so then his choice does not tend to show that his life is not autonomous. But if he chooses the right way and agrees to be an electrician in order to avoid becoming a murderer then his choice is forced.

I think it will be generally agreed that in this case the life of the person in my example is not autonomous and that his choice and the nature of his options are enough to show that he is not. That is, our judgment that he is not autonomous is unaffected even if the example is developed to show that his predicament is a result of a series of bizarre accidents and coincidences resulting from the breakdown and freak behaviour of several computers in some futuristic society. Autonomy requires a choice of goods. A choice between good and evil is not enough. (Remember that it is personal, not moral, autonomy we are concerned with. No doubt is cast on the fact that the person in the example is a moral agent and fully responsible for his actions. So are the inmates of concentration camps. But they do not have personal autonomy.)

Autonomy cannot be achieved by a person whose every action and thought must be bent to the task of survival, a person who will die if ever he puts a foot wrong. Similarly it cannot be obtained by a person who is constantly fighting

[1] S. I. Benn and W. L. Weinstein, 'Being Free to Act and being a Free Man', *Mind*, 80 (1971), 195.

for moral survival. If he is to be moral then he has no choice, just as the person struggling for physical survival has no choice if he is to stay alive.

This point raises an issue of great importance to the understanding of the relation between autonomy and other moral values. No one would deny that autonomy should be used for the good. The question is, has autonomy any value *qua* autonomy when it is abused? Is the autonomous wrongdoer a morally better person than the non-autonomous wrongdoer? Our intuitions rebel against such a view. It is surely the other way round. The wrongdoing casts a darker shadow on its perpetrator if it is autonomously done by him. A murderer who was led to his deed by the foreseen inner logic of his autonomously chosen career is morally worse than one who murders because he momentarily succumbs to the prospect of an easy gain. Nor are these considerations confined to gross breaches of duties. Demeaning, or narrow-minded, or ungenerous, or insensitive behaviour is worse when autonomously chosen and indulged in.

A second question presents itself now. Could it be that it is valuable to make evil and repugnant options available so that people should freely avoid them? Is the person who rejected a life of mindless idleness, for example, better than one who never had the chance of choosing it? Three reasons are often produced in support of this view. First, people must be tested and prove themselves by choosing good rather than evil. Second, the need to choose refines one's moral judgment and discrimination. Third, the presence of evil provides the occasion for developing certain moral virtues. Whatever sound sense there is in all three considerations derives from the thought that the morally good not only manages his life morally, but would have done so even if circumstances were less favourable or presented more temptations or pressures for evil.

Opportunities for the immoral and the repugnant cannot be eliminated from our world. It may be possible to develop a new form of tape that will make the copying of music from tape in breach of copyright impossible. One opportunity for immorality, let us assume, would thereby disappear. But the vice that it displayed, the vice of, let us say, dishonest dealing, will still have lots of opportunities to be practised. There may be some specialized vices opportunities for which can, at least in principle, be eliminated. But then in a world from which they were well and truly eradicated the corresponding specialist moral ability, that of being good in avoiding that vice, would not be one absence of which is a moral weakness or blemish. The morally good, in other words, are those who would have led a moral life even if the circumstances of their life were less favourable, but only in the sense of being able to cope with the temptations and pressures normal in their society.

For the most part the opportunities for dishonesty, indolence, insensitivity to the feelings of others, cruelty, pettiness and the other vices and moral weaknesses are logically inseparable from the conditions of a human life which can have any moral merit. Given their prevalence one cannot object to the elimination of opportunities for evil on the three grounds cited above. The same kind of considerations show that only very rarely will the non-availability of morally repugnant options reduce a person's choice sufficiently to affect his autonomy. Therefore, the availability of such options is not a requirement of respect for autonomy.

Autonomy is valuable only if exercised in pursuit of the good. The ideal of autonomy requires only the availability of morally acceptable options. This may sound a very rigoristic moral view, which it is not. A moral theory which recognizes the value of autonomy inevitably upholds a pluralistic view. It admits the value of a large number of greatly differing pursuits among which individuals are free to choose.

2.2 *Integrity.* Since the conditions of autonomy include both opportunity and the ability to use it, can a person who enjoys the conditions of autonomy nevertheless fail to lead an autonomous life? One can in fact fritter away one's opportunities, and fail to use (some of) one's abilities. To avail oneself of one's opportunities and abilities one has to be aware of them and make choices among them. This does not mean premeditation or a very deliberative style of life, nor does it necessitate any high degree of self-awareness or rationality. All it requires is the awareness of one's options and the knowledge that one's actions amount to charting a course which could have been otherwise.

As with the conditions of autonomy, so this awareness is a matter of degree. All one can say in the abstract is that one who drifts through life unawares is not leading an autonomous life. Simple ignorance of this kind is unlikely. But its more complex manifestations are common enough. Self-deception is pervasive. It disguises one's true situation from oneself. It is often a way of avoiding decisions, and an attempt to shirk responsibility. The self-deceiving has a way of 'surprising' himself. Only when it is too late to do anything about it does he discover where he has brought himself, excusing himself by saying 'I did not realize that all that was involved. I did not understand the situation. I did not mean to choose that, etc.' Self-deception prevents a person from being aware of his character and motivation. It may lead to repression of one's deeply felt aims, or to the pursuit of goals one is not aware of pursuing through means which are not one's conscious choice.

Various forms and degrees of self-deception are involved in other ways in which one may fail to be autonomous when the conditions for autonomy are met. An autonomous person is aware of his options and chooses between them rather than drifting along until they are lost, and his decision is made for him. He is also a person of integrity. There are two aspects to the connection between autonomy and integrity. To be autonomous one must identify with one's choices, and one must be loyal to them.[1]

A person who feels driven by forces which he disowns but cannot control, who hates or detests the desires which motivate him or the aims that he is pursuing, does not lead an autonomous life. The life he has is not his own. He is thoroughly alienated from it. The condition of alienation which I have in mind is not to be contrasted with smug satisfaction with oneself. Nor is it a state free from guilt and self-reproach. Though alienation is commonly accompanied by rejection of the alienated self it need not be. One can feel estranged from one's achievements. One may feel incapable

---

[1] The importance of identification with one's projects was emphasized and explored by H. Frankfurt.

of taking pride and pleasure in one's doings because one does not feel that they are one's own. In their more extreme manifestations these feelings border on the pathological. But in one degree or another they are part of the life of many.

Identification with one's life is a condition, or a pre-condition, of integrity, but it is not the whole of it. Another condition is loyalty to oneself, through loyalty to one's projects and relationships. In the last chapter I have emphasized how our projects and relationships depend on the form they acquire through social conventions. This means, as we saw, that they depend on complex patterns of expectations, on the symbolic significance of various actions, and in general on remaining loyal, within the recognized limits set for improvisation and change, to their basic shape. Failure to do so is failure to succeed, or even to engage, in the pursuits one has set oneself to make the content of one's life.

These failures are all too often dismissed as of no significance, as no more than simple cases of changing one's mind. The nature of a project or relationship may well be defined by social conventions. But these are, to borrow Searle's phrase,[1] constitutive rules. They define the activity. If by not following them you fail to engage in one activity this just means that you engage in another. You are playing chequers and not chess. How can that matter? It matters in part because of the expectations which one may have induced in others who may have adjusted their behaviour as a result. But it usually matters much more because it is a failure of the agent himself to do what he has decided upon. This failure is destructive of relationships because it involves letting down others. Beyond that it turns one's life into a life with failure in it. (Where one abandons a project because one comes to believe that it is worthless or morally wrong further considerations must be brought into play. But they do not change the basic account.) The more failures one accumulates in one's important pursuits the more of a failure one's life becomes.

Throughout this chapter I repeatedly sound the alarm to warn against confusing various valid ideas with apparently related but really distinct ideas. Here another warning may

[1] J. Searle, *Speech Acts*, Cambridge, 1969.

be in place against thinking that the previous remarks embrace a rigid, planned life, lacking spontaneity and hostile to the possibility of changing one's mind and dropping one pursuit to embrace another. Nothing is further from the truth. While some pursuits, e.g. various forms of monastic life, involve complete advance commitment to a very regimented and routine style of living, most are not of this kind. They allow for variations, encourage spontaneity, and some of the conventions governing their form delineate the (often plentiful) circumstances and reasons which are legitimate occasions for changing one's mind and abandoning the pursuit, without any whiff of failure in the air. An autonomous person is free to choose pursuits which are more short-term, less comprehensive in nature, and which maximize opportunities for change and variety.

Once all that has been taken as read it remains the case that every pursuit has its form, according to which certain modes of behaviour are disloyal to it, incompatible with dedication to it. These are the ones which signify more than a change of heart. They may come of that but they are, if persisted in, the marks of failure. Integrity consists, in part, in loyalty to one's projects and relationships. Compromising one's integrity exacts in these ways its own price. But what has it to do with autonomy? Surely an autonomous life can be a failure. Hence the failure which lack of integrity implies does not show any special connection with autonomy.

The connection is in the kind of failure it is. It is a failure of fidelity which sometimes raises doubt whether the agent was ever truly committed to the project. I do not wish to suggest that the doubt is always justified. If lack of integrity were always due to lack of initial commitment it would be a different failure. It would be a failure to commit oneself, an inability really to choose what one is superficially attracted to, and is trying to choose. The common cases are of a subsequent failure of fidelity, which follows an initial real commitment. That kind of failure is consistent with autonomy. But the other case also exists. The failure to make choices through lack of initial commitment disguised under the flurry of an initial infatuation, does diminish the autonomy of the agent's life. It resembles self-deception. It is a case where the opportunity to choose is missed by the agent thinking that he has made a choice and that he has committed himself, whereas in fact he failed to do so.

2.3 *Creating Value.* An autonomous life is neither necessarily planned nor is it necessarily unified. There is, however, a grain of truth in the view that autonomy gives life a unity. The autonomous person has or is gradually developing a conception of himself, and his actions are sensitive to his past. A person who has projects is sensitive to his past in at least two respects. He must be aware of having the pursuits he has, and he must be aware of his progress in them. Normally one needs to know of one's progress with one's projects in order to know how to proceed with them (and unless one tries to pursue them rationally then they are not one's projects any more). If I aim to teach a student Kant's moral philosophy I have to know where we have got to, in order to know how to proceed. I still pursue this goal even if I am often mistaken in my judgment. I am no longer pursuing it if I decide at random what to talk to him about or what to ask him to do next.

Even if my project in life is never to have the same experience twice, I will be sensitive to my past. I may decide at random what to do next, but I will be choosing from a pool of options from which the ones I have chosen before are excluded. Suppose I do talk to my student about Kant at random, because I believe that that is a good way of teaching Kant. I would still want to know whether I have been talking at random in the past in order to judge my student's progress. If he makes no progress I will have to change my plans for him. The same is true if my goal has been to have a random life. If I discover that I have not lived randomly until now it will be clear that I have failed in achieving my goal and there is no more point in proceeding with it. I may adopt for a second time the goal of having a random life from now on. But this would a fresh start. It is not to continue the pursuit of my old goal.

People do reach decisions which are insensitive to success in performance hitherto. Imagine that on New Year's Eve 1980 Joan decides to support her local charity as often as she can. A year later she suddenly recalls her decision, realizing with some embarrasment that it slipped out of her mind and she did nothing about it for a whole year. Does it matter? There is still as much reason for her now as there ever was to help the charity as often as possible. Her failure to do so in 1980 is no more reason not to do so in 1981 than was the fact that she did not help her charity in 1979 a reason for her not to decide to help it on New Year's Eve 1980. Nevertheless two changes have occurred. First, Joan has failed. Having decided to help her charity turns the fact that she did not into a failure which her not helping it before her decision was not. (If she had a moral duty to help the charity then not having done so in 1979 was a failure to do one's moral duty. But then her conduct in 1980 is a double failure: she failed to do her moral duty, and she failed to do as she resolved.) Second, the failure to behave as she decided in 1980 makes it impossible to start carrying out that decision now. All she can do now is decide again to help the charity.

The first of these facts is particularly important. Though the general reasons for helping the charity are now much as they were, Joan's failure to carry out her resolution to help the charity turns her conduct during 1980 into a failure, which but for her resolution it would not have been. This means that her resolution changed her reasons for action. Her commitment to a particular course of action created for her new reasons which she did not have before. This is a general feature of human life. It does not attach to deliberate or reasoned decisions only.[1] It is common to all cases in which one is committed to a project, a relationship or any pursuit, regardless of the way one came to be so committed. Our goals create for us new possibilities of success as well as of failure. Winning a prize, or winning the esteem of others for achievements in what one cares about and is committed to, is unlike winning a prize for something one happened to achieve almost accidentally while not really caring one way or another. Suppose someone entirely free from any literary aspirations won a prize for something scribbled in his bore-

[1] Therefore the explanation here given is independent of the explanation I gave in previous publications of the normative force of decisions. See 'Reasons for Action, Decisions and Norms', *Mind* 84 (1977), also in J. Raz (ed.) *Practical Reasoning*, Oxford 1978.

dom. It may put ideas into his head. But while indicating possibilities of future success, it is not a mark of any past success, as it would have been had the piece of writing which won the prize been the outcome of a committed engagement in writing.

Our life comprises the pursuit of various goals, and that means that it is sensitive to our past. Having embraced certain goals and commitments we create new ways of succeeding and new ways of failing. In embracing goals and commitments, in coming to care about one thing or another, one progressively gives shape to one's life, determines what would count as a successful life and what would be a failure. One creates values, generates, through one's developing commitments and pursuits, reasons which transcend the reasons one had for undertaking one's commitments and pursuits. In that way a person's life is (in part) of his own making. It is a normative creation, a creation of new values and reasons. It is the way our past forms the reasons which apply to us at present. But it is not like the change of reasons which is occasioned by loss of strength through age, or the absence of money due to past extravagances. Rather it is like the change occasioned by promising: a creation, in that case, of a duty one did not have before. For, whatever reasons one had to make the promise, its making transforms one's reasons, creating a new reason not previously there.[1] Similarly, the fact that one embraced goals and pursuits and has come to care about certain relationships and projects is a change not in the physical or mental circumstance in which one finds oneself, but in one's normative situation. It is the creation of one's life through the creation of reasons.

Some philosophical traditions emphasize self-creation.[2] Sometimes this has been exaggerated into a doctrine of arbitrary self-creation based on the belief that all value derives from choice which is itself not guided by value and is there-

[1] On promises see my 'Promises and Obligations' in P. M. S. Hacker and J. Raz (eds.), *Law, Morality and Society*, Oxford, 1977.

[2] Of discussions of the subject most congenial to my own point of view, and free of the exaggerations I draw attention to below, let me mention only two: A. Montefiore, 'Self-Reality, Self-Respect and Respect for Others', and J. L. Mackie, 'Can There Be a Right-based Moral Theory', both in *Midwest Studies in Philosophy*, 3 (1978).

fore free, i.e. arbitrary. The views explained above neither derive from nor support any such conception. On the contrary, they presuppose independently existing values which are transformed and added to by the development of one's projects and commitments. But, one may wonder, can one transform wrong into right simply by embracing it? If so what meaning is there to the assertion that embracing a project is done for a reason? Once one realizes that by embracing a project one makes its pursuit legitimate one would have no reason to care what antecedent reasons there are for embracing and pursuing it. The embracing cancels them out. If however embracing a project cannot turn it from wrong to right, what meaning is there to the claim that embracing it adds to its value for that person? Is it not always the case that he ought to pursue it only if he ought to have pursued it anyway, for reasons independent of his adoption of the goal?

I would claim, though I will not stop to illustrate the point at length, that sometimes one's choice does make it right for one to pursue a goal which but for one's commitment to it would have been a wrong goal to pursue. The analogy with promising can serve here as well. It may have been wrong to promise to give my son fireworks, for they are too dangerous. But having made the promise it may now be my duty to give him the fireworks. Of course if the danger is grave I should break my promise and seek to compensate him in some other way. It is not my contention that embracing a project can always tilt the balance of reasons the other way, only that sometimes it does so. Nor is it my claim that the typical function of commitments is to reverse the balance of reasons. Their typical, though not exclusive, function is to make indeterminate situations determined. In this lies also the answer to the second question above.

The previous chapter expanded on the prevalence of significant incommensurabilities. Choice between incommensurables is undetermined by reason. When we choose we choose for a reason. Whichever option we adopt we do so because of the factors which make it attractive. But those are not outweighed, given the disadvantages of the option, by the reasons for its alternative. Many of our decisions, in matters small and large, are under-determined by reason. The typical role of our decisions and choices, of having come to care about one thing rather than another, is to settle what was, prior to our commitment, unsettled. It makes the pursuit of the embraced option the right pursuit for us.

The emerging picture is of interplay between impersonal, i.e. choice-independent reasons which guide the choice, which then itself changes the balance of reasons and determines the contours of that person's well-being by creating new reasons which were not there before. This interplay of independent value and the self-creation of value by one's actions and one's past provides the clue to the role of the will in practical reasoning. Previously I have argued that wanting something is not a reason for doing it.[1] We can see now that, while fundamentally right, in one respect that claim was exaggerated. Saying 'I want to . . .' can be a way of indicating that one is committed to a project, that one has embraced a certain pursuit, cares about a relationship. It is, in the way explained, part of a valid reason for action, once the initial commitment has been made. To that extent talk of what one wants is relevant to practical reasoning. In this usage it does not signify the existence of a particular mental state, a desire. It signifies a commitment, deep or shallow, to a pursuit, which may be limited or lasting and comprehensive. There are other ways in which we talk of what people want, and the brief comment above is not meant in any way to be exhaustive. It does, however, capture the main practical relevance of wants.

Self-creation and the creation of values discussed here are not uniquely connected with the ideal of personal autonomy. They represent a necessary feature of practical reasoning. Their discussion adds to and complements the argument of the last two chapters. There is however a special connection between self-creation and the creation of values on the one hand and personal autonomy on the other. The ideal of autonomy picks on these features and demands that they be expanded. It requires that self-creation must proceed, in part, through choice among an adequate range of options;

[1] Especially in Chs. 5 and 9.

that the agent must be aware of his options and of the meaning of his choices; and that he must be independent of coercion and manipulation by others. The ideal of autonomy,
if you like, makes a virtue out of necessity. It picks on the
necessary features we discussed in this subsection and by
developing them in certain directions turns them into an
ideal. Personal autonomy is the ideal of free and conscious
self-creation. One must remember, though, that this remark
does not explain the ideal of personal autonomy, for our
notion of freedom is defined by personal autonomy and not
vice versa.

3. The Value of Autonomy

Is personal autonomy valuable? Its description in the first
two sections above may make it appear an appealing ideal.
But does its value derive from the fact that many people
desire to be autonomous? Is it valuable for those who do not
want to have it? The general drift of the argument hitherto
suggests that it cannot be valuable just because it is wanted.
On the contrary, those who desire it do so because they
believe that it is valuable, and only on condition that it is
valuable. What then is its value? And is it just one option
among several that one can choose or leave alone, or is it an
essential ingredient of the good life so that anyone's well-
being suffers if his autonomy is incomplete?

There are powerful reasons telling in favour of the view
that personal autonomy is only one valuable style of life,
valuable to those who choose it, but that those who reject it
are none the worse for that. Their refutation is important
to gain a proper understanding of the special features of
autonomy which distinguish it from ordinary valuable
options, such as playing golf, or becoming a nurse.

First, there is always the slow-acting poison of the thesis
of the transparency of values. If a person does not want to
be autonomous then how can being autonomous contribute
to his well-being, since he does not think that it does? I will
say nothing more on that issue. Second, it is tempting to
apply autonomy to itself. The life of the autonomous person
consists of pursuits freely chosen from various alternatives

which were open to him. Is not autonomy one of them? Does not its value in his life depend on its being freely chosen against a life without it? Finally, there is the most serious puzzle: the conditions of the well-being of a person, it was argued, are largely determined by his pursuits and goals. If he chooses to be autonomous then it becomes one of his goals and can contribute to his well-being. But it seems incapable of doing him any good if it is not wanted by him.

The last two arguments depend on assimilating autonomy to the goals and pursuits a person may have. Their refutation consists in showing that autonomy is not one project, or goal. As explained in the preceding sections a person lives autonomously if he conducts himself in a certain way (does not drift through life, is aware of his options, etc.) and lives in a certain environment, an environment which respects the condition of independence, and furnishes him with an adequate range of options. The autonomous life depends not on the availability of one option of freedom of choice. It depends on the general character of one's environment and culture. For those who live in an autonomy-supporting environment there is no choice but to be autonomous: there is no other way to prosper in such a society. Before defending this proposition let it be qualified by the reminder that autonomy is a matter of degree. Even for those who live in an autonomy-enhancing culture it is not always best to maximize the degree of their autonomy. All I am claiming is that their well-being depends on their ability to find their place in their environment which includes having what is basically an autonomous life.

Since our well-being depends on our goals, and our ability to pursue goals is limited by the social forms of our societies it is easy to see that an autonomy-enhancing culture may well be tilted in favour of the autonomous life. It may well make it much more difficult for one to avoid the lure of the autonomous life. But, one may wonder, does it follow that there are no possibilities of a successful non-autonomous life in such a society? After all the autonomous person is marked not by what he is but by how he came to be what he is. But his life prospers if he succeeds in what he is, regardless of how he became what he is. Therefore, autonomy cannot affect the well-being of those who do not pursue it as their goal except instrumentally. The mistake in this argument is the hidden assumption that while an environment supports autonomy through providing adequate opportunities to individuals, that fact does not affect the nature of the opportunities it provides. There are more of them, but they are themselves the same as the opportunities which can be available in a traditional society in which each person's course in life (occupation, marriage, place of residence) are determined by tradition or by his superiors. The opposite is the case. An autonomy-supporting culture offers its members opportunities which cannot be had in a non-autonomous environment, and lacks most of the opportunities available in the latter. This is yet again a matter of degree. Very few opportunities cannot exist at all outside an autonomy-supporting environment, and very few others cannot exist in it. The difference between the two types of environment is in the preponderance of one kind of opportunities in the one and of different kinds of opportunities in the other.

Consider the change in the Western attitude to marriage which accompanied the change from pre-arranged marriages being the norm, to the general convention that the married should choose each other. The change has gone so far that any action by a parent which might be seen as an attempt to influence the choice of a spouse is frowned upon, however innocent it may be. Parents have to be very careful before introducing to their children anyone who is of suitable age and status to be a candidate for marriage. The move away from pre-arranged marriages affects in a profound way the nature of the marriage bond. The free choice of partners is a major element determining the expectations spouses have of each other and the conventions which determine what is expected of their relations. The change to marriage as a self-chosen partnership increased personal autonomy. But it did so not by superimposing an external ideal of free choice on an otherwise unchanged relationship. It did so by substituting a relationship which allows much greater room for individual choice in determining the character of the relationship for one which restricted its scope.

More recent changes and tendencies in many countries legitimate not only choice of partner in marriage, but also choice whether to marry at all, cohabit without marriage, etc. These changes are uncertain and incomplete. Some tendencies, e.g. to communal families, or open marriages, may wither away. Others, e.g. homosexual families, may be here to stay. It is too early to have a clear view of the consequences of these developments. But one thing can be said with certainty. They will not be confined to adding new options to the familiar heterosexual monogamous family. They will change the character of that family. If these changes take root in our culture then the familiar marriage relations will disappear. They will not disappear suddenly. Rather they will be transformed into a somewhat different social form, which responds to the fact that it is one of several forms of bonding, and that bonding itself is much more easily and commonly dissoluble. All these factors are already working their way into the constitutive conventions which determine what is appropriate and expected within a conventional marriage and transforming its significance.

In a similar way, even though the skills and technology involved in certain crafts and professions may be identical in two societies, the significance of pursuing any of them differs greatly in a society in which everyone follows in his parents' footsteps from one in which there is free mobility of labour. Attitudes to work, expectations from it, and conceptions of its role in one's life generally are inescapably bound up with whether the different occupations are freely chosen or not. Therefore the very nature and value of these occupations depends on whether they exist in an autonomy-supporting environment or not.

The relations between parents and their children are an example of a relationship which is not based on choice of partners. It shows that an environment can be supportive of autonomy and yet include forms not based on choice (quite apart from the fact that no one has choice over which opportunities are available in his environment). It has to be admitted though that even here choice has tended to creep more and more into the relations. Parents have greater control over whether and when to have children, and to a certain extent over which children to have. The widespread use of contraception, abortion, adoption, *in vitro* fertilization and similar measures has increased choice but also affected the relations between parents and their children. The impact of the increased choice on the character of the family is only beginning to be felt.

It would be a mistake to think that those who believe, as I do, in the value of personal autonomy necessarily desire the extension of personal choice in all relationships and pursuits. They may consistently with their belief in personal autonomy wish to see an end to this process, or even its reversal. The value of personal autonomy is a fact of life. Since we live in a society whose social forms are to a considerable extent based on individual choice, and since our options are limited by what is available in our society, we can prosper in it only if we can be successfully autonomous. We may do so to various degrees. Some people may base more of their lives on those aspects, such as parenthood, where choice is more limited. Others may improvise in their own lives and vary common forms to minimize the degree of choice in them. But ultimately those who live in an autonomy-enhancing culture can prosper only by being autonomous.

The value of autonomy does not depend on choice, except to the very limited extent indicated. Throughout the preceding remarks I was assuming, of course, that it is generally agreed that an autonomous life is not inherently and necessarily evil or worthless. If it is, one cannot prosper by being autonomous. But my argument was aimed at those who regard autonomy as valuable, but as merely one option among many. Their mistake is in disregarding the degree to which the conditions of autonomy concern a central aspect of the whole system of values of a society, which affects its general character. The conditions of autonomy do not add an independent element to the social forms of a society. They are a central aspect in the character of the bulk of its social forms.

We can now see more clearly the strength and the ultimate failure of the revisionist challenge to the ideal of personal freedom. Taking autonomy as the concrete form of freedom (the next chapter will deal with political freedom and will include a further discussion of the relations between freedom and autonomy) the strength of the challenge is all too evident. Does not our analysis reinforce the view that freedom is not an independent separate ideal, that freedom consists in the pursuit of valuable forms of life, and that its value derives from the value of that pursuit? Our analysis certainly shows that autonomy is bound up with the availability of valuable options. But it concentrates on certain aspects of those options, those we identified as constituting the conditions of autonomy, those which are, as we saw in the present section, bound up with them. But the inseparability of autonomy does not mean that it is not a distinct ideal. Its distinctness is evidenced by the fact that it was described without commitment to the substance of the valuable forms of life with which it is bound up.

Autonomy is a distinct ideal, and it can be pursued in different societies which vary considerably in the other aspects of the pursuits and opportunities which they afford their members. Autonomy is, to be sure, inconsistent with various alternative forms of valuable lives. It cannot be obtained within societies which support social forms which do not leave enough room for individual choice. But it is compatible with any valuable set of social forms which conforms with the general conditions specified above. In that lies the distinctiveness of the ideal as a separate ideal, though one which cannot be obtained just in any environment.

4. Value Pluralism

Moral pluralism is the view that there are various forms and styles of life which exemplify different virtues and which are incompatible. Forms or styles of life are incompatible if, given reasonable assumptions about human nature, they cannot normally be exemplified in the same life. There is nothing to stop a person from being both an ideal teacher and an ideal family person. But a person cannot normally lead the life both of action and of contemplation, to use one of the traditionally recognized contrasts, nor can one person possess all the virtues of a nun and of a mother.

To establish moral or value-pluralism, however, the existence of a plurality of incompatible but morally acceptable forms of life is not enough. Moral pluralism claims not merely that incompatible forms of life are morally acceptable but that they display distinct virtues, each capable of being pursued for its own sake. If the active and contemplative lives are not merely incompatible but also display distinctive virtues then complete moral perfection is unattainable. Whichever form of life one is pursuing there are virtues which elude one because they are available only to people pursuing alternative and incompatible forms of life.

Such descriptions of moral pluralism are often viewed with suspicion, at least in part because of the elusiveness of the notion of a form of life. How much must one life differ from another in order to be an instance of a different form of life? The question seems unanswerable because we lack a suitable test of relevance. Indeed there is no test of relevance which would be suitable for all the purposes for which the expression 'a form of life' was or may be used. But this does not matter as the test of relevance we require is plain. For the purpose of understanding moral or value-pluralism, forms of life differ in their moral features.

Two lives must differ in the virtues they display, or in the degree that they display them, if they are to count as belonging to different forms of life. A form of life is maximal if, under normal circumstances, a person whose life is of that kind cannot improve it by acquiring additional virtues, nor by enhancing the degree to which he possesses any virtue, without sacrificing another virtue he possesses or the degree to which it is present in his life. Belief in value-pluralism is the belief that there are several maximal forms of life.

Moral pluralism thus defined is weak moral pluralism. It can be strengthened by the addition of one or more of the following three claims (and there are further ways of refining and subdividing them). *First*, the incompatible virtues are not completely ranked relative to each individual. That is, it is not the case that for each person all the incompatible virtues can be strictly ordered according to their moral worth, so that he ought to pursue the one which for him has the highest worth, and his failure to do so disfigures him with a moral blemish, regardless of his success in pursuing other, incompatible, moral virtues.

Second, the incompatible virtues are not completely ranked by some impersonal criteria of moral worth. Even if the first condition obtains it is still possible to claim that, though there is no moral blemish on me if I am a soldier and excel in courage because I am made of bronze, excellence in dialectics, which is incompatible with courage and is open only to those made of gold, is a superior excellence by some moral standards which are not relative to the character or conditions of life of individuals. The second thesis denies that such impersonal strict ordering of incompatible virtues is possible.

Third, the incompatible virtues exemplify diverse fundamental concerns. They do not derive from a common source, or from common ultimate principles. Some forms of two-level and indirect utilitarianism are morally pluralistic in the weak sense, and may also accept the first two strong forms of moral pluralism. But they are incompatible with the third.

There is yet another sense in which the value-pluralism explained above is weak. 'Moral' is here employed in a wide sense in which it encompasses the complete art of the good life, as Mill might have said.[1] It is in fact used in a sense which encompasses all values. The point of keeping the expression 'moral value', rather than talking simply of values, is to avoid two possible misunderstandings. First, 'value' is sometimes used in a relativized sense, to indicate not what is of value but what is held to be so by some person, group, culture, etc. Secondly, some people hold that some kinds of values, e.g. aesthetic ones, provide no reasons for action: that they are relevant merely to appreciation. In this article 'value' is non-relativized and is understood to constitute or imply the existence of reasons for action.

[1] This use of 'moral' is compatible with the one described in Chapter Twelve. There we noted that from the perspective of an agent certain reasons are not normally regarded as moral. Here we note that when considering practical reason generally, without being in the position of any agent in particular, all values and reasons are moral. Those which are personal rather than moral reasons to one agent, e.g. his concern for the welfare of his child, are moral reasons to impartial by-standers.

The argument of the last chapter supports strong pluralism, combining all the features we mentioned. Incommensurability supports the first two senses of strong pluralism and renders the third one very plausible. The dependence of value on social forms in itself supports all three conditions of strong pluralism. The existence of certain social forms is a contingent matter likely to frustrate any attempt at comprehensive ranking from any point of view, and making the existence of any underlying unifying concern most unlikely.

If valuing autonomy commits one to the creation of value which in turn presupposes strong pluralism, then assuming the value of autonomy one can prove strong value-pluralism. I shall not pursue this argument here any further. Instead I shall suggest, by a different route, that valuing autonomy commits one to weak value pluralism (and henceforth by 'value-pluralism' I will refer to the weak variety). Autonomy is exercised through choice, and choice requires a variety of options to choose from. To satisfy the conditions of the adequacy of the range of options the options available must differ in respects which may rationally affect choice. If all the choices in a life are like the choice between two identical-looking cherries from a fruit bowl, then that life is not autonomous. Choices are guided by reasons and to present the chooser with an adequate variety there must be a difference between the reasons for the different options.

Furthermore, as was argued above, the options must include a variety of morally acceptable options. So the morally acceptable options must themselves vary in the reasons which speak in favour of each of them. There are, in other words, more valuable options than can be chosen, and they must be significantly different or else the requirements of variety which is a precondition of the adequacy of options will not be met.

The upshot of the above is that autonomy presupposes a variety of conflicting considerations. It presupposes choices involving trade-offs, which require relinquishing one good for the sake of another. Excellence in the pursuit of goods involves possession of the appropriate virtues. Where the goods are varied in character, so that they display varied merits or advantages, their successful pursuit requires different virtues. The existence of more goods than can be chosen by one person, which are of widely differing character, speaks of the existence of more virtues than can be perfected by one person. It tells of the existence of incompatible virtues, that is of value-pluralism. A person may have an autonomous life without attaining any virtue to any high degree. However, he inhabits a world where the pursuit of many virtues was open to him, but where he would not have been able to achieve them all, at least not to their highest degree. To put it more precisely, if autonomy is an ideal then we are committed to such a view of morality: valuing autonomy leads to the endorsement of moral pluralism.

15
Freedom and Autonomy

The doctrine of political freedom with which this book concludes is based on the values of pluralism and autonomy
which were discussed in the last chapter. My purpose is to
show that a powerful argument in support of political freedom is derivable from the value of personal autonomy. This
is not a surprising conclusion. It is sometimes thought that
the argument from autonomy is the specifically liberal argument for freedom, the one argument which is not shared
by non-liberals, and which displays the spirit of the liberal
approach to politics. The chapter contributes to an exploration of this view. It does so in two ways.

First, it is sometimes assumed that respect for autonomy
requires governments to avoid pursuing any conception of
the good life. In other words the ideal of autonomy is used
to support a doctrine of political freedom reflecting anti-
perfectionism, the exclusion of ideals from politics. I argued
against such views in Chapters Five and Six. The present
chapter will reinforce these conclusions.

Another well known liberal argument for freedom is based
on the harm principle. This principle, first formulated by J.
S. Mill, has found a powerful champion in our times in H.
L. A. Hart.[1] The principle asserts that the only purpose for
which the law may use its coercive power is to prevent harm.
I shall argue that the autonomy-based principle of freedom
is best regarded as providing the moral foundation for the
harm principle. It explains why liberals are sometimes willing to employ coercion to prevent harm, as well as why they
refuse to use coercion for other purposes. Thus viewed the
principle helps assess the relative seriousness of various
harms, as well as to answer potentially damaging criticisms
of the harm principle which claim that it reflects the ideology

[1] J. S. Mill, *On Liberty*. H. L. A. Hart, *Law, Liberty, and Morality*, Oxford,
1963.

of the night watchman state. At the same time it has to be admitted that the interpretation to be here given to the harm principle differs from that it has received at the hands of individualistic liberals.

Before dealing with the core issues, the first section points to a generally overlooked source of intolerance, a source which is of special interest in the context of this book. For, I shall contend, pluralism has an inherent tendency to generate intolerance, a tendency which ought to be guarded against. Section 2 sets out the outlines of the autonomy-based doctrine of political freedom, and points to some of its limitations. Section 3 examines the relations between this doctrine and the harm principle. The argument is continued in the following section which touches on some of the issues raised by the question: to what extent, if at all, should politics and the law support paternalistic measures? The last concluding section compares our conclusions with some other familiar answers to the same questions.

1. Pluralism and Intolerance

It is sometimes supposed that value-pluralism by itself, through its approval of many incompatible forms of life, establishes the value of toleration. However, refraining from persecuting or harassing people who possess moral virtues which we lack is not in itself toleration. I do not tolerate people whom I admire and respect because they are generous, kind or courageous, whereas I am not. Toleration implies the suppression or containment of an inclination or desire to persecute, harrass, harm or react in an unwelcome way to a person. But even this does not yet capture the essence of toleration. I do not tolerate the courageous, the generous and the kind even if I am inclined to persecute them and restrain myself because I realize that my desires are entirely evil.

Toleration is a distinctive moral virtue only if it curbs desires, inclinations and convictions which are thought by the tolerant person to be in themselves desirable. Typically a person is tolerant if and only if he suppresses a desire to cause to another a harm or hurt which he thinks the other deserves. The clearest case of toleration, whether justified or not, is where a person restrains his indignation at the sight of injustice or some other moral evil, or rather at the sight of behaviour which he takes to be of this character. Whether a person is tolerant or not depends on his reasons for action. Himmler did not tolerate Hitler when he did not kill him. But an anti-Nazi may have spared his life out of a misconceived sense of duty to let people carry on even when they are in the wrong.

Notice that to claim to act out of toleration is to claim that one's action is justified, though in fact it may not be, perhaps because toleration is out of place in the circumstances.

I emphasized the tolerant person's view that in being tolerant he is restraining an inclination which is in itself desirable. The typical cases are those in which the intolerant inclination is in itself desirable because it is a reaction to wrongful behaviour. Is it then part of our notion of toleration that only the wrongful or bad can be tolerated? Many writers on the subject assume so. But this view seems unwarranted. To be sure one cannot tolerate other people because of their virtues. But one can tolerate their limitations. A person can tolerate another's very deliberate manner of speech, or his slow and methodical way of considering every issue, and so on. In all such cases what is tolerated is neither wrong nor necessarily bad. It is the absence of a certain accomplishment. This is not an attempt at hair-splitting. The reason people lack certain virtues or accomplishments may be, and often is, that they possess other and incompatible virtues and accomplishments. When we tolerate the limitations of others we may be aware that these are but the other side of their virtues and personal strengths. This may indeed be the reason why we tolerate them.

Toleration, then, is the curbing of an activity likely to be unwelcome to its recipient or of an inclination so to act which is in itself morally valuable and which is based on a dislike or an antagonism towards that person or a feature of his life, reflecting a judgment that these represent limitations or deficiencies in him, in order to let that person have his way or in order for him to gain or keep some advantage.[1]

---

[1] As was pointed out to me by P. M. S. Hacker, mercy is sometimes a special case of toleration. One can tolerate out of mercy.

This characterization of toleration deviates from the view which is most common in writing on political theory in two respects. My explanation relies on four features. First, only behaviour which is either unwelcome to the person towards whom it is addressed or behaviour which is normally seen as unwelcome is intolerant behaviour. Secondly, one is tolerant only if one inclines or is tempted not to be. Thirdly, that inclination is based on dislike or antagonism to the behaviour, character or some feature of the existence of its object. Finally, the intolerant inclination is in itself, at least in the eyes of the person experiencing it, worth while or desirable.

Political theorists tend to concentrate on one hostile reaction as the only possible manifestation of intolerance: the use of coercion. They are resistant to the thought that an expression of a hostile view, for example, may be intolerant behaviour. Secondly, as was observed above, it is often thought that only if a person judges another or his behaviour to be wrong or evil can he be tolerant of that person or of his behaviour.

I shall say little about the first point. If there is a concept of intolerance according to which only coercive interventions are intolerant, then this is not the ordinary notion of intolerance but one developed by political theorists to express a particular point of view. I know of no reason for sharing that point of view. The ideas of toleration and of intolerance identify modes of behaviour by their grounds and object. They do not identify them by the means employed. Saying this is not saying that all the manifestations of intolerance are either equally acceptable or equally unacceptable. It is merely to point out that here are concepts that identify actions by their motives and not by the means those motives lead to.

I have already explained the reasons for rejecting the view that only the bad or the wrong can be tolerated. The fact that intolerance can be directed at people's limitations and that those can be aspects of some other virtues which those people possess acquires special significance for those who believe in value-pluralism. It provides the link between pluralism and toleration.

Later in the chapter I shall argue that, within bounds,

respect for personal autonomy requires tolerating bad or evil actions. But toleration can also be of the good and valuable when it curbs inclinations which, though valuable in themselves, are intolerant of other people's morally acceptable tastes and pursuits. While pluralism as such need not give rise to occasions where toleration is called for, some very common kinds of pluralistic moralities do. Let us call them competitive pluralistic moralities (there are competitive moralities which are not pluralistic but they do not concern us).

Competitive pluralism not only admits the validity of distinct and incompatible moral virtues, but also of virtues which tend, given human nature, to encourage intolerance of other virtues. That is, competitive pluralism admits the value of virtues possession of which normally leads to a tendency not to suffer certain limitations in other people which are themselves inevitable if those people possess certain other, equally valid, virtues. The traits of character which make for excellence in chairing committees and getting things done, when this involves reconciling points of view and overcoming personal differences, those very traits of character also tend to make people intolerant of single-minded dedication to a cause. And there are many other examples, the prevalence of which suggests that most common forms of pluralism are of the competitive kind.

It is worth dwelling on this point, for it is often misunderstood. People who come to realize that their intolerant tendencies have to be curbed may conclude that they are bad in themselves, rather than merely in their expression. If they were, no virtue of toleration would be called upon to restrain them. This point applies to tolerating people's bad tendencies as much as to tolerating their limitations. I am not simply wrong in inclining to be intolerant of another person's meanness or vulgarity. These rightly trigger intolerant responses. A person who does not react to them in this way lacks in moral sensibility. Yet it is a response which should be curbed. This view presupposes a certain conception of moral conflict. It regards some conflicts as real conflicts between independent moral considerations, rather than as merely conflicting partial judgments which simply give way without trace to an all-things-considered judgment. It further assumes that some prima facie moral judgments, and not merely conclusive judgments, may have appropriate emotional or attitudinal concomitants or components.

The question of the appropriate emotional response to moral judgment is still relatively neglected in much of the writing on moral philosophy. It is generally admitted that certain judgments should be accompanied by appropriate emotional responses. Feelings of gratitude, resentment, anger, regret, guilt, and many others, play an important role in sound moral lives. A frequent implicit assumption is that they are properly attached only to conclusive judgments. If one's conclusive judgment is that another person was knowingly or recklessly in the wrong one may feel, and perhaps also display, anger. But if the overall judgment absolves him of blame then the fact that aspects of his behaviour were repulsive does not justify feeling repulsion towards him. This is a mistake in moral psychology. It underestimates the intimate connection between judgment and feeling in various areas of morality.

Those who recognize the reality of moral conflict hold that a judgment that an action is intrinsically bad can be, for example, compatible with a conclusive judgment that all things considered it is justified. It may both be justified and be intrinsically bad. If emotional responses attach to some moral judgments they attach to prima facie judgments. Conclusive judgments merely adjudicate between prima facie ones. They declare which of the prima facie judgments is of greater weight or urgency in the situation. They do not add concrete colour to our moral estimate of the action under consideration. If emotional responses can legitimately attach only to conclusive judgments they can only be undifferentiated feelings of approval or disapproval. The full range of moral emotions is comprehensible only because they attach to prima facie judgments. We admire courageous actions, are warmed by generous ones, are repelled by ruthless acts, etc., regardless of whether or not they are justified overall. Nor should we be expected to erase the emotions once it is established that the judgment to which they attach is overridden and the ruthless, repulsive, or cruel action was justified in the circumstances. Belief in moral conflict means that its being justified does not necessarily deprive it of these unattractive characteristics. By the same token it does not necessarily deprive the relevant emotions of their aptness. There are genuine and ineradicable conflicts of moral emotions just as there are genuine conflicts of moral reasons.

It is possible that all viable forms of pluralism are competitive. Failing that, it is likely that the variety of valuable options which is required by the ideal of autonomy can only be satisfied by competitive value-pluralism. This view is plausible given the range of abilities many people have. We assume that moral life will be possible only within human communities, and that means that the range of capacities, development of which is to be made possible in order for all members of the community to be autonomous, is greater than the range necessary to assure an individual of autonomy. That is a consequence of the fact that both the genetic differences between people and the social needs for variety and for a division of labour lead to a diversity of abilities among people. The moral virtues associated with the diverse forms of life allowed by a morality which enables all normal persons to attain autonomy by moral means are very likely to depend on character traits many of which lead to intolerance of other acceptable forms of life. All those forms of life are not only morally legitimate but also ones which need to be available if all persons are to have autonomy. Therefore respect for autonomy by requiring competitive value-pluralism also establishes the necessity for toleration.

Even if one rejects my supposition that, given human nature, autonomy can only be realized within a community which endorses a competitive pluralistic morality, even if one thinks that that supposition is based on a misguided view of human nature, that it is perhaps too pessimistic, even if one believes that autonomy and pluralism are possible without conflict, the above conclusion is not undermined. Even on these optimistic assumptions it is still the case that competitive pluralism contributes, where it exists, to the realization of autonomy. Therefore, competitive pluralism provides an argument for a principle of toleration. The only modification is that on the more optimistic assumptions there may be circumstances in which there will be no need to rely on the principle, circumstances in which the conflicts which activate it do not arise. This does not invalidate the principle of toleration. And of course in our world it is not merely idly valid; the circumstances for its invocation are very much with us.

2. Autonomy-Based Freedom

The previous section argued that competitive value pluralism of the kind which is required by respect for autonomy generates conflicts between people pursuing valuable but incompatible forms of life. Given the necessity to make those forms of life available in order to secure autonomy there is a need to curb people's actions and their attitudes in those conflicts by principles of toleration. The duty of toleration, and the wider doctrine of freedom of which it is a part, are an aspect of the duty of respect for autonomy. To judge its scope and its limits we need to look at the extent of our autonomy-based duties generally.

Since autonomy is morally valuable there is reason for everyone to make himself and everyone else autonomous. But it is the special character of autonomy that one cannot make another person autonomous. One can bring the horse to the water but one cannot make it drink. One is autonomous if one determines the course of one's life by oneself. This is not to say that others cannot help, but their help is by and large confined to securing the background conditions which enable a person to be autonomous. This is why moral philosophers who regard morality as essentially other-regarding tend to concentrate on autonomy as a capacity for an autonomous life. Our duties towards our fellows are for the most part to secure for them autonomy in its capacity sense. Where some of these writers are wrong is in overlooking the reason for the value of autonomy as a capacity, which is in the use its possessor can make of it, i.e. in the autonomous life it enables him to have.

There is more one can do to help another person have an autonomous life than stand off and refrain from coercing or manipulating him. There are two further categories of autonomy-based duties towards another person. One is to help in creating the inner capacities required for the conduct of an autonomous life. Some of these concern cognitive capacities, such as the power to absorb, remember and use information, reasoning abilities, and the like. Others concern one's emotional and imaginative make-up. Still others concern health, and physical abilities and skills. Finally, there are character traits essential or helpful for a life of autonomy. They include stability, loyalty and the ability to form personal attachments and to maintain intimate relationships. The third type of autonomy-based duty towards another concerns the creation of an adequate range of options for him to choose from.

As anticipated all these duties, though grounded in the value of the autonomous life, are aimed at securing autonomy as a capacity. Apart from cultivating a general awareness of the value of autonomy there is little more one can do. It is not surprising, however, that the principle of autonomy, as I shall call the principle requiring people to secure the conditions of autonomy for all people, yields duties which go far beyond the negative duties of non-interference, which are the only ones recognized by some defenders of autonomy. If the duties of non-interference are autonomy-based then the principle of autonomy provides reasons for holding that there are other autonomy-based duties as well. Every reason of autonomy which leads to the duties of non-interference would lead to other duties as well, unless, of course, it is counteracted by conflicting reasons. Such countervailing reasons are likely to be sometimes present, but they are most unlikely to confine the duties of autonomy to non-interference only.

These reflections clarify the relation between autonomy and freedom. Autonomy is a constituent element of the good life. A person's life is autonomous if it is to a considerable extent his own creation. Naturally the autonomous person has the capacity to control and create his own life. I called this the capacity sense of autonomy, for 'autonomy' is sometimes used to refer to that capacity alone. That capacity, which involves both the possession of certain mental and physical abilities and the availability of an adequate range of options, is sometimes referred to as positive freedom. That notion, like all notions which have become slogans in intellectual battles, is notoriously elusive. I prefer to discuss it in relation to the ideal of personal autonomy because positive freedom derives its value from its contribution to personal autonomy. Positive freedom is intrinsically valuable because it is an essential ingredient and a necessary condition of the autonomous life. It is a capacity whose value derives from its exercise. This provides the clue to its definition.

One's positive freedom is enhanced by whatever enhances one's ability to lead an autonomous life. Disputes concerning the scope and content of positive freedom should be settled by reference to the contribution of the disputed element to autonomy. Since autonomy admits of various degrees so does positive freedom. Since the impact of various courses of action on autonomy is incommensurate so is their impact on positive freedom. This 'imprecision' explains many people's exasperation with such 'woolly' concepts, and their reluctance to use them when engaged in serious theoretical or political arguments. Such reluctance would have been in place had these concepts been blocking our view of something more precise behind them. They do not. They mark features of life which are intrinsically valuable. The imprecision they import is ultimate imprecision. That is it is no imprecision at all but a reflection of the incommensurabilities with which life abounds.

Can negative freedom, i.e. freedom from coercion, be viewed as an aspect of positive freedom, i.e. of autonomy as a capacity? This view is liable to mislead. Autonomy and positive freedom relate primarily to pervasive goals, projects or relationships. The autonomous person freely develops friendships and other ties with people and animals. But that he is not free to talk to Jones now does not diminish his autonomy. The autonomous person chooses his own profession or trade. He may be denied the chance to cut down trees in the next field without any diminution to his autonomy. In other words, autonomy and positive freedom bear directly on relatively pervasive goals and relationships and affect more restricted options only inasmuch as they affect one's ability to pursue the more pervasive ones. Enrolling in a university or standing for Parliament in the general election, are examples of specific actions which affect pervasive choices. Denying one the ability to engage in them curtails to a significant degree one's ability to choose one's career and to feel a full member of a political community. Other specific actions affect one's autonomy not at all. Denying someone a certain choice of ice-cream is generally admitted to be insignificant to the degree of autonomy enjoyed by that person.

Discussions of negative freedom and of coercion usually concentrate on coercing people to perform or avoid specific actions. That is the natural context of coercion. But it may mask its moral significance and has on occasion led to a blind obsession with the avoidance of coercion. Negative freedom, freedom from coercive interferences, is valuable inasmuch as it serves positive freedom and autonomy. It does so in several ways.[1] Coercing another may express contempt, or at any rate disrespect for his autonomy. Secondly, it reduces his options and therefore may be to his disadvantage. It may, in this way, also interfere with his autonomy. It may but it need not: some options one is better off not having. Others are denied one so that one will improve one's options in the future.[2] In judging the value of negative freedom one should never forget that it derives from its contribution to autonomy.

The significance of denial of options to one's autonomy depends on the circumstances one finds oneself in. In some countries the vote does not have the symbolic significance it has in our culture. Its denial to an individual may be a trivial matter. Such factors do not diminish the importance of negative freedom, but they make it more difficult to judge.

The autonomy-based doctrine of freedom is far-reaching in its implications. But it has clear limits to which we must turn.

First, while autonomy requires the availability of an adequate range of options it does not require the presence of any particular option among them. A person or a government can take action eventually to eliminate soccer and substitute

---

[1] This topic was discussed in some detail in Ch. 6.

[2] On this subject see Gerald Dworkin's very helpful article, 'Is more choice better than less', *Midwest Studies in Philosophy*, 7 (1982), 47.

for it American football, etc. The degree to which one would wish to tolerate such action will be affected by pragmatic considerations which can normally be expected to favour erring on the side of caution where governmental action or action by big organizations is concerned. But it has to be remembered that social, economic and technological processes are constantly changing the opportunities available in our society. Occupations and careers are being created while others disappear all the time. The acceptable shapes of personal relationships are equally in constant flux, and so is the public culture which colours much of what we can and cannot do. Not everyone would agree that such processes are unobjectionable so long as the government does not take a hand in shaping them. The requirements of autonomy as well as other considerations may well call for governmental intervention in directing or initiating such processes.

It is important in this context to distinguish between the effect of the elimination of an option on those already committed to it, and its effect on others. The longer and the more deeply one is committed to one's projects the less able one is to abandon them (before completion) and pick up some others as substitutes. But even if such a change is possible, denying a person the possibility of carrying on with his projects, commitments and relationships is preventing him from having the life he has chosen. A person who may but has not yet chosen the eliminated option is much less seriously affected. Since all he is entitled to is an adequate range of options the eliminated option can, from his point of view, be replaced by another without loss of autonomy. This accounts for the importance of changes being gradual so that they will not affect committed persons.

The *second* main limitation of autonomy-based freedom has already been mentioned. It does not extend to the morally bad and repugnant. Since autonomy is valuable only if it is directed at the good it supplies no reason to provide, nor any reason to protect, worthless let alone bad options. To be sure autonomy itself is blind to the quality of options chosen. A person is autonomous even if he chooses the bad. Autonomy is even partially blind to the quality of the options available. A person is autonomous, it was argued in the last chapter, only if he pursues the good as he sees it. He can be autonomous only if he believes that he has valuable options to choose from. That is consistent with many of his options being bad ones.[1] But while autonomy is consistent with the presence of bad options, they contribute nothing to its value. Indeed autonomously choosing the bad makes one's life worse than a comparable non-autonomous life is. Since our concern for autonomy is a concern to enable people to have a good life it furnishes us with reason to secure that autonomy which could be valuable. Providing, preserving or protecting bad options does not enable one to enjoy valuable autonomy.

This may sound very rigoristic and paternalistic. It conjures images of the state playing big brother forcing or manipulating people to do what it considers good for them against their will. Nothing could be further from the truth. First, one needs constant reminders that the fact that the state *considers* anything to be valuable or valueless is no reason for anything. Only its being valuable or valueless is a reason. If it is likely that the government will not judge such matters correctly then it has no authority to judge them at all.[2] Secondly, the autonomy-based doctrine of freedom rests primarily on the importance of autonomy and value-pluralism. Autonomy means that a good life is a life which is a free creation. Value-pluralism means that there will be a multiplicity of valuable options to choose from, and favourable conditions of choice. The resulting doctrine of freedom provides and protects those options and conditions. But is the principle of autonomy consistent with the legal enforcement of morality? To the examination of this question we must now turn.

3. Autonomy and the Harm Principle

Mill's harm principle states that the only justification for coercively interfering with a person is to prevent him from harming others. My discussion will revolve round the somewhat wider principle which regards the prevention of harm

---

[1] It is no more possible to eliminate all valuable options than it is to eliminate all bad ones. Cf. Ch. 13.

[2] This is the burden of the normal justification thesis of Ch. 3.

to anyone (himself included) as the only justifiable ground for coercive interference with a person. The harm principle is a principle of freedom. The common way of stating its point is to regard it as excluding considerations of private morality from politics. It restrains both individuals and the state from coercing people to refrain from certain activities or to undertake others on the ground that those activities are morally either repugnant or desirable. My purpose is to compare the scope and justification of the harm principle with those of autonomy-based freedom.

That there may be at least some connection between the autonomy and the harm principles is evident. Respect for the autonomy of others largely consists in securing for them adequate options, i.e. opportunities and the ability to use them. Depriving a person of opportunities or of the ability to use them is a way of causing him harm. Both the use-value and the exchange-value of property represent opportunities for their owner. Any harm to a person by denying him the use or the value of his property is a harm to him precisely because it diminishes his opportunities. Similarly injury to the person reduces his ability to act in ways which he may desire. Needless to say a harm to a person may consist not in depriving him of options but in frustrating his pursuit of the projects and relationships he has set upon.

Between them these cases cover most types of harm. Several forms of injury are, however, left out. Severe and persistent pain is incapacitating. But not all pain falls into this class and even pain which does incapacitate may be objected to as pain independently of its incapacitating results. The same is true of offence. Serious and persistent offence may well reduce a person's opportunities. It may even affect his ability to use the opportunities he has or frustrate his pursuit of his goals. But many cases of causing offence fall short of this. All offensive behaviour may be reprehensible as offensive, independently of its consequences to the affected person's options or projects. Similar considerations apply to other forms of injury such as hurting people's feelings, etc.

It is of interest to note that pain and offence, hurt and the like are harmful only when they do affect options or projects. For 'harm' in its ordinary use has a forward-looking aspect.

To harm a person is to diminish his prospects, to affect adversely his possibilities. It is clear that supporters of the harm principle are also concerned with the prevention of offence and pain. It is not clear whether they extend it to encompass all forms of hurting or adversely affecting people. For clarity's sake we could distinguish between the narrow harm principle which allows coercion only for the prevention of harm in the strict sense of the word and the somewhat open-ended broad harm principle which allows coercion for the prevention of pain, offence and perhaps some other injuries to a person as well.[1]

I hope that these observations are as uncontroversial as they are intended to be. I have tried to follow the common understanding of harm, but to describe it in terms which bring out the connection between harm and autonomy. They reinterpret the principle from the point of view of a morality which values autonomy. That is, they are not an account of the meaning of 'harm' (only the point about the forward-looking aspect of harm belongs to an account of its meaning). Roughly speaking, one harms another when one's action makes the other person worse off than he was, or is entitled to be, in a way which affects his future well-being. So much is a matter of meaning. But this makes much turn on the notion of individual well-being. It gives concrete content to the principle.

People who deny the moral value of autonomy will not be committed to denying that there are harms, nor that harming people is, as such, wrong. But they would have to provide a different understanding of what behaviour harms others. Since 'causing harm' entails by its very meaning that the action is prima facie wrong, it is a normative concept acquiring its specific meaning from the moral theory within which it is embedded. Without such a connection to a moral theory the harm principle is a formal principle lacking specific concrete content and leading to no policy conclusions.

This way of thinking of the harm principle may help re-

---

[1] I shall assume without discussion and explanation that the prevention of severe pain justifies coercion. The explanation of our concern to avoid pain is a fascinating subject which cannot be undertaken in this book.

solve our response to two potentially decisive objections to it. First, the principle seems to forbid redistribution through taxation, and the provision of public goods out of public funds on a non-voluntary basis, as well as to proscribe such familiar schemes as a tax-financed educational and national health systems, the subsidization of public transport, etc. Secondly, the only reason for coercively interfering with a person in order to prevent harm is that it is wrong to cause such harm. But if coercive interventions are justified on this ground then they are used to enforce morality. If so why stop with the prevention of harm? Why not enforce the rest of morality?

The argument of the book so far leads to the acceptance of the second objection. It maintains that it is the function of governments to promote morality. That means that governments should promote the moral quality of the life of those whose lives and actions they can affect. Does not this concession amount to a rejection of the harm principle? It does according to the common conception which regards the aim and function of the principle as being to curtail the freedom of governments to enforce morality. I wish to propose a different understanding of it, according to which it is a principle about the proper way to enforce morality. In other words I would suggest that the principle is derivable from a morality which regards personal autonomy as an essential ingredient of the good life, and regards the principle of autonomy, which imposes duties on people to secure for all the conditions of autonomy, as one of the most important moral principles.

To derive the harm principle from the principle of autonomy one has to establish that autonomy-based duties never justify coercion where there is no harm. This brings us immediately to the first objection. Governments are subject to autonomy-based duties to provide the conditions of autonomy for people who lack them. These extend beyond the duty to prevent loss of autonomy. This may seem as an endorsement of the first objection to the harm principle. But is it? It is a mistake to think that the harm principle recognizes only the duty of governments to prevent loss of autonomy. Sometimes failing to improve the situation of another is harming him.

One can harm another by denying him what is due to him. This is obscured by the common misconception which confines harming a person to acting in a way the result of which is that that person is worse off after the action than he was before. While such actions do indeed harm, so do acts or omissions the result of which is that a person is worse off after them than he should then be. One harms another by failing in one's duty to him, even though this is a duty to improve his situation and the failure does not leave him worse off than he was before. Consider a disabled person who has a legal right to be employed by any employer to whom he applies and who has fewer than four per cent disabled employees in his work force. If such an employer turns him down he harms him though he does not worsen his situation. If you owe me five pounds then you harm me by delaying its repayment by a month.

So if the government has a duty to promote the autonomy of people the harm principle allows it to use coercion both in order to stop people from actions which would diminish people's autonomy and in order to force them to take actions which are required to improve peoples' options and opportunities. It is true that an action harms a particular person only if it affects him directly and significantly by itself. It does not count as harming him if its undesirable consequences are indirect and depend on the intervention of other actions. I do not, for example, harm Johnson by failing to pay my income tax, nor does the government harm him by failing to impose a tax which it is its moral obligation to impose, even if it can be established that Johnson suffered as a result of such failures. In each case the culprit can claim that the fact that Johnson is the one who suffered was decided not by the guilty action but by other intervening actions (which may not have been guilty at all).

But even though I or the government did not harm Johnson we caused harm. If you like, call it harm to unassignable individuals. The point is that one causes harm if one fails in one's duty to a person or a class of persons and that person or a member of that class suffers as a result. That is so even when one cannot be blamed for harming the person who suffered because the allocation of the loss was determined by other hands. A government which has a moral duty to increase old age pensions harms old age pensioners if it fails to do so, even though it does not harm any particular pensioner.

The upshot of this discussion is that the first objection fails, for the harm principle allows full scope to autonomy-based duties. A person who fails to discharge his autonomy-based obligations towards others is harming them, even if those obligations are designed to promote the others' autonomy rather than to prevent its deterioration. It follows that a government whose responsibility is to promote the autonomy of its citizens is entitled to redistribute resources, to provide public goods and to engage in the provision of other services on a compulsory basis, provided its laws merely reflect and make concrete autonomy-based duties of its citizens. Coercion is used to ensure compliance with the law. If the law reflects autonomy-based duties then failure to comply harms others and the harm principle is satisfied.

But the autonomy principle is a perfectionist principle. Autonomous life is valuable only if it is spent in the pursuit of acceptable and valuable projects and relationships. The autonomy principle permits and even requires governments to create morally valuable opportunities, and to eliminate repugnant ones. Does not that show that it is incompatible with the harm principle? The impression of incompatibility is encouraged by the prevalent anti-perfectionist reading of the harm principle. That reading is at odds with the fact that the principle merely restricts the use of coercion. Perfectionist goals need not be pursued by the use of coercion. A government which subsidizes certain activities, rewards their pursuit, and advertises their availability encourages those activities without using coercion.

It is no objection to point out that the funds necessary for all these policies are raised by compulsory taxation. I assume that tax is raised to provide adequate opportunities, and is justified by the principle of autonomy in a way consistent with the harm principle in accordance with the considerations described a couple of paragraphs above. The

government has an obligation to create an environment providing individuals with an adequate range of options and the
opportunities to choose them. The duty arises out of people's
interest in having a valuable autonomous life. Its violation
will harm those it is meant to benefit. Therefore its fulfilment
is consistent with the harm principle. Not every tax can be
justified by this argument. But then not every tax is justified
by any argument. A tax which cannot be justified by the
argument here outlined should not be raised.

Autonomy-based duties, in conformity with the harm
principle, require the use of public power to promote the
conditions of autonomy, to secure an adequate range of options for the population. But as we saw in the previous section considerations of personal autonomy cannot dictate
which options should be promoted. There are many possible
options the provision of which can make the available options
adequate. It is in deciding which options to encourage more
than others that perfectionist considerations dominate. Here
they are limited by the availability of resources mobilized in
the above mentioned way. The harm principle is consistent
with many perfectionist policies of the kind required by
any moral theory which values autonomy highly. It does,
however, exclude the use of coercion to discourage non-
harmful opportunities. Can that exclusion be derived from
the principle of autonomy?

If the argument of Section 2 is sound then pursuit of
the morally repugnant cannot be defended from coercive
interference on the ground that being an autonomous choice
endows it with any value. It does not (except in special
circumstances where it is therapeutic or educational). And
yet the harm principle is defensible in the light of the principle of autonomy for one simple reason. The means used,
coercive interference, violates the autonomy of its victim.
First, it violates the condition of independence and expresses
a relation of domination and an attitude of disrespect for the
coerced individual. Second, coercion by criminal penalties
is a global and indiscriminate invasion of autonomy. Imprisoning a person prevents him from almost all autonomous
pursuits. Other forms of coercion may be less severe, but
they all invade autonomy, and they all, at least in this world,

do it in a fairly indiscriminate way. That is, there is no practical way of ensuring that the coercion will restrict the victims' choice of repugnant options but will not interfere with their other choices. A moral theory which values autonomy highly can justify restricting the autonomy of one person for the sake of the greater autonomy of others or even of that person himself in the future. That is why it can justify coercion to prevent harm, for harm interferes with autonomy. But it will not tolerate coercion for other reasons. The availability of repugnant options, and even their free pursuit by individuals, does not detract from their autonomy. Undesirable as those conditions are they may not be curbed by coercion.

Some defenders of the harm principle will be disappointed with this justification. One source of suspicion is that it depends on contingent facts: the non-existence at the present time of means of coercion which do not infringe autonomy, and the fact that conditions justify suspecting governments of lacking respect for individuals. What if it became possible to coerce people to avoid immoral but harmless conduct without restricting them in any other way; suppose we had institutions which could be relied to do so only to stop immoralities and would not mistake what is worth while for what is evil nor would they abuse their power? They would be free from suspicion that they do not respect their subjects. In such a case both the conditions of adequacy of options and of independence will be satisfied. Should governments then coerce people to avoid harmless immoralities? To my mind it is an advantage of my argument that it does depend on contingent features of our world. The temptation to make abstract a priori principles yield concrete practical policies is responsible for many bad arguments. I do share the reluctance of supporters of the harm principle to say that in the imagined circumstances the enforcement of harmless immorality is justified. My reasons are, however, not theirs. Modest though the supposed circumstances are compared with some philosophical speculations, they diverge from anything we have experience of sufficiently to make it impossible for us to say how the change would affect the merits of the issue. It is substantial enough to bring with it not only a change in the application of our values, but a change in these values themselves. Such changes are, as a matter of principle, unpredictable.

4. Beyond the Harm Principle

The previous section strove to vindicate the harm principle. But it also transformed the way it is sometimes understood. It interpreted it not as a restraint on the pursuit of moral goals by the state, but as indicating the right way in which the state could promote the well-being of people. Given that people should lead autonomous lives the state cannot force them to be moral. All it can do is to provide the conditions of autonomy. Using coercion invades autonomy and thus defeats the purpose of promoting it, unless it is done to promote autonomy by preventing harm.

Seen in this light the harm principle allows perfectionist policies so long as they do not require resort to coercion. It deserves its place as a liberal principle of freedom not because it is anti-perfectionist. For it is not. But because, as J. S. Mill, its original advocate, and H. L. A. Hart, its leading protagonist in recent times, clearly saw, it sets a limit on the means allowed in pursuit of moral ideals. While such ideals may indeed be pursued by political means, they may not be pursued by the use of coercion except when its use is called for to prevent harm. The principle sets a necessary condition only. It does not justify all uses of coercion to prevent harm, but it proscribes the use of coercion for other purposes.

This vindication of the principle goes hand in hand with its demotion. It is not to be seen as the whole but merely as a part of a doctrine of freedom, the core of which is the promotion of the conditions of autonomy. The harm principle is but one aspect of this enterprise. Manipulating people, for example, interferes with their autonomy, and does so in much the same way and to the same degree, as coercing them. Resort to manipulation should be subject to the same condition as resort to coercion. Both can be justified only to prevent harm. Thus while the harm principle is of lasting value, over-concentration on it neglects the other aspects of the doctrine of freedom. It encourages a false belief that political freedom is freedom from coercion, nothing less nor more. It blinds us to the valid reasons behind our concern about the use of coercion, i.e. that often though not always it is liable to be abused, and that political coercion infringes the autonomy of the coerced.[1]

In one way the conclusions of the previous section assign greater importance to the harm principle than it is often given. It is common to regard it as setting a necessary condition for the justification of coercion and nothing more. 'No conduct should be suppressed by law unless it can be shown to harm others.'[2] This is a counter-intuitive view. If the prevention of harm justifies punishment does not the prevention of more harm justify it to a greater degree than the prevention of less harm? Could it be that the amount and nature of the harm to be prevented, and the amount and nature of the harm coercion will inflict, are irrelevant to the justification? The derivation of the principle from autonomy-based considerations indicates the way the relative importance of harm is to be judged. It is to be judged by the degree of restriction of one's autonomy it represents.

Autonomy-based considerations do not allow extending the harm principle beyond its proper scope to legitimize the use of coercion to prevent offence. Coercion can be used to prevent extreme cases where severely offending or hurting another's feelings interferes with or diminishes that person's ability to lead a normal autonomous life in the community. But offence as such should be restrained and controlled by other means, ones which do not invade freedom.

Some of the results which are sometimes justified on grounds of preventing offence are approached in a different way by the autonomy-based doctrine of freedom. The conditions of autonomy, it was emphasized before, include the existence of a public culture which maintains and encourages

---

[1] Not all coercion must infringe autonomy. Many cases of private coercion are very localized. They deny the coerced one option without interfering with his ability to choose from many others. Where those others are adequate no loss of autonomy is involved. In many such cases the good intentions of the coercer are not in doubt, and therefore no insult or indignity is involved. Many cases of parental coercion fall into this class.

[2] *Report of the Committee on Obscenity and Film Censorship*, Chaired by B. Williams, Cmnd. 7772, HMSO, London, 1979.

the cultivation of certain tastes and the undertaking of certain pursuits. A public culture which inculcates respect for the environment, and for its transformation at the hands of past generations, and which cultivates agreeable design and good taste in landscaping and urban planning, while not positively required as a condition of autonomy, is consistent with it. Autonomy requires a public culture and is consistent with a tasteful rather than a vulgar and offensive environment. As was explained in the previous section the Harm Principle is no obstacle to the pursuit of such a policy.

One way in which the autonomy-based doctrine of freedom advocated here deviates from some liberal writings on the subject is in its ready embrace of various paternalistic measures. Paternalism has a bad name among some liberal thinkers. It conjures up images of individuals being manipulated for their own good by big brother. Major last ditch battles against paternalism are fought by some liberty lovers in resisting the compulsory wearing of seat-belts in cars, etc. Yet the liberal conscience is divided on the subject. A good deal of indirect paternalism is not only tolerated but is positively encouraged by many liberty lovers. They clamour for laws improving safety controls and quality controls of manufactured goods, and apply similar reasoning to demand strict qualifications as a condition for advertising one's services in medicine, law, or the other professions. These measures do not coerce those whom they protect. But neither are they designed to stop people from inflicting harm on others. Their net effect is to reduce people's choices on the ground that it is to their own good not to have those choices.

Reflection on the impact of paternalism on autonomy shows that it varies to a degree which makes it senseless to formulate either a general pro- or a general anti-paternalistic conclusion. In particular, paternalism affecting matters which are regarded by all as of merely instrumental value does not interfere with autonomy if its effect is to improve safety, thus making the activities affected more likely to realize their aim. There is a difference between risky sports, e.g. where the risk is part of the point of the activity or an inevitable by-product of its point and purpose, and the use of unsafe common consumer goods. Participation in sporting activities is intrinsically valuable. Consumer goods are normally used for instrumental reasons.

Where the perfectionism advocated here goes beyond means-related paternalism is in sanctioning measures which encourage the adoption of valuable ends and discourage the pursuit of base ones. Here there are two main restrictions on the perfectionist, if you like the paternalistic, policies. First, the perfectionist policies must be compatible with respect for autonomy. They must, therefore, be confined to the creation of the conditons of autonomy. Second, they must respect the limitation on the use of coercion that is imposed by the harm principle, as well as the analogous restriction on manipulation.

One particular troubling problem concerns the treatment of communities whose culture does not support autonomy. These may be immigrant communities, or indigenous peoples, or they may be religious sects. It is arguable that even the harm principle will not defend them from the 'cultural imperialism' of some liberal theories. Since they insist on bringing up their children in their own ways they are, in the eyes of liberals like myself, harming them. Therefore can coercion be used to break up their communities, which is the inevitable by-product of the destruction of their separate schools, etc.?

The general outlook advocated in this book seems to lead to a test of viability as the most important consideration in determining policy towards such groups. Let me explain. I am assuming that their own culture is morally worthy. That is, first, it does not lead them to harm others, nor to destroy the options available to those not members of these communities. Second, when their culture flourishes in any given society it enables members of that society to have an adequate and satisfying life. In that case their continued existence should be tolerated, despite its scant regard for autonomy. If those assumptions do not hold then the case for toleration is considerably weakened, or even disappears. I am further assuming that their culture is inferior to that of the dominant liberal society in the midst of which they live. Those who do not share that assumption have no problem. If one holds that the illiberal culture is at least as good as the dominant liberal one then clearly one should take whatever action is necessary to protect it. The difficulty arises for those who believe the illiberal culture to be inferior to theirs. Should they tolerate it?

The perfectionist principles espoused in this book suggest that people are justified in taking action to assimilate the minority group, at the cost of letting its culture die or at least be considerably changed by absorption. But that is easier said than done. Time and again I have emphasized that people can successfully enjoy an autonomous life only if they live in an environment which supports suitable social forms. By hypothesis members of the autonomy-rejecting group lack this support in their communities. Wrenching them out of their communities may well make it impossible for them to have any kind of normal rewarding life whatsoever because they have not built up any capacity for autonomy. Toleration is therefore the conclusion one must often reach. Gradual transformation of these minority communities is one thing, their precipitate disintegration is another. So long as they are viable communities offering acceptable prospects to their members, including their young, they should be allowed to continue in their ways. But many of them are not self-sustaining. Often it is clear that they cannot be expected to survive for long as an isolated group in a modern society. Sometimes they survive as a dwindling community through the forceful stand of some of their members who sometimes combine with misguided liberals and conservatives to condemn many of the young in such communities to an impoverished, unrewarding life by denying them the education and the opportunities to thrive outside the community. In such cases assimilationist policies may well be the only humane course, even if implemented by force of law.

These remarks are of course abstract and speculative. They are meant to indicate the direction in which the conclusions of this book lead, rather than to deal with the issue in depth.

5. The Shape of Freedom

The moral outlook the implications of which we have explored is one which holds personal autonomy to be an essential element of the good life. We saw that such a morality presupposes competitive pluralism. That is, it presupposes that people should have available to them many forms and styles of life incorporating incompatible virtues, which not only cannot all be realized in one life but tend to generate mutual intolerance. Such an autonomy-valuing pluralistic morality generates a doctrine of freedom. It protects people pursuing different styles of life from the intolerance which competitive pluralism has the inherent tendency to encourage, and it calls for the provision of the conditions of autonomy without which autonomous life is impossible.

Three main features characterize the autonomy-based doctrine of freedom. *First*, its primary concern is the promotion and protection of positive freedom which is understood as the capacity for autonomy, consisting of the availability of an adequate range of options, and of the mental abilities necessary for an autonomous life. *Second*, the state has the duty not merely to prevent denial of freedom, but also to promote it by creating the conditions of autonomy. *Third*, one may not pursue any goal by means which infringe people's autonomy unless such action is justified by the need to protect or promote the autonomy of those people or of others.

We explored the limits of the doctrine, which are two. First, it does not protect nor does it require any individual option. It merely requires the availability of an adequate range of options. We saw that this lends the principle a somewhat conservative aspect. No specific new options have a claim to be admitted. The adequacy of the range is all that matters, and any change should be gradual in order to protect 'vested interests'. Secondly, the principle does not protect morally repugnant activities or forms of life. In other respects the principle is a strong one. It requires positively encouraging the flourishing of a plurality of incompatible and competing pursuits, projects and relationships.

It turns out that this autonomy-based doctrine of freedom implies the harm principle. Like it it yields the conclusion that one may not use coercion except to prevent harm. It does so only by embedding the harm principle in a moral outlook which, by relating it to a particular conception of individual well-being, gives the notion of harm concrete content. Not all the traditional supporters of the harm principle will welcome its vindication in this form. It is embraced not as a complete doctrine of political liberty but as one element of a wider doctrine. It is a consequence of the third proposition in the enumeration above. It is itself part of a perfectionist doctrine which holds the state to be duty-bound to promote the good life. It stops at coercion and manipulation only where their use would not promote the ability of people to have a good life but frustrate or diminish it.

This view differs both from some common liberal and from some common collectivist beliefs. On the one hand some will protest that the perfectionist approach advocated here overlooks the need to shun paternalistic measures for they offend human dignity. Respect for people as responsible moral agents, it is said, is inconsistent with paternalism. It requires leaving people to make their own decisions. I have argued against the simplistic presuppositions of this view. It disregards the dependence of people's tastes and values on social forms, on conventions and practices which are the result of human action (though usually not of action designed to achieve these results).

Respect for persons requires concern for their well-being. It calls for a proper perception of the importance of agency reason. This means a conception of well-being assigning a central role to the agent's own activities in shaping his well-being. An autonomy-based morality is not only consistent with these precepts, it goes further in demanding that people should be allowed freely to create their own lives. This is not only consistent with perfectionism. It requires it. It calls for the creation of conditions of valuable autonomy through the pursuit of perfectionist policies.

Its perfectionist character, the rejection of moral individualism, and the emphasis placed on the importance of collective goods bring the views here advocated close to various collectivist, or communitarian doctrines. They differ from many collectivist doctrines in that they do not lead to strong centralist government, nor to a radical programme of change through political action. The espousal of a pluralistic culture, to the extent of supporting competitive pluralism, and the autonomy-oriented conception of personal well-being militate against support for a strong government. The role of government is extensive and important, but confined to maintaining framework conditions conducive to pluralism and autonomy.

Since values are grounded in concrete social forms there is no room for radical political action to secure a fundamental change of social conditions. Politics is the art of gradual amelioration. I mention these points briefly here because of their obvious bearing on the scope of legitimate government and therefore on individual freedom. They were not explored in this book, which was not concerned with the appropriate institutional framework suitable in the light of the moral outlook advocated above.

This brings us to the relation between the autonomy-based doctrine of freedom and the doctrine of legitimate authority espoused in the first part of the book. One way of explaining their relation views the autonomy-based doctrine of freedom as stating the ideal. The service conception of authority dampens expectations by bringing to mind the limited power governments have to do good, and the dangers that placing power in their hands will misfire and do more harm than good. The doctrine of autonomy-based freedom is not inimical to political authority. On the contrary, it looks to governments to take positive action to enhance the freedom of their subjects. This cannot disguise the dangers inherent in the concentration of power in few hands, the dangers of corruption, of bureaucratic distortions and insensitivities, of fallibility of judgment, and uncertainty of purpose, and, the limitation which perhaps goes deeper into the inherent weakness of all concentration of power, the insufficiency and the distortion of the information reaching the central organs of government.

These afflictions affect different countries and different constitutional structures in different ways. Each has its own weaknesses and its own strengths. Some governments can be entrusted with the running of schools which it would be wrong to entrust to another, and yet the second can be relied upon to encourage technological innovation in discriminating and imaginative ways, whereas the first cannot—to give one contextless example. My point is that such differences are not merely the result of personalities. They are conditioned by the political culture of a country, by its constitutional history, by its methods of recruiting its political élite, and its relations to social and economic élites, and similar factors.

The study of these issues belongs to the theory of political institutions which must supplement any inquiry into political morality to give it concrete content applicable to the circumstances of a particular country. I mention their relevance because their presence affects in a radical way the degree to which one is willing to entrust any government with the tasks whose existence is indicated by the doctrine of freedom advocated in this book. I said that the limitations of governments force one to compromise the purity of the ideal doctrine of freedom. At the same time these limitations can be and are presented as one of the foundations of political freedom. Since power is corruptible, fallible and inefficient it should not be trusted. It should be hedged and fenced. The impotence of politics to do good, the unreliability of governments, is the basis of the freedom of the individual. This picture is both true and false.

It is true that it justifies restricting the right of governments to govern. It is also true that that limitation is based on concern for individual freedom and autonomy. To that extent a balanced view of the shortcomings of governments will lead to much more extensive freedom from governmental action than is entailed by the doctrine of autonomy-based freedom explained here. But this extension of freedom from governmental action is, in most cases, a result of a failure to achieve the full measure of freedom as a capacity for autonomy. The extended freedom from governmental action is based on the practical inability of governments to discharge their duty to serve the freedom of their subjects. And in most cases the result is that that freedom remains lacking. In most cases there is no other body nor any other social process which can achieve what government action fails to, that is the existence of a full capacity for autonomy to all members of a community.

The shortcomings of governments are but one of the regrettable sources of political freedom. Another is the danger of civil strife. The pursuit of full-blooded perfectionist policies, even of those which are entirely sound and justified, is likely, in many countries if not in all, to backfire by arousing popular resistance leading to civil strife. In such circumstances compromise is the order of the day. There is no abstract doctrine which can delineate what the terms of the compromise should be. All one can say is that it will confine perfectionist measures to matters which command a large measure of social consensus, and it will further restrict the use of coercive and of greatly confining measure and will favour gentler measures favouring one trend or another. The main lesson is again the same. Such compromises promote freedom from government, and they do so because the adverse circumstances show that an attempt by the government to achieve more freedom will achieve less.

Freedom based on fear of civil strife, like freedom based on the unreliability of governments, depends on some doctrine of 'ideal' freedom. It presupposes an ideal doctrine of freedom, for it tells us when and how to compromise, just as the unreliability of government is measured by its inability to achieve the targets set by the doctrine of the 'ideal'. Furthermore these doctrines of freedom by necessity and compromise bring us the freedom of imperfection, the liberty from governmental action which all too often is an admission that perfect freedom is unobtainable.

Index

advice 52–4
agreements 80–1, 174–5
akrasia 141, 299, 338–9
alienation, *see* identification
Anscombe, G. E. M. 22, 300
anti-perfectionism 107–62
  some contributing errors 157–62
  see also ideals, exclusion of; neutrality
Atiyah, P. 95
authority 19, 21–105, 107, 165, 261–2
  a right to ~ 56, 76
  and community 34, 71–80
  and consent 88–94
  and co-ordination problems 30, 49–50, 56
  and duty to support just institutions 66–7, 101–2, 104
  and error 47–8, 60–2, 159
  and prisoners' dilemmas 50–1, 56
  and reasons 29
  as a right to rule 22
  as justified power 23–8, 30
  charismatic 33–4
  claim of duty to obey 23, 27
  de facto 26–7, 46, 47, 56, 65, 75–6
  divine 31–2
  flexibility of account of 73–4, 80
  influence direct and normative 28
  inspirational 31–5
  legislative v. adjudicative 43–4
  linguistic distinctions 64–5
  mediating role of 58–9
  political 24–7, 34, 56, 70–105 (justification of 70–80, 88–94, 97–9, 427–9)
  practical v. theoretical 29, 52–3
  service conception of 56, 59, 67
  'surrendering one's judgement' 39–42
  the recognitional conception 29–31
  to confer rights etc. 44–5
  to pass unjust laws 78–9
  unlimited claims of law 76–8
  see also dependence thesis; no difference thesis; normal justification thesis; pre-emptive thesis
autonomy 108, 132–3, 144, 246, 265, 267, 273, 368–95
  aiming at the good 378–81, 412
  a matter of degree 154, 156, 373
  and coercion 150–7, 207
  and collective goods 205–7, 247, 250

and creating value 385–90
and harm 413–14
and independence 155–7, 377–8
and integrity 381–5
and interests 189–91
and pluralism 398–9
and political freedom 246, 407–12
and rights 203–7
and the harm principle 415–20
as a capacity 204, 371–2
~-based duties 407–8, 415–17
characterized 154–5, 373
incompatible with individualism 205–7
its value 390–5
not exhausted by a right 207, 246–7
the adequacy of options 205–7, 373–7, 379–80, 406

Baker, G. 66
Barry, B. 137–8, 140, 144
Beardsley, E. L. 371
Benn, S. I. 8, 14, 371, 378–9
Bentham, J. 166
Berlin, I. 14
Blackburn, S. 294
Bramstead, E. K. 1
Brandt, R. 170–1
burden of proof 8–9

Campbell, K. 166
Campbell, T. 250
Chisholm, R. 364
coercion 28, 109, 165, 274, 285, 373, 377–8, 403, 409–10, 413
  action under—justified or excused 150
  and autonomy 150–7
  and being forced 151–2
  coercive threats 149, 153–4
  defined 148–9
  see also harm principle
collective goods 199, 202–9, 216
collective rights 207–9
commensurability 268, 271, 272, 276
  and consequentialism 357–8
  see also incommensurability
conscientious objection, right of 111, 252
consent 21–2, 80–94
  and participation 96–7
  and promises 82–3
  defined 81